Also by Richard P. Howe, Jr.

Legendary Locals of Lowell
(with Chaim M. Rosenberg)

Lowell: Images of Modern America

Lowell Municipal Elections: 1965-2015

Also by Paul Marion

Atop an Underwood: Early Stories and Other Writings by Jack Kerouac (editor)

What Is the City?

Mill Power: The Origin and Impact of Lowell National Historical Park

Union River: Poems and Sketches

HISTORY AS IT HAPPENS

HISTORY AS IT HAPPENS

CITIZEN BLOGGERS IN LOWELL, MASS.

EDITED BY
**RICHARD P. HOWE, JR.
& PAUL MARION**

LP

Loom Press
Lowell, Massachusetts
2017

© 2017 by Richard P. Howe, Jr.

ISBN 978-0-931507-09-0

All rights reserved. No part of this publication may be reproduced by any means existing or to be developed in the future without the written consent of the publisher, except in the case of brief quotations embodied in critical articles and reviews.

Published in the United States of America
First edition

Loom Press
P.O. Box 1394
Lowell, MA 01853
info@loompress.com
www.loompress.com

Design and chapter page images: Joseph Marion
Typefaces: Caslon, Akzidenz-Grotesk
Printing: King Printing, Lowell, Mass.
Maps: Joe Donovan, Management Information Systems, City of Lowell
Cover image: Detail from *Bird's Eye View of Lowell, Mass.* (1876), created by C.H. Vogt for Bailey & Hazen

To our readers and contributors

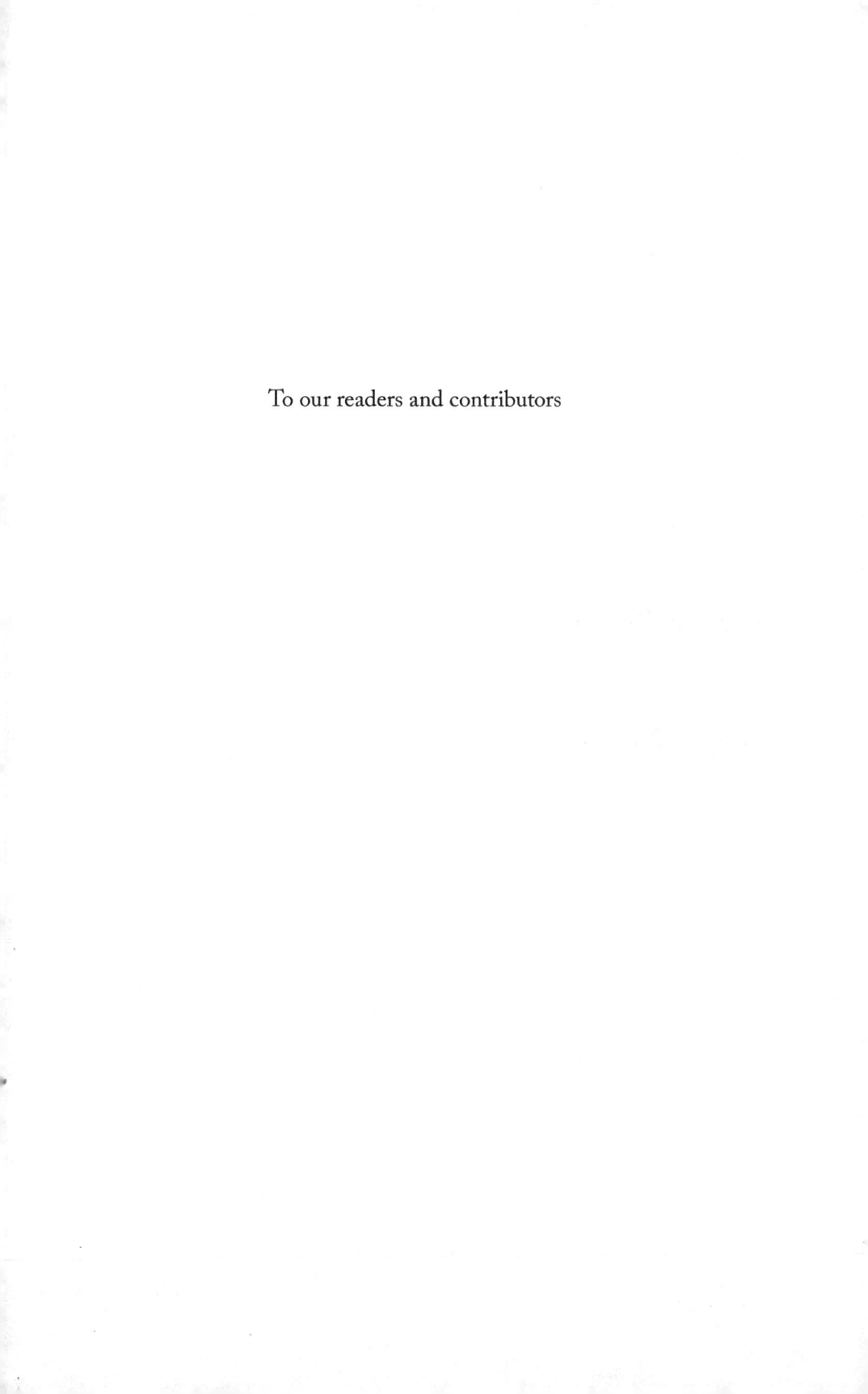

Foreword: Song of Ourselves, PAUL MARION i
Introduction: A Short, Local History of Blogging and Other Social Media, RICHARD P. HOWE, JR. iii

2007

D-Day for the Fifth, RICHARD P. HOWE, JR. 3
Congrats to Sen. Panagiotakos, RICHARD P. HOWE, JR. 4
Subprime Mortgage Crisis, RICHARD P. HOWE, JR. 5
Prayer and the City Council, RICHARD P. HOWE, JR. 6
Women in the 'Fabulous Fifth,' MARIE SWEENEY............................ 8
'Find a Way to Get in The Way,' RICHARD P. HOWE, JR. 10
Gay Marriage Vote, RICHARD P. HOWE, JR. 11
A Reply from the City Manager, RICHARD P. HOWE, JR. 13
Controversy at Folk Festival, RICHARD P. HOWE, JR. 15
Musing on Moxie's Lowell Roots, MARIE SWEENEY........................ 16
Dems Unity: Niki and Friends, MARIE SWEENEY............................ 17
Top Ten Lowell Political Events of 2007, RICHARD P. HOWE, JR. 19

2008

Obamamania in Nashua, TONY ACCARDI................................... 25
Pooh to the Pundits, MARIE SWEENEY.. 26
Bits and Bites, MARIE SWEENEY... 28
Sisters, HENRI MARCHAND 29
Adios, Aiello: A 'Third Place,' RICHARD P. HOWE, JR. 32
Remembering John, JACK NEARY... 33
Elliot's Closed?, MARIE SWEENEY 39
Casting My Vote, RICHARD P. HOWE, JR. 40
The Morning After, RICHARD P. HOWE, JR. 41
Ice Storm Report, RICHARD P. HOWE, JR. 43
Refugees Return, MARIE SWEENEY 44
New Year's Day and French Canadian-Americans, PAUL MARION....46

Back Pages, PAUL MARION 47
Top Ten Events of 2008, RICHARD P. HOWE, JR. 50

2009

Lowell Variety: History as It Happens, RICHARD P. HOWE, JR. 55
Out and About, MARIE SWEENEY 56
Riding the Rails: The 7:46 to Boston, RICHARD P. HOWE, JR. 57
Remembering Charlie Pierce, MARIE SWEENEY 59
Hamilton Canal Planning Meeting, JOE SMITH 60
Lowell Photography Weekend, PAUL MARION 63
House Fire at 62 Highland Street, PAUL MARION 65
Lisa Redmond and the Fire Cats, PAUL MARION 66
'Sampascoopies,' PAUL MARION 68
Breakfast-After-Dark, PAUL MARION 69
Walking Tour of the Acre, RICHARD P. HOWE, JR. 70
Writing on the Wall, PAUL MARION 72
Batman on Highland Street, PAUL MARION 74
Spring Sights, Sounds, & Thoughts, MARIE SWEENEY....................75
Swine Flu in Lowell, RICHARD P. HOWE, JR. 76
Scenes from a Redevelopment Zone, PAUL MARION 77
Latest on Home Sales, RICHARD P. HOWE, JR. 80
Immigrant Stories, RICHARD P. HOWE, JR. 81
Visiting With Two Very Special Veterans, STEVE O'CONNOR 83
Goodbye to the Doubletree, RICHARD P. HOWE, JR. 87
Lessons from Dad, BOB FORRANT 89
Ed McMahon, WLLH, Paul Sullivan, TONY ACCARDI...................92
Franco-American Connections, ANDREW HOWE 93
LaGrange, Lafayette, and the Acre, PAUL MARION 95
The Lowell Connector, RICHARD P. HOWE, JR. 97
Great Night at Elliot's, RICHARD P. HOWE, JR. 98
Lowell in the World War, RICHARD P. HOWE, JR. 99
Tony C., RICHARD P. HOWE, JR. 101
One of My Ted Kennedy Memories, MARIE SWEENEY 102

Mass Poetry Festival Rave, PAUL MARION 103
Lowell Bell Echoes the Pulse of Life, MARIE SWEENEY................. 105
Top Lowell Political Events of 2009, RICHARD P. HOWE, JR. 107

Photographs, TONY SAMPAS... 112

2010

The Apple iPad, TONY ACCARDI.. 127
35 Years Ago: Khmer Rouge Terror, GEORGE CHIGAS.................... 128
Post-Election Analysis, RICHARD P. HOWE, JR. 129
Welcome to the Tsongas Center, RICHARD P. HOWE, JR. 133
Eileen Donoghue for State Senate, MARIE SWEENEY..................... 134
Gov. Patrick at the Owl Diner, RICHARD P. HOWE, JR. 135
Common Sights, PAUL MARION 137
'Beast Underneath,' PAUL MARION 139
Ken Burns @ MCC, RICHARD P. HOWE, JR. 140
Frank Keefe: 'Lowell is a Beacon,' RICHARD P. HOWE, JR. 143
'Saturday, Saturday. . . ,' PAUL MARION 145
Who Gets Hurt?, PAUL MARION 147
Remembering Ed LeLacheur, JACK NEARY..................................... 149
All Hail Lyle Lovett, PAUL MARION.. 152
Neighborhood Schools, RICHARD P. HOWE, JR. 154
Maine Musings, NANCYE TUTTLE 157
Lowell Environmental Attorney Tries to Declare Care Independence!
Part 2, MATT DONAHUE 159
Maya Angelou & Joe Donahue, PAUL MARION 163
Willie, DAVE PERRY... 166
What Did I See @ the Meet-Up?, PAUL MARION 168
My Review of *The Fighter*, PAUL MARION 169

2011

Grand Street Peace Walk, PAUL MARION 175
The Pawtucketville Bibliophile, STEVE O'CONNOR 176
Blue Does Not Equal Liberal, JOHN EDWARD 179
Facebook Rookie, PAUL MARION 182
Live Tweet of the Bin Laden Attack, TONY ACCARDI 183
Your Old Car Can Go Home Again, RAY LAPORTE 185
Bruins Win Stanley Cup, RICHARD P. HOWE, JR. 186
Lowell Farmers Market Opens Today, MARIE SWEENEY 187
Final Shuttle Mission, ANDREW HOWE 188
Leymah Gbowee, Nobel Peace Prize, PAUL MARION 190
Electricity Restored! 106 Hours Out!, RICHARD P. HOWE, JR. 192
Lowell High Distinguished Alums, MARIE SWEENEY 194
Occupy Policy, JOHN EDWARD 197
Thanksgiving on the South Common, PAUL MARION 201
Joel-Lowell Rhymes, PAUL MARION 202
Top Ten of 2011, RICHARD P. HOWE, JR. 204

Poems

Rainbow Poem, TOM FITZSIMMONS 211
Coffee Truck, MICHAEL CASEY 212
Body Heat, JACQUELYN MALONE 213
Lowell's Irish Micky Ward, TOM SEXTON 214
23 October, PAUL HUDON 215
Memory of an Afternoon, MARY SAMPAS 216
Blue Dot Sign, MICHAEL CASEY 218
The Beauty of a Nail, MATT MILLER 219
The Way I Want to Remember My Cambodia, CHATH PIERSATH ... 220
Fog Lights, JOE MEEHAN 222
Patterns of a Prayer Town, PAUL MARION 223
Manny, TOM SEXTON 224
Billerica, Midnight, JEAN LEBLANC 225
Letters, KATE HANSON FOSTER 226

2012

Lowell Police Account of Downtown Riot, RICHARD P. HOWE, JR. ... 231
XFest and Puck Fest, PAUL MARION ... 232
Automobile Races, Technology, and the Lowell Connection,
MARIE SWEENEY ... 234
Tweet and Greet, RICHARD P. HOWE, JR. ... 236
'Dickens and Massachusetts' Exhibit, RICHARD P. HOWE, JR. ... 237
'This is Dalton Jones,' PAUL MARION ... 238
Texas Jack, Peerless Morlacchi, and the Lowell Connection,
TONY ACCARDI ... 239
Nobody Beats the Fizz, BOB FORRANT ... 241
On the Road with Apologies to Everyone, TOM SEXTON ... 245
Marcel's Laws of Politics, PAUL MARION ... 247
Remembering Peter Stamas, MARIE SWEENEY ... 248
Stephen King at UMass Lowell, PAUL MARION ... 252
Farewell, Dr. Patrick J. Mogan, PAUL MARION ... 254
Top Ten of 2012, RICHARD P. HOWE, JR. ... 255

2013

Dylan in Lowell, Another Side, PAUL MARION ... 263
Review of *Lost Child: Sayon's Journey*, RICHARD P. HOWE, JR. ... 265
Some Thoughts on the Marathon Bombing, RICHARD P. HOWE, JR. ... 267
Holding On to Those Self-Evident Truths, JOHN WOODING ... 271
Edward Snowden and Secret Intelligence, RICHARD P. HOWE, JR. ... 274
Lowell's Hidden Epidemic, DEREK MITCHELL ... 276
Cambodia Town of Lowell, SENGLY KONG ... 278
Remarks at Lowell Plan Breakfast,
FRANCEY SLATER AND COLLEEN BRADY ... 281
... And Howe, PAUL MARION ... 284
Lowell Celebrates Nelson Mandela, RICHARD P. HOWE, JR. ... 287
Goodbye to Recycling Boxes, RICHARD P. HOWE, JR. ... 288
Lowell Political Year in Review: 2013, RICHARD P. HOWE, JR. ... 289

2014

Moody Gardens, MEHMED ALI & BETH BRASSEL..........................297
Farewell, Joyce Denning, Teacher, PAUL MARION........................301
A Fun Bazaar at Mill No. 5, RICHARD P. HOWE, JR. 302
Bernie: Ideas Matter, PAUL MARION 303
Paul J. Sheehy: A Remembrance, MARTY MEEHAN 305
Dismantle the South Common? Hands Off, PAUL MARION 309
Chicago Lessons, PAUL MARION 310
Vigil in Memory of Fire Victims, RICHARD P. HOWE, JR. 314
'More For Your Dollar,' PAUL MARION 314
Market Basket Deal: Time to Celebrate,
MARJORIE ARONS-BARRON... 315
Rita Mercier Gets It Right, RICHARD P. HOWE, JR. 317
For Cassie, JOHN WOODING..320
Glass Half-Full and Filling Up, PAUL MARION 323
Open Campus: 1970s Lowell High, JIM PETERS.........................325
Parties, JACK McDONOUGH 328
Lowell Year in Review: 2014, RICHARD P. HOWE, JR. 330

2015

Whistler's Father, JULIET HAINES MOFFORD 337
Mayor Elliott and Human Rights, RICHARD P. HOWE, JR. 339
The Blizzard of 2015, RICHARD P. HOWE, JR. 341
Lowell Week in Review: March 8, 2015, RICHARD P. HOWE, JR. 350
Anam Cara Honor: Irish 'Soul Friend,' MARIE SWEENEY 354
Lowell's Nelson Mandela Overlook, RICHARD P. HOWE, JR. 358
Lowell Week in Review: Sept. 13, 2015, RICHARD P. HOWE, JR..... 359
Salute to Women Remarks, BOPHA MALONE 362
The Christmas Fruitcake: An Ageless Tradition, HENRI MARCHAND...366
Lowell Year in Review: 2015, RICHARD P. HOWE, JR. 369

Initiative

Sovanna, FRED FAUST 377
Sisson and Slater: Mill City Grows, FRED FAUST 382
George Duncan: The Kid and the Kool-Aid, FRED FAUST 387
Local Heroes Made a Splash, FRED FAUST 392
Dorcas Grigg-Saito: Low Key, High Success, FRED FAUST 398

2016

Anti-Trump Rally, 6:00 p.m. Report, PAUL MARION 411
Lowell Week in Review: Jan. 10, 2016, RICHARD P. HOWE, JR. 412
David Bowie and Bob Martin: The Lowell Connection,
PAUL MARION 415
Lowell: The Next Initiative, RICHARD P. HOWE, JR. 416
The Optics of Sanders: Is Bernie a Gandalf?, PAUL MARION 419
Lowell Week in Review: Feb. 14, 2016, RICHARD P. HOWE, JR. 419
Amazing Vision for a New Lord Overpass,
RICHARD P. HOWE, JR. 420
Lowell City Council Meeting, March 29, 2016,
RICHARD P. HOWE, JR. 422
Clemente Park: A History, RICHARD P. HOWE, JR. 427
Lowell City Council Meeting: Transgender Bathroom Debate,
RICHARD P. HOWE, JR. 430
Lowell Week in Review: Memorial Day Edition,
RICHARD P. HOWE, JR. 438
'A Special Place and a Special Park,' RICHARD P. HOWE, JR. 442
Compensation for Councilors, MIMI PARSEGHIAN 444
Carrying a Torch for *Ti Jean*, PAUL MARION 445
School Daze Lost in Time, BOB HODGE 446
Citizenship Is an Endless Job, PAUL MARION 450
President-Elect Trump, RICHARD P. HOWE, JR. 452

CONTRIBUTORS 457
LOWELL MAPS 464

FOREWORD

Song of Ourselves

Choral singing is a Lowell tradition. In the 1980s, the city hosted an annual choral festival showcasing church choirs and community choruses. Among French Canadian-Americans, the tradition dates from 100 years ago. Spiritual singing goes back to religious services in the freshly minted mill town. The original people here had their songs. Thinking about this book, I recalled Walt Whitman's line: "I hear American singing, the varied carols I hear." The words, ideas, and concerns that constitute this distinctive collection of posts for the *RichardHowe.com* blog make a democratic music.

Lowell is on the list with the Grand Canyon, Gettysburg Battlefield, and Statue of Liberty as a treasured place protected by the National Park Service. The Industrial Revolution took hold here on a grand scale. We have a microcosm of the country at the confluence of the Merrimack and Concord rivers. Dozens of languages are spoken by students in the Lowell public schools. Whitman, again, wrote, "I am large, I contain multitudes."

In the early 1800s, when a centuries-old Native American settlement and later colonial town was transformed into a commercial powerhouse, Lowell was a fount of ambition and ingenuity. Lowell-made innovations in applied science, engineering, and business practices energized the nation's economy. Thousands of workers and their families drawn by jobs in textile manufacturing wove the social fabric for a new city. As the factories produced cloth, the people nurtured a civic culture, a way of getting by and getting along that required its own imagination and passion. This innovative spirit was refreshed in the twenty-first century by a decision to seize upon new information technology to enrich the community dialogue.

A democratic republic will not function well if its citizens don't talk and listen to each other. They must express, converse, debate, propose, question, praise, and recollect. The public conversation feeds a shared sense of who we are and deepens our understanding of each other and the places we inhabit.

Our national experience is defined in part by the tension between independence and interdependence or liberty and "mutuality" as political scientist Mason Drukman writes in his *Community and Purpose in America*. The publisher of the blog that is the source of this book values both freedom and mutual support but with a pronounced tilt toward community engagement.

The *RichardHowe.com* writers make a noise that recalls Whitman's carolers, "singing what belongs to him or her and to none else." There is a song in the stories we tell, in the happenings we chronicle, in the dreams and concerns we describe, as well as in striving for the more robust humanitarianism that Drukman advocates. These are the carolers outside your door, composers of words and music for the local story, the voices of thinkers and doers.

—Paul Marion

INTRODUCTION

A Short, Local History of Blogging and Other Social Media

This book represents the best writing and images in the *RichardHowe.com* blog from 2007 to 2016. Together, the bloggers captured part of the city experience over ten years. Although the blog posts are archived online, their value is enhanced by this book. Organized in blog-like chronological order, the posts offer a history-as-it-happens account of life in Lowell, Massachusetts. The work may also be seen as a case study in hyperlocal reporting during a time when individuals, businesses, organizations, and members of the media industry were challenged to find the best way to use rapidly emerging communications technology to share news and information.

Lowell is well-known as a place that has transformed itself from a faded industrial town with one of the highest unemployment rates in the nation to a global model of urban revitalization. Politics played a big part in that transformation. So did the media. For most of that period "the media" consisted of the *Lowell Sun*, local AM radio stations WLLH and WCAP, and for a decade, cable television's NewsCenter 6. There were other forms of political communications: incessant phone calls, quiet conversations over coffee or louder ones over beer, mailed notes and clippings, and, once the City Council meetings were televised live, elected officials speaking directly to their constituents via cable TV. But the conversation was usually driven by those who were paid to write and talk about politics—the professional media.

Aside from the scale, that is pretty much how things worked nationally. At least that is how it worked until the summer of 2003. Earlier that year the United States and a handful of allies had invaded Iraq with the overwhelming support of the media, many Congressional Democrats, and a majority of the public. The chaotic post-invasion occupation of Iraq, however, gave strength to those who had opposed the war. By August 2003, the Iraq war and continued economic unease from the post-9/11 recession were becoming major issues for the emerging field of Democratic candidates for the 2004 presidential nomination.

In the early stages of that campaign, the nation's political class was stunned when Howard Dean, the little-known former governor of Vermont, bolted ahead of a Democratic field that included John Kerry, Joe Lieberman, John Edwards, Wesley Clark, Dick Gephardt, Al Sharpton, and Dennis Kucinich. While Dean's fervent opposition to the war and support for universal health coverage were sure to endear him to the most progressive members of the party, those things alone did not explain his skyrocketing popularity and the many millions of dollars contributed to his campaign.

Dean succeeded because his campaign was the first to fully harness the power of the internet as a campaign tool. Using online fund raising and Meetups, the Dean campaign raised more money and signed up more volunteers than any of its opponents.

They also blogged. *Blog for America* was the first presidential campaign blog. Hosted on the Dean campaign website and posting articles about campaign events and policy issues, *Blog for America* was interesting to read and gained much attention—especially from me. By December 2003, I was so fascinated by the role of blogging and the internet in the success of the Dean campaign that I decided to try it out for myself.

I had served as Register of Deeds of the Middlesex County Northern District since 1995. I embraced technology that changed much about the way land records were recorded and retrieved in Massachusetts. A blog seemed like a great way to communicate with registry users, and so on December 23, 2003, the *LowellDeeds* blog was born with the following post:

INTRODUCTION

"Welcome to the Lowell Registry of Deeds blog. For those of you unfamiliar with the term, 'blog' is short for 'weblog,' which is a frequently updated log on the internet about a particular subject. This site will have the latest news about what's going on at the Registry and in the real estate and land-recording business. I hope the blog proves to be useful and informative...."

I began writing every day about real estate matters and was soon joined by co-author and assistant Register of Deeds Tony Accardi. We used the blog to report trends in real estate, new policies at the Registry of Deeds, and global technological developments. The blog was well-received in the real estate community, but land records is not a topic to incite controversy.

The same could not be said of Lowell politics. By the close of 2003, the political structure in the city in some ways paralleled that of the country at the time of the invasion of Iraq. There was a powerful and popular leader—in the city's case, it was City Manager John Cox, who was overwhelmingly supported by the City Council and by the local media. That support was not unanimous, however, and the opposition found voice in a blog called *Left in Lowell*.

A New Hampshire native who came to Lowell with an English degree and skills in website design, Lynne Lupien launched *Left in Lowell* to add a voice to the national and state political debates that were waging at the time, but Lupien was not immune to local politics. She soon became a harsh critic of the Cox Administration and provided an electronic publishing platform for others who felt similarly.

Left in Lowell became a must-read for those interested in local politics. With a flood of anonymous, unmoderated comments, it became a raucous, profane, passionate platform for local political debate. It was also unsettling to those who had heretofore controlled the city's political power structure in the same way that Howard Dean's *Blog for America* had so disrupted the nation's political hierarchy.

As much as the substance of the local political debate on *Left in Lowell* fascinated me, that blog's utility as a communications platform intrigued me even more. For my entire life, I had witnessed the power of the media in Lowell to shape and influence the debate on public policy. Now, thanks to the internet and blogging software, anyone with a computer could have an influence on local events far beyond that ever before wielded by an individual citizen. This was light years beyond submitting a Letter to the Editor or calling a local radio talk show. While continuing to blog about real estate on the *LowellDeeds* website, I began to study blogging as a means of political activism.

Although the Dean campaign flamed out in the fields of Iowa in January 2004, blogging did not. Interest in citizen journalism was intense with frequent gatherings and conferences around the region such as "Beyond Broadcast 2006: Reinventing Public Media in a Participatory Culture" at Harvard Law School; "Democracy & Independence: Sharing News & Information in a Connected World" at UMass Amherst; and "Beyond Broadcast 2007: From Participatory Culture to Participatory Democracy" at MIT. Closer to home, blogging made its mark on statewide politics when in April 2006 a group of Massachusetts bloggers organized and conducted a debate of the Democratic candidates for Lieutenant Governor in that year's election. Televised and streamed live from the studios of Lowell Telecommunications Corporation, the blogger debate received extensive coverage in the *Boston Globe*, *Boston Herald* and *Lowell Sun*.

I leaped into political blogging in March, 2007, when Marty Meehan decided to leave Congress to seek the position of Chancellor of UMass Lowell. Having just witnessed the intense coverage of the 2006 gubernatorial election in both blogs and the mainstream media, I suspected that the upcoming special Congressional election would present a unique opportunity for politically attuned individuals on the ground to share their observations and opinions online. It did.

I already had a static website and the domain name *RichardHowe.com*, so once I figured out how to install and configure WordPress blogging software, *RichardHowe.com* was in business. With a hotly contested, five-person race for the Democratic nomination for Congress, the blog almost wrote itself. I quickly recruited friends and fellow political observers Tony Accardi and Marie Sweeney to be co-authors, and the three of us provided extensive coverage of the election which was ultimately won by Niki Tsongas, whose late husband, Paul, had held that Congressional seat on his way to the U.S. Senate and a presidential campaign (1991-92). Soon after the election, the blog masthead made a momentous pickup when writer, poet, and friend Paul Marion joined the team.

And "team" is a good word to describe the relationship that developed among the four of us. Tony, a former English teacher, real estate professional, and radio program producer, brought a level of technology and media savvy that was invaluable in a time when both of those fields underwent radical change and severe disruption. Marie, herself a former English teacher, Congressional staffer, and political activist brought a depth of understanding of Lowell and its people available only to someone possessed with a deep love of community. Paul is best described by museum and historical society consultant Julie Mofford in her review of his 2014 book *Mill Power: The Origin and Impact of Lowell National Historical Park*. Here is some of what Julie wrote about Paul:

> "The author leaves no brick or cobblestone unturned in this account of the development and success of Lowell National Historical Park. No one is more qualified than Paul Marion to tell the story of Lowell's renaissance. He has been directly involved since the onset of the city's transformation. He was on board from the founding of this urban national

park and responsible for many of Lowell's creative innovations and cultural achievements."

Elections provide powerful fuel to blogs. *RichardHowe.com* was fortunate to come to life at the start of an extraordinary stretch of political activity in Massachusetts. But my co-authors and I wanted *RichardHowe.com* to be about more than just politics. The four of us got into the habit of meeting for breakfast once each month, first at the River Road Café and, after it closed, at the Owl Diner, both in Lowell, or Cracker Barrel in neighboring Tewksbury. While the highlight of these breakfasts was often political gossip not suitable for blogging, we also devoted considerable time to strategic discussions about the blog.

From those gatherings came several initiatives. We saw the concept of place as a powerful connection between people and the community in which they live. By writing about neighborhoods, buildings, monuments, cemeteries, parks, and other components of the built and natural environments, we engaged current residents and those who had lived in Lowell previously. Another of our efforts was to recruit additional writers for the blog as a means of diversifying its voices but also to provide the constant stream of new content essential to a healthy blog. Through the years, at least 40 individuals have contributed prose, pictures or poems, some on a regular basis, others less frequently or even once only.

The blog has had a more complicated relationship with another group of guest contributors: people who make comments on a blog post. In the early days of blogging, the comment section became an "anything goes" arena for political commentary. The ability to make comments anonymously seemed to remove any sense of restraint or civility for some. The dominant view in the early blogging community was that such behavior should be tolerated in the name of free speech and dynamic discourse and that the nasty voices would be shouted down by other commenters. It occurred to me that the people who embraced this view were probably not the ones lending their names to blogs. I was less tolerant.

As the clearly identified host of the site, I found that many readers would attribute anything on the site to me. With a proven ability to make my own enemies, I did not need the help of anonymous commenters in that regard. Consequently, I implemented a "moderated comments" approach. Anyone could submit a comment, but it would hover in a queue until one of the co-authors of the site "approved" it. While Tony, Marie, and Paul each moderated their share of comments, the most inflammatory ones were held for my review. I allowed almost all of them. The few I rejected contained either vile language or personal attacks. I didn't like anonymous comments and wrote a post urging people to use their names. Some people disappeared; others continued to post in more temperate tones. Still, moderating the comments did deprive the site of some of the spontaneity and energy of earlier blogs, but I saw no alternative.

Despite the challenges noted above, problem comments were in the minority. Most people added information and insight to our blog posts. A few comments created some of the most memorable moments on *RichardHowe.com*. Here are a few examples.

On St. Patrick's Day one year, I wrote an innocuous post entitled "Red or Gray?" which queried readers on their color preference for corned beef. That unleashed a flurry of comments, some directly answering the question, but others adding to the traditions and memories of St. Patrick's Day through the city's history. One even offered a recipe for Irish soda bread.

Another post I wrote memorialized Manuel Martin, a young Portuguese immigrant from Lowell who was killed in action in France while serving in the United States Army during World War I. Within days, members of Mr. Martin's family from around the globe (Florida, California, Brazil, and Portugal) were leaving comments, thanking me for remembering their relative, with one writing "I am the last surviving nephew of Manuel Martin. I have the body-flag, his gold star, and his certificate signed by

President Woodrow Wilson."

I was a student at Providence College in Providence, Rhode Island, when a dormitory fire on December 13, 1977, killed ten students. On that date in 2010, I decided to share my memories of that tragedy. Every year since then, my post receives new comments from people identifying themselves as relatives or friends of the deceased students, as surviving residents of that dormitory, or simply individuals curious about the fire. A Lowell resident whose daughter recently graduated from Providence told me that while she was a student there, he heard something about the fire, Googled it, and had my blog post returned as the top result.

The experience with these comments and others brought home the power of the internet to bring people together. Others in Lowell made the same observation and acted upon it, because the end of the first decade of the twenty-first century was the golden age of blogging in Lowell. Besides *RichardHowe.com* and *Left in Lowell*, Gerry Nutter, Corey Sciuto, and Jackie Doherty all had self-named blogs. City Manager Bernie Lynch launched his own blog from City Hall. Greg Page and Cliff Krieger tackled broader issues on a *New Englander in Lowell* and *Right Side of Lowell*, respectively. Marianne Griese posted about culture and cooking on *Art is the Handmaid* while Anne Ruthman wrote about current events on *Lowell Handmade*. Anonymous writers launched sharp political commentary and satire on *Kad Barma*, *Mr. Mill City*, and the *Lowell Shallot*. The *Lowell Sun*, a bastion of the mainstream media, also jumped into the blogging pool with Chris Scott's *Column Blog*, Rob Mills' *Police Line Blog*, and others.

The crowded Lowell blogosphere era was short lived. Blogging on a regular basis requires a significant commitment of time and intellectual energy. Changes in circumstances and the ongoing demands of life caused many of the above-mentioned blogs to disappear or at least go on extended sabbatical.

However, the burgeoning online political world of Lowell

did not disappear; it shifted to social media. Both Facebook and Twitter reached maturity after the birth of *RichardHowe.com*. Before long, many of those who had been active in the Lowell blogosphere migrated their political commentary to Facebook. To me, that was a positive development. There was no moderation on Facebook, so people could write whatever they wished, but the terms of service required users to register by their true name so for the most part, everyone knew who was saying what. Facebook proved complementary to *RichardHowe.com*, becoming a delivery system of blog content to a wider audience while also serving as a platform for a more vibrant debate via comments than was offered by the slower-moving blog.

I have long believed that Twitter has the potential to become a powerful tool for sharing local information, but that remains an elusive goal. Like me, many use Twitter as a curated, continuous news feed, following political figures, major news organizations, their reporters, and sports teams. Unfortunately, the overall lack of locally focused tweets keeps Twitter from becoming a major source of local news and information.

Twitter got an enormous boost from Donald Trump in the 2016 presidential campaign. Trump used late night tweets to his millions of followers to set the tone of the campaign and to bypass traditional media outlets. Ironically, those same mainstream outlets often made Trump's tweets their lead news stories.

Video is another tool that has yet to realize its great potential as a means of sharing local information. Tony Accardi and I used to talk frequently about the power of video and how the obstacles to creating and sharing video had fallen so abruptly with the advent of tools like smart phones and YouTube. Tony agreed to become the video curator of *RichardHowe.com*, scouring the internet for short form videos that were created in Lowell or that otherwise might inspire blog readers to venture into video creation and sharing themselves. Since video does not translate well to print, Tony's video finds did not make it into this book. However, Tony agreed to share his thoughts on the democratization of video:

> "When Google purchased YouTube in 2006 for a staggering $1.65 billion, many technology observers thought the browser giant had made a huge mistake. Today, YouTube has over a billion users. The company itself estimates that one-third of people using the internet are registered YouTube users. These statistics are truly amazing and a testament to the popularity of video, especially of the home-grown style.
>
> Bloggers primarily use text and video to convey their message. Each provides advantages, but to paraphrase the British graffiti artist Bansky, video is democratic. A raw-cut video embedded in a blog post is a true presentation of reality. It is unadulterated, objective, and powerful. Video posts convey the emotional reaction of the participants and transfer these feelings to the audience. And video can do all of this while maintaining the integrity of the event.
>
> Of course, the effectiveness and popularity of videos in blogs are dependent on the material available to the blogger. When original video content is not available, the blogger often turns to video warehouses such as Vine (six-second videos) or YouTube.
>
> The advent of smart phones with video capability has revolutionized digital media by allowing the creation of a massive volume of content available to bloggers. Estimates are that the number of YouTube videos reach as high as one billion. As society has become more accustomed to technology, we have instinctively reached for our smart phones and become the collective recorders of history and unique moments in time. This trend will not change. As we create and upload more and more, the role of video in social media, our culture, and the work of bloggers, will only increase."

While the power of video is undeniable, the central act of blogging remains a writer at a computer keyboard. The practice has changed much since *RichardHowe.com* launched in 2007. By 2016, Facebook and Twitter had become big, commercialized, distribution engines, and other sites, like *The Drudge Report* and *The Huffington Post* wield power as aggregators of stories created by others. However, individual blogs have retained a niche in the electronic media landscape as delivery systems for longer form content that provides context for the abbreviated news world of social media.

Besides Donald Trump on Twitter, another major media story to emerge from the 2016 presidential election was the power of "fake news" sites which produced stories that were verifiably untrue. These falsehoods were often shared more than legitimate stories. One factor in this is confirmation bias, our willingness to believe things that fit within our view of the world. Another factor is the growing distrust of traditional media and of experts.

Tony Accardi, who has taught Citizen Journalism at Middlesex Community College for several years, believes that aggregation and filtering, which are even now being taught in college curriculums, will help sort through this deluge of content. Tony writes:

> "Today, few would disagree with the premise that information and news delivery is in a state of revolution. As an example, many young men and women in this current generation have never even read an ink newspaper. These are the students who fill the seats in our colleges today.
>
> Yet these same students are active participants in the gathering and dissemination of community information and news. Using Facebook, Twitter, blogs, Instagram and other social media tools, they have changed the communication landscape forever, and made college professors re-examine the

questions 'What is news?' and 'How do we assess its credibility?'

Just 15 years ago, college students were asking, 'What is a blog?' Today, their successors post countless items on Facebook, Twitter, and Instagram as casually as earlier generations talked with friends. This flood of citizen-generated content gushes at the public in a new, exciting, and overwhelming way.

Newly introduced college courses in digital media focus on the creation and effective use of the tools of 'the new trade,' helping to advance its popularity. Most students today know how to create and use social media tools. But now the sheer volume of information being produced threatens to drown out the effectiveness of citizen-generated content. This problem will most likely result in a shift in digital media instruction that includes utilities used for filtering the internet's vast quantity of information. As digital media classes seek to benefit more students who are already familiar with information creation, curriculum will concentrate on content 'mining' as opposed to content 'production.' Ultimately, the goal of collective knowledge can only be reached through the aggregation and filtering of digital information."

More than anything else, the 2016 election demonstrated the disruptive effect of the new media landscape on national politics. Whether it was Donald Trump tweeting directly to his millions of Twitter followers or "fake news" sites gaining more traffic on Facebook than stories from traditional news producers, the future role of the media in America is unclear.

So how does a blog fit into all of this? While there are fewer blogs today, those that survive retain the interest of many readers. One reason is that local bloggers are members of the community they cover. Familiarity gained through in-person contact with members of the community helps create a trusting relationship between bloggers and local readers. With the insatiable thirst for information about the places in which we live, there will always be room for those who provide credible news and insights.

Clay Shirky, a professor at New York University who writes and lectures frequently on the social and economic effects of the internet, maintains that throughout history new technology has tended to become available long before society figures out how to best use it. Shirky says that is exactly the case with the internet, which was a disruptive technology that drastically changed the media landscape. He also says that these disruptive phases of history are periods of intense experimentation. I see *RichardHowe.com* as an open-ended experiment in community communications.

—Richard P. Howe, Jr.

2007

D-Day for the Fifth

By **Dick** on March 13, 2007
—

The selection of U.S. Rep. Marty Meehan of Lowell as Chancellor of UMass Lowell led to a special election to choose his successor in Congress. It also helped launch this blog.

Frank Phillips reports in today's *Boston Globe* that UMass President Jack Wilson will announce his choice for UMass Lowell Chancellor later today, and all signs indicate that Marty Meehan will be that choice. The announcement will be made today, and not tomorrow as originally scheduled, to allow the new Chancellor to appear at a dinner of the UMass trustees tonight. (By way of background, Phillips is a former *Lowell Sun* reporter who, along with Kendall Wallace, made The Column the "must-read" section of the Sunday paper).

Even though the still unofficial race to succeed Marty has dominated political discussion in Lowell, most of us have severely underestimated the attention this race will draw from outside the district. For example, a post on the *Blue Mass Group* blog yesterday ignited a vigorous debate about the relative strengths of the candidates, and Adam Reilly criticized the Fifth District's state senators for not stepping up and joining this race. In other news, state Senator Steve Baddour (D-Methuen) announced yesterday that he would not run for Congress this time.

HISTORY AS IT HAPPENS

Congrats to Sen. Panagiotakos

By **Dick** on March 21, 2007
—

Lowell's Steve Panagiotakos, who was elected to the state Senate in 1996, ascended to what many consider the second most important post in the Senate, chair of the Ways and Means Committee. Unfortunately for him and for Lowell, his tenure in that position coincided with the country's worst economic crisis since the Great Depression. Steve chose not to seek re-election in 2010, and was succeeded by Eileen Donoghue.

It seems that state Sen. Therese Murray's first official act as the new president of the Senate was to name Steve Panagiotakos chair of the Senate Ways and Means Committee, a position second in importance to the president. Congratulations to Steve. Certainly, the participants in this Sunday's Greek Independence Day parade here in Lowell will have an added reason to be proud of their heritage. With the Senate on the verge of releasing its proposed budget for fiscal year 2008 with public hearings and tumultuous conference committee hearings to follow, the chair of Ways and Means will be in the eye of the budgetary storm for the next few months. Local political chatterers will have to divide their time between critiquing the Congressional campaign and speculating about all the state funds that will now flow into Lowell courtesy of the new Ways and Means chair. That kind of speculation is short-sighted, however. The senator from Lowell is in position to wield enormous influence on all aspects of state policy from education to health care to taxes, things that affect everyone each day. Maybe we should let him focus on that stuff first. He won't forget Lowell. And as the saying goes, If you feed the elephants, the mice will take care of themselves.

Subprime Mortgage Crisis

By **Dick** on April 9, 2007
—

During Saturday's Fifth District candidate question and answer session, Jim DiPaola, the Sheriff of Middlesex County, repeatedly alluded to the subprime mortgage crisis. His deputies are directly involved in the process of holding sheriff's sales and in evicting those who have been foreclosed from their homes, so he sees the human effect and is obviously (and appropriately) making it an issue in the Congressional campaign. The *Lowell Sun* adds a valuable view of the subprime foreclosure crisis with a major three-part series by Mike Lafleur that began yesterday. There have been many stories about foreclosure statistics, but not many that have put a human face on the problem. Lafleur succeeds in doing this by interviewing a gentleman who lost his Dracut home to foreclosure in January 2006. Using two related mortgages totaling $295,000 to finance the purchase of the home, this individual only earned $886 per month from his disability check and a part-time job. His monthly mortgage payment was $2,300. The math obviously doesn't work, so how did this happen? The print edition of the story provides a copy of the homeowner's loan application which shows his monthly income to be $6,158, not $886. This story is must reading for anyone searching for an explanation of how this crisis came about.

HISTORY AS IT HAPPENS

Prayer and the City Council

By **Dick** on April 25, 2007
—

The place of religion in city government has been a recurring theme at Lowell City Hall. This post is about the vote to open City Council meetings by reciting a nondenominational prayer instead of the Roman Catholic version of the "Our Father." In December 2013, emotions flared again when the City-owned Nativity Scene was erected on the grounds of nearby St. Anne's Church rather than on the grounds of City Hall.

A Lowell High School student recently told me of a debate that broke out while his Honors history class was studying the Reformation. What I found most fascinating was not the content of the discussion (which sounded the equal of any graduate school seminar) but the diversity of the participants. Among the eighteen or so classmates were Buddhists, Hindus, Muslims, Jews, Orthodox Christians, Protestants, and Roman Catholics—rather, one Roman Catholic (that being my correspondent). This year, students from that and other classes at Lowell High have already been admitted to Harvard, Yale, Brown, Notre Dame, and other elite universities. They are Lowell's future—but only if they choose to make Lowell their future.

It was these students that came to mind as I monitored last night's emotional debate on the future of the Lowell City Council's longstanding practice of opening each meeting with a recitation of the Roman Catholic version of the "Our Father." The council majority agreed to switch to a non-denominational prayer more likely to withstand Constitutional scrutiny. Predictably, the prevailing councilors were vilified this morning on the local AM radio station, WCAP. Why has this decision caused such a rabid reaction?

Partly, it's attributable to some justifiable resentment by Catholics who feel they belong to the one religious group in America that can be insulted with impunity. But I also think that the heated criticism on this issue is a subconscious reaction by those who feel a familiar and comfortable way of life slipping away. Some embrace change. Some are petrified by it.

Presumably, it was a similar mindset back in the nineteenth century that caused a Massachusetts bureaucrat in an official government report to slur French-Canadian immigrants by calling them the Chinese of the Eastern States (not to mention the insult to the Chinese). It was the same mindset that prompted some Lowell homeowners in the late nineteenth and early twentieth centuries to convey real estate on the express condition that the property never be conveyed to anyone born in Ireland or descended from anyone born in Ireland. While that report author and those deed grantors would undoubtedly argue that they meant no harm, they certainly did create harm by making Lowell a less welcoming place for the city's newest residents.

When the City Council in 2007 recites a prayer that is familiar only to a minority of residents, the council makes the city a less welcoming place for the rest. By voting as they did last night, the majority not only sent a message to Lowell's many non-Catholic residents that the council respects their religions and cultures and traditions, but the council also increased the likelihood, however slightly, that those top students from Lowell High won't migrate to a more welcoming community after college, but will return to Lowell as doctors, lawyers, engineers, scientists or teachers—and that will make this a better place for all of us.

HISTORY AS IT HAPPENS

Women in the 'Fabulous Fifth'

By **Marie** on May 8, 2007
—

Scot Lehigh's column in today's *Boston Globe*, focuses on the issue of women in elected positions of power in New England, past and present. Women hold two U.S. Senate seats in Maine (Snowe and Collins), the governorship in Connecticut (Rell), and one of two seats in Congress (Shea-Porter) from New Hampshire. The Democratic Party Chair (may have just stepped down), State Senate President, and Speaker of the House in N.H. are women. Connecticut, Vermont, and New Hampshire had women governors in the 1970s (Grasso), '80s (Kunin) and '90s (Shaheen). Of course, Massachusetts had Jane Swift as acting Governor, but she chose not to run in her own right when Mitt Romney appeared on the political scene. With women as Lt. Governor, State Treasurer, Attorney General, and Senate President, as well as three formerly in the U.S. Congress (Rogers, Heckler, Hicks) and Democratic Party Chair, Massachusetts has a good record with women in office. All this was a lead-in to a discussion of "a woman in the House" from the 5th District. The fact of Massachusetts having only sent three women to Congress seems to make the Massachusetts Fifth Congressional District especially intriguing to Lehigh. Which is why the Democratic race to fill Marty Meehan's seat promises to be such an interesting affair: The front-runner is a woman, as is the candidate best positioned to challenge her. As the special election scramble begins, the clear leader is Niki Tsongas, widow of Paul Tsongas, former U.S. Senator and a Lowell legend, who is a recognized community leader in her own right. But Eileen Donoghue, six-term Lowell city councilor and former Mayor, also enjoys considerable support in the city that is the heart of the district—

and the backing of some of the Fifth's pivotal power brokers. While listing prominent supporters of both women, it was clear that Lehigh couldn't resist taking a poke at the position of the "cagey congressional coyote"— Congressman Marty Meehan and his supposed neutrality in the race.

While heavy on the positives for Tsongas, Lehigh does credit Eileen Donoghue with her own strength and support. But although Tsongas supporters portray her as the only serious woman candidate, that undersells Donoghue, who is expected to be strong in Greater Lowell and who has the potential to grow in northern tier communities like Haverhill, Lawrence, and Methuen, places without local favorites in the fight. Donoghue already enjoys the support of important figures such as state Senator Steven Panagiotakos and Mayor Bill Martin, both of Lowell. Mayor Bill Manzi and state Senator Steven Baddour, both of Methuen, are expected to endorse her shortly. Lehigh gives the men in the Democratic race—Barry Finegold, Jamie Eldridge, and Jim Miceli—only a passing glance and little chance while positing that Republican Jim Ogonowki "just might mount a serious challenge." His conclusion: Still, at least at this point, the Fabulous Fifth seems likely to send a Democratic woman to Congress.

HISTORY AS IT HAPPENS

'Find A Way to Get in the Way'

By **Dick** on June 4, 2007
—

U.S. Rep. John Lewis (D-Georgia) gave an inspiring Commencement Address yesterday at the UMass Lowell graduation. Lacing his remarks with humor and history, Lewis traced his entry into the Civil Rights movement to his upbringing as the child of a sharecropper in rural Alabama. The posted signs that constantly reminded everyone of a divided society—White and Colored—disturbed him, but his parents counseled, Don't get in the way; don't get into trouble. But in 1955 at age 15, Lewis heard Martin Luther King, Jr., speaking on the radio from Montgomery, Alabama, and this inspired him to become a soldier in the non-violent revolution that was being waged for civil rights. Of course, the only ones practicing non-violence were Lewis and his companions, for they were often beaten and injured during their peaceful protests. Using the phrase "Find a way to get in the way" as the central theme of his remarks, here's a sampling of what Lewis told the graduates yesterday.

> "Be maladjusted to the problems of today. Get in the way. Get your voices heard. You have a mandate from all who came before you in this great struggle. In the Civil Rights Movement, we were prepared to put our bodies on the line. We studied Thoreau and Gandhi and followed the example of Martin Luther King, Jr. We created a non-violent revolution of values and ideas. Because of this, we live in a better country and we are a better people. We've made a lot of progress, but this is a struggle for a lifetime. Stand up for what you believe in. Never give up. Keep the faith."

Gay Marriage Vote

By **Dick** on June 14, 2007
—

As court rulings across the country sweep away bans on same sex marriage, it is easy to forget the controversy that erupted here when the Massachusetts Supreme Judicial Court ruled on November 18, 2003, that "barring an individual from the protections, benefits, and obligations of civil marriage solely because that person would marry a person of the same-sex violates the Massachusetts Constitution." Opponents of same-sex marriage sought to amend the Massachusetts Constitution to ban such marriages through the referendum process. This post describes the final act of that effort.

Today's Constitutional Convention defeated the ban on gay marriage by a vote of 45 to 151. To recap this issue, a petition to place a referendum that would amend the Massachusetts Constitution to ban gay marriage required the support of 25 percent of the state legislature at two successive Constitutional Conventions. It had already achieved that amount of support last year. If the ban had received the votes of 50 or more senators and representatives today, it would have appeared on the state ballot in 2008. By only receiving 45 votes, this referendum effort is dead.

The Lowell delegation was split with Tom Golden and Kevin Murphy voting against the measure and Steve Panagiotakos and Dave Nangle voting for it. The Democratic Congressional candidates have all weighed in on the ban on gay marriage. Representatives Jamie Eldridge and Barry Finegold voted against it. Jim Miceli voted for it. Niki Tsongas released this statement:

> "Three years ago, I rallied on the steps of the State House with my daughter in support of same-sex marriage, and today the work of thousands of people

dedicated to marriage equality has finally paid off. I am pleased that the legislature reflected the will of the majority of Massachusetts residents by recognizing that constitutional amendments should not limit rights but expand them. We can all be proud that we live in a state where the civil rights of all our citizens will be protected. Our state and nation are stronger for this commitment to defending the rights of all people and for putting a high value on the principles of tolerance and human dignity."

While Eileen Donoghue released this one:

"I applaud Massachusetts legislators today for their courageous vote against adding discrimination to the state Constitution. I have always supported equal marriage rights and will continue to fight for the extension of those rights as a representative in Congress."

While the supporters of gay marriage are jubilant, the pro-ban side will have much to say about the people being deprived of their right to vote. But the winning side played by the rules. Everyone had to publicly vote on it; it wasn't killed by some procedural shenanigans.

As for the right of the people to vote, no less of an authority than James Madison would be skeptical of such a procedure. In his famous essay on the U.S. Constitution, "Federalist No. 10," Madison wrote that in a pure democracy (where each person has an equal vote) "a common passion or interest will, in almost every case, be felt by a majority. . . and there is nothing to check the inducement to sacrifice the weaker party." Such democracies inevitably become "spectacles of turbulence and contention."

Madison argued that our republican form of government, where the power of the government is delegated to a small number of citizens elected by the rest, is far superior.

> [The effect of republican government] is to refine the public views by passing them through the medium of a chosen body of citizens, whose wisdom may best discern the true interest of their country, and whose patriotism and love of justice, will be least likely to sacrifice it to temporary or partial considerations. Under such a regulation, it may well happen that the public voice pronounced by the representatives of the people will be more consonant to the public good than if pronounced by the people themselves. . . .

A Reply from the City Manager

By **Dick** on June 19, 2007
—

My two recent posts about the plight of downtown Lowell elicited a cordial and informative email message from City Manager Bernie Lynch. After thanking me for recognizing and commending the efforts of the police department, he mentioned some of the other things the City is doing to help stem the rising tide of summertime violence. The centerpiece of this effort seems to be the Anti-Gang Task Force appointed by him last November. Composed of leaders from the police department, the District Attorney's office, the probation department, the school department, Middlesex Community College, and others, this group meets monthly.

> "Each meeting [of the Task Force] includes a review of gang-related incidents, possible response measures,

discussion of the dissemination of information, and development of initiatives to address the root causes that you note in your blog. For instance, we initiated a jobs-for-youth program whose purpose is to encourage businesses to create summer jobs. To date, we have established over 50 positions under this effort and are still trying to get more by reaching out to the business community. We've also increased our recreational offerings from the City through new programs and increasing the number of pools that will be open. We've reached out to our state and federal legislators on behalf of increased funding for things like the Shannon Grant program. In fact, Greg Croteau of the United Teen Equality Center just returned from a trip to D.C., where he testified before a Senate Committee on the issue of gang and youth violence and identified the City's and UTEC's efforts as models for other communities. Finally, the City Council Public Safety Subcommittee has a meeting next week to review this work and get an update on our plans for this summer and beyond. This follows an earlier meeting with the Youth Subcommittee where the jobs and recreation programs were outlined."

That's all very encouraging. Last summer, when I'd leave work, the neighborhood near the courthouse resembled the grandstand at Busch Stadium in St. Louis there were so many red shirts in view. (This year, the preferred color is brown, but there's less of it). Gangs account for many of our incidents of violence, so everything the City is doing is good. But gangs are just part of the problem. Yesterday, I wrote of an 1898 shooting on Market Street. Cities have always had problems and always will. Success is measured by shrinking problems enough to make them a nuisance instead of a threat. Do that, and vacant storefronts will take care of themselves.

Controversy at Folk Festival

By **Dick** on July 30, 2007
—

Matt Murphy must have a crystal ball. A day after his article on the political impact of YouTube appeared in the *Sun*, Constitutional Party candidate Kevin Thompson has launched a video attacking the Lowell Folk Festival for limiting his freedom of speech and a more pointed attack on Republican candidate Jim Ogonowski who had the misfortune to show up at JFK Plaza moments after Mr. Thompson had his confrontation with the National Park Service police. Like any good techno-capable citizen, Thompson had a video camera and documented the entire incident.

Here's a preview: The Lowell Folk Festival took place this past weekend. Stages are scattered throughout the downtown. This incident takes place in front of the stage at JFK Plaza (home to the Lowell Police Department), which is adjacent to Lowell City Hall. The National Park Service routinely designates spots within their facilities as free speech zones. Within these zones, political activity is permitted, but the rest of the national park is a non-free speech zone in which political activity is limited. From my own experience, I know that Lowell National Historical Park has designated free speech zones on a day-to-day basis, so this wasn't some recent contrivance. My assumption has always been that it has passed judicial scrutiny and has been judged to be Constitutional, but I digress.

When Mr. Thompson's effort to collect nomination form signatures was curtailed, he grabbed his camera and recorded (surreptitiously, it appears, and with poor audio) the park ranger explaining this to him. Then along comes Mr. Ogonowski and his entourage complete with a political sign. They stroll into the non-free speech zone. (The audio gets better here). Mr. Thompson alternatingly taunts Mr. Ogonowski for not showing up at debates and beseeches Park Service employees to apply the same rules to Republicans. While Mr. Ogonowski adopts an ignore-him-and-he'll-go-away approach towards Thompson, his staff seems befuddled. (They really ought to practice their immediate action drill for hecklers). One Ogonowski aide tried to push the camera away and another opened an umbrella and used it to try to shield the candidate from the camera. The video is just under eight minutes long—it's worth watching.

Musing on Moxie's Lowell Roots

By **Marie** on August 5, 2007
—

Today's *Boston Globe* story on Moxie reminded me not only of its "roots" in Lowell, but also of that whole world of "medicine" in the mid- to late-nineteenth century. Lowell's history as the home of patent medicines, tonics, and cures certainly laid the ground work for accepting the entrepreneurship of today in bio, nano, and many other technologies. Many tout these technologies as the future for Lowell in the twenty-first century. Lowell has historically been receptive and welcoming to those like Dr. J.C. Ayer, C.I. Hood, E.W. Hoyt, Dr. A. Thompson, and others who used their creativity and ingenuity to make Lowell a hub for more than textiles and related machinery. I think it might be time for my colleagues in the Lowell Historical Society to mount an exhibit for yet another look at the glory days of patent medicine companies in Lowell. Most are familiar with Moxie, but wouldn't you like to know about Fr. John's Medicine, Hood's sarsaparilla and cough cure, Ayer's cherry pectoral, Johnson's Brown Bottle, Rubiofoam, toothpowders, pills, and of course the renowned German Cologne? This industry, by the way, gave rise to a broad spectrum of advertising and later to a world of collectibles. There were giveaways of all kinds: postcards, trade cards, calendars, puzzles, cook books and posters. Patent medicine bottles are collected, traded, and sold—some are quite valuable. (Look on eBay under Lowell Collectibles). Along with cartoons and the political rhetoric of the day, they help to tell one of the many stories of Lowell.

Dems Unity: Niki and Friends

By **Marie** on September 5, 2007
—

Niki Tsongas prevailed in the special Democratic Primary to replace Marty Meehan in Congress. Here is Marie's report from the Democratic Party unity event held right after the election.

As an activist Democrat, I am very pleased with the talk, the turnout, and the commitments coming from this morning's Democratic Unity press conference at the Doubletree Hotel in downtown Lowell. The room was full of supporters from all the campaigns—movers, shakers, strategists, and the grassroots activists. The media, including Michael LaFleur of the *Sun*, Latoyia Foster Edwards from NECN and Victoria Block from Channel 7, was well represented.

Mass. Democratic Party Chair John Walsh took the platform followed by an impressive group of Democrats including Senators Steve Panagiotakos, Steve Baddour, Sue Tucker, and Susan Fargo; state Reps. Dave Nangle, Kevin Murphy, David Torrisi, Corey Atkins, Tom Golden, and Linda Dean Campbell; Mayor Bill

Martin, Mayor Bill Manzi, Attorney General Martha Coakley, Governor Deval Patrick, Niki Tsongas, Eileen Donoghue, Jaime Eldridge, Barry Finegold, and State AFL-CIO leader Bobby Haynes.

The cheers and applause were loud and sustained. Senator Kennedy connected to the event by phone announcing, "Ted Kennedy here with congratulations for Niki Tsongas. Vicky and I want to know what can we do to help?" The Senator praised the challengers by name and declared that Democrats all care about the issues. He commended everyone for coming together and looks forward to working with Niki Tsongas in Congress.

Governor Deval Patrick then took center stage and congratulated all candidates for "running a positive campaign on the issues, for not talking down to people, for addressing needs and anxieties. He emphasized that "We can't just be about what's wrong with Republicans. We have to talk about what's right about Democrats." He said the Republican candidate in this race was strong, but the voters in the Fifth District have a choice: to go back to the recent past or to go forward in pursuit of the American dream.

The Governor then introduced Niki who, after praising each of the other candidates said, "Make no mistake, this campaign is a referendum on the Presidency of George Bush and on the war in Iraq." Niki spoke of a timetable for withdrawal with a plan to care for our veterans. To the Republican candidate, she said, "You cannot run, and you cannot hide—the message to the White House is it's time to end the war. We spend $13 million per hour on the war." She also spoke of health care, global warming, education as a family value, and economic development. She thanked Senator Kennedy, "who shows how purpose can be put to work," and all who were present. She ended with what appears to be the thrust of the campaign: "Send the message to the White House that we want to go in a different direction."

Top Ten Lowell Political Events of 2007

By **Dick** on December 29, 2007
—

1. Marty Meehan resigned from Congress to become Chancellor of UMass Lowell.

2. Niki Tsongas won the Democratic primary in a Congressional special election, defeating Lowell City Councilor Eileen Donoghue and state Representatives Jamie Eldridge, Barry Finegold, and Jim Miceli.

3. Tsongas defeated Republican Jim Ogonowski in a surprisingly close special Congressional election.

4. Superintendent of Schools Karla Brooks Baehr opted out of a renewal of her contract to seek the state Commissioner of Education job.

5. Radio station WCAP (980 AM) was sold by long-time owner Maurice Cohen to Clark Smidt and Sam Poulten, who vow to retain the station's local focus.

6. For Lowell City Council, Alan Kazanjian and Mike Lenzi were elected to replace Eileen Donoghue and Joe Mendonca (who had replaced George Ramirez, who had resigned midterm to take a position in the Governor Deval Patrick administration).

7. The School Committee was shaken up as newcomer Dave Conway topped the ticket and Supt. Brooks Baehr-critic Regina Faticanti finished a strong second while five-term incumbent Kevin McHugh was defeated.

8. Cancer claimed the life of Paul Sullivan, who began his media career at WLLH as the host of *Morning Magazine*, became a force in local and state politics as a *Lowell Sun* columnist, and later hosted a talk show on WBZ radio.

9. Real estate market troubles worsened, with home sales down and foreclosures up, and the resulting credit crisis threatened to bring down the entire national economy.

10. The Boston Red Sox won the World Series (again with a team filled with former Lowell Spinners: Jonathan Papelbon, John Lester, Clay Buchholz, Dustin Pedroia, Kevin Youkilis, Jacoby , and Brandon Moss.)

2007

2008

Obamamania in Nashua

By **Tony** on January 6, 2008
—

By late 2007, Senator Barack Obama (D-Illinois) had developed serious momentum in his quest for the Democratic nomination for the Presidency. Tony Accardi experienced that tidal wave in Nashua, N.H.

Yesterday I attended the Barack Obama rally at Nashua High School. I intended to be a casual observer. My wife and I arrived approximately 45 minutes early for the 10:00 a.m. event. We figured this was ample cushion time. Oh, were we wrong! When we approached the school, we couldn't believe our eyes. The line to enter stretched at least three football fields, snaking down and around the parking lot. We wondered whether we would even get in because there were so many people waiting. But the excitement in the atmosphere easily strengthened our patience. There had to be more than a thousand people in front of us as we took our place in the line. After thirty minutes of waiting, I looked back and saw what I estimated to be another thousand people behind us.

When the doors opened, Obama workers filled the gymnasium quickly and efficiently. My wife and I were lucky enough to be directed to remain on the floor and take a position in the front row to the side of the podium (I did mention we were in the front row, right?). The atmosphere was electric. I imagined that this was the kind of energy that John and Robert Kennedy generated in the '60s.

Obama's people were fabulous. They were courteous, energetic, and organized. Within twenty minutes of filling the gym every pair of able hands was holding an Obama sign (yes, I kept mine). The crowd was so large (I estimated 3,000), that some unfortunates were directed to an overflow room. This is the only way I can describe what it was like when Obama entered the room: in 1965, I saw the Beatles perform at Suffolk Downs in East Boston; that is the only time I heard a louder roar of excitement and enthusiasm. The candidate delivered a rousing speech filled with the messages of hope and change, firing up the crowd until it crescendoed in a chant of O-bam-a, O-bam-a, O-bam-a. Before I knew it, I was jumping up and down yelling O-bam-a, O-bam-a, and demanding change. I was in the grip of Obamamania. Today? Well, I almost feel hung over. Yes, I still have my Stand for Change sign, but I've calmed down. Here's a message to you disbelievers out there: This guy's got something special, and he radiates it.

Pooh to the Pundits

By **Marie** on January 9, 2008
—

When Hillary Clinton won the New Hampshire Democratic primary, Marie Sweeney was thrilled and a little resentful of the prognosticators who had already awarded Obama the Democratic nomination.

This is personal! As the debate wore on last Saturday night I reversed my decision to skip the Hillary Clinton rally in Nashua on Sunday. There was something about Clinton that night that touched me at the core—obviously now, in hindsight I see that others, particularly women, were also affected. The excitement, the electricity, the energy in the room on Sunday afternoon buoyed my feelings for better than predicted results on Primary Day. Once home I went online and sent money.

On Monday I spent three hours on a local radio program—devoted to all things New Hampshire primary. When a caller told us of a media report that a candidate had a meltdown in Portsmouth and named Hillary Clinton, I was stunned and said very little—letting the host and others react. My gut reaction was that the woman who moved me over the weekend wouldn't be in a Monday morning meltdown. She was strong, focused, and determined. She answered all questions asked—on a full range of topics, not shying from anything or anyone. So, no damn question about her hair would rock her boat. I was more than right! I felt that she was caught by the concern and interest expressed for her personally. That's a novelty on the campaign trail. I think she was touched by it, not in the throes of a staged moment.

The resulting vitriol, venom, and downright wackiness spewed around the blogosphere. The talk shows and places beyond were medieval. I admit I'm in HRC's best demographic—woman of a certain age. I was angry and dismayed to think that the issue of gender was a rope to be wrapped around the neck of Hillary Clinton in of all places New Hampshire. Apparently, enough N.H. voters decided differently. They defied the pundits, pollsters, and prognosticators. Kudos to those voters who stayed the course or who took a second thoughtful look. One way or another, history will be made on November 4, 2008.

Note: I wrote this piece early this morning but held-off posting until returning from doing some personal business. While in the car I moved all over the AM/FM "dial" and heard some outrageous treatment of women voters who were calling in to express their views. Also, the Public Policy Polling guys were floundering around spouting all kinds of reasons for the Hillary win. For me it was women—women from all demographic categories—women who listened and reasoned—and it was Hillary herself who made the connection and closed the deal. Go, Hillary.

HISTORY AS IT HAPPENS

Bits and Bites

By **Marie** on January 25, 2008
—

For those of you who thought you spotted newly-elected Lowell Mayor Edward "Bud" Caulfield in the audience at Governor Deval Patrick's State of the State address last night, you saw correctly. The Mayor was there seated right next to Boston Mayor Tom Menino. That is a coveted seat. It wasn't originally designated for the Lowell Mayor, however. Mayor Caulfield was in Senator Panagiotakos' office while waiting to join other guests in the House Chamber, and his presence was made know to the "powers that be." Before you know it, he was invited to sit next to Mayor Menino. The original designee was unable to attend: Senator John Kerry.

At this morning's "Today's Knowledge Economy: Renewing the Connection in Merrimack Valley Cities" forum at UMass Lowell that focused on MassINC's Gateway Cities report, UML professor Bob Forrant was scheduled to present the challenges and strengths and offer suggestions to the participants. As he began, he looked to the front row and with a twinkle in his eye expressed some concern that the Lowell City Manager, the Mayor of Lowell, and his boss (Marty Meehan) were there. Marty in his ever-typical way immediately quipped, "Bob, I didn't think you had a boss." It made great comic relief! Chancellor Meehan in his remarks referred to the mortgage/foreclosure report prepared by my "boss" here, blogger Dick Howe. Meehan called the study "valuable information" and an "important analysis" and a useful "tool." Dick's report was a front page story in the Sun this morning. The *Sun* editorial also praised Howe's position on the transparency surrounding the Superintendent's Search Committee process. Readers of this blog know that Dick is an advocate for a fully open procedure, including most importantly public interviews by the screening committee of the finalists. Mayor Caulfield, too, supports a fully open process. Dick must be surprised at all that "positiveness" coming from the Dutton Street office of the daily paper.

Sisters

By **Henri Marchand** on June 15, 2008
—

The following essay premiered on UMass Lowell's Sunrise *radio program on WUML in June 2006. The author retraced the trip this past Memorial Day Weekend, again with his brother and cousin, in what has become a family tradition.*

For the past three years, I've joined my brother Rene and my cousin Rick on the long weekend pilgrimage north to Canada, to the Quebec village of Lac au Saumon (Salmon Lake) situated at the beginning of the Gaspe Peninsula. Our destination was the motherhouse of the Sisters of Notre Dame, Queen of the Clergy. As usual, the 700-mile trip began at six o'clock on Saturday morning. We took turns driving and dozing, reading and calling out crossword clues, debating politics, and recalling family history. And snacking. We drove up Route 95 northeast to where it ends in Houlton, Maine, and from there we took Route 1 North past endless potato fields and forests of pine and birch until we reached the quiet border town of Van Buren at twelve-thirty. After lunch, we crossed into New Brunswick and barreled along pastoral Route 17 for four hours through rolling fields, hill country, and villages named after saints. At Campbellton, we headed north on Route 132, also known as the Route of the Pioneers, following the Matapedia River that runs below steep ridges. We passed through lumber forests alternately clear-cut and thickly planted and where there is always the promise of a moose materializing by the side of the road. At five-thirty, we arrived at Lac au Saumon. We turned off the main street running along the lake and climbed through the tiny village to the motherhouse, an impressive building overlooking the village below and the hills beyond the lake.

Waiting anxiously, Aunt Rita greeted us with her ever-cheerful spirit at the front door. Walking the long hall of the east wing towards the cafeteria, Rick said that he'd never seen so many holy pictures in one place. The walls were covered with images of the saints. Jesus was on countless illustrations and calendars, on crucifixes and in the wide smiles and warm welcomes of the aging sisters. They greeted us with a hearty chorus of *Bonjour!* as we entered the dining hall and moved along the buffet line. Every year the community's average age rises and its numbers diminish, but the sisters' hospitality remains constant. Several stopped by our table to wish Aunt Rita "*une bonne vacance*" and to chatter in fast French. We tried to keep up, to recall enough of the language of our parents and grandparents to get by, but mostly we faked it, nodding and smiling and hoping that Aunt Rita and her friend, Sr. Monique, could interpret for us. They were kind and laughed with us at our fumbling, and we somehow understood most of what was conveyed.

There are few televisions in the house, all in community rooms, so after our aunt bid us goodnight about eight o'clock, we broke out a couple of beers Rene had smuggled in. Except for our tired talk and squeaking of our rocking chairs, the house was silent. We had traveled nearly 700 miles in 12 hours, but it seemed a journey of even greater distance.

We were on the road back to Lowell the next morning, and arrived at my mother's house in time for dinner. We described our road adventures and listened to the actual sisters begin their long vacation conversation. At 81, our aunt has been retired for eight years. She returns to Lowell for her annual vacation to spend six weeks with her sister. Known for her spunkiness, Aunt Rita will tease. Listening to her and my mother, I sometimes hear two teenage girls sharing secrets, giggling, and whispering in conspiratorial tones. When they were younger, my mother was the serious, studious sister, known for following the rules; Aunt Rita was the prankster, always trying to get her older sister into trouble and known for having an eye for the boys. But at age 15, she says, she received her calling and entered the convent two years later. She left Lowell in the spring of 1942, traveling by train to Lac au Saumon, where it was still winter, to begin a two-year novitiate. A horse-drawn sled carried her and her trunk from the station to the motherhouse. "There was a lot of snow!" she recalls. Some in the family didn't give her six months, but she stayed and made her final vows in 1949, and has been assigned to parishes from Massachusetts to Quebec.

The closer she was stationed to Lowell, the more often she visited. For six weeks, the two sisters will be inseparable as they make the most of their time together before saying goodbye in mid-July. They will attend Sunday Mass and graduation and birthday parties, and friends and distant relatives will visit. They will watch *Jeopardy*, discuss their latest ailments without complaint, and recall their younger days. They will play cards, dominoes, and a cutthroat game called Tuck, a favorite of my aunt's that she plays without mercy. Laughter will come easily and heartily and often. And, of course, they will pray every day. I imagine that they pray that these next six weeks pass more slowly than the last six decades.

HISTORY AS IT HAPPENS

Adios, Aiello: A 'Third Place'

By **Dick** on July 23, 2008
—

The closing of Café Aiello is a loss. The staff made a great cup of coffee, and it was a comfortable, convenient place to meet, especially for those of us who work on the south side of downtown (and in proximity to the new downtown development frontier, the Hamilton Canal District). Urban theorists, sociologists, and others have long identified the importance of the "third place" in society. The first place is your home, the second place is where you work, and the third place is somewhere else, an informal meeting place where you can exchange ideas with others. For centuries, perhaps, local coffee shops and pubs served this purpose. Today, it's Starbucks and places like Brew'd Awakening and Café Aiello that fulfill that role. Third places are essential in post-industrial communities like Lowell where promoting the creative economy is a key to future economic progress. Creative types like artists, computer programmers, and inventors often work in isolation, which means places to socialize and interact with others are especially important for them. While Aiello offered good things to drink and eat and provided appealing space, it faced steep challenges, not the least of which was a Dunkin Donuts across the street. But the entire Hamilton Canal District has challenges, and the ability for places like Aiello to stay in business during the formative stages of this development area will be a big measure of whether this it succeeds.

Remembering John

By **Jack Neary** on September 30, 2008
—

The following originally appeared in St. Anthony Messenger.

One day, the bullying stopped.

And it took a catastrophe of epic proportions to remind me why.

On the morning of September 11, 2001, I was in my home office, about to check my email and log on to the electronic news. The phone rang. A friend called to tell me to turn on my television because a small plane had flown into one of the World Trade Center buildings in Manhattan. News, to be sure, though it didn't seem to be the kind of news one would drop everything to check out. But my friend was not the overreacting type, so I went into the living room and clicked on the Panasonic. I'm sure I went right to CNN, which was the network of immediacy back then. Nowadays, virtually every television network is immediate, shoving each other's airwaves out of the way to get the hot picture or sound byte. But the network of choice during national crises in '01 was CNN, so that's where I went.

And that's where it was. The fiery tower jutting up into the impeccably blue late summer morning sky. My friend's report didn't seem accurate. Or sufficient. A small plane did this? Not likely. Both of the principal structures at the WTC were imposing buildings. And the hole that appeared to have been blown into the side of one of those iconic edifices was a hole that probably was not made by a small plane. I watched with tense fascination as the ugly, world-shattering story unfolded, point-by-point, update-by-update, talking head by talking head.

The buildings only represented the real horror we all felt, the horror we couldn't know, the horror confronted by the people inside those buildings. There'd be no more work in the home office that day, certainly. It was one of those times when the often brain-numbingly unpredictable life of the freelance writer/theater director allowed me to shift gears midstream and just stare at the world event spinning out of control on the television.

What was not spinning out of control on the television, however, was the persistent crawl at the bottom of the CNN screen, rigidly and unsparingly updating me second to second on the various details of the morning's disaster.

About three hours after I began watching, as I sat leaning forward in my living room chair drinking in all the information, a stunning piece of news on the CNN crawl brought me unexpectedly back to high school. To Keith Academy, an all-boys Xaverian Brothers institution in Lowell, Massachusetts.

At Keith, I was one of those kids, as a freshman at least, who was imposed upon. Maybe "stepped on" is a more accurate characterization of my daily routine. I was overweight, shy, and dynamically challenged. The agenda for each school day employed by the most cloddish among my classmates was written boldly on my face, flashing in my eyes, perhaps even emblazoned on my forehead:

"This kid is a pushover. Bullies, start your engines!"

There was nothing terribly original about the bullies of Keith Academy. Their method was standard operating procedure. Exactly what you'd expect from hulking, insecure fifteen-year-olds more full of themselves than they were of compassion. They were walking clichés, heisting lunch money from my locker, shoving me out of the cafeteria line, creating uncomplimentary nicknames to holler at me down the hallway. Future literary managers scribbled "Kick me" on PostIts and slapped them on my unsuspecting suit-jacketed back. My bullies were not clever, but they were vigilant. And I wouldn't fight back. I wouldn't report them to Brother Patrician, the burly, no-nonsense principal. Maybe I thought he'd just tell me to take it like a man, I don't know. But I would not react visibly at all. I was such an easy mark for them, I think they used me for practice. A warm up act before taking on the kids who might retaliate. For the first few months of my freshman year at Keith Academy, the bully onslaught was unrelenting.

And all I could think of when I saw what I saw on the crawl on CNN about three hours into 9/11 were those bullies and why they stopped bullying me.

The day progressed, the televised drama intensified. The ultimate reality show, years ahead of its time. The first building collapsed. Then the second. The mountain range of smoke and cinder and flying rubble stretched from the Battery to the Bronx. I had been there, in that embattled city, only a day and a half earlier, sitting in the right field stands at Yankee Stadium, watching the Red Sox lose, as they usually did back in those pre-2004 Septembers. I had parked my Sentra in Manhattan, right there as I saw it on the TV screen, where the mammoth tuft of smoke now enveloped the streets. A day and a half ago, I was there, and now the city was. . . what? Exploding? Imploding? Under attack? Nobody knew for sure. Speculation about terrorism stopped being speculation when the second airliner plowed into the second tower. Inconceivable. But actually happening, right there, on CNN.

He was just a kid. Back at Keith. Taller than some, but not a towering figure. In fact, he walked with a kind of loping slouch, his mop of blond hair seemed to shove his head and neck down into his torso, emphasizing his powerful shoulders. Not small. Not large. But not put upon, that's for sure. The bullies took one look at him and said, "Nah, let's go after the short fat kid who sits in front of him."

That would be me.

His last name fell immediately after mine in the alphabet, so in homeroom he sat directly behind me in Brother Theodore's Religion class. "Teddy" was great, a sports lunatic who allowed us to watch the Red Sox in the '67 World Series during class time, back when they actually played weekday games in the

Fall Classic. Brother Theodore set us up alphabetically, thus contributing to my eventual escape from the bullies, and, in a very odd way, to this article.

It wasn't an instant friendship, the one that developed between me and the kid farmer who sat behind me. He was, in fact, a farmer, from Dracut, Massachusetts, a town just outside my hometown of Lowell. Later, after we'd become friends, he invited me and another classmate to visit him on his small farm just outside of Lowell. He neglected to tell us it was spreading season, when all the manure that... accumulated... in the barn over the long winter was excised from its bovine cache and tossed from the gratingly roaring John Deere every which way over field and meadow on the farm. It made for a memorable olfactory sensation. To my friend and his family, it was business as usual. To me and the other kid who came along with me for the visit, it was an eye-wateringly pungent assault on our nostrils. When I remember my day on my friend's farm, I remember the first time I walked into that barn. It was the only time I walked into that barn. I made certain of that. And I walked out really fast.

In any case, my farmer friend and I were both the reticent, shy type, so, despite our classroom proximity, ours was not an instant camaraderie.

It took the bullies to make that happen.

I sat there in front of my television staring in disbelief at the crawl, even though the information had moved on and the breathtaking moment I experienced seconds earlier was instant history. They had run a picture of him, and he looked just as he did in high school. Fuller face, maybe, but not much else was different. The hair looked the same. Just as blond, maybe not quite as floppy. It looked like a professional photo, one that his airline must have taken for his identification card. Smile broad, but not overly so. Eyes calm, calming, confident. He looked like a contented man.

The way I'd want my pilot to look if I were taking a commercial flight out of Boston to L.A.

At school, it wasn't any specific incident that triggered our friendship and the bullies' abandonment of Project Fat Kid. He just started sitting with me at lunchtime. I'd been the kid who sat alone, the solitude inviting ridicule and abuse. He sat alone, too, usually, but in a different kind of non-threatened way. One day, he just sat down next to me and we ate our lunch together, chatted a bit, and started hanging out at lunch every day. Once that happened, because he was who he was, the bullying stopped. Maybe he was bigger than I remember him, and they were afraid. I don't know. It just stopped. We became school friends. And that was it.

When we graduated, we went to separate colleges, and did not stay in touch. After school, he remained in Dracut, just a few miles from my house, but... our relationship simply did not extend beyond Keith Academy. He went his way. I went mine. He ran the family farm. I went into theater. Life happened.

And then, the crawl.

I learned more about him after 9/11, of course. The world did. We discovered that he had inherited his family's farm and turned it into a very successful business in Dracut. We also found out that he had joined the Air Force after college and had become a pilot. He somehow managed to combine two careers—flying commercial jets and running a farm—into what everybody described as an exemplary family life. On September 11, 2001, he started his day the way he always did when he had a cross-continental flight—he'd get up at dawn, have breakfast, and hop in his truck to drive to Logan. On the way, he'd honk his horn as he drove past his uncle's house. He was a family man.

I think about sitting there, in the Keith Academy gymnasium, an aging leather-and-sweat-smelling space that was used for everything from lunch to assemblies to basketball games to football pep rallies. I think about my friend, and I can't remember what we talked about at lunch. I have a brain like a sieve. I wish I could remember. I wish a lot of things. I wish I had kept in touch. I wish I had been part of his life, because it became clear that the people who knew him loved him. I wish it had occurred to me before 9/11 to let him know how important he'd been to me when I was fourteen, trying to survive in a difficult environment, dealing with idiot schoolboys and, also, incidentally, with my father's death. But when you're a kid, you don't think about the effect another kid has on you. Only time provides that enlightenment. And, if you're lucky, you get the opportunity to say thanks.

His name was John Ogonowski, and Brother Theodore, CFX, seated him behind me in Religion class, homeroom, at Keith Academy in 1964, because that's the way the alphabet dictated it should be. His name was John Ogonowski, and he was the pilot of American Airlines Flight Eleven out of Logan Airport in Boston, September 11, 2001.

I couldn't get anywhere near his funeral at St. Francis Church because by that time he belonged to the world and the world press covered the funeral. When the world press covers a funeral in Dracut, Massachusetts, there is no parking. So, I watched on television. Probably on CNN.

I wrote a letter to the local newspaper, and the local newspaper printed it. In it, I thanked John for being such a nice kid in high school. Years too late. But I imagine his family read it. His wife. His kids. So they'd know. I hope so, anyway.

And I'm thinking that maybe my friendship with him, way back then, was something of a thank you in and of itself. John seemed to be the kind of kid who didn't need to be thanked out loud, the kind of man who knew when he was doing a good thing, but never making a major deal out of it. I think he knew about my bullies, and I think it made him happy that they backed off.

A virtual thank you.

In the end, he became a major deal. World-renowned. For doing his job at the center of what turned out to be a life-altering event for all of us.

But by then, John Ogonowski had long since made his mark on his friends and family in Dracut.

Just as he had made his mark on me, when he took my out-of-order high school existence and provided it with some semblance of normality.

Just by sitting down with me for lunch.

Elliot's Closed?

By **Marie** on October 31, 2008
—

Just heard that Elliot's Famous Hot Dogs in all its locations was shut down today! This Lowell culinary institution opened its doors in 1920. Long a staple for hot dog lovers—including the venerable Johnny Carson sidekick Ed McMahon of Lowell—it's hard to imagine Lowell without access to an Elliot's hot dog. Rumors also abound about the relocation or maybe even the demise of the Lawrence landmark for hot dogs—Laughton's. Remember the Dutch Tea Room, the B.C., the Epicure, the Speare House, Bishop's, the Prince Grotto, D.L. Page, the Rex, and so many more? Let's hope that the Owl Diner, Good Thymes, River Road Cafe, Club Diner, and others continue with business as usual.

HISTORY AS IT HAPPENS

Casting My Vote

By **Dick** on November 4, 2008
—

I got to the Daley School shortly after 7:30 a.m. to cast my vote for Obama and Biden. There were waves of people entering the school, but with two separate precincts and an efficient check-in system there was only a short line. It took five minutes to get my ballot and start darkening in the ovals. The act of voting went smoothly, but the voting machine was broken. Usually you slide your ballot into the top, where automatic rollers grab and pull it in; the machine tallies your vote internally while indicating the number of your ballot. Instead, we had to drop ballots into an open slot in the side of the box. Maybe the automatic tabulator will be fixed during the day and the ballots will be fed through; but if they're not and the ballots have to be counted by hand, it will take a while to get the results from Ward 8, Precinct 3.

My son Andrew turned 18 at the end of the summer, so this was the first election in which he was eligible to vote. Wanting to cast his first-ever vote in person rather than by absentee ballot, he came home from college yesterday, and I drove him back after voting this morning. As we headed down Massachusetts Ave. in Cambridge at about 8:30 a.m., I noticed a long line of people snaking along the sidewalk and around a corner. Thinking that perhaps tickets were about to go on sale for an exceedingly popular concert, I blurted out, "I wonder what that line is for?" He replied, in the type of kind and understanding tone an 18-year-old uses to inform his father of the obvious, "They're waiting to vote." Mistaking a long line waiting to vote for people waiting for concert tickets—maybe our democracy is healthier than we thought.

The Morning After

By **Dick** on November 5, 2008
—

On November 4, 2008, Barack Obama was elected President of the United States. I was pleased.

Some thoughts the morning after the election. With the outcome of the vote in four states still in doubt (North Carolina and Missouri are too close to call, while Indiana is leaning Barack Obama and Montana is leaning John McCain), it's good that the race was not any closer. Our country didn't need another presidential election decided by post-balloting maneuvers by lawyers.

Obama won 68 percent of the "youth vote" (ages 18-29). As someone pointed out to me this morning, an 18-year-old who was able to vote for the first time yesterday was in the fifth grade when George Bush defeated Al Gore in 2000. The historic turbulence of that election and all of its consequences undoubtedly taught those kids that elections count. Indeed, the Florida 2000 vote taught them that every vote counts. Another factor in the youth vote is technology. Most young voters were using computers before they could walk. When McCain, early in the campaign, said he was "learning about the internet," he lost the youth vote. For most of us, computers are an integral part of our everyday lives; voting for someone who was clueless about the potential of such technology was never an option.

The pundits are saying Obama "blasted through a racial barrier," which is true, but anyone who asserts that race is no longer an issue in America is delusional. Between an increased turnout of African Americans and votes by white Americans who considered race in a positive way—that is, it would be a huge step forward for America to elect a black President—history may show that race was a net plus for Obama. But make no mistake, racial animosity simmers unabated in America. The outcome of this race suggests it is eroding, but it is still there. I hope the performance of the Obama administration will zap that tumor like a massive dose of radiation, and that ugly part of America will lapse into permanent remission.

Three years ago, I read an article about the discontent many Democratic Party leaders felt towards Howard Dean and his "50-state strategy." Dean believed that Democrats had to make an attempt in every state, no matter how much the Republicans dominated it. Democratic insiders saw this as a waste of money, advocating the same "two coasts plus one" strategy that had worked so well in 2000 and 2004 (resulting, of course, in eight years of George W. Bush). Fortunately, Dean prevailed. Obama was of like mind, which is why he won states like Virginia, Colorado, and Nevada.

The post-election spin from both Fox News and much of the mainstream media is, "Will Obama govern as a centrist or as a socialist with his fellow travelers Nancy Pelosi and Harry Reid?" Anyone who seriously asks that question has had blinders on for the past two years. Obama beat the Clinton machine and the Republican machine that, even though wounded, was still potent and dangerous. Now he's going to be rolled by Pelosi and Reid, two "leaders" who have accomplished nothing in the two years in which their respective bodies have held majorities in Congress? It will be the other way around.

And if you have listened to Obama's policy positions, he intends to lead squarely from the center. That's not just an electoral bait and switch, either. It's his core philosophy. Obama's victory is a devastating blow to our enemies. The war on terror will not be won by superior fire power, but by superior ideas.

Around the world today, the results of this election are causing suicide-bombers-to-be to question their motives. Every rational being in the world wants to live cooperatively and in peace. Other nations will see this as the opportunity for a fresh start.

As for the economy, that will be our new President's biggest challenge. Unfortunately, our financial crisis is bound to get worse before it gets better (although my guess is the stock market will experience a pretty good bounce today). Hopefully, we will see a New Deal-like infusion of public works projects that provide employment while strengthening our infrastructure along with extensions of unemployment benefits, health insurance for the unemployed and uninsured, and serious attempts to remake our economy for the twenty-first century. History tells us that in a recession, you must increase government spending, not cut it.

That's it for now. There will be plenty of additional reaction in the days to come.

Ice Storm Report

By **Paul** on December 13, 2008
—

Branches started snapping about 2:00 a.m. Friday. Cracking limbs and the loud thuds of boughs hitting the yard and pavement woke us. Daylight revealed the damage. The top of a tall cedar had broken off and crashed onto one of our cars, which was unscathed because thick green tufts cushioned the fall. Nearby cars were not spared when a huge maple tree split at the vee, sending one half smashing onto and over a backyard fence—and onto seven cars in the adjoining parking lot. One car's rear quarter was punctured by a sharp broken branch and another had glass damage. Amazingly, most of the cars came away with minor nicks and bruises. Fifty feet away a thick limb from an ancient cherry tree squashed another section of the backyard fence. Pine boughs were strewn around the yards. Our driveway looked like an evergreen carpet full of shattered glass, with about three inches of pine needles, cones, and spurs of fir all encrusted with ice.

Overnight the power had blinked out two or three times, but we were fortunate to have not suffered an outage. At Enterprise Bank's branch on Gorham Street I spoke to a friend who does our snow-plowing; he was told the power would be out at his house in Lowell until Monday. I heard the same from two landscape company workers who were cutting up downed trees with chainsaws. They were from Hudson, Mass., and had been clearing debris since midnight. They had seen electrical transformers blowing up in showers of blue sparks as they drove around in the dark. Wires and trees were down all over, the worst ice damage since a storm in 1998.

When, finally, the sun shone strongly for a while yesterday afternoon, the trees in our yard started raining ice as they shed their crystal shells. The new worry is freezing weather that will make utility repairs much more difficult and prevent the drying.

Refugees Return

By **Marie** on December 15, 2008
—

It's amazing how quickly you can disconnect from the broader world when you have no electricity. The pump doesn't work, so the water seeps into the basement, then rapidly rises. A damp coldness permeates your home, and the stark reality of having to leave hits you on the side of the head!

With a certain age comes an inability to tolerate the cold and the isolation. With "no room" in any local inn and only with the intercession of our "connected" son, we trekked to Burlington for a three-night stay. (Unlike our mall neighbor to the north, the Burlington Mall with no loss of electricity was a hot spot for shopping, Santa, and sales. In fact, traffic was so heavy when we returned to the inn on Saturday afternoon that turning left off the ramp rather than right towards the Mall was a tremendous relief!) We were joined by my 86-year-old mother who suffered from the same heat, light, and water deprivation. And did I mention the downed trees in both yards? As we turned into our Tewksbury driveway at noon Sunday to get a situation update, the outdoor garage light went on, an amazing reconnect to the rest of the world.

Fortunately, outer Belvidere "turned-on" as well. Allowing the heat to catch up seems a wise choice, so after another night with many other electricity-deprived refugees and families from as far away as Maine and central New Hampshire, as well as towns in the Merrimack Valley, we returned home today. As we talked over the last 72-plus hours and checked-in with family, we remembered the hurricanes of the early 1950s, the Blizzard of '78, and other times when we were cut-off or isolated from the broader world and how we coped. Was it easier? Did we take it more in stride? Of course, no electricity in August or September is a different kettle of fish. My mother remembered the closeness and helping each other, not just family but the neighbors too. She talked of growing up in the Highlands and of family and friends. We did, too, but in another time and generation (for us it was the Sacred Heart/Grove and outer Belvidere). Back to normal tomorrow? Well, it may take a bit longer, and then there's Christmas coming next week, and we have stories to share!

HISTORY AS IT HAPPENS

New Year's Day and French Canadian-Americans

By **Paul** on December 28, 2008
—

This is from *The French-Canadian Heritage in New England* by Gerard J. Brault (Univ. Press of New England and McGill-Queen's Univ. Press, 1986): "January 1 was one of the most important feasts of the year. The family gathered early at the grandparents' or parents' home, and the eldest son asked for the blessing [from the grandfather]. . . . The blessing (similar to one given by a priest) was followed by a wish along the following lines: . . . *Je vous souhaite une bonne et heureuse anneé, une bonne santé, et le paradis a la fin de vos jours!'* ('I wish you a prosperous and happy New Year, good health, and eternal bliss when you pass on!') . . . After attending New Year's mass, the family returned home for drinks and food, often including roast beef or turkey; mashed potatoes; peas, pickles, beets, and onions; *tourtieres* [pork pies]; *croquignoles*; and other desserts."

The day concluded with visits to relatives. Massachusetts state Representative Henri Achin of Lowell served for 25 years in the legislature (1912 - 1937). A lawmaker who was deeply faithful to his cultural roots, Rep. Achin succeeded in making New Year's Day an official holiday in the Commonwealth, which it has been since 1917. (For these facts, thanks to Richard Santerre's pamphlet *The Franco-Americans of Lowell, Massachusetts* [The Franco-American Day Committee of Lowell, 1972].)

Back Pages

By **Paul,** December 31, 2008
—

My family's house in the South Common Historic District was bought by my wife's grandfather in the 1930s. The house was built for managers of the Appleton Mill Company in 1869. Occupants in the first 60 years left things behind. One curiosity is a shelf of books from the 1800s—random titles from personal libraries that got passed down as the house changed hands. That's my guess, unless one past occupant collected the mixed bag of books. Poking through the books again this morning, I was struck by some coincidental dates.

There's a beautiful, four-inch-thick copy of *Byron's Complete Works, Illustrated* (Phillips, Sampson and Company: Boston, 1854) signed: "Mrs. Sarah E. M. Goodrich, January 1st, 1855." This volume contains "unabridged, line for line, word for word, the complete works of Lord Byron" in 1,071 gilt-edged pages, including "his suppressed poems and a sketch of his life." We have a two-volume set of *The Ingoldsby Legends; or, Mirth and Marvels* by Thomas Ingoldsby, Esq. (The Rev. Richard Harris Barham), published by W. J. Widdleton of New York in 1866. These are illustrated stories in verse about French musketeers, knights and ladies, the Merchant of Venice, smugglers and buccaneers, jackdaws, witches, milkmaids and nurses, and ghosts. What caught my eye today is the inscription on the title page: "F. P. Putnam, Lowell, Dec. 31, 1867"—signed 141 years ago to this day. Sometimes History jumps into your hand.

This is the same Mr. Putnam who inscribed another book "Frank P. Putnam, Christmas 1872, from Eliza." Frank received as a gift *Rambles of an Archaeologist among Old Books and Old Places* by Frederick William Fairholt, F.S.A., published by Virtue and Co. of London in 1871. A book written in French that seems to go with this one is *L'Age du Bronze: Instruments, Armes, et Ornaments* par John Evans D. C. L., L. L. D., published by Librarie Germer Bailliere et cie. of Paris in 1882. There's also *The Monumental History of Egypt as Recorded on the Ruins of Her Temples, Palaces, and Tombs* by William Osburn, R. S. L. (London: Trubner and Co., 1854). In the style of the time, several of these volumes have marbled or feather-design end papers in rich greens, blues, reds, and gold.

Mr. P. had other interests also, because his name shows up in an unusual book, *The Hasheesh Eater: Being Passages from the Life of a Pythagorean*. In the vein of tales from the East, this mysterious author recounts the secret to the "Eastern narrative" and mind. His subject is "Cannabis Indica," the resin of which is hasheesh. He writes: "From time immemorial it has been known among all the nations of the East as possessing a powerful stimulant and narcotic properties. . . ." Harper & Brothers of New York published the book in 1857. The explorer proceeds with his narrative through stages of curiosity, ecstasy, pain, and torture to, finally, "abandonment of the indulgence." Sounds a little like a nineteenth-century version of the 1936 film classic *Reefer Madness*. Forget what you may have heard about Jack Kerouac. Is Putnam the missing link in "Beat" attitude in Lowell? In an Appendix, J.W. Palmer, M.D., citing medical journal articles and experiments in India, makes a case for medical use of the herb, all of which is oddly timely given the new law in Massachusetts regarding use of the substance.

Putnam appears in real time in *The History of Lowell and Its People* by Frederick W. Coburn, volume III (Lewis Historical Publishing Company: New York, 1920). There's a full-page photo of him in business attire with a white handlebar mustache and a cigar in his hand. Here's his profile:

"Frank P. Putnam was born in Lowell, Massachusetts, November 15, 1848, and has ever resided in his native city and added to her mercantile greatness. He attended the public schools of the city, but at the age of fifteen years left high school to go into his father's store, business life greatly attracting him from boyhood. This was in 1863, or 1864, the clothing store of Addison Putnam [the oldest of Lowell's men's clothing and furnishing stores] then being located at the corner of Market and Central streets. He rapidly absorbed the principles upon which the business was conducted . . . and upon arriving at legal age [became his father's] partner, the firm trading as Putnam & Son. [He later became president of Putnam & Son Company at 166-168 Central Street.]

"Addison Putnam was a member of the Board of Aldermen for a time, but Frank P. has accepted no political office, but served the city for twenty-one years as a trustee of the Public Library. He is a director of the Appleton National Bank; trustee and vice-president of the Lowell Five Cents Savings Bank; director of the Traders' and Mechanics' Insurance Company of Lowell; and is a member of the Board of Trade. He is a thoroughly public-minded citizen, one who can be relied upon to aid in any movement promising better things for Lowell or the country-at-large. He is a Republican in politics.

"In the not always peaceful arts of trade he has won eminence, and in his native city of Lowell is well known and highly esteemed as merchant and citizen. There are few men, who, if fortune had been kind to them in a financial way, but would develop some special interest which often amounts to a passion, sometimes a hobby. Mr. Putnam is not an exception, his passion being the cultivation of flowers, carnations, and single chrysanthemums being his specialty. Many are the prizes and first premiums which adorn his home, where four large greenhouses are stocked with the specimens and varieties which most appeal to the owner's tastes.

"Mr. Putnam married, in Lowell, November 1, 1898 (at the age of 50), Sarah Barry. The family residence is at North Tewksbury, where the greenhouses are Mr. Putnam's especial pleasure, and a generous hospitality is extended."

Top Ten Events of 2008

By **Dick** on January 2, 2009
—

1. The Lowell School Committee hired Dr. Chris Scott to follow Dr. Karla Brooks Baehr as Superintendent of Schools.

2. The future of the Tsongas Arena and LeLacheur Park was murky, due to questions about who will own the arena and manage the baseball park.

3. In the local media, the *Sunrise* public affairs program ended on WUML at the university, George Anthes left the air on WCAP Radio, but went on cable TV with *City Life*, and Lowell City Manager Bernie Lynch and Republican activist Cliff Krieger launch their own blogs.

4. The most controversial issues for the city council were procedural: changing from weekly to biweekly meetings; a residency ordinance proposal that died a quick and quiet death; and an initial defeat of the City Manager's proposed reorganization of the Office of Cultural Affairs.

5. One of the most dangerous traffic intersections in Massachusetts, Plain-Chelmsford-Powell streets, was reconfigured, and the University Avenue Bridge was closed for emergency repairs.

6. Register of Probate John Buonomo was filmed by a security camera allegedly taking cash from copying machines at the Cambridge Registry of Deeds Office; and state Senator James Marzilli is facing charges arising from bizarre personal behavior in Lowell.

7. The national election took much of our attention with Hillary Clinton winning the state Democratic primary in February and Barack Obama defeating John McCain in November's presidential election.

8. Gasoline topped $4.00 per gallon early in the year, however, the price fell to $1.65 by Christmas.

9. Foreclosures increased while home sales and house values declined.

10. The New York Giants defeated the Patriots in the Super Bowl; the Dracut Middies won the state football crown for high schools; and the Celtics won the NBA championship for the first time in 20 years.

2009

2009

Lowell Variety: History as It Happens

by **Dick** on January 1, 2009
—

Today we introduce a special feature for the new year. In addition to our normal coverage of politics and current events, we will also use this blog to capture Lowell's history as it happens. History is defined by the *American Heritage Dictionary* as "A narrative of events; a story; chronicle; a chronological record of events, as of the life or development of a people, country, or institution." To produce our "chronological record of events" about Lowell in 2009, we will devote at least one blog post each day portraying life in our city.

At one time Lowell was dotted with neighborhood variety stores like Marie's, Mickey's, Lowell, Parker Street, Patty's Kitchen, Salem Street, Sunny, 1300, Village, and Yim. Just as the ideal variety store had all the daily staples and a little of almost everything you might want or need, we hope that our online journal will reflect the variety of Lowell life.

We hope to capture that variety by inviting our readers to become contributors to this dynamic journal. Please become more than a reader by adding your own reports, observations and recordings of daily life in Lowell. Have the buses stopped running up Christian Hill because of the snowstorm? How big was the crowd at last evening's Tyler Park concert? How did the baseball game go at Shedd Park? What did you think of the restaurant you tried for lunch today?

These are just a few examples of the infinite variety of topics that will make up this year-long record of our city. Check out the "writing prompts" section of our Lowell-2009 page on the upper menu bar for more ideas.

We ask that you limit entries to 250 words or less so that the posts make for a brisk read. Send your composition to the

55

blog editor by email for posting. While we don't promise to post everything that is received, we seek great variety. Speaking of variety, if you prefer pictures or video to tell your story, tag everything "Lowell-2009" and send us the links to your flickr or YouTube uploads. Join us in this community documentation experiment. A year from today, we expect to have a remarkable, unique account of one year in the life of a city known for its history. We are asking you to be self-conscious as a group, as Lowellians, to see what we can make together.

Out and About

By **Marie** on January 5, 2009
—

I was out and about in the late morning today doing errands, some in Downtown. On this ordinary morning trek down Route 133 I found myself behind a funeral procession on its way to St. Mary's Cemetery. Slowing down made checking out my surroundings easy. There are still trees down from the great ice storm of December '08, but none were obstacles. Despite the recent weather and the reality of winter, there are repair, restore, and replace projects in high gear. On Andover Street, the renovation and restyling of the Freeman Ballard Shedd manse, one of the twin or mirror-image Victorian houses, continues. At first I expected the results to look more armory than residence, but to my surprise, as the work continues and the new look unfolds, I've changed my mind. It looks elegant and quite at home on this street. On East Merrimack Street stone work and other repairs on the Immaculate Conception Church exterior continue under Fr. Nick Sanella's watchful eye. Next door at Lowell Memorial Auditorium men converged on the roof and elsewhere doing long-awaited infrastructure repairs for the long-term good health of that 1922 building. Downtown was quiet but dressed for the holidays. The full parking lot at Pollard Memorial Library reminded me that school was back in session, including the nearby Adult Education program. The new Jeanne d'Arc Credit Union building rising between the Wannalancit/Suffolk mill complex and the U.S. Post Office on Fr. Morissette Boulevard is all glass and clear to the eye. No hint today of the exterior cover. A sign adjacent to Cobblestones Restaurant reminded me that Winterfest '09 is drawing near. I think a day has been added to the schedule as the dates posted are February 5-7. Thursdays are good nights for Lowell events and celebrations. No big rush at Market Basket in Stadium Plaza on the Tewksbury line. With snow predicted for Tuesday night and Wednesday, I guess that will happen tomorrow. Errands done, after a stop to see my mother, I was home to Tewksbury to finish-up my un-decorating chores.

Riding the Rails: The 7:46 to Boston

By **Dick** on January 10, 2009

When traveling to Boston on a weekday, taking the train always seems like the best option. It's not cheap: a round-trip ticket from Lowell costs $13.50 plus $5 to park, but it still costs less than driving. (The underground garage at North Station charges $19, plus there's the cost of gas). So with a meeting "in town" this morning, I joined the one hundred-plus commuters boarding Train No. 310 shortly before its 7:46 a.m. departure from Lowell's Gallagher Terminal.

I rode the train almost every day for two years while attending school in Boston 25 years ago. From that experience, combined with watching the behavior of "regulars" on my less frequent trips since then, I know that critical decisions are required within seconds of boarding. Do you sit on the two-place bench seat on the left side or on the three-place bench seat on the right side? Since the morning trains are packed, I opt for the left side. I'm by nature an optimist, but the commuter rail is a place for minding your own business, not for meeting new and interesting people. It's easier to do the former when you're sharing a seat with one neighbor, not two. However, from April through September such considerations get trumped by the morning sun that blazes through the left-side windows, making it difficult to see, let alone read. It's January, though, and the sun is so far in the southern sky that only the engineer needs Ray-Bans.

Another question immediately arises. Where on the left side should I sit? The optimist in me prefers seeing where I'm going rather than where I've been, so the rear-facing seats are out. If you're in a hurry, sitting in the first few rows in one of the first few cars makes for a speedy exit, but that has a downside, too. At subsequent stops, new passengers come streaming through your car bound for the front-most places. As they pass through, they yank open the heavy sliding door at the front with such force that it sticks in the open position, allowing freezing cold air laced with diesel fumes to stream into the car. Often, a seated passenger will arise and tug the door shut, but then a straggler from the last stop wanders up the aisle and reopens the door, frustrating the Good Samaritan and ratifying everyone else's decision to stay stoic and seated.

As is evident from their dress, the morning riders are a business-like group. The ratio of *Heralds* to *Financial Times* and backpacks to brief cases flip flop the closer you get to Boston. Exiting the train is orderly, but fast-paced, as experienced riders steel themselves for the blast of arctic wind that hits them when they exit North Station and begin the trek up Beacon Hill.

The midday return trip is different. There are far fewer

passengers, but also fewer conductors on the train, so all but one or two cars are closed off. Still, it's rare not to have an entire bench to oneself. Fellow passengers are much more diverse: racially, ethnically, chronologically, and sartorially. My only complaint is with the one or two passengers seated nearby who inevitably spend the duration of the ride engaged in loud, seemingly pointless cell phone conversations. If you're going to make everyone in your car an aural witness to your side of the discussion, at least make it about something interesting. No matter. Soon you're rolling Lowell-ward from North Billerica, searching for the back of Fay-McCabe Funeral Home, trying to pick out which of the rusting, graffiti-spattered tank cars idling behind the Shaughnessey School contain hazardous substances, crossing the Spaghettiville Bridge, and then you hear "Lowell, last and final stop." You're home.

Remembering Charlie Pierce

By **Marie** on January 17, 2009
—

The survival of all the passengers and crew of the US Airways flight that "landed" on the Hudson River yesterday brought back memories of the Eastern Airlines Electra crash at Logan Airport on October 4, 1960. A flock of starlings caused of the 1960 crash; another "bird" incident involving both engines of the US Airways Airbus caused yesterday's crash. There was no miracle for 61 of the passengers in the Logan crash. Aboard the six-minute flight was a contingent of 15 Marine Corps recruits bound for boot camp at Parris Island, South Carolina. Three of the inductees who died were area young men—Charles

T. Pierce, Jr., and Edward H. Robinson, Jr., were from Lowell and Leroy W. Boyes was from Tewksbury.

Charles T. Pierce, age 18, while born in Louisiana, lived most of his life in Lowell. He was educated in Lowell schools, attending the Immaculate Conception School and graduating from Lowell High School in 1960. He was active in sports. He competed in the Silver Mittens and the *Lowell Sun* Golden Gloves tournament. He was survived by his parents Charles and Alma and two sisters, Cheryl Ann Pierce and Madelyn Sheehan. He was a communicant at St. Peter's Church in Lowell. He will always be remembered by his classmates—I was one of them at the Immaculate—as a great guy.

Hamilton Canal Planning Meeting

by **Joe Smith** on January 23, 2009
—

The Hamilton Canal District (HCD) Redevelopment Vision Session #5 was convened at the Lowell Senior Center on January 22nd. It was the last in the series of open meetings where City officials and the developer, Trinity Financial, interacted with the public to evolve an exceptional plan that has the potential of achieving transformational change.

For background, the HCD is a 13-acre parcel of land adjacent to the downtown that is mostly vacant, certainly underutilized, and with historic mill buildings that have been wasted to decay from the elements. The plan consists of two somewhat separate, but integrated by planning, developments. One is public, the Trial Court complex that will consume about 3.3 acres, and one private, a mixed-use project by Trinity Financial that includes housing, retail, commercial, and open space. For the community, it offers the hope of a livable, expanded center city while converting wasted land into productive real estate.

Hank Keating, the project manager from Trinity, updated the audience on significant changes since the previous session in May, 2008. The function of Middlesex Street through the Lord Overpass has been retained with traffic improvements, whereas initial plans, not well-received by most abutters, called for elimination of the Middlesex link through the Overpass. A parking garage, deemed critical for a significant commercial development, was modified in design to mitigate the intrusion into Canal Place 3 housing. With great support of the State House delegation, the Transportation Bond bill designates $10 million for the project infrastructure efforts, of which $3 million was released through Lt. Governor Murray last week. The National Park Service has a planning consultant to start the feasibility study for extending the trolley system through the district connecting to the Gallagher Transportation Center. The initial phase of the project calls for restoring the historic Appleton Mills for approximately 135 units of artist live/work housing and for a third party to develop the historic Freudenberg building for its own purposes. Keating announced that they have selected a Newton-based developer, CWC Builders, as the prime contractor for the Appleton Mills to contain the risk associated with renewing the decaying structure. Local subcontractors will be invited to participate in this work, and local contractors/subcontractors will participate in the succeeding, less risky, developments.

An interesting aspect of the work to be done is a Memorandum of Understanding (MOU) agreed between CWC, Trinity, the Cambodian Mutual Assistance Association, and the Building Trades to engage local workers in an Apprentice Program that would serve to grow the workforce while providing good-paying jobs. This redevelopment is not just an end in itself, and its process should help in the creation of an educated, productive workforce in the area.

Nancy Ludwig of ICON Architecture reviewed the private-sector development, not only showing the conceptual design of each building, park, bridge, and roadway, but also explaining the design rationale used to settle each concept. After the parcel-by-parcel presentation, she provided moving views of the district with fly-overs that gave the audience a better perspective of how all the parcels linked with each other. Jenn Campbell, state Division of Capital Asset Management, and prime architect Maurice (Mo) Finegold updated the audience on the status of the public portion of the HCD, the Trial Court Complex. Preliminary site work must be done, but the hope is that the site acquisition will be complete in time for a mid-May start of work with demolition of existing buildings and preparation of the site. The site is 3.3 acres, and the building design that has been developed will cover nearly one acre, with eight stories, each of exceptional height for a total of about 140 feet. The architect has taken great care to make this a "green" building, with some very interesting on-site, renewable energy sources, natural lighting, and air handling.

George Proakis of the City Division of Planning and Development described the Form Based Code (FBC) that has been developed for the HCD. The FBC provides greater emphasis on form than the typical zoning codes that emphasize use. As a mixed-use development, the FBC has been segregated into a number of codes applicable to various parcels in the district. Each one of these codes contains a set of rules that precludes bad uses and encourages designs consistent with the overall project goals. The FBC is in its final stages and will hopefully be accepted by the City agencies and ready for the developer in early March. With that and other actions completed, Trinity plans to start work in May of this year on the Appleton Mill complex, with a target completion date of October 2010.

Ms. Ludwig then gave a more detailed look at the design concept of the Appleton Mills, where they retained the main wall of the mill aside the Hamilton Canal and preserved the water-power raceways and equipment in the lower level of the mill. The significant decay of the mill provides the opportunity to phase in a more modern design to the parts of the building that are not salvageable, creating an interesting complex for the artist colony. James Keefe, CEO of Trinity Financial, closed out the meeting saying that we are now at the end of the beginning of this project, with the challenging next phase ahead of us.

Lowell Photography Weekend

by **Paul** on February 1, 2009
—

My wife, son, and I enjoyed the exhibitions of photography at three locations today: The Brush Gallery and Arts League of Lowell Gallery at Market Mills and the Whistler House Museum of Art/Parker Gallery. At about 1:00 p.m., the Brush was packed with people for the reception and announcement of four prize winners. This show featured classic black-and-white photographs of a variety of subject matter, from architectural studies to portraits.

The entries were the work of people from across the state and beyond. One winner was from St. Louis. Across the mill yard, the ALL Gallery featured a mix of color and black-and-white work. My brother Richard had two prints in the show—one image from the North Shore and another of a sagging outbuilding near the former Hub Hosiery in Lowell. A distant cousin of mine, Greg M., had a color shot of a distressed person sprawled on a city street. There were two selections by Karen Westphalen who has been shooting the bridges in Lowell. She had a one-person show at the Mogan Cultural Center a few months ago. She uses distinctive heavy metal frames that allude to the steel work on bridges.

Our next stop was the Whistler House Museum, where there was a small but impressive display of Polaroid transfer prints. One group of prints was made from archival images shot by a man who traveled in the early 1900s to Cambodia, China, Egypt, and other countries. The small prints were fascinating moments in time with familiar icons of these cultures: the Sphinx, Chinese junks, a Buddhist temple.

We were also impressed by the fine pastel works in the Parker Gallery in an exhibition curated by Jim Dyment of the Whistler House. People streamed in to see the Polaroids, and museum director Michael Lally greeted everyone. Afterwards, we toured the house itself, which is as vital as ever. Paintings from the permanent collection were displayed in all the rooms. It's always special to see the Aldro Hibbard winter scenes when there is snow outside on Worthen Street.

We topped off our tour with a stop in the third-floor studio of resident artist Meredith Fife Day. She was in and welcoming visitors to the jewel of a work-space with the big window looking out on the Holy Trinity gold dome and St. Patrick's stone steeple. The gold leaf of the dome was on fire with sunlight against a background of pure powder-blue sky. She had a series of paintings, collages, and drawings all inspired by a remarkable blue bridge in France that she had seen on a recent visit. I was also interested in her paint-and-pencil studies of buildings and rooftops in the Acre. Kudos to the organizers of the Photography Weekend.

2009

House Fire at 62 Highland Street

By **Paul** on February 6, 2009
—

I'm back in the house after being on the sidewalk for more than an hour witnessing a powerful fire in the three-story white house on the corner of Thorndike and Highland streets: 62 Highland Street. Fire fighters have been attacking the flames with hoses in the freezing air. They were busting upper floor windows with axes. Heavy black smoke poured from the roof. It appears that all the residents got out safely, but I don't have first-hand knowledge of that fact. A neighbor said she heard the fire fighters had swept through all the rooms when they arrived. Flames spread upward and ate through the roof. I hear news helicopters circling. I haven't seen the live reports on Boston news channels, but relatives told us they had seen the breaking news when they called to check on us at our place just a few doors down the street.

Several of the residents who had been taken in by a neighbor in sat at the kitchen table reading the Bible. The owner of the house was worried that she would have to evacuate if the wind pushed the fire any closer. I told her to bring everyone to our house if the situation worsened. A young man who lives on the lower floor worried about his parents and their losses. All their artworks and writings were in danger. One woman cried hard as she watched the smoke thicken. I spoke with another man whose apartment is on the third floor. He said, "There's no saving that building." He had run out wearing just a shirt and pants. Somebody later gave him a sweater and sweatshirt after seeing him standing in the ice and snow.

At one point, there must have been six hoses streaming water onto the Thorndike side of the house. One neighbor from two houses down had come out with a sophisticated video camera to film the tragedy. Police officers took statements from residents of the building. I heard a fire fighter say he was having trouble with a pump on one truck. The fire fighters worked methodically to contain and then beat back the fire. I just got a phone call from a friend saying a TV reporter described the scene as almost under control. My wife and son have gone back out to see what is happening.

The house is one of the treasures of the South Common Historic District. Known as the Asahel Puffer House (ca. 1871), here's a description from the Lowell Historic Board brochure: "This Second Empire-style residence's slate mansard roof is pierced by arched dormers while an ornate portico and side porch illustrate other popular features of the period." This is the house Paul Tsongas grew up in and from which he launched his political career as a city councilor in 1969. My wife and son are back in. They heard that funeral home director John McDonough's son Jack had called in the report of a fire in the building after he saw smoke in one of the windows.

Lisa Redmond and the Fire Cats

By **Paul** on February 7, 2009
—

I appreciated reading *Sun* reporter Lisa Redmond's article about the fire at 62 Highland Street fire in this morning's paper. It was good to read a confirmation that all nine residents of the house made it through the ordeal without being hurt. The material damage to each of them is immense. This becomes a hinge moment in their lives with something very different coming next.

One additional detail in the story meant something special. Three cats survived the fire. I'm pretty sure those are the three cats belonging to a kind woman whose apartment is or was on the second floor. My family and I had helped raise those cats from the time they were born to a stray mother in our back yard. They were born last August in a small cave-like section of a pile of granite foundation blocks out back where a barn once stood. The litter included two grayish tiger cats and a three-colored money cat, like the mother. The mother kept them out of reach of anyone and raised them with amazing care. They survived the elements and who knows what else. I started bringing food and water to her so she wouldn't have to hunt for mice or birds in the small woods abutting South Highland Street. When they were up on their feet, she moved them to a new home under our garden shed. I began feeding them every day. They were slightly wild and nervous, so I was not able to gather them up to bring them to the Humane Society or a no-kill cat shelter. I was also concerned about taking them away from their mother. On fall afternoons we'd see them curled up on top of one another in a patch of sun near the shed. They had survived a skunk trying to get at them under the shed and drenching rain storms. I began thinking about arranging an adoption, asking around to see who might be interested in taking one or more of the kittens.

In October, I heard about the kindly woman at 62 Highland Street who loves cats. Her own long-time pet had recently died. She agreed to take the whole group and try to find a home for them. With some difficulty, we finally got them over to her place before the first frost. She had them checked by a vet, neutered and spayed, and got them their health shots. She placed one of the young cats with a friend out of state, but still had the mother and two tigers when the fire struck. Their owner was away the day of the fire, but returned in the evening. Fire fighters helped her get in to the building to check her apartment. I heard the rescued cats had icicles on their fur from the water that had poured into the house.

HISTORY AS IT HAPPENS

'Sampascoopies'

By **Paul** on February 20, 2009
—

Every day for more than 40 years, Charles G. Sampas wrote a newspaper column for the *Lowell Sun*. Everyone who read the paper knew about "Sampascoopies." He was a proto-blogger in before www. In 1986, his daughter, Marina Sampas Schell, published her edited collection of his columns on Lowell history, just a sampling, in the book *That Was the Way It Was. . .*(Lowell Historical Society, 1986). Here's a quote from the back cover:

> "How can Lowelltown ever be dull? It is dull minds that make it dull—in their minds...Lowell is an endless panegyric of the good life...Stand at the Square here. . . and watch the parade of faces. . . No two alike. . . Infinite variety. . . Here, if you stand long enough, you will meet all the people you've ever known. . . ."

Charles Sampas was a human website, an aggregator of historical and contemporary information that he would refashion and offer up in daily doses. His writing was documentary, impressionistic, narrative, celebratory, meta-personal, and kind of postmodern and pop art-like in the way he appropriated information and data and re-purposed it in the democratic format of a newspaper.

Breakfast-After-Dark

By **Paul** on February 27, 2009
—

The Owl Diner last night was transformed into a combination revival tent and Hollywood after-Oscar party hot spot as Sen. Steve Panagiotakos hosted a community appreciation rally for some of the leading community organizations in Lowell. More than 100 people converged on the popular eating place on Appleton Street at the invitation of the Senator, who called for the local huddle to remind everyone of the contributions made every day by the non-profit groups and neighborhood associations. Community Teamwork Inc., Girls Inc., Alternative House, Lowell Family Y, Lowell Parks & Conservation Trust, Boys & Girls Club, House of Hope, Salvation Army, Wish Project, Transitional Living Center (Shelter), Merrimack Valley Housing Project, United Teen Equality Center, all the neighborhood organizations, and a few others got a shout-out and rousing applause as the Senator offered capsule descriptions of their services and gave thanks for their efforts.

Waitresses buzzed around with plates of pancakes, scrambled eggs, and ham-steaks. Somebody said, "This is like eating backwards—having dessert first." Other folks recalled their mothers flipping the menu and making French toast and omelets for supper. Standing in the middle of the main eating room with the Senator were state Representatives Golden, Murphy, and Nangle, along with Mayor Caulfield and regional School Committeeman Hayden. Many members of the Lowell City Council and School Committee were in the room as were City Manager Lynch and School Supt. Scott. Congresswoman Tsongas flew in from Washington, D.C., and drove straight to the Owl from Logan so that she could express her gratitude to the community heroes and give folks a first-hand report on the atmosphere in Congress, which she said is serious and sobering, but also filled with a sense of possibility and Obama-brand hope.

Sen. Panagiotakos told the assembled leaders that the state fiscal situation would have been extremely difficult had the federal recovery act legislation (economic stimulus money) not been approved. He encouraged everyone to stick together and keep the sense of community strong during these challenging economic times. The *Lowell Sun* is preparing a series of articles about what it was like in Lowell during the Great Depression, which some folks say arrived earlier and left later in Lowell than anywhere else in the U.S. When we look back on the Great Recession of 2008-09, local historians may point to last night's town meeting at the Owl Diner as an important event that recharged the spirit of the Lowell team and prepared people for difficult months ahead.

Walking Tour of the Acre

By **Dick** on March 14, 2009
—

At least 25 people joined Dave McKean's 90-minute walking tour of the Acre this morning. None were disappointed. The tour commenced at the National Park Visitor Center on Market Street then proceeded across to *The Worker* statue on Mack Plaza at the corner of Market and Shattuck streets. Dave told how almost every day new research is refining and in some cases revising the history of the Irish in Lowell. Dave's own examination of the burial records at St Patrick's Cemetery (known simply as the Catholic Burial Grounds through its early existence) showed that young Irish men frequently were drowned, crushed, buried in cave-ins, and otherwise met their end in every type of construction accident imaginable, often linked to canal-building.

The tour wandered up Shattuck Street and across Merrimack to St Anne's Church. There, Dave talked about the work, social, and religious lives of Lowell's early Irish, explaining that the No Irish Need Apply phenomenon, at least in the mid-nineteenth century, was more myth than reality, an assertion that drew vigorous but good-natured rejections from several in the group. The discourse at St Anne's ended when Dave posed this question: What profession enabled the Irish to lift themselves out of the lower working class construction jobs that so many of them held? He silently answered by turning up Merrimack Street and pointing at City Hall. Yes, politics provided the pathway to the middle class for many Irish, although the city's first Irish mayor was not elected until the 1880s. Dave also pointed out the Ladd & Whitney Monument, the resting place of Luther Ladd and Addison Whitney, the first Union soldiers killed in the Civil War during a riot in Baltimore on April 19, 1861. While neither Ladd nor Whitney was Irish, one of the heroes of the day, Sgt. Timothy Crowley, who carried the colors and rallied the troops when they came under fire, was of Irish descent. Dave explained that when the textile mills closed at the start of the war, most of Lowell's male Irish residents joined the army both for employment and to show their patriotism.

The tour continued up Merrimack to Hanover and then over to Market where we saw the historic building at 493 Market Street which, a century and a half ago, was a thriving store run by Patrick Keyes. Every day Keyes held court on the first floor while on the upper floors lived his wife and 12 children. Dave expressed his hope that the building, currently dilapidated and boarded up, can be saved and restored as one of the most important examples of a structure from early Lowell.

From there, the tour proceeded down Lewis Street and across the Western Canal to the front of St. Patrick's Church. Opened originally in 1831 as a wooden structure on the same site as the present church, the current church was built in 1854 in a

13th-Century Gothic style. In 1904, a fire caused the collapse of the steeple and the roof, but the walls remained intact and the structure was fully repaired. During the floods of two years ago, the lower church was ruined; when the floor was pulled up for repairs, the outline of the original wood church was clearly visible in the dirt. The bigger stone church had been constructed over and around the smaller wooden church. Workers disassembled that structure once the outer shell of the bigger structure was completed. Dave also told us some of the history of St. Patrick's School, the Sisters of Notre Dame who still teach there, the famous O'Brien family of priests that made St. Patrick's such a strong and vibrant parish, and a variety of other fascinating historical facts. The Acre tour was an excellent way to spend a sunny and brisk late winter Saturday in Lowell.

Writing on the Wall

By **Paul** on March 24, 2009
—

This past Saturday, I stopped at the Bangkok Market on the corner of Chelmsford and Sheldon streets. It was a little early in the season for their impressive outdoor produce display, a mini-Haymarket in the Highlands, but there were lots of Asian vegetables whose names I don't know, along with cartons of grapefruits shining like yellow softballs and trays of green grapes and limes (3/$1.00).

To the right of the entrance on the Sheldon St. side, the store wall serves as a community bulletin board. Two colorful posters promoted music events on March 21, each one with text in English and Khmer. One poster featured the Shaolin Band and Minnesotan singer Rotana, a beautiful young woman, and a clean-cut young pop music "Super Star from Cambodia," Sen Ranut. Presented by SAVA, the event took place at Sompao Meas at 450 Chelmsford St. (tickets $20 or $25 at the door). Also performing last Saturday were "two sexy stars from Seattle" at the Pailin Restaurant, 6 Branch St, plus the six alluring members of the H2O Band (tickets $20, food included). A third poster advertised a Khmer New Year party on Saturday, April 11, at the Lowell Elks Lodge, 40 Old Ferry Road. This is a "Charity Fundraiser for Angkor Hospital for Children" (tickets $15 or $20 at the door). The dress code: "Proper attire or your best Khmer outfit." Other notices or announcements taped on the wall ranged from census information and tax preparation services to apartments available and help wanted in a nails shop.

Customers filled plastic baskets with fruits, vegetables, meats, and other groceries. I bought scallions, cilantro, pickling cucumbers, and green grapes. I was reminded of my grandfather's market in Little Canada and what Saturday mornings must have been like in that ethnic enclave years ago—the special foods and local talk that come with such places. These stores are information clearinghouses, too. It's the same at the Indian grocery next to University Music off Middlesex Street. There, it's Basmati rice and Bollywood film DVDs. In Little Canada in the 1920s, it would have been *tourtieres* (meat pies) and *L'Étoile* with the news in French.

HISTORY AS IT HAPPENS

Batman on Highland Street

By **Paul,** April 10-12, 2009
—

A movie convoy for the boxing film *The Fighter* took over the entire front lot of the Rogers School on Highland Street across the street from my house. The congregation of trailers, trucks, and assorted vehicles looks like a carnival round-up on Regatta Field in Pawtucketville. Security cars buzz around the long school driveway all day. Two cranes at the courthouse a block away today held up dark screens, which from Twitter reports I learned were raised to keep the sun from blasting in the south-facing windows upstairs where scenes were being shot.

On Elm Street earlier, a few residents sat on their steps, away from the stifling air inside. I asked one man if he'd seen any movie stars. He said, "I wasn't home to look—I was working all day." At work today a colleague I've known since high school said he can't believe Hollywood is making a movie based on the experiences of the Lowell boxers: "They could never tell the real story." Milling around the court parking area were people from the film crew, the ones whose names scroll up for minutes after the end of the film: drivers, caterers, sound guys and girls, and technicians in motion-picture craft unions.

One guy labored up the sidewalk with a pile of bottled-water cases on a hand-truck. The water man is part of the team, alongside the screenwriter, personal assistants, grips, deputy cinematographer, and the woman rolling the wardrobe rack across Gorham Street. The water-guy. He pushed the hand-truck up the sidewalk from Linden to Elm streets, where he stopped to light a cigarette and take a few drags before heading toward the tent-covered food station.

There wasn't anything more to see, so I walked home and turned on the TV. Surfing through the channels I caught a glimpse of Mark Wahlberg making a guest appearance on the latest episode of the HBO series *Entourage*, which he produces, and then in the movie channels came upon the Western *3:10 to Yuma*, starring Christian Bale—the two actors who today ate lunch across the street in one of the catering stations at the Rogers School. Batman was in the gym.

Spring Sights, Sounds, & Thoughts

By **Marie** on April 25, 2009
—

My morning trip into Lowell to the Pollard Memorial Library (PML) was a spring awakening. The blue sunny sky with the temp in the low 70s framed masses of striking yellow forsythia dotted along Route 133. Magnificent magnolia trees, some small in yards and others large and luminous in front of the Immaculate Conception Church. Shrubs and small flowering trees offer soft pinks and shades of lavender; low beds light up with yellow daffodils and jonquils. The garden gateway at River Road and Andover Street heralds multiple seasons of carefully tended colorful plants and flowers with its sunny blossoms and welcoming greenery.

There were walkers (notably former School Superintendent George Tsapatsaris), runners, joggers, bikers, and baby-carriage pushers along the route with traffic snarls at East Merrimack and Nesmith streets—two lanes struggling off the Quinn-Holmes/Hunt's Falls Bridge—and later bumper-to-bumper vehicles at the intersection of Gorham and Appleton streets. At Middlesex Community College stands of white flowering trees flanked the campus buildings at an unusually quiet pedestrian crosswalk.

No Saturday morning classes? The front area of City Hall was full of celebrants at the Armenian flag-raising where a white-gloved man in uniform gracefully gestured, and soon after the sound of Mayor Caulfield's voice singing the national anthem resounded even behind both City and Memorial halls to the Pollard Memorial Library parking lot. A fire truck engine roared and then purred on its way to duty. The yellow trolley ready to shuttle a group of tourists along the city's historic track. Car tops down; music rocking; long line at the Central Street free food offering; sun worshippers at Brew'd Awakening; too early for the politicos at Cafe Paradiso; there's pollen in the air. Home with my bag of library books, leaving for the Democratic State Committee meeting in Bridgewater soon. Curtis LeMay tells me that the 2010 Massachusetts Democratic Constitutional Offices Nominating Convention will be in Worcester—no surprise. "There's a lot to like about Lowell" for the other annual Democratic conventions. They'll be back if UMass Lowell Chancellor Marty Meehan will let them in at the Inn and the arena. Enjoy this wonderful spring weekend.

Swine Flu in Lowell

By **Dick** on April 28, 2009
—

When I drove past the Lowell Health Department on my way home from work last night, the sight of six Boston TV trucks parked there ready for their remote broadcasts suddenly transported the current swine flu scare from Mexico to Pine Street. As I write this, there is no public report on whether the two Lowell students tested for the virus are indeed infected by it, so as President Obama put it, there is cause for concern and a heightened state of alert, but it's not cause for alarm. We're in the midst of tough fiscal times and anger-induced calls for cutbacks in government spending proliferate, however, this current public health scare should remind everyone that government has an important role to play in keeping us safe, and that's got to be worth something.

Scenes from a Redevelopment Zone

By **Paul** on May 9, 2009
—

This morning I went walking and looking in the area once referred to as "Uptown," but which has been recast by the city planners as the JAM (Jackson-Appleton-Middlesex streets) area, and the adjacent in-progress Hamilton Canal District.

1. From the high ground of the Lord Overpass near Durkin's Carpeting and Interiors you see to the north the Textile Museum's white-suited astronaut reaching for a big ball of woolen yarn floating in space on a huge banner over Dutton Street. We ought to have that spaceman banner on every parking garage for a couple of months while the museum rolls out its new permanent exhibition—"Textile Revolution: An Exploration Through Space and Time." In a single image, the museum pushed the mill story into the twenty-first century.

2. The rocking blue graffiti'd letters on Sun Electric in a subterranean area off shore of the Lord Overpass, the agitated letters on the fully painted side of the building set against a night cityscape backdrop. Electric Motors & Pumps. The left side of the mural done in peach, lavender, and greens, picking up the early spring colors, new-leafed trees, and spiky weeds. In the grassy path on the safe side of the guard rail the manhole cover is in sync with the theme: "Lowell Electric Light Corporation."

3. King St. Revere St. Garnet St. Middlesex St. Pearl St. Freddy's Auto Repair, Domestic and Foreign (under new management—old sign). Ocean State Nails & Hair Salon and across the way the closed Best Buy Sea Foods (a connection?). The massive warehouse reminiscent of the former Curran-Morton behemoth on Bridge Street that was demolished to make way for Kerouac Park, an almost indestructible bunker of concrete and steel re-bar. U.S. Dry Cleaners. KWG PC, Computer Repairs & Sales. La Tijera de Oro Barbershop with its poster of artfully cut hair/shaved heads featuring tattoo-type designs, a real body-art shop. La Differencia Restaurant promises "The Best Caribbean Flavors." The Law Offices of George P. Jeffreys. An iron front grate pulled down tight to the sidewalk. Court House Deli by the Livingstone family—door propped open. Two guys eating breakfast. Construction underway at Garcia-Brogan's, the Mex-Celtic eatery "getting in on the ground floor" of the Early Garage.

4. Garrity's Antiques (Always Buying Estates). Sailboat-cover sheet music of "Bobbin' Up and Down" on a wooden table. An amateur painting of JFK in a blue polo shirt, holding sunglasses, looking at the ocean from his Cape Cod compound. A poster from the Metropolitan Opera's 1981 production of *Parade* in NY. Framed Monet maritime scene print and a City of Medford Fire Department Certificate. Lamps. A wooden sled. Trunks and chairs. Mirrors and out-of-state plates and dishes and white figure skates. 1950s model cars. A gold metal troubadour, slightly damaged like a broken *Aphrodite*.

5. At the Lowell Transitional Living Center clusters of people waking to the day, talking excitedly under the blooming dogwood trees. The sidewalk is a trail of pink petals. A black man steps up and sweeps a blonde woman off her feet and into his arms with a loud "Good Morning," and everyone laughs.

6. Ever notice that the WCAP radio sign is between two signs for Cappy's Copper Kettle? WCAPPY?

7. Major's Pub. Loft 27. The Lowell Gallery. Ray Robinson's Sandwich Shoppe. Mr. Al sitting in a chair reading the paper when a Saturday morning customer steps in for a haircut. A block away at the Majestic Barbershop there's one guy in the chair and two young guys waiting. Washington Bank. Sim's Driving School. Electrical Distribution. The Club.

8. Garnick's Music Center. Classic used album sleeves pinned up on the side wall: *Songs by Ricky*, *The Buddy Holly Story*, *The Beatles Yesterday and Today*, *Orpheus Ascending*, *Glad All Over* by the Dave Clark Five, Elvis's *Blue Hawaii*, The Beatles' *Something New*, and *Surf City* by Jan & Dean. In the 1960s, Record Lane on Central Street and Garnick's on Middlesex were the hot-spots for the latest music. Bins and bins of albums. Aisles of music in between Garnick's television sets and phonograph consoles (hi-fi and stereo). What's left is an echo of its hey-day. There was a straight line to Garnick's from "J. C.'s Golden Oldies" on WLLH and TV's *American Bandstand*, *Shindig*, and *Don Kirshner's Rock Concert*.

9. Romeo and Juliet Cafe. Allied Retail Systems, Specialists in Service, Sales, and Supplies since 1959. The closed Elliot's Famous Hot Dogs stand. Cars and trucks nosed in against the Owl Diner, advertising Haddock and at least one job available. Favor Street and the Eliot Church (Could they sell hot dogs on Sundays and call them Eliot's with one "l"?).

10. All the other places and things that I missed.

Latest on Home Sales

By **Dick** on May 5, 2009
—

In my neighborhood, spring always brings dandelions and For Sale signs. This year's no different, so now is a good time to look at what's happening with real estate. This April's statistics send a mixed message. The number of deeds recorded in Lowell in April 2009 (106) was 30 percent less than the number recorded in April 2008 (151). More encouraging news came from a substantial decline in foreclosures: In April 2009 there were 20; in April 2008 there were 37, a drop of 47 percent. More than anything else, the 1000+ foreclosures that have occurred in Lowell since the beginning of 2007 have driven down home values throughout the city. During 2007, for example, 251 properties went through foreclosure. In almost every case, the foreclosing lender (i.e., the bank) was the high bidder at the auction and therefore became the new owner of the home. But banks are in the business of lending money, not owning property, so these homes were immediately put back on the market.

By mid-April 2009, almost every one of those 2007 foreclosures had been resold to new buyers, but for prices that were 36 percent less than the pre-foreclosure purchase price of the home. The heavily discounted prices of these post-foreclosure properties tend to make the asking prices of other homes on the market seem high. Under normal circumstances, sellers of non-distressed properties would lower their asking prices to reflect the declining values of the real estate market. But because many of those sellers bought their properties when the market was at or near its peak, their mortgages were equally high, so they must obtain a high enough resale price to pay off their existing mortgages. This inability to reduce asking prices further could account for this April's decline in the number of sales relative to last year: potential buyers still believe that asking prices are too high. Despite all of that, the substantial drop in the number of foreclosures is a good sign. Foreclosures drive down values, so fewer foreclosures may mean prices will begin to stabilize, which is the first step in any real estate recovery.

Immigrant Stories

by **Dick** on May 15, 2009

More than 50 people gathered tonight at the Revolving Museum to discuss a research project about recent immigrants to Lowell. The study, commissioned by Lowell National Historical Park and being conducted by UMass Lowell faculty and students, represents an effort by the park to update its story of Lowell by documenting the stories of those who have come to the city from other countries during the past quarter century and comparing their experiences to those of earlier people.

Many of the interview subjects present tonight shared stories with the audience. The individuals we heard from came from Cambodia, Vietnam, Sierra Leone, Ghana, Ivory Coast, Brazil, Mexico, Puerto Rico, Greece, and Armenia (by way of France). There were several recurring themes that united the experience of folks who came from distant corners of the earth. One was the preservation of native culture that is done most often with food from the old country, but also through festivals and holiday traditions. Another theme was the value of a support system formed by earlier arrivals from the same place. One speaker told of settling in Portland, Oregon, after a long exodus from Cambodia, but then relocating to Lowell a few years later after hearing of the large, vibrant Cambodian community here.

Another speaker, who came from Greece as a 19-year-old who had just graduated from fashion school and spoke not a word of English, told of an early trip to buy fabric. She struggled to make herself understood with gestures supplementing her few words of English until the proprietor of the store, George's Textile, realized she was from Greece and effortlessly reverted to his native Greek, making this young immigrant feel embraced by her new community.

Someone asked about immigrants refraining from political involvement. Several said that recent arrivals are so focused on survival that they don't have time to devote to public policy matters. But others said that in many of the countries they come from there was no democracy, and any attempt to be politically active was risky in the extreme. This leads to a culture of non-involvement that persists here. Other factors are that many immigrants are not citizens and not eligible to vote and that older immigrants often retain strong ties to ancestral nations and so follow politics there more than in America.

It was an amazing evening filled with important insights. The completion of this study is many months away, and an event similar to this evening's will be held to celebrate the outcome. Whenever it is, it will be well worth attending.

Visiting With Two Very Special Veterans

By **Steve O'Connor** on May 24, 2009
—

In the following essay, originally read on UMass Lowell's Sunrise *program on WUML, Steve O'Connor remembers a day spent with two veterans, Edwin Poitras and Jack Flood, both of whom survived dire circumstances during World War II. Both are real American heroes. Poitras died in 2006. Flood died in 2013.*

While doing some research on the internet lately, I came across a website dedicated to the Museum of World War II, in Natick, Massachusetts. It's possible to take a virtual tour of the museum, but I learned that it is not open to the public; an invitation is required. Prospective visitors must write an explanation of who they are and why they would like to see the private collection. This is just the sort of mysterious affair to pique my curiosity, so I immediately sent an email explaining that I was doing research for a novel and wanted to visit with a couple of decorated WWII veterans to commemorate VE day. A few days later, I received a call from the curator, asking if May 7 would be convenient. He gave me directions, explaining that the building was unmarked, but that there was a 14-inch shell on either side of the front entrance. In police circles, he said, we call that a clue.

When I asked Edwin Poitras and Jack Flood if they'd like to go, both accepted readily. Jack Flood survived the North African campaign against Rommel, only to find himself wading through waist-deep water toward a little piece of hell on a beach in Normandy on June 6, 1944. Edwin Poitras, a Lowell resident who speaks French, was selected for spy training, and was dropped into Nazi-occupied France to prepare the way for invading soldiers like Jack.

The weather forecast for May 7, like the report for D-Day,

called for a storm. The weatherman predicted high winds and torrential rains. My wife said, "Maybe you should postpone the trip." I just couldn't imagine telling a guy who stormed Omaha Beach and another guy whose plane was shot down shortly after he parachuted out of it that we couldn't go because it was raining. They had been to places where it was raining fire and lead. So, I set off with Edwin and Jack for Natick. The old fellas talked a little bit about the war on the way down, and a lot about their boyhoods in Lowell. Neither man had an easy life.

Edwin's father died when he was a boy, but he got a job with the carnival, selling popcorn and candy apples for a dollar a day, plus food. He sent all the money home to his mother, because he only needed food. Later, he worked five days a week in the Boott Mills and on Saturdays helped the ice man deliver blocks of ice for the ice boxes people used to keep food from spoiling.

Jack worked at the A&P Market beside the *Sun* Building in Kearney Square. He said that someone there knew a lot of the kids from Upper Broadway and got them jobs there. He also later drove a *Lowell Sun* truck with Pugsy Walsh and Buster Meehan, father of the current UMass Lowell Chancellor. Guess where Jack's seven dollars a week went? You got it. To his mother. "Your grandfather," Jack Flood tells me, "was working up in Tyngsboro painting a house. He could take the train back to Lowell for five cents, but he preferred to walk back to Lowell, so that he could stop in North Chelmsford and spend the five cents on a cold glass of beer." He told me how my grandfather and father would leave their house in the Acre, carrying a ladder, one at each end, over to Pawtucketville or Centralville, or up to Belvidere, to paint a house. "And that's as true as there's a God in heaven," he says.

Edwin turns around in the front seat and says, "Hey Jack, how about hot water heaters? Wasn't that a blessing? We hooked them up to the stove," he explains to me. It's difficult to believe that the two men with me come from a time before hot water, before electricity in homes, and when painters carried their ladders on their shoulders across the city. They discover that they were both friendly with the blacksmith whose business was near the School Street cemetery. "You know where they buried all the dead horses?" Edwin asks, "Over at Dead Horse Lane." There's a colorful address for you.

I can't help wondering if their hard lives and simple faith were part of what made the Greatest Generation so great. They seem to have had so little, and yet they seem to have had so much. We arrived at the Museum of World War II by mid-morning. Predictably, neither man had bothered with an umbrella, and both scoffed at the idea that I could drop them off at the front door, and go park the car. "We'll go with you, Okie," Jack says. And Edwin adds that a little water never hurt anyone.

Touring the museum with these two old soldiers 60 years after the conclusion of their war is something I'll never forget. We had to show identification and sign a form that if we injured ourselves in the museum we would not hold the owners responsible. We were given a hand-held speaker phone; each room and each individual display had a number, and by punching in that number, we could hear an explanation of the exhibits. The voice from the hand-held speaker warned us that some people found the first room upsetting and might want to skip it. It was full of artifacts from Nazi Germany, including life-sized wax SS soldiers in black uniform, replete with Totenkopf or Death's Head insignias, and a wax Hitler wearing Hitler's actual shirt. There was a massive gold swastika that once hung behind Hitler at a rally. There was a ten-foot painting of Adolph, which he gave as a present to Goering. There was a sign in German, which translated, read "Swing Dancing is Forbidden." There was also, of course, a lot of anti-Semitic and anti-British and -American propaganda.

Edwin Poitras was in his element in the room dedicated to the OSS, the American version of Britain's SOE, an elite network of spies and undercover operatives. He was immediately drawn to a suitcase radio like the one he used to send and receive messages in occupied France. "We used to move 70 miles every seven days, because the Germans would begin to home in on the source of the transmission with their direction finders." He points out the tiny Minox cameras that look like cigarette lighters, flat blades that can be taped to the body so that they will not be noticed in a pat down; a device that looks like a pen, but fires one .22 caliber bullet; and a double-edged knife whose handle contained an L pill. L for lethal. "I carried two," Edwin says. In case of imminent capture the L pill was the only guarantee that an agent would not talk, and death would be quicker and less painful than death by Gestapo methods.

One other room contained a tank the size of a Hummer on top of another Hummer. I was surprised to hear the voice on my hand-held speaker phone say that if you chose you could mount the tank and even get inside, so long as you put on one of the two army helmets that sat on the front of the tank. "No wonder they wanted us to sign that form, Jack," I said, but when I turned around, I saw that 83-year-old Jack Flood had the helmet on and was climbing up the front of the tank as if he were back with the 88th regiment, the tank killers, in 1943. "Come on up here, Okie." So the two of us were perched on top of the tank in army helmets, looking down the barrel of an 88-millimeter cannon. Never having been a soldier, I honestly felt a little like Mike Dukakis up there, but Floody was right at home, and I had to wonder what scenes were playing out in his mind. There were machine gun nests full of weaponry. It amazed me how much these men still remembered after 60 years, but I suppose there are some things you don't forget. Edwin picked up a Thompson machine gun and said, "This was a lousy gun. Couldn't hit anything unless it was right in front of you." There are other guns they admire and praise, as dependable old friends that helped them win the war and get home. "This is really something else Steve, I'm glad we came," Jack says, but then he adds quietly, "but I bet I'll have nightmares tonight."

The nightmare in Europe that began on September 1, 1939, with the Nazi invasion of Poland, ended on May 8, 1945, 60 years ago. Once, while waiting for a ferry in Le Havre, France, I ducked into a store to buy a newspaper. I got talking to the old fellow who worked there, and when he heard my accent, he asked, "Etes-vous Americain?" "Oui, je suis Americain." He extended a hand across the counter and took mine.

Goodbye to the Doubletree

By **Dick** on June 11, 2009
—

The imminent transfer of the Doubletree Hotel to UMass Lowell is welcome news. Twenty years ago, a key factor in Providence-based developer Arthur Robbins's decision to build a luxury hotel in downtown Lowell—it was a Hilton back then—was a guarantee from Wang that business executives training at Wang's worldwide training headquarters (now Middlesex Community College's main building in Lowell) would all stay at the Hilton. My recollection is that Wang promised 60 percent occupancy of the hotel. Soon after the hotel was constructed, however, Wang Laboratories collapsed and the hotel never really recovered. In the early 1990s, I worked in Kearney Square but parked my car in the Lower Locks Garage. Each night as I walked across the pedestrian bridge on my way to the garage I would glance up at the hundred or so room windows on the north side of the hotel and try to gauge how many were occupied by the number of lights that were on. It was rarely more than a dozen.

Through the years, the hotel has changed hands several times. Each new management team arrived with promises that this new effort would be different, but the result was always the same on a day-to-day basis; there just wasn't enough going on to support a hotel of that size in that location. As it became apparent that running a traditional hotel on that site just wasn't feasible, there was often talk of converting the building into a long-term care facility of some kind. This newest development is far better than that option.

In fact, the UMass Lowell Inn & Conference Center has the potential to remake yet again the image of downtown Lowell. The city's embracing of the creative economy has transformed much of the downtown, but the constituent elements of that economy are by their very nature small and widely dispersed. They're the kind of businesses that independently bubble up when you put a lot of creative and industrious people together in the same place. There's no central location that catches the eye of a visitor or serves as the entryway into the city's creative economy. The hotel's latest manifestation has the potential to serve in that role. Beyond the obvious benefits that the infusion of new student-residents should bring to many of the downtown's small businesses, the Inn & Conference Center can become the hub of downtown activity by hosting conferences, meetings, and other events that are compatible with the city's attempts to embrace (and capture the benefits of) the creative economy.

Lessons from Dad

By **Bob Forrant** on June 21, 2009
—

Here's a Father's Day essay from guest contributor Bob Forrant, who's a professor in UMass Lowell's Department of History:

As Father's Day approaches I think a lot about my dad and the life lessons he provided me. And, I wonder what he would have made of our country's current state of affairs. I wish I could talk to him about the Red Sox and the travails of "Big Papi," the Bruins all too predictable end to their hockey season, and the federal government's ownership of most of the nation's automobile industry! I also wish I could thank him for providing me with a terrific role model for being a dad.

My dad worked hard for 40 years as a meat cutter for the Great Atlantic & Pacific Tea Company, otherwise known as the A&P, once one of the country's leading grocery chains. It's difficult to imagine anyone working so many years for one company ever again. His father built machines for nearly that many years at a place called Reid Brothers in Beverly, Mass. Growing up, I used to cut my grandfather's lawn, but I never got the precise pattern right that I was supposed to follow with the lawnmower. Even so, he still paid me in silver dollars!

Having three younger sisters and a brother in a good Catholic household, I joined the working world at age 14, bagging groceries and stocking shelves in Henry's Market in North Beverly. I needed to earn money for clothes, the movies, a new Rolling Stones album, and Red Sox and Bruins tickets. My dad took me to my first game at Fenway Park and my first Bruins game at the real Boston Garden, not the luxury-suite palace that stands on the same sacred ground today. I suspect my dad would not like the new building, and he would be disgusted with the hideous new $1.5 billion Yankee Stadium. I was born to despise the Yankees. In fact, according to family legend when I was four years old a woman in a grocery store asked me "Whose little boy are you?" My response: "I'm Johnny Pesky's son!" Pesky played second base for the Red Sox at the time. Sorry, Dad.

We used to take the train in to Boston for Sunday night hockey games, and we always sat on a corner in the balcony. For my dad, the best place to see a hockey game was high on a corner so you could see plays developing from one end of the ice to the other. Rich folks, he said, sat up close because they did not understand the game at all. And anyway, if you sat low to the ice you could not see the puck at all. I passed the same profound knowledge on to my son; when he buys Bruins tickets every year for my birthday they are high on a corner! Thanks, Dad.

When I was 14, I faced what was for the time a large dilemma. With my hard-earned money, I had purchased tickets for a Rolling Stones concert. When the day of the concert rolled around the baseball team I played for had a rained-out game rescheduled for the same time as the concert. What to do? My dad was crazy about baseball and played catch with me in the crib. I loved the game too, but the Rolling Stones? I asked him to tell me what I should do, but he said, No way.

So, I decided to go to the concert. He never brought this up again other than to say life would eventually fill up with far tougher choices, so I might as well start making them. Thanks, Dad, for that valuable lesson. My dad, active in the Amalgamated Meatcutters union, often took me to his union meetings, sometime talking during the car ride about the importance of sticking together. On some of these rides he also informed me that working people voted Democrat because Republicans were for the bosses. At age ten a lot of these political lessons were lost on me, but later in life when I took a job at American Bosch, a large metalworking plant in Western Massachusetts, the light went on and I recalled his words. In fact, many workmates in that factory reminded me of my dad: hardworking, dedicated to supporting their families, scrupulously fair, and desperately reliant on their weekly paycheck to "make ends meet," a phrase I heard often at my kitchen table growing up. Thanks, Dad, for that valuable lesson.

My dad would certainly find it difficult to fathom how the economy got so messed up, how so many people went overboard with their credit cards and how so many union autoworkers were out of their jobs. Every Friday evening, he always worked until 9:00 p.m. On Fridays, he brought home his white pay envelope and handed it to my mother who took care of the household budget. Then, he would open a can of sardines, get a bunch of Saltine crackers, and a Narragansett Beer ("Hi-Neighbor, have a 'Gansett") and sit in front of the TV to watch the Friday night fights sponsored by Gillette. When I was small, I used to sneak down stairs from my bedroom, hide behind his chair and watch the fights, too. On Saturday mornings, I would wake up in my bed and not recall how I got there. Dad, thanks for letting me believe I was putting one over on you all those years.

My dad never went to college, but he loved to read, as did my mom. We bought an encyclopedia set when I was pretty young. We got the *Readers' Digest*, and I devoured it cover to cover every month, and we were also in the Book-of-the Month Club. One of my favorite pictures of my father is of him reading a book to my two children when they were ages four and two. Thanks, Dad, for passing on your love of a good book.

I recently published a book myself and dearly wish my dad could have read it. I dedicated it to my children Leah and Nate, and I also dedicated it to Tony Fonseca, Donald Staples, and Dad. I worked for years with Tony and Don at American Bosch. The three men epitomize everything good about blue-collar workers, men whose lives remind us of the quiet dignity found in hard toil. These three men would have nothing but disdain for the scam artists who preside over Wall Street and our Massachusetts State House; the CEOs at places like Chrysler and General Motors, who take down millions of dollars in salary while wrecking their companies; the talk radio shouters who act like they care about working people but really don't; and the forever posing baseball players who take more than a minute to get around the bases after hitting a home run.

Ed McMahon, WLLH, Paul Sullivan

By **Tony** on June 24, 2009
—

The passing of Ed McMahon brought back memories to me, but none as vivid as the day the late talk show host Paul Sullivan brought Ed to Lowell. The details of how and why McMahon came to Lowell is a story for another day. At the time of McMahon's visit Paul was hosting the local radio show *Morning Magazine* on WLLH and I was his producer/sidekick. The show was a ball, both on and off the air, that's all I'll say.

Fast forward this story. With the help of Middlesex Community College and its President, Dr. Carole Cowan, McMahon's visit was a great success. Middlesex made all the arrangements and dedicated a bench outside its main building to Ed. Today, the bench still sits overlooking the canal. Paul being Paul arranged for McMahon to be brought to and from Lowell by limo (of course, this was a radio trade). The morning before Ed arrived, Paul Sullivan proudly announced to me, "Tony, you and I are going to ride in the limo with Ed on the trip back to Logan." I loved it.

After the bench dedication, Ed went up to the WLLH studio in the old Hilton Hotel and recorded several WLLH promos, one of which was "Heeerrrreeee's Sully" (guess whose idea that was?). The ride back to Logan with Ed McMahon was great. He and his wife were extremely friendly, although McMahon spent a lot of time on his cell phone. Ed McMahon at the time was hosting the popular TV show *Star Search* with the legendary Dick Clark. During the ride, Ed received a call from Dick Clark's "people" asking to change the date of a *Star Search* recording because of a conflict. Anyway, when we arrived at the airport both Paul and I got out of the car with McMahon and his wife. As the limo driver unloaded their luggage other people began to recognize the star. Some pointed at us and some just stared for a while. Before leaving, Ed shook both my hand and Paul's and put his hand on our shoulders. His friendly wife embraced us both with two arms in front of a large crowd of "spectators" that had assembled. As the McMahons walked toward the departure terminal, Ed and his wife were swamped with admirers. Paul and I re-entered the limo in the back seat. As Ed stopped to sign a few autographs, our limo began to slowly pull away. Paul rolled down the passenger-seat window, stuck out his head and arm, began waving enthusiastically, then yelled out to Ed McMahon, "Bye, Dad, see you soon." With Sullivan's shout the entire crowd turned their heads to the future WBZ radio star and "gazed" at him. It was a day I'll never forget.

Franco-American Connections

By **Andrew** on July 15, 2009
—

Today marks the anniversary of the storming of the Bastille in Paris on July 14, 1789. What the English-speaking world knows as Bastille Day is actually the anniversary of the *Fête de la Fédération*, which was held on the first anniversary of the storming of the Bastille in 1790 and established the short-lived constitutional monarchy in France. While the constitution did not last very long (due to opposition on all sides), one of the men who worked to uphold the constitution, and who was later punished by the Republican government for doing so, was Marie-Joseph Paul Yves Roch Gilbert du Motier, Marquis de Lafayette, a figure familiar to students of American history.

Lafayette arrived in America at the age of 19 in 1777, having defied the orders of King Louis XVI not to leave France. On July 31, Lafayette was commissioned as a major general in the Continental Army after having offered to serve without pay. He soon became General Washington's aide-de-camp. Because of his bravery at the battle of Brandywine, Pennsylvania, in September, Washington asked the Congress to grant Lafayette the command of a division in the Continental Army. Congress agreed. Lafayette went on to serve in the battles of Gloucester, Barren Hill, Monmouth, Rhode Island, Green Spring, and the Siege of Yorktown.

After the war, Lafayette returned home to France where he took part in his own country's revolution. On July 15, 1789, he was named commander-in-chief of the National Guard of France, the militia that served the National Assembly, which had been formed by dissidents in the Estates-General to create a constitutional monarchy. As the revolution progressed, Lafayette was branded as a traitor by its leaders for his loyalty to the idea of a constitutional monarchy and was forced into exile. While in exile, Lafayette was imprisoned for five years before Napoleon finally negotiated his release. In 1790, Lafayette sent the key to the Bastille to George Washington, a tribute "as a son to my adoptive father; as a Missionary of liberty to its Patriarch."

It was quite easy for Americans to forget the service France rendered to our young country. (Remember "freedom fries?"). French soldiers and sailors fought and died alongside Americans during our War of Independence and, perhaps more importantly, the French government financed much of the war. The Marquis de Lafayette is a clear symbol of this service rendered to our country. And he in turn brought what he had learned from his time in America to France and took part in the French Revolution, hoping to spread the American ideals of liberty and equality. This exchange of service and ideas is a constant reminder to the fact that we as a nation can always benefit from helping other countries.

LaGrange, Lafayette, and the Acre

By **Paul** on July 15, 2009
—

Thanks to Andrew for his Francophile posting. After returning to France from America, Lafayette lived near Paris in a house called La Grange. Why do I mention this? Because we used to have a LaGrange Street in Lowell, in the Acre, close to Marion Street, both of which were wiped off the city map a few years ago by a City Council vote in response to a citizens' request to rename the streets Cork and Dublin streets (based on evidence that those streets or public ways of an earlier time in the neighborhood had those names).

Lost in the discussion at the time, in my opinion, is that LaGrange and Marion streets were of a piece with Adams-, Jefferson-, and Franklin-named "streets" in the neighborhood that were clearly a tribute to heroic figures associated with the founding of our nation. At the time of the debate, at least one person said to me that the "Marion" and "LaGrange" names had something to do with a French-Canadian building contractor. Taking away LaGrange was like taking away a street named Mount Vernon or Monticello, two other names of family homes connected to leaders of the Revolution. Marion is, of course, General Francis Marion of South Carolina, "the Swamp Fox" whose Revolutionary War exploits were popularized by Walt Disney in the 1960s when he was looking for another folk hero like Davy Crockett (a visitor to Lowell, by the way). Marion is sometimes credited with inventing "guerrilla warfare," which he and his band of men practiced with success against the British in the swamps of the South.

While the proponents of LaGrange and Marion lost the argument in the Council chamber to advocates for righting a wrong that was seen to have been done to the founding Irish in Lowell, the compromise was supposed to lead to a historical marker on site that noted the longstanding street names of LaGrange and Marion and background about why the streets had been so named. I haven't seen the marker if there is one. A better alternative all around might have been to do what some other communities do in this situation, which is to keep the current name and add another sign plaque under the current street sign, saying "Formerly Cork Street" or "Formerly Dublin Street." That would have shown respect for the historical record and not required current residents to change all documents on which their permanent address appears.

So, thanks, Andrew, for raising the French flag on Bastille Day and reminding all of us of the bond between the two nations. And we must remember the American sacrifices in France in World War II, before and after D-Day, 1944, as well as the bravery of World War II soldiers and fliers in France, and those who served before them in World War I.

The Lowell Connector

By **Dick** on July 31, 2009
—

When giving people directions to the Superior Courthouse, I find it hard to describe their exit from the Lowell Connector. "The highway just ends in a T-shaped intersection" is about the best I can do. But the Connector wasn't supposed to end like that. Back in 1968 there was a proposal to extend the Connector into the heart of downtown Lowell. The highway would have continued over Gorham Street (by bridge) and through the Back Central neighborhood, with entrance and exit ramps onto Central Street. The highway would have then proceeded in a northeasterly direction until it reached Lawrence Street where the Whipple Café is located and then would have curved to the north and followed the line of the Concord River (about where Lawrence Street now runs). The state's plan for the road would have taken it across Church Street in a surface intersection controlled by traffic lights, through the space now occupied by the Lower Locks Parking Garage, over the Concord River, through the Davidson Street Parking Lot with an end point at East Merrimack Street, right in front of the Lowell Memorial Auditorium.

This plan would have required the taking and demolition of 208 buildings that housed 405 families and 28 businesses. (I've been told of follow-on phases that would have had the Connector continue on towards the Merrimack River, curving to the left through what is now Kerouac Park to tie in with Father Morrissette Boulevard or that another plan would have had the Connector cross the Merrimack and continue on through Dracut where it would eventually tie-in to an extended Route 213).

The business community lobbied hard for the Connector Extension. The following is from a pamphlet published by the

Lowell Chamber of Commerce:

> Lowell needs a highway connector so that the Route 495 Business Spur will not abruptly end on Gorham Street. Our downtown businesses cannot remain a healthy and viable force in the economy of the area without high speed access and egress to the heart of the central business district; some of our major merchants face serious financial problems, and these merchants provide thousands in taxes and millions, YES, MILLIONS, in payrolls. Access, egress and ease of travel play one of the major roles in attracting and keeping shoppers and business alive. While the Greater Lowell area has grown 30 percent in the last 10 years, the sales in Lowell have grown only 1 percent.

On September 10, 1968, the City Council rejected the proposal by a 7 to 2 vote.

Great Night at Elliot's

By **Dick** on August 5, 2009
—

Thanks to all who gathered at Elliot's this evening to enjoy a hot dog and some company in an authentic Lowell setting. I say gathered rather than stopped by because it was a true gathering. People arrived, ate, and lingered. It was a diverse group with many who write on blogs, either as authors or comment-makers, plenty of blog readers, and lots of people who are connected through Facebook. Plus, there was a squad of city council candidates.

And Walter Garside, his family, and his staff were furiously dispensing hot dogs and fries all evening after a day that saw lines out the door at noon. They must be exhausted, but they did a great job. We'll all be back soon. Despite the political nature of the crowd, politics did not dominate conversation. While early arrivers ate inside, everyone eventually congregated on the sidewalk and the grassy space on the Middlesex Street side of the restaurant. It was a perfect setting. The buildings provided the shade, a cool breeze blew up Elliot Street, and everyone just stood (and sat for those who were prudent enough to bring lawn chairs) and talked and enjoyed each other's company.

If I was asked to describe the gathering, I would use one word: FUN. It was a throwback to the day when houses were built close together, and neighbors, who knew one another's names, congregated on someone's front porch each night to enjoy the cool early evening air and talk. It's the kind of thing that half-acre lots and home entertainment centers have evolved out of our lives today. And that's what I see as the real value of blogs and websites and Facebook and Twitter at the community level. They provide us with the tools to stay connected with people and facilitate meet-ups like tonight's.

Lowell in the World War

By **Dick** on August 14, 2009
—

During my recent walk along the Western Canal I came upon the Michalopoulos Monument. Regarding that monument, reader Eileen Loucraft left this comment: "I did a little digging on Athanasios C. Michalopoulos in the *Lowell Sun* archives.

He was killed in action July 12, 1918, as a private in the 102nd infantry, Company K at Château-Thierry in France. His body was returned to Lowell in July 1923 along with two other soldiers, Privates Walter Marr and Frank McOsker. The square was dedicated in May 1931."

Eileen also emailed me a copy of a page from the November 11, 1921, Sun that listed all the men from Lowell who died while serving in the military during World War I. The title of the article, "Lowell's Death Toll in World War" reminds us that in 1921 the term "World War" was still singular. The list is lengthier than I would have expected, and many who died succumbed to pneumonia.

From the list, I picked out some familiar names. They're familiar because places around the city bear the names of these deceased veterans, however, only few of us know how these places acquired these names. Here are some examples: Cupples Square is named for Lt. Lorne L. Cupples who died of wounds in France in October 1918; Gallagher Square is named for Private William Gallagher, 302d Machine Gun Battalion, who died of wounds in France, October 7, 1918; Kearney Square is named for Lt. Paul Kearney who was killed in action in France on October 3, 1918; Kittredge Park is named for Capt. Paul E. Kittredge who was killed in action in November, 1918; McOsker Circle (behind St Margaret's Church on Stevens Street) is named for Private Francis M. McOsker, Headquarters Company, 101st Infantry, who was killed in action July 13, 1918. And then there was Anthanasios Michalopoulos, Co. I, 102d Regiment, who died in France of wounds received in action, July 12, 1918, and for whom the monument in the heart of the Acre is named.

Tony C.

By **Dick** on August 18, 2009
—

Forty-two years ago, I headed to bed at whatever time seven-year-olds went to bed and tuned my bedside AM-only clock radio to 850 AM to hear Ken Coleman and Ned Martin call the last few innings of that night's Red Sox game on the old WHDH. I soon heard the crack of the bat and Coleman's melodious voice, saying "Fly ball to right field, Tartabull's under it, and he makes the catch." What was Jose Tartabull doing in right field? Where was Tony Conigliaro? Tartabull was a serviceable backup, but Tony C was one of the stars of the team. Why wasn't he playing?

As the game progressed, I pieced it together. Conigliaro had been hit in the face by a Jack Hamilton fastball and had been taken to the hospital. His injuries were severe: a broken cheek bone, a dislocated jaw, and a damaged retina. His season was over. The Sox eventually picked up the colorful and talented Ken "Hawk" Harrelson to play right field, and the team won the American League pennant after an amazing stretch drive, but lost the seven-game World Series to the St. Louis Cardinals.

Conigliaro rejoined the Red Sox for the 1969 season, played several more years, and occasionally exhibited the pop in his bat that made him the American League home run leader in 1965. But he was never the same, and his baseball career soon ended. In 1982, he suffered a heart attack and a stroke that left him incapacitated for the rest of his life. He died in 1990 at age 45.

The amazing last place-to-first place accomplishments of the 1967 Impossible Dream season helped our memories of Conigliaro's loss fade from our collective consciousness. But I think other things contributed to that. Here was a kid who was born in Massachusetts (Revere) and not only made the Boston Red Sox, but was a star. He was one of us. If he could make it, why couldn't we? But that all changed in an instant. With one pitch, this talented athlete's career was forever altered for the worse. Tony C became a symbol of the randomness of life. He was embraced when he returned, but it was never quite the same for him or for us.

One of My Ted Kennedy Memories

By **Marie** on August 27, 2009
—

We were Kennedy people! No surprise there—Irish, Catholic, Democrats, living in Massachusetts. In my mind's eye I can still see my beloved and revered grandmother, Agnes Meehan Kirwin, swaddled in towels, big very dark sun glasses peeking beneath a huge sun hat, proudly wearing at least two large JFK campaign buttons. She was comfortably ensconced in a chair on Craigville Beach. It was the summer of 1961, and she was awaiting the helicopter fly-over as President Kennedy was brought home to the summer White House on Cape Cod. Knowing she was that close to JFK was so meaningful—and of course the rosary in her hand was being said for him. No political neophyte—she was herself the sister of a politician—Lowell Mayor, state Representative and Postmaster—The Honorable John F. Meehan. She understood the reality and the mystique, and I followed her lead.

It was 1964, and a coup for higher education in Lowell. Then and there I began my personal 45-year-long political and ideological romance with Ted Kennedy. On June 7, 1964, Senator Ted Kennedy came to Lowell to be the Commencement speaker at Lowell Technological Institute and receive an honorary degree. The Senator later came across the river to Lowell State College to speak at that Commencement. I was one of 132 graduates that day who heard his rebuke to those critics of the "war on poverty" who didn't seem to get the problem of poverty in America and the need for education, jobs, and job training. We were all trained to be teachers, and he admonished us to give our students "not just knowledge but a commitment." He noted that education "makes the difference between a helpless burden on society and a useful citizen." He stood beside our class gift to the college—a bronze bust of President Kennedy—and thanked us for spearheading a fundraising drive for the Kennedy Memorial Library. We were all inspired that afternoon. I still carry the image of the young man of that day carrying the mantle of family, duty, and service.

Mass Poetry Festival Rave

By **Paul** on October 18, 2009
—

Here's one poet's reaction to the events yesterday at the Massachusetts Poetry Festival: "I spent six hours at the festival and enjoyed every minute. Many thanks for such a great event ... I'll read anywhere, a barn or a shoe factory, but that crowd at Cobblestones was as good as it gets. Wow! Onward." Lowell had a wild weekend with today's Bay State Marathon and yesterday's Poetry Festival and American Studies Association Conference at the Boott Mills Museum. There was a statewide cheerleading competition at Lowell High School in the afternoon as well.

Thanks to all the volunteers, donors, participants, writers, and everyone who helped make the Poetry Festival a success. Festival organizers report that the attendance topped 2,000 from Thursday through Saturday (not including today's events at the Boston Children's Museum and Harvard University). The highlight for me was the opening program of Favorite Poems in simple, but stately St. Anne's Church, including Mayor Caulfield reading a somber Lucy Larcom poem about President Lincoln's death, standing only yards away from Lucy Larcom Park; MassINC's public-policy-guy John Schneider of Lowell reading W.H. Auden's "The Unknown Citizen"; Sayon Soeun of the Light of Cambodia's Children organization giving us Frost's "The Road Not Taken" and breaking everyone's heart with his dignified explanation of what the poem means to him as a survivor of the Khmer Rouge genocide; arts leader and humanitarian Nancy Donahue sharing a poem by Jake, an 11-year-old writer from Lowell; attorney and public speaker extraordinaire Michael Gallagher reciting from memory a funny fable-poem and a few lines from Lewis Carroll; Mike's father (Charles, I think), reading Henley's "Invictus" and another classic, "In Flanders Field," by WWI Lt. Col. John McCrae, a Canadian surgeon; web guru Nicco Mele reciting, again by heart/mind, an Eamon Grennan poem; UMass Lowell professor and Lowell resident Tony Szczesiul reading a John Ashbery poem; Amy Gorin of Wellesley reading a touching poem by her son in remembrance of his grandfather; host Maggie Dietz of the Favorite Poem Project at Boston University reading a virtuoso sound poem by Gerard Manley Hopkins; and Melissa Ballard of Lowell and Middlesex Academy Charter High School with a surprise, reading "The Cut"—a poem of mine about nature's relentless self-repair. I hope I didn't forget anyone.

The Thursday night kick-off event in Lowell, at the National Park Visitor Center, was another memorable edition of The Cultural Lines of Poetry, which is becoming a literary tradition in the city. The Hellenic Culture and Heritage Society hosted an array of writers who shared their work on the theme of "Poetry in Hard Times," presented through the filter of their heritages. More than 70 people listened to readings by a former political prisoner in Iran, a refugee of the Liberian civil war, a young Greek immigrant writing about Greece in World War II, a nineteen-year-old Cambodian woman who is part of a youth poetry slam team that performed in Chicago (both of the young writers are first-year students at UMass Lowell), a nephew of legendary Lowell newspaperman Charles Sampas reading his uncle's poem of Lowell vignettes, and a handful of other writers from the area.

Another highlight for me was the program "Poèmes du Monde Francophone; Poèmes from the Francophone World" at Pollard Memorial Library with poets of Haitian heritage, including Danielle Legros-Georges of Lesley University and Cambridge "Poet Populist" Jean-Dany Joachim. Their beautifully rendered readings in two languages made the seminar-size gathering seem even more intimate.

The Small Press Fair organized by Derek Fenner and Ryan Gallagher of Bootstrap Press of Lowell in the former Bombay Mahal restaurant space on Middle Street was a huge success. We need a space like that open 52 weeks a year. The literary products were dazzling—and people spent money because you just don't see those beautifully designed and printed books and journals full of fresh writing in one place anywhere.

Lowell Bell Echoes the Pulse of Life

By **Marie** on November 24, 2009
—

The weather was cold and misty for the unveiling ceremony for the "Lowell Bell" sited in the small park at Prescott and Central streets earlier today. The speeches and thanks were given in the lobby of the nearby Eastern Bank by Lowell Heritage Partnership (LHP) President Richard Lockhart, Mayor Bud Caulfield, and Eastern Bank President Robert Rivers. The reclamation, restoration, and installation of this historic nineteenth-century fire bell was a joint project of the LHP with Eastern Bank, the Rotary Club, the Theodore Edson Parker Foundation, Enterprise Bank, Lowell National Historical Park, and others.

Bells are such a great symbol of the life and times of people in Lowell. From a signal to a planter to a symbol—this bell reminds us of "the pulse of life" that beat throughout Lowell's history.

As a member of the LHP, I was surprised but pleased at the outpouring of support and interest at the morning ceremony as officials pulled back the blue tarp to reveal the bell and its mounting. It looked wonderful and appealing as an anchor to that very busy and high-traffic intersection. The mounting is reminiscent of the public art piece a short walk away on either side of Central Street titled *Human Construction*. The event was covered by the Boston media as well as the *Sun*. I just chatted on the phone with an editor from the *Boston Globe* looking for some information about the bell. It certainly was a "better news" story than the last few that have brought these newsies to the city.

When the wayside informational kiosk is installed, it will tell the story of the bell. This is a draft of that story, which starts with a diary entry of Ellen Collins, a Lowell mill girl:

> "'Up before day at the clang of the bell and out of the mill by the clang of the bell into the mill and at work in obedience to that ding dong of a bell just as if we were so many living machines.
>
> 'The pulse of life in nineteenth-century Lowell moved to the peal and chime of bells overhead. Clock towers, church steeples, mill buildings, fire and police stations all sounded their bells to broadcast their many messages. Mill bells would ring eight times a day. Lowell was known as the Bell City.'
>
> This bell was discovered partly buried, upside down, in a yard in a Centralville neighborhood home across the river from Downtown. It was being used as a garden container for flowers. It is believed

that a mill employee in 1923 brought this bell to his home from a demolished mill. Recent research points to service as a fire alarm signal in the tower of the Old Market House, once a market and later a police station. Featured in a *Sun* newspaper story about the 'Mystery Bell,' it still holds some of its secrets.

The Naylor Vickers Company of Sheffield, England, supplied many of Lowell's bells, including those still hanging at the former Central Fire Station on Palmer Street and the Boott Cotton Mills. Made in 1859, this bell is steel rather than the more expensive bronze and produced a sharper sound that was more effective for emergency communications. The bell stands here to remind us of those days when 'Cotton was King' and the world looked to Lowell as the model for planned urban living."

Top Lowell Political Events of 2009

By **Dick** on December 28, 2009

It was a busy year in Lowell politics, so I won't limit myself to just ten items. Here is my list of the top political events in Lowell in 2009:

Local incumbents lost in all three elected boards this November. On the city council, Alan Kazanjian and Armand Mercier failed to win re-election. They (and Mike Lenzi who did not run) were replaced by Franky Descoteaux, Joe Mendonca, and Patrick Murphy. On the school committee, Regina Faticanti, the longest-serving elected official in Lowell at the time, was not re-elected. She was replaced by first-time candidate Alison

Lariba. And on the Vocational High School committee, long-time incumbent Mike Hayden was not re-elected, with the voters choosing Fred Bahou.

A ballot referendum to change the method by which Lowell voters chose their city councilors called Choice Voting was defeated by 6841 against to 5174 in favor.

The world fiscal crisis forced the City government to make substantial cuts to its FY09 budget, including many layoffs.

Arguing that more budget cuts were needed, a majority on the city council voted to eliminate funding for the position of Assistant to the City Manager (held by Andy Sheehan). The same councilors also voted to eliminate the City's primary election. At election time, many voters later identified the outcome of these two matters as a cause for dissatisfaction with some members of the council.

The school committee also made substantial cuts, eliminating more than 120 jobs. In a controversial move (to some), the committee also voted to move the school department headquarters from the Bon Marché building downtown to the newly vacated Rogers School on Highland Street (which was also closed in a cost-cutting measure).

The University of Massachusetts Lowell became the owner of two of the anchor buildings of downtown Lowell, the Doubletree Hotel (which was purchased from private owners in April to become the UMass Lowell Inn & Conference Center) and the Tsongas Arena (which was transferred by the City to the university in October) and renamed the Paul E. Tsongas Center at UMass Lowell.

In economic development news, the new Target store on Plain Street opened in October, the official ground-breaking for the Hamilton Canal development area occurred in November, and by Christmas the Lowe's on Chelmsford Street is rapidly taking shape. In addition, the new Jeanne d'Arc Credit Union headquarters opened, and several new stores, shops, and markets opened in downtown. And Elliot's Hot Dog stand re-opened.

Massachusetts Senator Ted Kennedy died in August after an extended illness. Controversy arose when the state legislature voted to alter the method of filling a vacancy in the U. S. Senate. Formerly, the governor would appoint someone to fill the seat until the next state election, but in the expectation of John Kerry becoming president in 2004 with a Republican governor in office, the legislature changed the law to have the seat filled by a special election. But this year, with health care reform possibly hanging on a single vote, the governor and legislature decided to change the law once again by allowing the governor to name an interim Senator until a successor could be elected. Governor Patrick appointed Paul Kirk who did, in fact, cast a critical vote on health care reform just last week.

As for the special election, after former Congressman Joe Kennedy and present Congressmen Marty Meehan and Steve Lynch all decided not to run, the Democratic field ended up with Martha Coakley, Mike Capuano, Steve Pagliuca, and Alan Khazai, with Coakley winning by a wide margin in the December primary. In January 2010, she will face Scott Brown who defeated Jack E. Robinson in the Republican primary.

In April, TV trucks from Boston descended on the Pine Street headquarters of the Lowell Health Department to report on the first cases of the H1N1 flu in Massachusetts, which were diagnosed in two boys here in Lowell.

Hollywood came to Lowell this summer as Mark Wahlberg, Christian Bale, Amy Adams, and a large production company spent several weeks on location filming *The Fighter*, the story of Lowell boxer Micky Ward.

In March, the City administration issued homeowners cranberry-colored barrels and changed the way the city's trash was collected.

In May, the City government and the Lowell Spinners minor league baseball club executed a new 10-year lease for Lelacheur Park.

A town hall meeting on health care reform in Chelmsford

hosted by Niki Tsongas featured many opponents of reforms and previewed emotional confrontations around the country throughout the summer and fall.

Old media continued to suffer with the *Boston Globe* being threatened with closure if its labor unions didn't make major salary and benefit concessions (which they did). The *Lowell Sun* required all employees to take furloughs in February, laid off some employees in April, raised the newsstand price of the daily paper from 50 to 75 cents, and removed "The Column" from its website in a move preparatory to charging for content delivered on its website.

The influence of new media continued to grow as local candidates made YouTube and other social networking sites major components of their campaigns. New blogs such as *MrMillCity*, *Lowell Shallot*, *Lowell Handmade*, and *Art is the Handmaid of Human Good* appeared on the scene.

2009

Photographs by Tony Sampas

"The Eagle and the Moon"

"Spring's Return"

PHOTOS

"Along French Street"

"Passaconaway, Edson Cemetery"

"A Place of Illumination, Pollard Memorial Library"

HISTORY AS IT HAPPENS

"The Northern Canal from the Richard Howe Bridge"

"Along School Street"

"Beneath the Bridge"

"Kerouac Park"

"Cote's Market"

PHOTOS

"Holy Trinity"

2010

The Apple iPad

By **Tony** on January 19, 2010

Wednesday, Apple released its new "tablet" called the iPad. The iPad is 10 inches long and only .5 inch thick. The device offers several internet connection options ranging from Wi-Fi to 3G. It plays videos, displays pictures, surfs the internet, and runs all Apple Apps. The iPad price is between $500 and $1,000.

Since the iPad was released on Wednesday, I've had two days to think about this thing. On the first day, I couldn't get myself beyond the idea that the iPad was just a big iTouch. "This product is going nowhere," I thought. Then I did a little reading and discovered that both Google and HP were also developing their own versions of a tablet. OK, I must be missing something if these two giants want into the tablet market.

Yesterday, as I talked to people about the iPad features it hit me. The iPad may very well be a revolutionary device. First off, the tablet will not replace the smart phone nor was it meant to. But it just might be what is needed to speed up the world's transition from ink text to electronic text. For newspapers, it might be the perfect path to integrated multi-media features and articles.

Trust me, I do not own stock in Apple and am not trying to sell this thing. Why would someone would buy an eReader like a Kindle or Nook that can only download black-and-white text when he or she can get an Apple iPad that downloads sharp color text, and does much more?

I saw its real value when I started to think of the iPad more as a "home device" and less as a "mobile device." Don't get me wrong. It has mobility. The iPad has ten hours of battery life, weighs 1.5 pounds, and hits a 3G network.

But me? I'm a homebody, so I see myself using the iPad to read an electronic version of the newspaper while eating breakfast. I see myself downloading an eBook about John F. Kennedy with text that's hyper-linked directly to a video of his inaugural address. I see myself showing off my granddaughter in a slick slide show. I see myself getting driving directions while easily switching from a Google Earth view to a street view of where I am going. All on the iPad.

35 Years Ago: Khmer Rouge Terror

By **George Chigas** on January 28, 2010
—

Scholar and writer George Chigas, a Lowell native, published a collection of poems in 1986 that drew on the experiences of his wife, Thida Loeung, as a refugee who escaped the genocidal Khmer Rouge in Cambodia. This coming April will mark 35 years since the Khmer Rouge captured Phnom Penh and terrorized the Cambodian people. George Chigas's book Chanthy's Garden *chronicles the experiences of refugees who resettled in Lowell.*

DREAMING OF SUGAR CANE

In a photograph of Khao I Dang
I saw the mountains you crossed over to escape.
Through the night
you lugged baby sister on your hip
across a bridge of bones and hair
laid down by soldiers' land mines.
Waiting in the camp

you drifted back over those mountains
to a ruby morning
when your father taught a smiling girl
exact movements of hands and feet
to perform Angkor's old time dance;
and went door to door
selling baskets of corn
balanced with a pole on your shoulder
as your father walked alongside
eating sugar cane and lychee fruit.
Your father sat engoldened upon the lotus
amused by the cricket's gossip
while you learned English in the camp,
dreaming of sugar cane.

Post-Election Analysis

By **Dick** on January 20, 2010
—

Posted the day after state Senator Scott Brown defeated Attorney General Martha Coakley to fill the U.S. Senate seat vacated by the death of Ted Kennedy.

After the Coakley rally in Lowell on Saturday night, it seemed that Brown's momentum had been checked and that he may have peaked too soon, but that was clearly not the case. As anyone who has run a road race knows, when you commence your finishing kick to overtake the runner in front of you that runner sometimes has a kick of his or her own. Although you catch up momentarily, the racer quickly surges back into the lead and bolts across the finish line far in front of you. That's what happened in this election.

Now that it's over, and Scott Brown is our new U.S. Senator from Massachusetts, it's time to talk about why things happened as they did. Brown ran a near flawless campaign and caught the imagination and the hopes of a wide range of Massachusetts voters in a way no one including Brown, I presume, could have foreseen in early December. Here are some of the factors that I see contributing to Coakley's defeat:

To the extent Republican candidates have been successful in Massachusetts, it's been in statewide races. In gubernatorial elections, William Weld beat John Silber, Paul Cellucci beat Scott Harshbarger, and Mitt Romney beat Shannon O'Brien. In U.S. Senate races, Romney gave Ted Kennedy a scare in 1994, and Bill Weld nearly defeated John Kerry in 1996. For whatever reason, when Massachusetts voters get angry enough to enact change via the ballot box, they seem to think statewide rather than State House.

That said, I don't see this as a Republican victory as much as it's a populist revolt against the party in power. As Pete-in-Lowell wrote in response to a recent post here, Scott Brown's momentum is not only a tribute to his abilities, but also to how smoothly things can go without heavy involvement from party machinery. I don't think he'd be in this position if he had the full-throated support of the GOP from the outset. Many of those who streamed to the polls in record numbers were ordinary citizens not obsessed with politics. They're mostly unenrolled, and two Novembers ago they mostly voted for Barack Obama and his promise of change. Instead of change, however, they've been bombarded with endless headlines about the obscene bonuses now being paid to the very same bankers who are most responsible for causing the recession. Wall Street gets bailed out and rewarded, but the homeowner who is underwater on his mortgage gets nothing. No wonder everyone is so angry. No wonder they again voted against the party in power (even though it's the party they voted for just 14 months ago).

Then there's health care reform. The old saying that there are two things you never want to watch—the making of sausage and the making of legislation—was never more applicable than it is to the current health care reform efforts in Congress. President Obama's strategy seemed to be to get anything possible passed now as a kind of foot-in-the-door first step, and then the rest would fall into place later. In the process, deals were made with individual Senators, drug companies, insurance companies, and unions. And the benefits to the average person (the same one frustrated by the bank bailout) were never described well or persuasively.

Two factors unique to this race made health care a particularly potent issue. First, the election is now, in the ugliest part of the legislative process. If there had been no Senate special election here and Congress enacts something soon, its proponents will have the rest of the year to promote its benefits and perhaps win over some skeptical voters. The second problem is that the Senate race is in Massachusetts where we already have good health insurance. Many I've talked to were suspicious that our costs will go up and our care will worsen as we subsidize the rest of the country.

The approach to governing used by both President Obama and Governor Patrick played a role in this election, not to mention in their own sagging popularity. Both see compromise and incremental change as the surest path to reform. In the legal profession, it's said that you can't gain the best settlement for your client unless the other side is convinced that you're ready to go to trial. If your goal is settlement at all costs, you end up with a lousy settlement. The same is true when it comes to legislation. If Obama and Patrick had taken the policy fight to the public earlier in the process, the substantial discontent that exists now may not have materialized.

Speaking of legislation, many of the random Brown supporters I heard from included "We need to shake things up on Beacon Hill" in their reasons for voting Republican. The collective impact of Speaker of the House Sal DiMasi's indictment, Tom Finneran's disbarment, Anthony Gallucio's probation revocation, and James Marzilli's conviction cannot be discounted. Neither did the voters ignore the change the legislature made to the method of filling a vacant U.S. Senate seat (allowing the governor to appoint an interim Senator until the special election) after the death of Senator Ted Kennedy, a procedural change voters may have resented. And that change is on top of the previous change in 2004 when the legislature stripped the governor of the power to make an appointment to a Senate vacancy when it appeared that John Kerry was about to be elected president. It's supreme irony that had they left the law as it was, Deval Patrick would have been able to appoint someone to fill Kennedy's vacancy at least until next fall's regular state election.

Even the special election process worked against the Democrats, whose most reliable voters, urban residents, may have already spent their energy in hard-fought municipal elections in November while more conservative suburban voters hadn't been to the polls since last spring.

Then there's Martha Coakley and her campaign. Events since the primary certainly corroborate the old saying that there are only two ways to run: scared and unopposed. But blaming Coakley and her campaign would be a mistake. This was not just a tactical victory by Brown; it was one of those electoral tidal waves that periodically upend the political status quo. Democrats who blame the outcome on the candidate just ignore strategic weaknesses and set themselves up for more defeats down the road.

Still, even Coakley herself would probably agree that she could have run a better campaign. While it's true that she has run statewide before, it was never in a contested race. When Tom Reilly left the Attorney General's office in 2006 to run for governor, Coakley ran for Attorney General and had no opponent in the primary or in the general election. Her only contested race was when she was elected Middlesex District Attorney back in 1998 when she defeated Michael Sullivan and Tim Flaherty in the primary and Lee Johnson in the general election. Finally, there was one thing about this election that I thought demonstrated the double standard applied to female candidates. A woman who had posed nude in a national magazine centerfold would have been treated far differently for that decision than was Scott Brown for doing the same thing.

Welcome to the Tsongas Center

By **Dick** on February 6, 2010
—

Despite UMass Lowell's 3-2 loss to Boston University, this was a great night at the newly renamed Tsongas Center at UMass Lowell (formerly known as the Tsongas Arena). The night began with a short speaking program with university Chancellor Marty Meehan sharing his vision of how the arena will continue to benefit the city while becoming an integral part of the university. City Manager Bernie Lynch said everyone could be sure that UMass Lowell got a good deal because Chancellor Meehan had been such a tenacious negotiator. UMass President Jack Wilson commended state Senator Steve Panagiotakos for brokering the deal between the city and school. Wilson said Steve had a future as a psychiatrist after what he went through to pull this agreement together. Congresswoman Niki Tsongas and Senator Panagiotakos both spoke. Chancellor Meehan finished by thanking several in attendance whose work in the early 1990s made the arena possible including then-*Sun* publisher Jack Costello, former Mayor Dick Howe, and former state Senators Paul Sheehy and Dan Leahy.

And then the game started with a flurry of scoring. Lowell put the first goal in just 22 seconds into the period. Less than a minute later, BU tied it. When BU was whistled for a penalty at nine minutes of the first period, a hopeful buzz seeped from the stands, but BU quieted that with a shorthanded goal at 9:49. About a minute later, perhaps even on the same penalty, BU scored another shorthanded goal, making the score BU 3, UML 1 at 10:25 of the first period. UML played more aggressively in the second period and scored that period's only goal at seven minutes, making the score BU 3, UML 2, which is how the game ended a full period later. UML pulled the goalie with 47 seconds left and had several shots which were not strong scoring chances.

Eileen Donoghue for State Senate

By **Marie** on April 6, 2010
—

After Steve Panagiotakos announced that he would not seek re-election as state Senator in the 1st Middlesex District, former Lowell Mayor Eileen Donoghue and Middlesex County Assistant District Attorney Chris Doherty faced off in the Democratic Primary. Here's Marie's post about Donoghue's announcement event.—RPH

Former Lowell Mayor Eileen Donoghue made her official entry into the race for the First Middlesex state Senate seat today at a noontime gathering at Cobblestones restaurant downtown. She was introduced by Hieng Chhay, who met Eileen in 1998 when she was mayor and he was a counselor at the Light of Cambodian Children's "Future Stars" camp. Now a UMass Lowell grad, Chhay lauded Donoghue's support to help young people avoid violence.

Amid praise for retiring Senator Panagiotakos and before a

crowd of well over 100 supporters, Donoghue pledged to "earn every vote" in her run for this office. She noted that in her past dealings with the Senator and others in the area delegation she learned that active partnership "is a model for how to get things done."

Gov. Patrick at the Owl Diner

By **Dick** on April 10, 2010

At about 8:20 a.m. on this breezy, chilly but sun-soaked morning, a dark green Peter Pan coach rolled down Appleton Street and slowed to a stop in front of Lowell's iconic Owl Diner. In front of the diner were dozens of supporters waving "Deval Patrick - Tim Murray - 2010" signs; across the street were more than a hundred members of the Lowell Police union, all clad in white t-shirts with "LPA" on the back; and all holding signs bearing slogans such as "Deval hates cops" and "Treat us fair." The governor exited the bus and worked his way inside the diner, which was packed with supporters and regular patrons. Among the elected officials present were state Senator Panagiotakos, Lowell Mayor Jim Milinazzo, City Councilor Bill Martin, School Committee member Jackie Doherty, and candidates for state Senate Eileen Donoghue and Chris Doherty.

After working his way around the room, shaking hands with everyone and even helping to clean up a plate that slid off a waitress' tray due to the crush of bodies inside, the governor spoke about the police protesters outside and the issues at stake in this election. Here is some of what he said:

"You may be concerned about some of the police who are outside protesting. These are good people. They're worried about their livelihoods and the public's investment in them, and so am I. But let me be clear: when we changed from police details to civilian flaggers, that was not about some policy point, that was about you, about efficiency, about simplicity, about how we do well and better what, frankly, 49 other states are already doing. When you hear issues around the Quinn Bill, for example, that's not because the Quinn Bill is evil; it's because we're at a place right now where we're having to make a lot of hard choices.

"There is nothing about what we've proposed that puts anyone's collective bargaining rights in jeopardy. Nothing. And you've got to know that, because you're not going to always hear that or get that from somebody's sign or slogan.

"There are going to be a lot of things said in this campaign that are about tearing people down. That is not what this campaign is about. And that is not what this administration is about. It's about lifting us all up; and if you want to be a part of that, you've got to bring that out. In each decision we have made and will make, I want you to be absolutely certain who is on my mind and in my heart—and it's these three kids right here (gestures towards three children sitting at a nearby table). The point is, generational responsibility is what we must get to. We must be about that ancient idea that each of us in our time is responsible for doing everything we can to leave society better for the generation to come. That characterizes every decision we have made, we will make—and, with your help and with the help and blessing of the people of the Commonwealth, every decision we will make in the next four years. Thank you all for coming."

Before leaving the Owl, Governor Patrick had a quick sit-down meeting with police union officials Jerry Flynn and Bryan McMahon, facilitated no doubt by Senator Panagiotakos. Once in the parking lot, the governor dipped into his wallet and slipped a bill into a donation can held by a fund-raising member of the PYO Little League, spoke with Senator Panagiotakos for a few minutes, and then boarded the bus, bound for his next rally in Newburyport.

Common Sights

By **Paul** on June 7, 2010
—

I've lived near the South Common since 1992, not going to the park much until the early 2000s when I started using the oval around the playing field on the floor of the Common as an exercise track. Something is different this spring, however. There's a noticeable uptick in activity on the Common, and I mean good activity. When I first moved into the neighborhood I was regularly calling the Back Central Police Precinct to report drug deals going on in front of the Rogers School and hookers drifting up South Street to the backside of the former St. Peter Church rectory. In those days, the only grown men riding bikes were messengers in the underground economy. Now even I've got a bicycle, and some mornings ride the streets bordering the park.

Early on weekday mornings, on the weekends, and after work the Common is alive with sports players, families using the playground, dog-walkers, joggers and health-hikers, young basketball and tennis players, couples sitting on blankets under the pines on the hill—all this and more. The closing of the Rogers School was a loss of vitality, but the school department offices have brought new folks to the park. When I walk my family's Boston Terrier at 6:30 a.m., I still find too many "empties" in the darker recesses of the sprawling green space and step around too much broken glass on the paved walkways, but overall the Common seems to have found its constituency.

For a long time, it appeared to be a largely abandoned park except for the soccer players who raced back and forth in the dirt-bowl that was once a green field. Although the Rogers School was on the Common, I never sensed that the school meshed with the park. Yes, the students would be out there for physical education classes, but the school was oriented toward Highland Street—not unlike the way the mills downtown were built with their backs to the river. The busiest I would see it was during the annual carnivals and the well-attended Puerto Rican Festival. Long gone were the memorable nights when the South Common hosted the climax of the Lowell Folk Festival with more than 5,000 people arrayed around the natural amphitheater sloping up from the sports field. The other lively times were post-snowstorms when the hill dipping down from the Eliot Church turned into one of the best sledding runs in the city.

This change is all for the best and just in time for the City's plan to renovate the South Common. The sidewalk upgrade along Thorndike Street is well along, with lots of granite curbing in place. The spring, City workers spread a heavy layer of loam on the center of the playing field to make up for the damage done by huge piles of snow deposited during the winter. I'd like to see the City haul the snow somewhere else. The salty snow is not good for the soil. The trees look as healthy as ever even if there are a few too many. That will be addressed when the park redevelopment begins. I hope the City allocates money to move the plans forward. As one daily observer, I see the community embracing the Common more vigorously—and just in time.

'Beast Underneath'

By **Paul,** June 30, 2010

—

I wake up early every day, but today I got up even earlier to check on our young cat that came home from the vet's yesterday after being spayed. We were told to watch her closely for several days to be sure she is recovering as expected. I was awake, listening to New Hampshire Public Radio's overnight broadcast of the BBC World Service, when I heard the rattle of cans and cart wheels on the street through the open window. It was barely first light, but a middle-aged couple was making the rounds on trash pick-up day. They fished in the recycle bin for redeemables. A tall, thin older jogger passed them on his way toward the courthouse. He was alone, but there are guys the same age as him who run this route in a group, probably jumping off from the "Y" on Thorndike Street. The clock read 4:32. Big cities like New York and Boston come to mind when you think about cities that don't sleep, but Lowell has its own 24/7 tempo—ask any police officer about the night rhythm. This time of year the birds keep time in the trees. Their music rises with the light.

The news as usual was angled toward war, money, and politics. The Republic of Congo is marking its 50th year of independence from Belgium. Chaos and brutality have dominated the nation for five decades. At one point, ten African nations were fighting with or against political factions in Congo in what was called "Africa's World War." I also heard a report about Hamid Ismailov, an Uzbek novelist and poet from Kyrgystan now living in London. He's a writer-in-residence for the BBC who has been blogging about the turmoil in his homeland, where the Kyrgyzs are fighting people with roots in Uzbekistan who live in Kyrgystan. Listening to him, I was reminded of my friend Steve talking about the Irish Civil War and the more recent indiscriminate bombings when he was studying at Trinity College in Dublin. Ismailov was asked if he was losing faith in human nature, given all the violence. About the inter-ethnic strife in his nation, he said, "I felt as if my hands were cutting my legs." He had written on his blog, "Are the crows that do not peck out each other's eyes more human than us?" and "Is civilization as thin as the shirt we wear, covering a beast underneath?" He said the stories of human kindness coming out of the war zone make him feel hopeful.

You don't have to cross an ocean to encounter violence. Last week, a 19-year-old man from downriver in Lawrence was killed in the Back Central neighborhood, a short walk from where my family lives. Juan Ferrer's death was a page one story in the newspaper. Two days after the shooting, yellow police tape lay on the pavement in the alley outside the building where he had been visiting friends. He was at a barbecue, according to a news report. A black kettle-top grill stood in the alley, and dark curtains blew in one of the open windows above. I asked a neighbor who knew him what happened. "There was an argument. Somebody had a gun."

Ken Burns @ MCC

By **Dick** on June 16, 2010
—

Congratulations to Middlesex Community College (MCC) for tonight's 12th MCC Celebrity Forum at Lowell Memorial Auditorium. Ken Burns was outstanding. He entered from the rear of the hall, accompanied by a vintage recording of "This Land is Your Land," and quickly mounted the stage that was decorated by foliage, a canoe, and a tent in recognition of his latest film,

Our National Parks: America's Greatest Idea. Burns spoke from a solid wooden podium at center stage with his image projected on a large video screen to his rear.

Burns began by describing the central themes that run through all his films. Foremost is the exploration of the question "Who are we?", closely followed by examinations of race and space, particularly how the sheer size of our country shaped us as a people. He spoke glowingly of our national parks, calling them "the Declaration of Independence applied to the landscape." Several times he returned to a point made in the 14-minute introduction to *National Parks* that was shown before he took the stage: That we fail to appreciate the fact that we, as American citizens, own the most magnificent and beautiful natural spaces in our country. This was a radical notion. In the rest of the world, such spots were the sole domain of kings and nobles. Without the national park system, Burns suggested, Yellowstone would be a gated community reserved for the wealthiest in our country.

Burns closed with a compelling personal story. His mother died of cancer when he was very young, and his father was distant and stingy with his affection (which Burns readily identifies as a consequence of his mom's illness). Once when Burns was only six years old, his dad took him on a drive and then a hike along Skyline Drive at the mouth of the Shenandoah Valley. The filmmaker said that this long-forgotten memory, brought back to life while filming *National Parks*, reminded him that part of that story is an intensely personal one: it's about who we see these places with and how we pass along our love of these parks to the next generation.

After his prepared remarks, Burns took questions for half an hour. When asked which film has had the biggest impact on him, he replied that since all the movies follow similar themes, whatever one he's working on most recently would be the one, although he conceded that the amazing response to *The Civil War* made that one stand out. How does he choose the subject for a film? He said, "The topics choose me," and that he's finished every project he's began.

Burns observed that it's often in the financial interest of many to keep us divided, so one of his goals is to identify things that bring us together. He said, "Nostalgia and sentimentality are the enemies of everything that's good," but he criticized academic historians for rejecting the narrative form of history which in turn negatively influences the teaching of history. The biggest part of the word "history" after all is "story," and if you don't tell a good story, no one's going to pay much attention. He also said that too often we retreat to pure rationality, to a world where 1 plus 1 always equals 2. His objective is to take us to a higher plane, one where emotion and inspiration play a bigger role.

Audience member Paul Sheehy next asked Burns, the creator of a film called *Baseball*, to comment on any changes that should be made to baseball rules after a blown call by an umpire cost Detriot Tigers pitcher Armando Galarraga a perfect game a few weeks ago. Burns said, "The outcome was exactly right." He said that two other pitchers have already thrown no-hitters this year, but their names will soon be forgotten. Galarraga, on the other hand, by his tremendous show of grace, class, and fortitude, will forever be remembered. After all, said Burns, Life is not about everything going right: it's about loss and failure as well as success. Burns then explained that his next film, which he is doing the final editing of right now, is a sequel to *Baseball* called *The 10th Inning*. He said that New England fans will especially enjoy this one since the story that binds it together is the 2004 baseball season.

Ken Burns fielded a few more questions and then departed to a standing ovation after first receiving a Middlesex Community College sweatshirt from President Carole Cowan. Burns was an excellent speaker, thought provoking at so many levels. I walked out of the Auditorium determined to get onto Netflix and fill up the queue with his films.

Frank Keefe: 'Lowell is a Beacon'

By **Dick** on June 23, 2010
—

The concluding session of the 2010 "Public Matters: Empowering Lowell's Leaders" program took place this evening at Middlesex Community College. Urban planning guru Frank Keefe (Lowell's chief city planner a long time ago) was the keynote speaker. I found his remarks fascinating, uplifting, and, to anyone interested in Lowell's developmental trajectory over the past 40 years, invaluable.

Keefe said that when he first got to Lowell, the prevailing "vision of Lowell" was "amorphous and divided" with at least one scenario advocating the demolition of all remaining mill buildings with the resulting rubble used to fill in the canals. He praised the city councilors who killed the plan to extend the Lowell Connector through the Back Central Street neighborhood, but said a key event came when Richard Nixon ended funding for Urban Renewal in 1973. Without federal funds, there was no way to finance the demolition and rebuilding plans. The turning point within the city came with the establishment of the Center City Committee. Up to that point, "the politics of patronage and negativity prevailed," but Center City brought together representatives of every sector of Lowell and forced folks to grapple with a shared vision for the future of the city. That committee decided that Lowell should find its future in its past. Keefe explained that up until that point, historic preservation was all about the colonial era with all available funding going to Federalist buildings and Revolutionary War sites. The notion of spending preservation dollars in a gritty industrial city such as Lowell was unheard of.

Keefe gives Pat Mogan much of the credit for the selected strategy. Mogan said that after hearing incessant negativity from parents about their community, it was no wonder that kids grew up wanting to leave. By teaching young people to respect, embrace, and have pride in their past, the kids would stick around. As for the tactics employed, Keefe described a unique "Lowell formula" that consisted of (1) a shared vision arrived at by consensus building with every constituency and (2) every City agency following complementary policies (by which he meant the shared vision identified the specific missions of each department and each of those missions advanced the overall vision). Keefe said the results have been "magical" and that Lowell has done these "complementary projects" better than any other city for the past forty years. He said Lowell had long ago mastered the knack of "getting stuff from the state." Before Lowell, state parks were in forested areas such as Carlisle; Lowell proposed and got a "Heritage State Park" in the middle of the city. Community colleges were another example: before Lowell they were in sparsely populated areas unlike any shared image of "community." In Lowell, the community college is in the middle of the city.

Lowell also benefited through the years from being the target of affection of two powerful politicians: Mike Dukakis and Paul Tsongas. Keefe explained that Dukakis's father was a graduate of Lowell High School who went on to Harvard and Harvard Medical School. Consequently, "Dukakis loved Lowell." Tsongas added two key features: (1) he made sure that the private sector was "fully engaged" and (2) helped create the Lowell Plan and the Lowell Development & Financial Corporation whose members were active partners in all subsequent developments. Tsongas also recognized that there had to be an emphasis on culture, the arts, and education. The result of all this effort was "a new politics" that valued "projects not patronage," all of which was sustained by the leadership and cooperation of the City Council, city managers, and city planners.

"No other city in the Commonwealth has had the sustained vision and commitment that Lowell has had." Keefe closed by speculating how tempting it must be for state and federal politicians to say, "Lowell's done well and gotten its share so let's help another city." But Keefe emphatically urged that the temptation be resisted. "Lowell is a beacon," he said, "that must be sustained as a role model for the rest of the cities in the Commonwealth."

'Saturday, Saturday. . .'

By **Paul** on July 25, 2010
—

I've been to every Folk Festival since the first National Folk Festival in Lowell in 1987, and the 2010 Saturday portion was as good as I've seen it—the talent, street life, audience size, urban energy. I spent a lot of time at Boarding House Park with the UMass Lowell booth. The crowd never quit from 12 noon to 9 p.m., when we folded our tent for the day. We answered hundreds of questions about university programs. We handed out about 1,000 free foam visors printed with the school logo.

At Boarding House Park the acts were top notch, particularly the Steep Canyon Rangers (a strong candidate for best group name this year), Bua (traditional Irish, introduced by Seamus Connolly), De Temps Antan (French-Canadian roots music), and the Kings of Harmony, who paraded their jazzy brass sounds into the park. I heard Cape Verdean songstress Maria de Barros and her band at the Dutton Street Pavilion, where she had the dancers swinging to "funana," which the festival website describes as a "zydeco-like dance form with strong African roots, rhythmically powered by the 'ferro,' a piece of metal scraped with a smaller metal object."

A few observations: The transformation of the national park

parking lot into the Dutton Street festival area is one of the best changes that has been made in recent years. The area rivals the Boarding House Park zone for dynamism, and it's great to have the activity on the doorstep of the Market Mills complex and the park Visitor Center. It functions as a vibrant front plaza and lively back yard at the same time, depending on which direction you enter the festival zone from.

The people-watching was Olympics-level all day. If this isn't a people's festival now, I'll eat my foam visor. In the early years of the festival, the audience tilted toward the Channel 2/WGBH Radio-type folk aficionados—not that there's anything wrong with that. Now, the great American mosaic is on display—and there's everything right about that. Walking through downtown at about 9 p.m., I heard (and saw) music pouring out of every business that had a cup or a table to its name. In front of Mambo Grill, a reggae band featuring horns powered through bouncy covers of Bob Dylan and Bob Marley. The frontman wore a black t-shirt with a big John Lennon image on the front. There was a woman in a white sun-dress on the side slow-dancing with a gray-beard vet in a wheelchair. The guy was twirling his chair to spin her around. Merrimack Street was still a pedestrian way at that hour and became a performance canyon as the music climbed the building facades and deflected off tall windows.

2010

Who Gets Hurt?

By **Paul,** August 4, 2010
—

In Christianity we are taught that Jesus died for our sins. There is also the suffering of those who are maimed by the sins of others. Blogging for *Time* magazine on August 2, Joe Klein offered up a sober assessment of President Obama's speech to the disabled vets a few days ago that marked the end of "major combat operations" in Iraq by our country. It's not unusual for a writer to have an idea he or she wants to write about, but cannot find a way in to the subject. Klein's blogging, as well as this past week's *Time* cover with the young Afghan woman, Bibi Aisha, whose nose had been sliced off by her husband, opened a path into something I've been thinking about for a month.

On Sunday, July 4, I saved the front page of the *New York Times*. It's been folded and sitting on my desk since then. The lead photograph on page one is of 23-year-old Brendan Marrocco of Staten Island, N.Y., at Walter Reed Army Medical Center. He's in a rehabilitation room with a medical aide who is helping him with an artificial leg. On Easter Sunday, 2009, Brendan was riding in a vehicle that was blown up by a roadside bomb in Iraq. According to the *Times*, "he became the first veteran of the wars in Iraq and Afghanistan to lose all four limbs in combat and survive." He has four artificial limbs, but is hoping for a double arm transplant, "a rare and risky procedure." He has a brother who is with him almost constantly and a girlfriend.

Brendan's image brought to mind another photograph that I will never forget. When the war in Iraq began the media published a picture of a boy whose two arms had been amputated after being horrifically burned during the bombardment of Baghdad. I searched the web for details to remind myself what had happened to him. Twelve days into the official start of the war in March 2003, 12-year-old Ali Abbas was maimed when what was described as either a "stray American bomb" (CBS News) or "a coalition missile attack" (BBC) wiped out 16 members of his immediate and extended family, including his parents, at the family home outside Baghdad. Ali Abbas survived and, according to the most recent report I could find (2007), now lives in England. Donations that flooded in after his photo was seen around the world were used for medical procedures, rehabilitation, and schooling.

In an interview in 2007, he said "I still remember my family and I still blame the person who bombed my house. Because when he bombed the house there weren't any soldiers or weapons. We were farmers; we had cows and sheep. There's no reason that [the bombing] should have happened." He grew to be a teenager who learned to use his feet as hands (he has artificial arms) for everything from brushing his teeth to painting pictures of flowers. He rides a three-wheel bike that he steers with his shoulders. When he's older, he says he'd like to do some kind of work to promote peace.

Bibi Aisha is the new "Afghan girl"—a heart-wrenching counterpart to the famous *National Geographic* magazine cover photograph of a beautiful young woman that is one of the iconic portraits of the past 30 years. Her story of abuse at the hands of a husband from the Taliban is difficult to hear and read. There's hope for her with facial reconstruction surgery. Her visibility has drawn attention and support, however, there are other girls and boys and women and men whom we will never hear about.

We are approaching the ninth anniversary of 9/11. It seems beyond the capacity of any one of us to comprehend the scale of death and destruction that have resulted from that day. And atrocities such as the one involving Bibi Aisha aren't tied to 9/11; we know about them because we are hearing more about Afghanistan. This week President Obama presented a medal to Susan Retik, who, with Patricia Fleming Quigley of the Lowell Flemings, founded "Beyond the 11th," after losing their husbands in the 9/11 attacks, to reach out to and help Afghan widows. The late Patrick Quigley's name is carved into the UMass Lowell 9/11 memorial along the Riverwalk behind the university residence halls close to the hydro-electric plant off Pawtucket Street.

The people mentioned here have paid a huge price. They are alive, but scarred physically and psychologically. Why? Because of conflicts rooted in religious friction, political power struggles, and competition for resources and riches. They didn't ask for trouble, but trouble found them. I was looking for a way in to this post when I wanted to write about Brendan Marrocco. Now I'm wondering if there is a way out.

Remembering Ed LeLacheur

By **Jack Neary** on August 11, 2010
—

So much has been written over the past few days about my friend—our friend, everybody's friend—former state Rep. Ed LeLacheur and his boundless enthusiasm for life and service, that nothing I can contribute here can really add much to his legacy. I do have two stories, though, from my experience with Ed, to pass along.

If you played baseball at any time in your life, you remember that one play that is the "best" you ever made. Some of you are lucky, in that the "best" play happened in a real game, a sanctioned game, maybe even a playoff game. Not me. The "best" play I ever made happened in batting practice. We were at Manning Field. Probably a Saturday. The Sacred Heart Parish ("The Haht") was putting together a softball team to play in the church league. Maybe the late '70s, early '80s, something like that. A bunch of guys were fiddling around before the first practice started, and the fiddling evolved into something of an organized batting practice session. You know—guy grabs a bat, takes a few swings, another guy grabs a bat. Not all that formal, but. . . organized nonetheless. For some reason, I planted myself at third base to shag whatever came off the various bats as I awaited my own turn. All I remember about the rest of that day is Eddie, taking his swings, lifting a pop foul behind the bag at third, which then drifted toward the corner in left. I sized it up, and started back to shag the fly. Shagging flies in batting practice usually means picking the ball up off the ground after the fly lands. But I saw that I could get to this pop up. It would not be easy, but. . . I don't know. . . for some reason I felt I needed to make the play. So, I turned on the jets—don't laugh, I had jets then and when push comes to shove I have jets now—and I kept the soaring sphere (yeah, I've read purple baseball prose before, too) in sight as I peeked when I could at the chain-link fence that separated the field from the parking lot down the left field line. I wasn't going to make it. The ball was going to hit the ground and my effort was going to be all for naught. (I try to do as little as possible for naught in my life.) My back was completely turned from the field. LeLacheur was probably leaning into the next batting practice pitch. Nobody was watching me. Still—I had to catch this ball. And just before it was to scrape the fence, I lunged forward and Willie Mays-ed the thing into my glove. Without question, the best baseball play I ever made. Nobody cared then. Nobody cares now. I know this. But Eddie's passing allows me to tell the story, because he was the guy who hit the ball.

 My second and favorite recollection of Ed deals with his infectious sense of humor. It's another "Haht" story. This time, again in the '70s, it's the Sacred Heart Bowling League that met weekly at the Brentwood Lanes. A machine of a league coordinated by the late, great Frank Flynn, and we all had a terrific time. From this point on in the story, except for LeLacheur, I'm not going to name names. I think everybody's dead, but I'm still clamming up on the names. People have relatives. Anyway, it's early in the evening and LeLacheur is there, yukking it up with the rest of the guys. At one point, one of the older guys in the league—big, blustery, pipe-smokin' Irishman—points to another guy about to roll. The other guy is also older, but smaller, quieter, and probably not all that Irish. Kinda reminded me of Donald Meek in the movies or John Fiedler on TV. Anyway, the blustery Irishman looks at Donald Meek and says to LeLacheur, "That's the pastor, isn't it?" Of course, it was not the pastor. Not even close. But Eddie saw an opportunity and took it. "Sure," says Eddie. "That's the pastor. Absolutely." And that was it. For a while. The evening wore on and, for all intents and purposes, Donald Meek-guy was the pastor to the Blustery Irishman-guy. The rest of the bowlers in LeLacheur's group got into it, too, deferring all evening to Donald Meek-guy—"Nice one, Father!" "Way to go, Father!" "Which Mass are you saying on Sunday, Father?" LeLacheur, the instigator, just let it keep going. Until the end of the evening approached. At that point, Eddie pulled Donald Meek-guy aside just before he was about to try for a spare and whispered something into his ear. Donald Meek-guy nodded, and made his way to the lane. He took his duckpin ball and lined up his shot. Blustery Irish-guy watched. Donald Meek-guy made his approach, rolled the ball, and missed the spare. (In the interest of keeping the blog relatively clean, I'm misspelling the featured word in this upcoming rant.) "What the eff was that?" Donald Meek-guy roared! "Did you guys see that effin' ball! The effin' lane is effin' warped! I'm not bowlin' at this effin' place ever again!" Blustery Irish-guy blanched. I think he may have even dropped his pipe into his lap. Every bowler in the place, by that time, was in on the joke. Everybody roared. Nobody, though, more than LeLacheur. I had never seen anybody more ecstatic in my life. His laughter thrust him away from the lanes, over by the bench near the front door, where he collapsed in an avalanche of guffaws. To me, it wasn't just the idea of the gag that was brilliant. It was the execution. The timing. The patience it took to get from the set up to the delivery.

I will remember Ed LeLacheur for many things—including the fact that the last time I saw him, he came to see my play *The Porch* in Stoneham, Mass., and I believe he had a great time. But this memory—which I call "That's the pastor, isn't it?"—is my favorite.

All Hail Lyle Lovett

By **Paul** on August 14, 2010
—

At one point last night, Lyle Lovett had 15 musicians and singers on the Boarding House Park stage. I never once thought of Lawrence Welk. I had not seen/heard Lyle Lovett in concert. What was I missing? What I was missing! Where to begin? The twin dynamos of the music series, Peter Aucella and John Marciano, keep outdoing themselves. For shows in recent years, Lyle Lovett & His Large Band ranks with the appearance of Joan Baez at the French Street pergola for sheer musicianship and performance power. For energy and lift and proliferation of fun, the edge goes to Lyle.

The *Sun* this week reported that his troupe has played in Boston and on Cape Cod, but I can't believe those shows were better than the one last night. The recording gods should have been at their machines because a live album/cd/download of the show last night in Lowell would be a mega-hit. The band played for more than two hours after a catchy opening set by song-stylist Kat Edmonson, whose voice wraps around standards like "Summertime" as if genetically engineered for them. I can't remember the names of the players in the "Large Band" or the four fabulous older guys singing on the side, but each of them deserves to have his name etched into the steel of the performance pavilion for history's sake. The temperature was perfect. A searchlight swept the sky all night for added glamour. Am I too enthusiastic? Sitting there with my wife and some close friends, I was dual-tracking in my head, enjoying every well-played note and beautifully sung word while trying to put what was going on in experiential context. Like the labels on science displays in the Exploratorium in San Francisco that ask, "What's going on here?"—I was thinking, this is the essence of art-induced joy and why people say they "love" music, not too strong a word.

How many people attended the show? About 2,000. And there were moments when the artists and audience bonded in pleasure that explain why people have been beating on drums and plucking strings and trying to make harmonious sounds for thousands of years. The show was a tour through American music, from rock and roll to jazz, from country and gospel to the pop songbook, from alt-country to blues and swing and the other variations. We witnessed a unit at its peak. When the lights came on at the end of the show the grounds buzzed and bubbled with chatter as people folded up blankets and chairs and moved toward the exits. To the organizers and sponsors: "Well done, well done." To the band-leader and the band: "Forget Cape Cod; come back to Lowell next summer."

Neighborhood Schools

By **Dick** on September 5, 2010
—

Earlier this week I posted on Facebook regarding the start of school, which prompted a conservative friend to comment on the benefits of neighborhood schools, a term I haven't heard in a few years. It might surprise readers to learn that I am a proponent of neighborhood schools, only my idea of a neighborhood school differs greatly from that of most who use the term.

Transporting kids to schools outside their neighborhoods was first used as a tool to integrate schools. Overwhelming evidence that wealthier neighborhoods had wealthier schools while poorer neighborhoods had poorer schools exposed the lie of separate but equal and prompted courts to act where local officials would not. In addition to the equities involved, all students who attend schools with diverse student bodies derive great benefits from that experience. For that reason, I would support making integration a bigger factor in school assignment than place of residence, if everything else was equal.

But all things aren't equal. Any child who arrives in a classroom in a Lowell public school who is well-fed, well-rested, well-clothed, well-cared for and comes from a safe and supportive home—regardless of how traditional or non-traditional the occupants of that home may be—will receive an excellent education. For too many kids, some or all of those prerequisites of learning are simply not available. If you're now tempted to say, "It's the parents' responsibility," please don't, because that would just show that you're unwilling to have a serious discussion on this topic. Of course, it's the parents' responsibility, but a depressingly large number of parents are either unable or unwilling to provide those prerequisites to learning.

The only way to break out of this pattern is for society to

provide these things to the kids who need them. We've been trying to do that for nearly a half century. There have been some successes, but not enough to keep pace with the scale of the needs. While more money would certainly help, it's not an option and, more importantly, I'm not sure that it's necessary. What is necessary is a more efficient way of delivering existing resources and services to those who need them. And that's where the neighborhood school comes in.

Here are some of the characteristics of my neighborhood school: It would have free day care both before and after the formal school day started and ended. In most families, parents work, whether it's both of them or the one in a single-parent household. Juggling a work schedule and school drop-off and pick-up times creates an incredible amount of stress on both kids and their parents. Once the child gets to school, a nutritious breakfast and snacks would be available at a reasonable price to those who could afford it and free to those who could not. For many children, the food they eat at school is their only decent nutrition of the day. After-school care would not be a simple babysitting service but would be a mixture of homework and physical activity. Almost every kid would benefit from more exercise and having access to a homework center. Staffed by college students pursuing education degrees as part of formal partnerships with UMass Lowell and Middlesex Community College, this would be a huge benefit to the students. The homework centers and gyms would also be available in the evening. If it's a neighborhood school, then some kids, at least, should be able to return easily after dinner.

Besides the basics of food, day care, and homework help, each school would have medical professionals from community health centers assigned on a regular basis. Why should a child miss an entire day of school for a routine medical appointment when the medical professional might be able to be at the child's school in the first place? And (non-school department) social workers and counselors would play a critical role and should also be consistently present. If a child is in crisis, interventions could happen immediately.

By keeping the schools open all the time, they could also serve as neighborhood centers. Instead of having police substations in rented space, put them in schools. What better way of building relations between the police and the community? Neighborhood groups could hold their meetings at the schools, young adults could use the gyms later at night, community cookouts and gatherings could be organized on the school grounds. The possibilities are endless. And best of all, since this approach just reallocates existing resources, it would not require significant new spending.

So why hasn't stuff like this happened already? Any initiatives like those I describe above that have been tried in the past have been stifled by the bureaucracy and its rules. I refer to existing resources, but those resources all are dispersed among independent agencies—local government, local schools, state government, federal government, and non-profits that are funded by government—with no one in charge, no one responsible for the big picture. Each of those agencies operates within its own universe and the concept of sharing resources is usually seen as a threat rather than an opportunity. We all know it's easier to kill an idea than it is to implement it.

That's my view of a neighborhood school. As much as I value the benefits of integration, I think the benefits of the school-centric/neighborhood centric model of delivering services that I describe above outweigh all other considerations.

Maine Musings

by **Nancye Tuttle** on September 20, 2010

—

Nancye Tuttle writes about the start of school and Merrimack Valley–Hollywood connections in the following post, which originally appeared on Nancye's World.

It's been several weeks since I've posted, but it isn't because I'm lazy, just particularly busy as school got underway. Right now, I'm enjoying the sunshine and bright blue ocean in Kennebunkport, Maine, where my daughter and son-in-law have a cozy abode that's a perfect getaway, even on a chilly September weekend. Amazing how a couple of space heaters warm up a cool room on a nippy night. So, here's a few things I've noticed, enjoyed, or thought about since last posting: Back to school always fills me with excitement and a bit of nostalgia. I guess it's because my mother was a teacher and my daughter is a teacher and the call of the classroom always beckons me, too. I love the anticipation of new books, backpacks, lunch boxes, and friends. And I feel truly blessed and honored that for the past six, almost seven, years that I've been able to teach at Middlesex Community College. I met my new students last week in my Film, Video, and Society class. They seem like a bright, inquisitive bunch and are already into the semester, sharing their thoughts and insight on film. We've started with the movie *School Ties*, shot in Lowell, Concord, Groton, and Acton 19 years ago. It's a well-made small film, accurately depicting the 1950s at an elite prep school, where prejudice was the norm. I like to think things have changed on that front, but sadly, I don't think it's that much different. It's always fun to point out local "locations" in the movie, though, including Danas' Market on Gorham Street in the opening segment. If you haven't seen *School Ties*, I recommend it. And, hopefully this time next year, I'll be recommending *The Fighter* as another great example of a locally made film.

Austin Tichenor, Reed Martin, and Matt Rippy, the guys in the Reduced Shakespeare Company's T*he Complete World of Sports* (abridged), now playing at Merrimack Repertory Theatre (MRT), are a hoot to talk to. I enjoyed interviewing them a couple of weeks ago for my column in *The Sun*. And, according to positive reviews in *The Globe* and *The Sun*, it's a must-see show for its raucous ribbing of sportscasters, sports fans, and sports, in general. Haven't seen it yet, since I no longer review for *The Sun* (Lifestyle editor Suzanne Dion took over the job with my retirement in August). But I hope to get there sometime before it ends on Oct. 3 to offer a few comments on this blog. It's nice to know MRT's 32nd season's off to a winning start—at least according to the critics. Scott Grimes still loves Dracut, his old neighborhood, and the Lo-Kai. And after talking to him for a 10 Questions column in *The Sun* last week, it seemed to me that he hasn't gone Hollywood, despite his success on TV and in the movies. Scott came back to town last week for a few days to play in the Dracut firefighters golf tournament at Meadow Creek. He brought memorabilia from such shows as *Band of Brothers* and *E.R.*, which helped him achieve fame. These were to be auctioned at a special event at the Lo-Kai to benefit the Dracut food pantry. I wish I could have gone, but Maine beckoned that weekend. But it was good to talk to Scott and share his story with *Sun* readers. Anyone see him? I'd love to hear how he was in person.

Finally, on the arts scene, the Addison Gallery of American Art in Andover is now officially reopened after a two-year closure for renovations, upgrades, and the addition of new classroom and office space. Here you'll see significant works by Whistler, Sargent, Hopper, de Kooning, Homer, O'Keeffe, and Wegman, plus significant works of modern art. I love wandering the galleries and experiencing the intimacy of this fine small museum, one of the gems of the Merrimack Valley. Located on the campus of Phillips Academy, it's close to Andover's downtown with its nifty restaurants and shops. Make it a point to visit the Addison, which hosts it official re-opening next Saturday. Free and open to all. Also next weekend, Lowell Open Studios celebrates its 10th anniversary with nearly 140 local artists showcasing their work at venues around the city. I'll preview it in the *Sun's* Stepping Out section on Thursday, Sept. 23. Look forward to seeing you around town.

Lowell Environmental Attorney Tries to Declare Car Independence! Part 2

By **Matt Donahue** on September 23, 2010
—

Last month Lowell attorney Matt Donahue wrote about his plan to "shed his car." Thirty days into the experiment he files this report:

Well, my first reaction is of course the caliber of the Richard Howe blog. Thanks for the positive feedback and the fascinating discussion of how we become "Car independent," which would of course lead to energy independence. I appreciate the loyalty to the car; it is tough to stare it down each day and take public transportation or bike or walk. I have become so lazy about it that the best part of this exercise—no pun intended—is that you must think about your transportation choices and plan accordingly. Yes, that sounds silly, but those things that we take for granted we do not think about; we just do it or go, and the car helps us do things more conveniently. But what is the problem with waiting a bit? Well, that's a topic for another day. . . .

THE NEW ECONOMY

The fact is that with a laptop and now a Droid, I have access to my paralegals, secretaries, and associates in my law firm via phone, internet, and e-mail all the time. So, if I am on a bus or waiting for a bus, or a ride, I can review e-mail and respond. In fact, many things are done before I even arrive at the office. When staff arrives at 8:00 a.m., I can provide them a list of things to do and they can ask me questions upon my arrival. These things I could not do if I was in a car, although I could talk on the phone, which I did for ten years, but that was adding more neck and shoulder pain. It was not as effective as a well-thought out conversation or e-mail planning your day or managing staff. It has become more than not driving a car. It is a way of life; and is there really any waiting any more when you have electronic hand-held devices? (I recently waited at the Registry of Motor Vehicles for an hour registering the new car and did my reading online of the *New York Times*, *Reuters*, and, of course, the *RichardHowe* blog . . .). What is time now and what is place and why crowd out that space and time with self-transportation? Why not exercise, bike and walk, or hook a ride publically or privately (a taxi is an option, but does not take a car off the road). This is my 30-day report on my transportation travels over the last month since the death of the suburban. (Post-Suburban Life)

CAR LOW LITES

To quickly recap, our Suburban died in the last week of July 2010. We had a neighborhood camping trip planned, so I had to rent a minivan and borrow a trailer to fit all the stuff—14 kids and five adults to get to a campsite in Vermont. We needed a car to return two sons to college on the weekend of August 27-30—one to Vermont and the other to Connecticut. We incorporated a few days of vacation with the kids before the drop-off to Vermont on the 28th.

NO-CAR HIGHLIGHTS

The more time I spend away from car, the more I enjoy it and the more I really do not like driving. It gives me back, shoulder, and neck pain. I have more pain sitting in a car than I do after a good session of exercise, the difference being that I get no benefit from driving. My chiropractor loves me when I drive and my spinal column gets all messed up! The guy at the gas station hates my new smaller more energy efficient car: "What happened to the Suburban? I used to love those $75.00 fill ups!" Ouch! No sitting in traffic. Have you been on Rte. 495 lately? Better you than me!

UNINTENDED CONSEQUENCES

For about two weeks, we did not have a third car; we juggled, and there were unintended consequences. For example, my son Matt, who typically took the car to his job at Meadowlands Ice Cream, started to bike to work. In the end, he really liked the biking. He is back in school. Matt's biking was partially the result of son Greg's landscaping job in Westford, for which he needed a car. Matt, who sleeps late, decided he did not want to drive Greg to work—then requiring him to be picked up—so he opted for the bike.

CATCHING A LIFT

Because my wife, Lisa, works downtown she requires a car for her work as a nurse with the Visiting Nurses Association. She drives as part of her job in the Greater Lowell area to see her patients. Since her office is next door to mine, I would frequently catch a lift to the office with her. We may have created the first Belvidere to Downtown Lowell 1.3-mile carpool!

BORROWING

My in-laws frequently had a car available that I could use for appearances at court or meetings outside of the city or pick-ups of non-driving children from camps, summer school, or other activities. We did buy a car, but it is sitting in the driveway more often than in the past, because I take the bus, walk, or bike to work. I gave in to Lisa's common sense and realistic advice—also commented on in my August 24 entry in which I wrote that you can have a car to give you peace of mind, but leave it in the driveway.

OBSERVATIONS

Riding the bus is nice, simple, and the AC is cranking as I use the 15 to 20 minutes to organize my thoughts for the day or tackle my "To Do list." On the way home I veg out and watch the scenery and close my eyes or sometimes do some light reading. People are still looking at me funny, and sometimes the bus drivers are not sure that I am in fact waiting for the bus. Though I saw several people recently who said they took the bus for a while or rode their bikes to work in the past. If I was in a city like Cambridge or Somerville, both less populous than Lowell or even Lexington, no one would think twice about taking the bus to the train or the MBTA. If this is an issue for Lowell, is this an issue? I have walked to the office, biked to the office, carpooled to the office, taken the bus, and borrowed a car to get to the office and then use for appointments on days I needed a car. I am waiting for a call back from Zip Car; nothing yet, but I will call the CEO to request a meeting. The corporate headquarters is in East Cambridge. Inspired by Marianne's comments on your blog, Dick, I expect to bike more—it is too quick, easy, enjoyable, and good for me to ignore.

TRANSPORTATION CHALLENGES

I look forward to getting from point A to point B without a car. In requires thought and planning and scheduling. With a car in the driveway though, there is less havoc if domestic emergency transportation issues arise—like a call from Lisa saying, I am stuck with a patient and Peter needs to get to the dentist in 15 minutes!

Maya Angelou & Joe Donahue

By **Paul** on October 27, 2010
—

Today's New York Times *includes an article about the Harlem-based Schomburg Center for Research in Black Culture of the N.Y. Public Library acquiring a massive archive of papers from author and performer Maya Angelou. The story prompted me to recall Maya Angelou's visit to Lowell in 1989 as a guest of Middlesex Community College. On the same day, poet Joe Donahue launched a book at the Whistler House Museum of Art. Following is an op-ed piece I wrote at the time for the* Lowell Sun, *but which never appeared because of a change of editors.*

A DAY THAT STARCHED OUR BACKBONES

Two writers read and recited their work to a combined audience of almost 1,500 people on an otherwise ordinary Thursday in Lowell. October 19th turned out to be a day of roses and accolades. Renaissance woman Maya Angelou stunned a packed house at a noontime program at the Smith Baker Center, a converted nineteenth-century church across from City Hall; in the evening poet Joseph Donahue launched his first collection of poems at the Whistler House Museum of Art. Maya Angelou sang, recited, preached, acted, and danced her way through a fast-paced 90-minute performance in the crescent-shaped hall ringed by stained-glass windows. "I have not come for nothing!" she declared, ordering the college students to take out pen and paper to write the names of authors she was about to reveal: Georgia Douglas Johnson, Paul Laurence Dunbar, and Mari Evans were a few of the African-American writers whose poems she shared, along with her own work.

Remembering her grandmother's wisdom, Angelou said, "Poetry puts starch in your backbone." She described her love of reading and vast appetite for great works, from Shakespeare to Countee Cullen. "All knowledge is spendable currency—read, read, read!" Hers is a message of liberation from the small, mean life that threatens to debase us. "Everyone in this hall has been paid for by ancestors of every color," she told the students. "Your assignment is to prepare yourselves to pay for those who will come after." Angelou scolded, laughed, and clapped, offering bold, musical poems of her own about love and the nature of women and a hilarious piece about a "smoking carnivore" who cannot abide the natural food crowd. She advised writers in the audience to "tell the truth, but not necessarily all the facts." A professor at Wake Forest University, Angelou is the author of *I Know Why the Caged Bird Sings* and other works of prose and poetry. Selected as the "common book" of the year at Middlesex Community College, her memoir was read by students across disciplines. Television viewers will remember her playing the mother of Kunte Kinte in the television mini-series *Roots*.

Joseph Donahue traveled to Lowell from New York City to introduce his first book of poems, *Before Creation*, to his extensive family and old friends. The Whistler House's Parker Gallery was filled with a crowd eager to hear the words of a poet who is an important voice of his generation of writers. The author's keen mind and the fine craftsmanship shone through the spoken words. A professor at Stevens Institute of Technology in New Jersey, Donahue offered a choice wedge of contemporary poetry: the style of his work, at its best, is a combination of "neo-Language Poetry and high lyricism," according to a colleague.

Standing in a room hung with Don Quixote etchings by Salvador Dali, he delivered his poems very much as is, not cluttering the presentation with extensive set-up or paraphrase. Beginning with a long prose poem, "Purple Ritual," he guided the audience on a tour of the American psyche, using the assassination of John F. Kennedy and his own family's history as an armature on which to fix his meditations about myth, fate, loss, and recovery. Explaining that he had tried to find a way to write about New York City while living there, he then read several poems about the city, works reflecting the edgy and exotic terrain of our most modern metropolis.

Opening Joseph Donahue's new book is like slicing open a ripe pomegranate—poems filled with brilliant, jeweled, densely packed, sweet, and sometimes acid language and images are as tasty one by one as in clusters. The shape of the whole work satisfies even before the juicy nuggets are chewed to the dry seed. The surprise of the evening was his reading of three moving elegies not included in the book. The local audience took to heart his remembrances of Lowell journalist and family friend Jim Droney, the Droneys' daughter Sarah, and a figure whom no author with Lowell ties can ignore—Jack Kerouac. These poems telegraph the strength of his next collection. Donald Hall insists that poetry is not dead, even though, he says, some critics and commentators are trying to murder it. Hall claims, "More people read poetry now in the United States than ever did before." And their spines are better for it.

HISTORY AS IT HAPPENS

Willie

By **Dave Perry** on November 2, 2010
—

I dreamt of Willie Mays last night. It was the first time in many years Mays' slightly bowlegged visage showed up in my sleep, but there you are. It was a strange dream, the greatest baseball player cast in newsreel black-and-white, in full San Francisco Giants uniform, including the turtleneck that probably kept him alive as he roamed the frozen tundra of Candlestick Park. I thought of my father, too. This is what we do in moments like Monday's. The Giants brought home the first World Series to San Francisco.

Fifty-six years. My, my. I was born into Giants fandom, in Santa Rosa, Calif., two years after the Giants last won it all in New York, two years before they packed up for Baghdad by the Bay. We, too, moved. Dad was a Navy pilot, so every year or two we made a new home. Florida; Washington state; Coronado, Calif.; Hawaii; even Texas, where Marc Brown used to chase me home from sixth grade each day, because I wasn't from Texas. Always, the Giants were an emotional anchor, something to remind me I had roots. Marichal, McCovey, the Alous, Orlando Cepeda, Jim Davenport, sweet Tito Fuentes, and of course, Mays.

Over the past decade, when we visited San Francisco each summer, a former boss got me the MediaNews seats two rows behind home plate. AT&T isn't a ballpark, but another architectural dream in a city overflowing with them. I got my father there twice before he died in September 2007, thanks to my old boss Kevin. During a particularly confused time in my younger life, my dad and I drove cross-country from Connecticut to California. I was defeated by college, then factory work, and was returning west to resume school. He had timed our trip to coincide with a Cubs-Giants doubleheader at Wrigley Field in

Chicago. Four summers ago, we were at AT&T Park. Best seats in the house. His grandsons sat with him. There are no words for things like this.

Another time at AT&T park, we were ushered down into the hallway that runs beneath the grandstands. Shea Hillenbrand, the former Lowell Spinner, had been traded to the Giants, and had adopted a child with his wife. My wife bought a baby blanket as a gift, and greetings from Lowell, and there we stood in the dank hallway, waiting for Hillenbrand to cross from the locker room to the field entrance. I kept thinking, I could die here. I nearly did. And down the hallway in the distance, an usher slowly led a piece of machinery. "We'll need to move aside as much as you can," said the usher with us. "Mr. McCovey is coming through." And toward us came Willie "Stretch" McCovey, an immense man with baseball's most disarming smile. I froze. All I heard was my heartbeat, pounding in my eardrums. An usher asked if Willie would sign autographs for a couple of kids, my sons. McCovey smiled. I backed up to the wall behind me. Where could a guy get a new pair of pants, I thought. "You ain't no kid," McCovey said with a smile to my oldest son, Ben. He signed. My old job took me to plenty of places where I met celebrities. Never once a problem, save for meeting Steve Cropper, my favorite guitarist, at the Grammys. But Stretch? I tried to form words, but could not. I made little groaning noises, I think, as McCovey drove off, smiling.

Being a Giants fan never felt like suffering, or torture. It was more like glee, something that connected me and my dad when nothing else did. Yes, there was heartbreak when they lost. But you knew they would. So, last night crept up on me. I wore out Giants caps for years. Sometimes, folks around here offered kind glances, but the sentiment attached to them was certain ... pity. Others held me responsible for the sins of Barry Bonds. I listened to Lawrence Ferlinghetti's "Baseball Canto" before the final game Monday night. There was always poetry in baseball, but not baseball in poetry until Ferlinghetti wrote this brilliant poem about sitting in the stands at Candlestick, watching black and Latin players turn the old order upside-down. Everything is political in San Francisco. Everything. Expect a parade like you've never seen.

So, there was Willie Mays in my dream, and I was on the field next to him, and he smiled, and was chatting with someone. I was a reporter, I guess, and had a few questions with him. And then he walked off, slipping his arm around another man, who never turned around but from the back looked very much like my father. Then I woke up. Of course, Marc Brown, the Texas bully who chased me home each day, he only saw the back of me. And I was mostly fast enough to beat him home. Mostly. But Marc, that skinny little corduroy butt you chased back in Texas? Today, you can kiss it, my friend.

What Did I See @ the Meet-Up?

By **Paul** on December 4, 2010
—

This morning's bloggers' meet-up at Top Donut in Centralville exceeded my expectations. People arrived before 9:00 a.m., and the crowd grew to about 50, according to Dick's count. It was a high-spirited bunch of writers, readers, photographers, designers, and comment-makers. People stayed until almost 11.30 a.m., well past the posted wrap-up time. I was also glad to see how busy the donut shop was without our group. The walk-in and drive-up business was steady all morning. All Lowell businesses would be doing well at that pace.

I think the most active blogs were all represented, including the City Life LTC video bloggers, with John McDonough on hand. Dick used his phone to make a video record of the event, so I'll let him show who was on hand. I met a man from Tyngsboro who wanted to tell me how much he appreciated my post in favor of preserving the Pawtucket Falls Dam. I learned from Alex and Anne Ruthmann that UMass Lowell students "blog" via Facebook and are less interested in the now-traditional type blogging that I'm doing. I talked to Corey Sciuto about the car wreck-appeal of the anonymous blogging/mugging via Topix on the *Sun* site. There was a sidebar conversation with Phil Lupsiewicz and Allegra Williams about organizing a short-form video contest for Lowell videos as part of the "Lowell 175" celebration planned for 2011-12 in honor of the city's 175th anniversary. I met Sopheak Sam, one of the activists from fobclothing.com at Western Ave Studios, who told me about the group's "premier urban t-shirt line." I learned that Lynne Lupien is teaching in the Business of Music program at UMass Lowell, which I should have known, being in the same building.

Our virtual community became an actual community.

My Review of *The Fighter*

By **Paul** on December 29, 2010
—

Tonight, with my wife and two friends I saw "the movie" at the Showcase Cinema, just a slap shot away from Micky Ward Circle. The film ended two hours ago, and I'm still in a kind of shock from the hyper-realism on screen. Lowell appeared to be under a colossal magnifying glass. The film felt as much like a documentary as it did a drama, and is a family story more than a boxing movie. More than a family story, though—a cultural story about people and lives and aspirations that are common across a certain segment of the social spectrum. My immigrant roots are in that segment.

The film bangs a gong for anyone who knows Lowell. You walk out of the Showcase Cinema, drive out of the parking lot, and you are on the movie set. I suppose that must be how lots of people in Los Angeles or New York City feel about being in TV-land or movie-land. The locations are like the back of your hand. Knowing the outcome of the real-life story didn't dilute any of the impact of the screen story. The casting was note perfect. The portrayals of George Ward and Officer Mickey O'Keefe (as himself) were outstanding. Melissa Leo as Alice Ward dominated her scenes, even when backed by the seven weird sisters. My favorite fight scene was Amy Adams' smackdown of one of the sisters during the attempted home invasion or sibling intervention (choose one) on Christian Hill.

Christian Bale deserves a prize for his work—just the physical aspect would be enough to win, never mind the talk. My favorite Lowell scene was Bale running across the Ouellette (Aiken St.) Bridge. And Mark Wahlberg holds the social cyclone all together as the steady, modest moral center of this fractured but winning parable. I've worked with a lot of folklorists in my career. This film is a field day of deeply local popular culture in a postindustrial city. Speaking of which, the Industrial Revolution that some people like me have made so much of as part of Lowell's revitalization is tossed off as a joke when it comes up in the notorious HBO documentary about Lowell being "crack street."

The ending is more complex than someone might expect, mostly because of the inner life of the hero. Just when the viewer expects him to pull out of the tribal quicksand, he reaches back for what he knows best and finds a middle ground or third way through his own will power. Humanity in many but not all its shades is on display. I've long said the whole world is in Lowell if you look hard enough. *The Fighter* is film art in peak condition. Let's have more of it, more Lowell stories, more cinema visions, more movie art for more human good.

2011

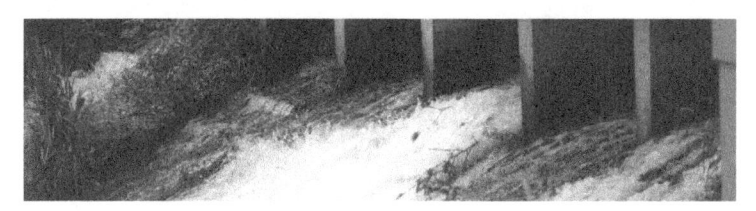

Grand Street Peace Walk

By **Paul** on January 2, 2011
—

Standing on the old Armory site with about 60 other people at 2:00 p.m., I couldn't help thinking that Armory Park was being used for another kind of conflict, even war in the broadest sense—a war against violence like the war against poverty championed by Rev. Dr. Martin Luther King, Jr., whom we'll be remembering and honoring in two weeks.

Taya Dixon Mullane of the Lower Highlands Neighborhood Group (LHNG) called everyone into a loose circle and said a few words, offering condolences to the families of Corinna Ouer, the young woman who was killed yesterday on Grand Street, and the other young people who were shot and wounded in an attack at a house party nearby. Captain Kevin Sullivan, commander of the district's police activities, spoke about the senselessness of the shootings and the daily efforts of City police to keep the peace. He praised the neighborhood leaders and encouraged everyone to increase their involvement in neighborhood issues. He commented on the diversity of the group, people from all backgrounds and heritages, a good sign.

Mayor Jim Milinazzo offered his sympathy to the families and friends of the victims on behalf of residents of Lowell and his colleagues on the City Council. Greg Croteau of the United Teen Equality Center spoke briefly about UTEC's effort to prevent violence and engage the youth in the city in positive ways. Walter and Marianne from 119 Gallery at the corner of Chelmsford Street and Grand stood up with their neighbors. I saw other familiar faces in the crowd.

The LHNG distributed strips of long wide purple ribbon for people to tie to utility poles and street posts up and down Grand Street, a symbol of respect and remembrance for the victims. A police car with whirling blue lights crawled ahead of the loose procession and stopped in front of the house where the shots had been fired. Several of the young people who knew the victims walked up the front steps of the white duplex and tied ribbons on the iron railings on both sides of the stairs. A young man wearing a white dust mask covering his nose and mouth kept up his work, carrying plastic bags of something out of the basement of the house. People watched from the porches and windows of houses up and down the street. When we passed the Bethel AME Church everyone heard the live music inside. Somebody was playing drums. A light rain fell on the procession, adding to the grim, gray mood.

The Pawtucketville Bibliophile

By **Steve O'Connor** on January 9, 2011
—

A few years ago, while browsing through the *Lowell Sun*, I read a small announcement in the classified section under Free Offers. "Sherlock Holmes Books Free to Interested Party." I was intrigued by the announcement, which seemed like one of those mysterious events that might begin a Sherlock Holmes story. "Look here Watson! What do you make of that?" asks the great consulting detective, one hand in the pocket of his smoking jacket, the other holding a meerschaum pipe which he waves toward the Lowell Sun, his eyes squinting through a wreath of gray smoke. "Hmmm. What a singular advertisement, Holmes!"

With these suggestive images in mind, I called the number. A young woman answered. She explained that her late grandfather had been a great fan of Sherlock Holmes and had bought several editions of his adventures, as well as commentaries, guidebooks, and other Holmes literary memorabilia. She and her father had decided that they would like to give the books to someone who would appreciate them.

"That's me," I said. She gave me her address, which was in the Pawtucketville neighborhood across the river, and I drove over on a fine summer afternoon. The young woman, baby in arms, greeted me, and introduced me to her father. A stack of books on the back porch caught my attention, principal among which was *The Annotated Sherlock Holmes*—two large volumes containing the four novels and 56 short stories in which Conan Doyle related the adventures of the amazing London sleuth, illustrated with maps, diagrams, photographs, and drawings. If I had had my own Doctor Watson to accompany me on that trip, I'm sure that I would have copious and detailed notes on the case: the exact address, the names of the woman and her father, and, in particular, the name of the deceased, who is really the subject of the case, as you shall see. When the father and daughter saw how delighted I was with the work I've just described, they asked me if I was a lover of books in general, because the old man had left quite a few books behind, which I was free to examine upstairs.

No cat ever leaped with greater alacrity toward a saucer of milk than I flew up those stairs, but I was unprepared for what I found there. It was an apartment full of books. I was like Ali-Baba in the cave of the 40 thieves—a treasure of tomes lining the walls and strewn everywhere. "We've already given a lot away," the man said. I scanned the titles. There were histories and compilations: *English Essayists, The Romantic Poets, The Age of Enlightenment, History of Philosophy, Quarrels That Shaped the Constitution, The Story of Islam,* Toynbee's *Civilization.* Then there was the literature: Dante's *Inferno,* Chekov's stories, Joyce, Proust, Tolstoy, Shakespeare, Milton. Philosophers, orators, poets. In all this world of riches, I happened to pick up a beautiful copy of *The Rubaiyat of Omar Khayyam,* and opened it: "The Moving Finger writes; and, having writ,/ Moves on: Nor all thy Piety nor Wit/Shall lure it back to cancel half a line,/Nor all thy Tears wash out a Word of it."

The room in which I stood contained much of the accumulated wisdom of the world. I turned to the man who stood behind me and asked, "Who was your father? Was he a professor at the university? A historian? A scholar?" The man smiled, a little sadly, I thought, and said, "No, he was a lineman for the telephone company." He explained to me that his father had come to this country as a young man from Holland. When he arrived, with little formal education, he began to study English. He was soon speaking it, but some of the young men he worked with laughed at the mistakes he made when he spoke. They told him he would never learn to speak proper English. He resolved then and there that he would not only master the English language, but also would know it better than those who laughed at him, and be better educated than they. And he began to read. And he read, and read, and read. All his life. He read everything: science, law, literature, history, and, of course, Arthur Conan Doyle, who remained his favorite.

I left with a few boxes of books, and with a profound respect for this man because he was more than a lineman; he was a Renaissance man.

Doctor Watson closed his notebook, and tucked it with his pencil into the pocket of his tweed jacket. "A fascinating case, Holmes. What an extraordinary individual. Exceptionally intelligent and highly motivated."

"Precisely, Watson. It is a fact of human nature that I have often remarked. We assume that the best way to motivate human beings is to encourage them and tell them they can do something. In fact, the opposite is often true. When others told this uneducated man that he could not learn, he resolved with stalwart determination to prove them wrong. And he not only succeeded in outdoing them," said the great detective, "but transformed himself in the process," and he added with a modest smile, "I'm only glad that I was of some small assistance."

Blue Does Not Equal Liberal

By **John Edward** on January 12, 2011
—

The state of Massachusetts bucked the national trend in the 2010 elections. While most states were trending "red," Massachusetts preserved its "blue" identity. The mistake in reading these results is to assume that confirms Massachusetts is a liberal state. Public policy defines liberalism, not political party affiliation. In addition to electing Democrats to all the statewide offices, and electing an entirely Democratic delegation to the U. S. House of Representatives, we still have Democrats in firm control of both branches of the State Legislature. However, in many cases the policies adopted by our blue legislature, and blue Governor, are far from liberal. Tax policy says a lot about how liberal a government is. In *The Conscience of a Conservative*, Senator Barry Goldwater said: "Government has a right to claim an equal percentage of each man's wealth, and no more."

In Massachusetts, we fall far short of this conservative goal. Massachusetts is one of only seven states that have a personal income tax without progressive rates. The state taxes your income at 5.3 percent whether you make $40,000 or $400,000 or $4 million. A progressive income tax is necessary to offset other taxes that are regressive—where low-income earners pay more of their income than the wealthy. In Massachusetts, the personal income tax represents only about one-third of state and local tax revenue. We rely heavily on regressive sales and property taxes. Overall, the tax structure of the Commonwealth of Massachusetts is very regressive. Low-income earners pay taxes at a rate twice as high as the wealthy. Massachusetts may be blue, but a regressive tax structure is not liberal.

If it were not for a dispute over slots at racetracks, things would have been much worse. We rely heavily on lottery income, which, while not officially labeled a tax, is extremely regressive. The Democratic governor and Democratic legislature came very close to expanding state-sponsored gambling by approving casinos. House Speaker DeLeo promised to try again in the new legislative session. Not what you should expect from a so-called liberal state. In addition to going blue in 2010, the voters of Massachusetts approved making Massachusetts the only state to not apply a sales tax to alcoholic beverages. Voters were apparently willing to ignore the social costs incurred by consumption of these products. I could argue that approving the exemption for alcohol was the more liberal position. Most people associate liberalism with government intervention. In this case, voters decided they thought government is smart enough to intervene and give one industry special treatment with respect to what is supposed to be a general sales tax.

Inequality in the United States is more severe than it ever has been. In *The Conscience of a Liberal*, Senator Paul Wellstone observed that there is a very high correlation between wealth status and educational success, and between resources allocated and success. Education is the great equalizer. Improving education, from early childhood through the university system, is essential in promoting both economic growth and making sure more people benefit from the growth. Massachusetts cut higher education funding by an inflation-adjusted 18 percent over the last decade—more than any other state. Massachusetts now ranks 45th in the nation on how much of our state budget is invested in higher education. Tuition and fees in the UMass system have doubled in the last decade. The National Center for Public Policy and Higher Education graded Massachusetts an "F" on affordability. Meanwhile, our blue legislature refuses to extend in-state tuition rates to the children of illegal immigrants even though it would increase revenues for the state and lead to significant increases in earning capacity.

Massachusetts may be Democratic-blue, but we showed our true colors in how state government responded to the recession.

My brother lost his job last year. That might not seem unusual, especially given he worked in the Fall River-New Bedford area where the unemployment rate was over 18 percent. However, his job was helping people find jobs. During a severe recession with very high unemployment, the state cut job placement programs. The next big litmus test will be how the state handles a projected $2 billion budget shortfall. The blue Governor, blue Speaker of the House, and blue Senate President all say they have no plan to raise taxes. Increasing tax rates might not be a good idea right now. However, the state could generate up to $1 billion in new revenue by closing tax loopholes. For example, the film industry tax credit will cost the state an estimated $125 million this year, and return very little. We cut job programs but we make sure Mark Wahlberg gets a nice parting gift after spending a few days here filming. Instead of closing loopholes, the Democrats on Beacon Hill will slash human services budgets—again. They may cut local aid—again. Spending on education will take another hit.

Then-Senator John F. Kennedy said, "if by a 'Liberal' they mean someone who looks ahead and not behind, someone who welcomes new ideas without rigid reactions, someone who cares about the welfare of the people—their health, their housing, their schools, their jobs. . . ," then he was proud to be called a liberal. If you are that kind of liberal, if you care about the common wealth, the policies of our Democratic Party-controlled Commonwealth of Massachusetts should have you seeing red. Last year, Governor Patrick said he would like to see a progressive income tax but that it would take a multiyear campaign. We re-elected him for another four-year term. Now is a good time to remind him that if he cares about the welfare of the people, the Democratic leadership needs to look ahead and welcome "new" and progressive ideas.

Facebook Rookie

By **Paul** on January 16, 2011
—

I joined the 500-million-member club called Facebook after delaying for a long time because it looked to me like another form of media to keep up with. When I was a kid, my family was late getting a color TV, so maybe there's a pattern. However, my first week has been an adventure in learning how to use a new tool, connecting with far-flung people whom I know, and starting to use it for communication. Overall, it feels like I'm at a virtual amusement park with a whirling social merry-go-round in the middle, the News Feed. When to jump off and on? The biggest surprise was finding out that my 80-something uncle from the Centralville neighborhood has a page. He listed me in the family category. I got a vintage Yardbirds music video clip from poet Joe Donahue. Corey Sciuto and I traded messages and did a little business. My son posted a doctored photo on my Wall. I began adding content to my pages. Music was easy. Write the name of the performer, and a picture pops up. I discovered that my college-teaching brother in Virginia has a page—never would have guessed that. I easily reached the number for friends that is about average, according to FB statistics, about 130. I learned from a few people that FB is old enough to have lost some people for various reasons: too time consuming, somewhat susceptible to hacking, and can lull users into letting their guards down regarding mail with infected attachments. So far, it's like traveling to a new place. I'll see how it goes.

Live Tweet of the Bin Laden Attack

By **Tony** on May 3, 2011
—

An IT contractor named Sohaib Athar unknowingly tweeted the American assault on Osama Bin Laden's compound in Pakistan. Below is Athar's tweet thread from the night of the attack. To make the text easier to understand, I reversed the timeline of the posts so they read from earliest to latest, and I skipped some of the lesser related tweets by Sohaib Athar.

@ReallyVirtual
ABBOTTABAD LAHORE PAKISTAN
An IT consultant taking a break from the rat-race by hiding in the mountains with his laptops.

@ReallyVirtual Sohaib Athar: Helicopter hovering above Abbottabad at 1AM (is a rare event).

@ReallyVirtual Sohaib Athar: A huge window shaking bang here in Abbottabad Cantt. I hope its not the start of something nasty :-S

@ReallyVirtual Sohaib Athar: @m0hcin all silent after the blast, but a friend heard it 6 km away too. . .the helicopter is gone too.

@HaniaAhmed by ReallyVirtual: OMG :S Bomb Blasts in Abbottabad.. I hope everyone is fine :(

@ReallyVirtual Sohaib Athar: Since taliban (probably) don't have helicopters, and since they're saying it was not "ours", so must be a complicated situation #abbottabad

@ReallyVirtual Sohaib Athar: The abbottabad helicopter/UFO was shot down near the Bilal Town area, and there's report of a flash. People saying it could be a drone.

@ReallyVirtual Sohaib Athar: @smedica people are saying it was not a technical fault and it was shot down. I heard it CIRCLE 3-4 times above, sounded purposeful.

@ReallyVirtual: A Major of the #Pakistan #Army's 19 FF, Platoon CO says incident at #Abbottabad where #helicopter crashed is accidental and not an "attack"

@terminalxpkTerminalX by ReallyVirtual: The Major also says no "missiles" were fired and all such exaggerated reports are nothing but rumours #Pakistan

@ReallyVirtual Sohaib Athar: And now, a plane flying over Abbottabad. . .

@naqvi MunzirNaqvi by ReallyVirtual: I think the helicopter crash in Abbottabad, Pakistan and the President Obama breaking news address are connected.

@ReallyVirtual Sohaib Athar: Report from a taxi driver: The army has cordoned off the crash area and is conducting door-to-door search in the surrounding

@ReallyVirtual Sohaib Athar: @kursed Well, there were at least two copters last night, I heard one but a friend heard two, for 15-20 minutes.

@ReallyVirtual Sohaib Athar: RT @ISuckBigTime: Osama Bin Laden killed in Abbottabad, Pakistan.: ISI has confirmed it; Uh oh, there goes the neighborhood :-/

@ReallyVirtual Sohaib Athar: Uh oh, now I'm the guy who liveblogged the Osama raid without knowing it.

@ReallyVirtual Sohaib Athar: and here come the mails from the mainstream media. . .*sigh*

Your Old Car Can Go Home Again

By **Ray LaPorte** on May 21, 2011

I left my old hometown for good nearly 25 years ago, after spending a rich early career helping to rebuild its historic structures and fading reputation. And, although I have few opportunities to walk her streets or visit old haunts, friends, or family, I have recently and inexplicably found myself going there in vivid dreams. Last year, out of the blue, my first Lowell dream in memory saw me getting up the courage to finally kiss my 8th grade crush on the corner of Textile and 4th avenues. And this winter I awoke after cruising Pawtucketville in my 1961 MGA, a car that I bought from a Lowell friend 14 years ago, but had never driven in Lowell. I recently and reluctantly decided in February to sell her, as my Martha's Vineyard life is a bounty of playful distractions. The car's diminishing use was inadequate to justify monopolizing precious winter garage space that my wife needs. I was ready to sell the old beauty to a guy in Rhode Island, but decided first to give her prior owner and old Lowell friend a call to see if he would want her back. And after a flurry of enthusiastic phone calls, e-mails, and car pictures that included one with my two-year-old grandson in the driver's seat, it was agreed that she would journey back home to her old Lowell family. "Maggie" left the island on Tuesday atop a flat bed and now is happy back in Lowell with Dave, Mary, and their grown girls, taking up residence next door to my former family home on Andover Street and 50 feet from my old bedroom where I first dreamed. They will be joyfully driving Miss Maggie around Lowell again, and so my recent dream of her there has come true, except I'm not in the driver's seat. However, and happily, I have been promised that she could return home to me when my grandson is ready to drive her. Indeed, going home again isn't just a dream. . . .

Bruins win Stanley Cup

By **Dick** on June 15, 2011
—

Congratulations to the Boston Bruins who defeated the Vancouver Canucks 4-0 in a game seven victory. It's been an incredible decade for professional sports teams in Boston. Consider: New England Patriots won the Super Bowl in 2001, 2003, and 2004. Boston Red Sox won the World Series in 2004 and 2007. Boston Celtics won the NBA championship in 2008. Boston Bruins won the Stanley Cup in 2011.

Lowell Farmers Market Opens Today

By **Marie** on July 8, 2011
—

The Lowell Farmers Market opens for the season today, July 8, from 2:00 to 6:00 p.m. Still in its easily accessible location on the JFK Plaza next to Lowell City Hall, the market has expanded opportunities for locavores, offering a vast array of vegetables; breads; and sustainably farmed pork, chicken, beef, eggs, and dairy products; as well as crafts, prepared foods, coffee, desserts, and other specialties. Look for cooking demonstrations and entertainment as the season rolls out. Since 1979, Community Teamwork, Inc. (CTI) has sponsored the Outdoor Farmers Market in downtown Lowell. Open every Friday from early July through late October, the Market provides residents, workers, and visitors an opportunity to buy fresh fruits, vegetables, flowers, homemade preserves, and even homemade crafts from local farmers and artisans. The market features weekly theme events like Children's Day or Senior Citizens Day, and offers live entertainment, food demonstrations, and discounts on quality products. Women, Infants & Children federal food coupons may be redeemed for fresh produce. For more information, call CTI at (978) 459-0551. Stay tuned for updates.

HISTORY AS IT HAPPENS

Final Shuttle Mission

By **Andrew** on July 8, 2011
—

On Friday July 8, at 11:26 a.m., NASA will launch the space shuttle *Atlantis* on STS-135, the final shuttle mission. It marks the end of an era that began on April 12, 1981, with the first flight of *Columbia*. 135 missions later, the United States' fourth great space program, the successor to Mercury, Gemini, and Apollo, has come to its end.

I was born between STS-31 and STS-41, the 35th and 36th shuttle missions, both flights of the shuttle *Discovery*. STS-31 was the mission to deploy the Hubble Telescope. I have never known anything but the shuttle program. Quite frankly, I have taken it for granted; I cannot imagine it being over. But after tomorrow the United States will no longer have the ability to put astronauts into orbit; we will be reliant on Russian Soyuz rockets for the foreseeable future. Not only is there no plan to replace the shuttle, but now Congress is preparing to cancel the Webb Telescope, which was to be the successor to the Hubble, taking us back even closer to the Big Bang than Hubble is capable of.

The shuttle is the most complicated machine ever built, consisting of more than a million moving parts. The time and work involved in preparing a shuttle for launch is unimaginable. The shuttles have given us the Hubble and the International Space Station. And they have given us more technological and scientific breakthroughs than most of us will ever know.

In the early 1990s, Congress halted plans to build a supercollider in Texas, opening the door for Europe's CERN to build the largest supercollider in the world. Cutting-edge particle physics is now done in Europe; European labs will be the ones to unlock the next great secrets of the fundamental building blocks of nature. Now the future of both American astronomy and cosmology, in the form of the Webb telescope, and spaceflight are in question. At a time when more and more countries are developing the means to reach space, we have focused our attention elsewhere. It could be said that we have greater priorities to focus on; a space program is simply too expensive for our time. But we know that the Apollo program gave back far more to the economy than the government spent. We also know that many of the greatest discoveries in science were mere accidents, the results of exploration for exploration's sake.

However, for my generation at least, I think there is a more important argument to be made. The shuttles represented one of America's greatest achievements in its history. They were a symbol of national pride and an inspiration to us all. Now where will that inspiration come from? How inspired will we feel when it is Chinese astronauts, not American, who become the first humans to land on Mars? Will we stand idly by while the other nations of the world surpass us in technical capability?

NASA's future remains uncertain, as does the future of the American scientific community as a whole. Our schools are failing to teach students basic science. Half of our graduate students in science and engineering are foreigners. And we have no vision for the future. When President Kennedy gave his famous speech in 1961 declaring that, by the end of the decade, the United States would put a man on the Moon, we did not have the rockets to get there. We did not have a design for a lunar lander, never mind had we built one. We had not even yet put a man into space. My hope is that another President Kennedy will step forward and call on us to surpass what we think is possible. But, in the meantime, you can watch Friday's launch on NASA's website and, if you wish, NASA has released an amazing documentary about the shuttle program, which can be watched on YouTube. I urge you to watch both; they mark the end of one of the finest periods in American history. They also mark the end of one of the greatest scientific achievements in human history.

HISTORY AS IT HAPPENS

Leymah Gbowee, Nobel Peace Prize

By **Paul** on October 7, 2011
—

Winning the Nobel Peace Prize is a big deal. When I learned this morning that Leymah Gbowee of Liberia, now living in Ghana, had been awarded the Prize in a three-way share with President Ellen Johnson Sirleaf of Liberia and democracy activist Tawakkul Karmen of Yemen, I felt good for her—and excited because I know this person. I met her when she was in Lowell for three weeks last April, serving as UMass Lowell's Greeley Scholar for Peace Studies.

Each year the University invites an outstanding individual who has advanced peace and social justice for a multi-week residence on campus. Leymah organized women to use nonviolent tactics to oppose the tyrant Charles Taylor during a long civil war in Liberia. They forced fighters on both sides to resolve the conflict. We reached Leymah through Kathy Reticker of our Greeley program advisory committee, whose sister, Gini, directed a film about Leymah's peace-building work in Liberia, *Pray the Devil Back to Hell*. Kathy is the executive director of Acre Family Day Care.

The lesson I took from Leymah is that there are times in your life when you should put yourself on the line. You should risk what's important to you when the cause is more important than your own comfort, your reputation, and even possibly your safety. She was determined to do what she could to stop the killing. She had the vision to imagine bringing together women of Christian and Muslim faiths in a mutual effort to stop the violence that was destroying the lives of their children. She was confident that the women had more common sense and decency than the angry, hostile, power-hungry men who were fighting.

She was with us for about three weeks, living at the UMass

Lowell Inn & Conference Center with her young daughter. Her husband joined her for the final week. She spoke in a dozen settings on campus and in the area. Her daughter stayed during the day with one of the women who works for Acre Family Day Care. Kathy had arranged this. One day the woman who took care of the little girl told Leymah about a women's shelter in the city where she volunteered. Leymah told her she would like to go there. It was the end of a busy day of meeting people and talking, but she insisted on going over to the shelter and meeting the women.

A group of us from the university had lunch with her the day she arrived. We were captivated by her accounts of the struggle in Liberia and the work she was doing at that moment in the nearby country of Côte d'Ivoire (Ivory Coast). She was trying to organize the women there the way it had worked in Liberia, but she was having trouble getting people to cooperate. Sitting at the long table in the gallery at the Allen House on campus, I remember thinking that this person has come to us from a war zone where people are jailed or murdered for challenging the authorities. Her calmness and self-assurance was inspiring. She is articulate and knowledgeable, but down-to-earth at the same time. Another day at a lunch downtown she talked enthusiastically about NBA players. She knows the basketball team rosters better than I do, following the games on satellite broadcasts in Africa.

Everyone who met her in Lowell was deeply impressed by her determination to help people resolve conflicts. She spoke about reaching young people while their minds are still open to finding a better way to behave than resorting to violence to solve problems or gain advantages. We knew that we were in the presence of someone special. The Nobel Peace Prize announcement today confirmed it.

Electricity Restored! 106 Hours Out!

By **Dick** on November 4, 2011
—

Somehow I thought the moment of power restoration would be more dramatic. Instead, I received a hurried phone call at work. "National Grid trucks are on our street now." I hopped in my car with its "collision wrapped" rear window (see below) and zipped home, happy that all the traffic lights en route were functioning. Flipping the switch in the front hall, the ceiling light came on, a signal that our 106 hours of primitive living had come to an end.

The observations and lessons-learned from this episode are many and will be the subject of a later post. Power outages are nothing new around here. What I found is new is the unreasonably long time it takes to restore power. My sense is that in years past, electricity was usually restored well within 24 hours. If it went 48, it was very unusual. But then came the ice storm of December 2008. People in the Highlands neighborhood who lost power during that event went without for several days. Earlier this year, neighbors who had power knocked out during Hurricane Irene waited four days to have it restored. This time, we lost power at 1:12 a.m. on Sunday, October 30, and had it restored five days later on November 3.

Why does it take so long to restore power to so many people? I suspect National Grid has pared back its workforce to such an extent that it has insufficient resources to effectively respond to predictable regional outages. The company seems to have made a cost/benefit calculation that it is more profitable to incur the fleeting wrath of those who lost power than to maintain a workforce adequate to handle the task in a timely manner. In this the company is engaging in a type of bureaucratic rope-a-dope. Rope-a-dope is a boxing tactic made famous by Muhammad Ali in his 1974 fight against George Foreman. Early in the fight, Ali simply covered up and leaned back against the ropes, letting Foreman pound away without mounting an active defense. Protected from the damaging blows by the flexibility of the ropes and his own forearms, Ali endured the early rounds unharmed. Not so Foreman. His early flurry of punches left him exhausted and, when Ali finally shifted to the attack, Foreman lacked the energy to defend himself, and Ali won the fight.

"Bureaucratic rope-a-dope" is a tactic in which the bureaucracy, either governmental or corporate, figuratively leans back against the ropes and covers up, allowing its critics to pound away until they grow tired and go away, leaving the bureaucracy and its infuriating practices completely intact. With power outages, we have bursts of outrage from the public, echoed by the media, and picked up by the legislature. But the outrage, both real and feigned, soon dissipates in the face of other concerns or interests. Months pass until the next outage occurs and, odds are, a different group of citizens will feel the impact of the next one, and the process starts anew with nothing meaningful ever getting done.

It's ironic that as we become more dependent on electricity for things that are critical to safe, not to mention comfortable, living, our electrical service has become less reliable. We're at the point where having generator back-up for your home is the new norm of life in the twenty-first century.

HISTORY AS IT HAPPENS

Lowell High Distinguished Alums

By **Marie** on November 4, 2011
—

It was time again to honor that special group of people who have been declared "Distinguished Alums" of Lowell High School (LHS). The group that gathered last night is the eighth class of alums so honored. The first class was in 2005—this illustrious group who set the tone to follow—included Jack Kerouac, Class of 1939; George Behrakis, Class of 1951; Paul E. Tsongas, Class of 1958; and Donna Lavigne McCallum and her husband and classmate Elkin McCallum, Class of 1961—grads in a close cluster of years, grads who made their mark, grads who excelled in the arts, business, politics, public service, and philanthropy. Others who carry the mantle of Distinguished Alumni include surgeon Dr. Brendan Leahey, Metropolitan Opera mezzo-soprano Rosalind Elias, UMass Lowell Chancellor and former Congressman Marty Meehan, General and Governor Benjamin F. Butler of the first LHS graduating class of 1831, entrepreneur Ted Leonsis, and author Elinor Lipman.

The Class of 2011 is another special group covering a broad time frame in the history of Lowell High School: William Henry O'Connell, Class of 1876—prelate of the Roman Catholic Church serving as Cardinal/Archbishop of Boston from 1907 to his death in 1944—O'Connell was described by his great nephew former U. S. Senator Paul Kirk (D-MA) as presiding during the "Golden Age of Catholicism" in America. Kirk talked of "Will O'Connell" and his triumph in overcoming and learning from the hard lessons of ethnic and religious discrimination. It emboldened him later to help transform the American Catholic Church into more "public Catholicism." He built more churches, schools, and hospitals, and ordained more priests than at any other time in Massachusetts history. More interesting for this particular event though—was Kirk's assertion that Will O' Connell's time at Lowell High School was a time of great happiness where, unlike in his early school experience, his faculty mentors helped grow his love of books and learning—where his desire for a college life grew, and where his vocation grew. This November 27, 2011, will be the 100th anniversary of O'Connell's elevation to the College of Cardinals.

John Stack, Class of 1924, was an eminent Fulbright Scholar, aeronautical engineer, and a chief researcher at Langley Field, working to pave the way for transonic aircraft. He designed the Bell-X, the first plane to break the sound barrier. So outstanding was Stack in his field of supersonic flight that he—along with pilot Chuck Yeager—was awarded the Collier Trophy—the highest award given in aviation. His daughter—Martha Stack Sim—was charming in her recollecting of her father who loved Lowell and loved his large extended local family—especially his cousins—both Stacks and O'Connors. She told the audience that her words for the students earlier in the day were to be like her father who would say: "Make that thing work right!"

George N. Tsapatsaris, Class of 1949—had a remarkable 41-year career in public education and stands one of the longest-serving Superintendents of the Lowell schools. His legacy of new school buildings and renovated spaces is unparalleled. His goal to bring equal quality instructional service to all students is a mark of his legacy. George told us that the first time he stood on that stage in the Cyrus Irish Auditorium was as president of his ninth grade class—he hoped that 65 years later he was wiser and smarter—he did know that his passion for making a difference was still as strong! He praised the influence of his Lowell High School history teacher and mentor Frank McHugh; he credited LHS for reinforcing the strong values of discipline, honesty, and perseverance; he acknowledged the "can do" attitude he learned from an officer in the 4th Army; and noting that it really does "take a village" to shape a child in a school system, he lauded in particular the team of Mayor Dick Howe, City Solicitor Tom

Sweeney, City Manager Jim Campbell, and state Representative Steve Panagiotakos, along with the UMass Lowell College of Education, for what they did for the schools in important times in the late 1980s when a refugee and immigrant influx brought great challenges. It was truly George's audience (it was full of family, friends, and School Department colleagues) as he stood to the loudest and warmest applause and even some hoots, hollers, and cheers!

Robert J. Goldberg, Class of 1968—teacher, professor, UMass Medical School department director and world-renowned epidemiologist whose study and research greatly affected the understanding and treatment of coronary artery disease, venous thromboembolism, and chronic heart failure. He directed the landmark Worcester Heart Attack Study. Dr. Goldberg spoke with wit and nostalgia of his Lowell High days—remembering his escapades in Fred Gallagher's science lab, teachers Helen Shea (English), Arthur Pard (Math), Wyman Trull (who took him and others up to his alma mater Bowdoin College for a look-see), and Coach Ray Riddick. He remembered large classes, lots of student energy, and solid structure at Lowell High. His wife, Ellie Heifetz, was a classmate—LBJ was President—his dad owned Allen Cosmetics on Merrimack Street—and he once as a young kid got a hit off a Brian Martin pitch!

Patti Fleming Quigley, Class of 1982, honored as a humanitarian for her work and commitment to empowering widows affected by war, terrorism, and oppression—a cause that inspired her. She found herself a widow with a young child and eight months pregnant when her beloved husband, Patrick, perished on September 11, 2001, a passenger on United Flight 175. She was perhaps the most emotional as she declared herself "honored and humbled" to be with her group. Comparing herself to winning football's Heisman Trophy—an individual person with a great team behind her—raised by her parents and mentors, the late Bernice and Brendan, the former Mayor of Lowell. He was in the audience sitting beside me along with her brother Tom, director of the Lowell Police Academy, her super siblings, her friends from Wellesley, Massachusetts, her two daughters, Rachel and Leah, all allowing her to be the best that she could be! She spoke of moving forward in the face of adversity and using her voice for positive change.

All honorees spent the day in Lowell, touring the high school, speaking to students, and enjoying a special lunch. Thanks to class of 1960 alum Nick Sarris, the names of the Class of 2011 Distinguished Alumni are already on the wall of honor in the lobby of the Cyrus W. Irish Auditorium. It was a wonderful evening of tribute and memory!

Occupy Policy

By **John Edward** on November 7, 2011
—

So far, the Occupy Wall Street movement is just that, a social movement. The protestors have much to protest. Our socioeconomic system suffers from acute illnesses. At some point, the protests need to evolve into policy prescriptions.

The slogan "We are the 99 percent" seems to be catching on. The just released report on inequality from the Congressional Budget Office helps explain why. The top one percent of wealth holders now includes incomes of $350,000 or more per year. In the last thirty years, after-tax income for the top one percent increased by 275 percent, or about seven times as much as the rest of us. At the beginning of the period, the top one percent made as much as the entire bottom 20 percent. Now they make as much as the bottom 40 percent.

The problem has been 30 years in the making. It was too easy to ignore increasing inequality when the overall economy appeared to be doing well. Now the Census Bureau reports that over 20 million in the United States are not just living in poverty, but in deep poverty. These are people making less than half the poverty level. These are, for example, families of four making less than $11,157.

The national unemployment rate has been in the 9 to 10 percent range for two-and-a-half years. The unofficial underemployment rate is over 17 percent. More than six million people, almost half of the unemployed, have been out of work for six months or more.

Meanwhile, the financial firms that caused the Great Recession and took government help are not helping us. The New York State Comptroller reported that Wall Street firms last year paid bonuses that averaged $128,000. Yet, financial firms cannot find a way to allow homeowners who have never missed a payment to refinance. Eleven million homeowners are trapped "underwater" because the market value of their home is less than the outstanding debt.

Meanwhile, the government continues to offer preferential treatment to the one percent. One of the most egregious examples is "carried interest." Hedge fund managers take this cut out of shareholder gains. It can add up to billions of dollars a year of income for a fund manager while shareholders take the investment risk. The federal government taxes carried interest as capital gains. Instead of paying the top rate of 35 percent, or even a typical 25 percent paid by working families, these millionaires and billionaires pay only 15 percent on their unearned income.

The top one percent also gets preferential treatment from financial firms. Just two years ago, one out of three checking accounts had fees. Now more than half do. Not only do the wealthy not pay these fees, they get better rates and preferred service.

Last year, the Supreme Court overturned bipartisan legislation and court precedent to make it much easier for the top one percent to influence elections. Candidates for public office need big money for the media to take them seriously. Elizabeth

Warren may end up being a fine choice as the Democratic nominee for Senator. Marisa DeFranco may be a good choice as well, but we will probably never know because she cannot raise money from the top one percent.

When anyone has the temerity to suggest even modest attempts at fairness, defenders of the top one percent accuse reformers of starting "class warfare." See, for example, President Obama's proposal to return the top tax rates to the slightly higher rates of the Clinton years, a time when economic growth was quite strong and budgets were balanced.

I offer the following response, free of charge, to candidates who want to embrace Occupy Wall Street and their cause:

You are correct, it is class warfare, it has been going on for 30 years, and now we are finally fighting back!

Further, I offer the following suggestions to candidates who want to occupy policy.

Everyone is talking about jobs. The latest jobs report shows progress is still insufficient. We need a two-pronged approach.

One, in the short run the federal government needs to continue stimulating the economy and creating jobs. They should focus on investing in our crumbling transportation infrastructure and our underfunded education infrastructure.

Two, the government needs to give private businesses the confidence to invest. In the long run, the private sector will be the engine of job creation. Corporations do not need lower taxes as an incentive. The evidence makes is clear that approach is ineffective. Companies need less uncertainty. They need to see a serious long-range plan to balance the budget. It worked for President Clinton. As for taxes, what is required is a simpler and more equitable tax code (more on that in my next column).

Creating more jobs is a good thing. Jobs that pay more equitably are better. Education and taxes are the keys.

A well-educated work force is a well-paid workforce. When I graduated from a Massachusetts state university a little over 30 years ago, tuition increased by over 13 percent in my senior year.

It went from $300 per academic year to $340. Even adjusting for inflation, that is only about $1,300 per year in today's dollars. In-state tuition and fees (but not room and board, and textbooks) at UMass Lowell is now $11,300. In the last year alone, public universities nationwide increased tuition by 8.5 percent.

Not everyone needs to go to a four-year college. Community colleges, technical training programs, computer and financial literacy, and job placement services are all part of the equation.

Early childhood education is essential. Investing in small children has the best payoff of any long-term investment we can make.

People in top one percent claim we need lower taxes to encourage investment. Does that mean we need higher taxes that may discourage work? If legislators insist on using taxes to encourage investment, they must base the incentives on the number of decent paying jobs created. Federal and state governments should expand very successful earned income tax credit programs that encourage work.

Lack of proper financial regulation led to the Great Recession. In 2010, Congress passed financial reform legislation that offered modest steps toward addressing the worst of Wall Street abuses. There is much more work to do.

President Obama gave up on Elizabeth Warren heading the Bureau of Consumer Financial Protection she helped form. He must not give up on this agency having the power to enforce his vision where "there are clear rules and basic safeguards that prevent abuse, that check excess, that ensure that it is more profitable to play by the rules than to game the system."

Finally, campaign finance reform must be part of the agenda. Running for public office should not require being in the one percent, being financially obligated to the one percent, or even giving the appearance of being obligated.

Our forefathers warned us about tyranny of the majority. Now we need public policy that protects the 99 percent from the tyranny of a vastly wealthy and inordinately powerful minority.

Thanksgiving on the South Common

By **Paul** on November 24, 2011
—

It was quiet on the Common at 7:00 a.m. when I made the circuit with our Boston Terrier, Ringo. How cold was it? Not very. Enough for a seasonal edge. The leaf-trees are empty. Color has drained from fallen leaves, which from a distance resemble light brown scatter rugs under the grayish trees. The firs and pines are darker green for being the remaining filled-out tree tops. The grass is still green but not as lush as in high summer. In the shade, frost whitened the paper leaves. Across on the north rim, under the classic Eliot Church spire, volunteers had gathered to prepare the vast community meal that is a tradition on Summer Street, at the spot where a seventeenth-century Christian preacher from Boston approached the local peoples who had been coming to the fishing grounds between the two rivers for hundreds of years.

There's a big brass sign from 1930 that was installed in front of the church on the 300th anniversary of the Massachusetts Bay Colony. Rev. John Eliot translated the Bible into the local language of pre-Lowell, Wamesit, being the Algonquian language, and later wrote a book calling for an elected theocracy to be the ideal form of government. Considered a religious extremist in England, he had shipped out to Massachusetts in 1631, which means he was a peer of the pilgrims who got involved with the natives down Plymouth way and cooked up the first Thanksgiving feed, which some contrary historians locate in 1565 St. Augustine, Fla., or 1619 at the Virginia Colony, both of which celebrated good harvests with feasts according to the sources at Wikipedia. So, there's a little bit of Puritan dust in the dirt along the edge of the South Common. The spirit of charity prevails in the good deeds at today's church that gathers its congregation from contemporary pilgrims of a different kind, people from far lands who found their way to America to start over, people who sit in the wooden benches alongside parishioners with long roots in this place. They're all there today making a meal for their neighbors who will be thankful to have one this mid-day.

Joel-Lowell Rhymes

By **Paul** on December 15, 2011
—

Just back from an inspiring "performance" by Billy Joel in Durgin Concert Hall on UMass Lowell's South Campus. For two hours the music mega-star engaged in a lively conversation with the audience, using a green laser pointer to call on this or that eager person in a sea of hands. The stage talk format is Joel's preferred situation for college visits these days. He says he found his route into the music business by trial and error, with a lot of mistakes, so this is his way of giving back to those who are thinking of music as a way to make a living or to make a life. There was no "book" to follow back in 1964 when he joined his first band in the days of Beatlemania. He says he "fell hard" for the music life and didn't look back, playing obsessively during his teenage years, so much so that he didn't finish high school. He doesn't point to himself as a model of anything, he says, but he has plenty to offer from the school of learning-by-doing.

Joel was at ease, joking with the audience and making himself the butt of most of the fooling, including the unlikely pairing of an "incredibly not good-looking guy" who used to be five-foot-seven, and supermodels like Elle Macpherson (six-foot-two inches) and the Brinkley woman who agreed to marry him, the "Innocent Man." He goofed on some of his classic songs like

"Piano Man" and "We Didn't Start the Fire." But in between the banter and storytelling, Billy Joel gave trade secrets of his business and told the truth about what it took to become a rock star. He said luck and timing were key ingredients, on top of the dogged performing night after night that sharpened his art and allowed him to master the craft.

Responding to questions, he hopped from the standing mic to one of the two pianos, illustrating at times the point he was making. When a guy in the balcony asked if he started with music or words, Joel said, "Ninety-nine percent of the time it was music, which was and is what I like best." But he had an example of starting with words, the lyrics to "We Didn't Start the Fire," a recitation of key names and phrases that summarize his life and times up to 1989. He played all or part of a dozen songs, including "Piano Man" and Elton John's "Candle in the Wind."

For me, the highlight of the night occurred near the end when a young guy hollered out "Leningrad," hoping that Joel would play the song. Joel had earlier replied to a woman who asked about his greatest achievement, saying he was proud of his visit to the USSR in 1987 when Mikhail Gorbachev was the nation's leader. He said the Russians went crazy when they heard his songs on the supersonic sound system Joel had brought from the USA. When Joel heard "Leningrad," he paused and, I think, said, "I haven't played that live." Maybe he said he hadn't played it live for a while. Anyway, the student yelled out, "Let me play it." Joel, who had been a good sport all night with all kinds of requests, said OK and invited the student on stage to take the smaller piano while he sat at the grand piano. Joel asked the student if he knew the intro. "Of course," came the answer, and they were off. The audience hung on every note and word of the song about an American who grew up during the Cold War with the Soviets finally meeting face-to-face a Russian of about the same age. It was exhilarating to watch the two piano players, note perfect as far as I could tell. When the song ended, the audience erupted, some standing and cheering. Joel said, "He played it better than I did," and called him over to the microphone and announced the student's name—I missed it in the uproar. Not about to miss his opportunity, the tall, thin young guy handed Joel a CD in a case, no doubt his own recordings.

Joel closed out the evening with a few Christmas songs, starting with a rich version of "Have Yourself a Merry Little Christmas," and then inviting the music student-loaded audience to harmonize on a sing-along as he played and sang "Angels We Have Heard on High." It was a major coup to have earned the rare visit by Billy Joel. The power of what he has created was reflected back to him in the sincere applause and warm statements made by many of those he called on tonight.

Top Ten of 2011

By **Dick** on January 1, 2012
—

Here is my own eclectic list of important things that happened in 2011.

1. The local political lineup changed considerably in 2011. Steve Panagiotakos, who was elected to the Lowell School Committee in 1989, the Massachusetts House of Representatives in 1992, the state Senate in 1996, most recently serving as chair of the Ways and Means Committee, chose not to run again in 2010, and so spent his final days in the state Senate in January 2011. He was replaced by Eileen Donoghue, a former six-term Lowell city councilor (1996-2008) and two-term mayor (1998 and 2000), who won the 2010 state Senate race after running unsuccessfully for Congress in 2007. The Lowell City Council lost its

longest serving member when Bud Caulfield, who had been elected to twelve consecutive terms beginning in 1987 (with two, 1995 & 2007, as mayor), chose not to seek re-election. Jim Milinazzo, who had served four council terms beginning in 2003 (mayor in 2009), was defeated, and first-term Councilor Franky Descoteaux, stepped off the council. John Leahy, who was elected to five terms on the Lowell School Committee beginning in 2001, lost his bid to join the council. Jackie Doherty, who was elected to four terms on the school committee beginning in 2003, lost as did first-term committee member Alison Laraba.

2. Weather was a top story throughout 2011. Major snowstorms hit Lowell on January 12, January 18, January 21, January 27, and February 1. A fall snowstorm at Halloween knocked down countless trees and electrical wires, leaving many residents without power for five or more days. Many others experienced similar power outages at the end of August due to high winds from Hurricane Irene.

3. The once-per-decade Congressional redistricting substantially altered the map and the lineup in Massachusetts. The historic, Lowell-centric Fifth Congressional District is now the Third, gaining Fitchburg and other communities in northern Worcester County while keeping the core Merrimack Valley portion of the district largely intact, aside from Billerica and Tewksbury, which are now part of the Sixth District. Outside of our area, redistricting caused two long-time incumbents, John Olver and Barney Frank, to not seek reelection.

4. The UMass Lowell physical renaissance continued with the construction of the Health and Social Sciences Building on South Campus and the Saab Emerging Technologies and Innovation Center on North Campus. In January,

UML purchased the former St Joseph's Hospital, while the revitalized Tsongas Center and UML Inn & Conference are drawing more and more folks to downtown Lowell.

5. After a contentious and controversial period of negotiations with the school committee, Lowell Public Schools Superintendent Chris Scott decided not to seek a renewal of her contract. She was succeeded by Jean Franco, who was an administrator in the system.

6. Former City Councilor Mike Geary was elected City Clerk after Rick Johnson resigned.

7. Mike McLaughlin, whose strong ties with Greater Lowell include past employment with the Lowell Housing Authority and Dracut Public Schools, and who was formerly a candidate for Lowell City Council and Lowell City Manager, was the subject of a *Boston Globe* expose on the astounding salary and benefits he received as director of the Chelsea Housing Authority. The negative publicity surrounding McLaughlin may have tainted the future political prospects of Lt. Governor Tim Murray, who had close contacts with McLaughlin and perhaps even Scott Harshbarger, who allegedly sought to intervene with Governor Patrick on McLaughlin's behalf.

8. Lowell City Manager Bernie Lynch and 19 city unions reached an agreement on the future of health insurance coverage for city employees. This is a huge, long-term accomplishment that has yet to receive the positive attention it deserves.

9. UMass Lowell became a player in national politics with the creation of its Center for Public Opinion, the polls of which are frequently quoted by media outlets around the country.

And UML's Massachusetts Democratic Senate debate gained national acclaim. The initial debate appearance of Elizabeth Warren, whose strong performance at Durgin Hall cemented her standing as the front-runner in the Democratic race, caused the strongest of her Democratic opponents to drop out, and allowed the focus to shift to a Warren v. Scott Brown race next November.

10. It was a great year for what I might clump together as local and regional celebrity news and entertainment. Leymah Gbowee, who resided at UMass Lowell as a Greeley Scholar for Peace Studies, was awarded the Nobel Peace Prize. In Hollywood, performers in *The Fighter* won Academy Awards for Best Supporting Actor and Actress. The Bruins won the Stanley Cup, and the Red Sox collapsed, losing Theo Epstein and Terry Francona in the process. Billy Joel and the Dropkick Murphys played at UML venues. The legislature authorized casinos. Lowell celebrated the 175th anniversary of its incorporation as a city and the 150th anniversary of the start of the Civil War.

Poems

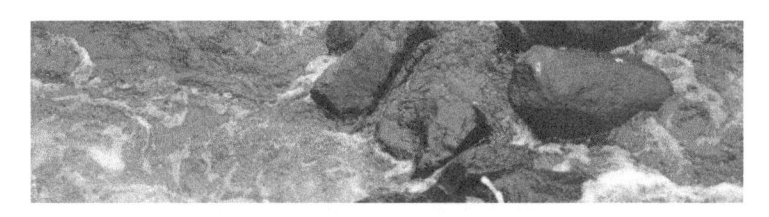

Rainbow Poem

by **Thomas Fitzsimmons**
Sept. 14, 2008

When I was a kid
Playing hooky
Spending my dime on a loaf of Greek bread
To eat dry
High on a hillside above the Merrimack River
Outside Lowell, Massachusetts,
I did not think I
Would be sitting on Parnassus slope
Above Delphi
Eating my loaf of Greek bread
With feta, black olives,
& retsina
Looking down thru temple valley and time
To when I was a kid
Playing hooky eating my bread
Dry on the hills above the Merrimack River
Outside Lowell, Massachusetts

Delphi, 1976

This poem appeared as a Loom Press broadside in 1982.

Coffee Truck

By **Michael Casey**
August 18, 2010

the coffee truck once ran out
of Tahitian Treat at the mill
so for a long time I used to get Wink
and the coffee truck guy told me a story
he said the mending room girls
always used to get
Halfnhalf with their lunch
then for a long time
he couldn't get Halfnhalf
only Polynesian Punch
and when the guy got Halfnhalf back
they wouldn't touch it
they was so used
to getting Polynesian Punch
so when the guy got back Tahitian Treat
he thought I wasn't gonna touch it either
but I went right back
to getting Tahitian Treat
no more Wink for me after that
I fooled the guy
and he was surprised too

Body Heat

By **Jacquelyn Malone**
August 26, 2010

The Farm Beneath the Sand is called the Viking Pompeii.
—New York Times *article*

The climate hardened, and the Norse left
the forty rooms where, under one roof, the last
residue huddled—to conserve body heat. Then
for centuries the Farm Beneath the Sand lay buried
in a river of glacial grit.
All waters run to Lethe,
the great stream that takes in farms, hopes, genes
in the same bed. Civilizations swirl in its eddies,
going—in the water's turns—from conqueror to conquered
before they sink amid clay pots, a shred of cloth, the stone
marker no one left can read, animal bones, body lice—all
going down like the rumored feats of dragon prows
that cut the Arctic seas, like Atlantis, the Easter gods,
or the Library of Alexandria—memory of mankind—going
under, washed as clean of human dreams as time, as sand.

Lowell's Irish Micky Ward

By **Tom Sexton**
January 6, 2011

Round 2. Ward's left eye is already cut,
but he keeps moving toward Arturo Gatti.
My wife's gone to bed and turned out the light.
Gatti's left hook sounds like a thunderclap.
I haven't watched a fight in many years,
not since I moved away from Lowell.
A Celtic Cross glistens on Ward's shoulder.
I wince as he shakes off blow after blow.
He has my uncle Leo's fighter's face,
with features almost as flat as a stone.
Staggered by a right, he picks up the pace.
I want to see a hurt Gatti go down.
They fight to a draw. Closed eye for closed eye.
I go to bed shamefaced and stubbornly tribal.

23 October

By **Paul Hudon**
January 4, 2013

the one was courting my sister back when
we lived on Melvin the far end of Little Canada
nice kid and not a mean bone in his body which
let me tell you was an attractive little arrangement
of muscle and need propelled around our kitchen
limbic byways gone juicy with hormonal download
not that we could see that of course when it was
him in our face all the time jokey always on his toes
dancing around Alice like Alice was the only thing
on the planet going his direction leaving him no piece
of mind Alice devoid and irrevocably ignorant
of the wall the bounce and the other side where
unconscionable as gravity the Merrimack takes aim at
the Atlantic like the meaning of life is counting on it

Memory of an Afternoon

By **Mary Sampas**
January 11, 2011

Hot humid Manhattan afternoon.
Broadway's din is ear splittingly loud.
Suddenly, from somewhere on high,
as though from heaven,
a hugely amplified voice booms
that all traffic must now stop.
The first hospital ship is in, the voice says,
and it's carrying the first wounded
from D-Day.
Ambulances are to cross Broadway
en route to a hospital in Brooklyn.
The silence is complete, and eerie.
Cars stop.
People stop.
Some whisper prayerfully.
Some bless themselves.
Some weep. The long convoy begins.
The ambulances are olive drab trucks,
covered, but with open backs.
A chill strikes from within,
banishing the heat and humidity,
and we shiver.
The tension is intense as broken bodies
pass by us in those trucks,
but we can't see them.
We can only imagine.
And now we feel wild waves on a black beach
and hear shells bursting and see bombs dropping.
We hear the screaming
and taste the blood

and feel the awful pain.
After the 20th truck passes us,
the total silence is pierced
by a hoarse but joyful cry:
"Hello, hello, Sampascoopies!"
We are stunned, but it is already too late.
That ambulance is quickly succeeded
by another, and another.
We gasp that some wounded lad,
back in his country,
sees a familiar face as he is borne to the hospital.
My husband described
this incredibly moving moment
in his column,
hoping to hear news of the wounded man
from his family
or anyone who knew him.
He sounded so happy
that one fleeting moment,
to see someone from home,
but we never found out
who he was, and if he lived
or if he died.

Blue Dot Sign

By **Michael Casey**
April 6, 2011

she was walking down Bridge Street
to the Blue Dot
buy a half pound
for Sister Vincent Ferrer's
Saint Patrick's Day gift
box of candy
she was already in the car
when she told me that
or I wouldn't have offered her
a ride in my pink cadillac
for Sister Vincent Ferrer?
Sister Vincent not my favorite person
Sister Vincent an Irishman?
you must have to be kidding me
but my passenger, Sister James, asks me
Albert, how'd you get
the money for such a nice car
like I stole it
well I stall
it is something like a secret, Sister
you have to be discreet
wouldn't spread this around
promise you won't tell anyone, Sister?
y'af to keep this quiet
I mean this is like confessional, you know
you won't tell anybody? promise, right?
so she promises silence
as she gets out of the car
and I says
Sister

I rob banks
and she starts crossing herself
really really fast
looking up to heaven
after every sign

The Beauty of a Nail

By **Matt Miller**
January 28, 2013

hangs on it being
unseen as when
it suspends a
painting or some
caught on camera
moment on a plain wall
or the way within
the wall it holds up
the house, the pipes,
the unrolled
insulation or even
when somewhat seen
as when it holds a man
up to martyrdom—
always it is the tool,
not the meaning.

The Way I Want to Remember My Cambodia

By **Chath PierSath**
January 12, 2013

I want to remember how I was free to run in the field
eyeing the sky—my handmade kite flying high,
loving the wind, loving the clear white cloud.

I want to remember how I was free to run in the sun,
free to own and roam the fields, free to walk and sing
to myself or to God of the hills full of trees, to the green
rice paddies, to the pink lotus in my pond, and to the black
muddy swamp, to the white crystal tune of an overflowing
river, to the rainbow of my felicity and the wild dogs' red
mating call.

I want to feel the flirtatious air caressing my naked body
in childhood innocence wrapped in the arms of my brothers,
free of hate, free of war.

I want to remember the shrilling cry of crickets hidden
under broken planks, the way I went earring for them
in the mist of dawn to capture them in my jar. My chase
after dragonflies, my sling pebbles passing birds, how I
spent day after day fishing, netting grasshoppers in the sun,
and in its burning heat, how I went searching for beetles in
cow manure while herding cattle and water buffalo
away from home.

I recall my mother's cooking fire, her salted fish grilled
on burning charcoal, the smell of her boiling stew, her
sharp knife drumming the cutting board. In her outdoor
kitchen, the smoke of her art hissed out of her wok, moving
into the air like a cobra shedding its skin on our fence.

I want to feel my dark Cambodian skin crack from playing
with earth, my boyish brown eyes to stare again at the green
bamboo, leaning to soak in the fragrance
of the yellow, flowered hills.

I want the serenity of the blue ponds and the white river of
childhood and to feel the winds wiping away the dewdrops,
still clinging to my naked body.

I want my peasant home, to still be in that village among
the surviving people on that laboring earth where I was born
into my Cambodia. My Cambodia, tell me
again the stories of how the old
ghosts take possession of human souls, how monsters
shape the art of death.

I want to hear how the Goddesses
turn what is ugly into what is beautiful.

Make me part of that secret. Let me dance in your sun.

Fog Lights

By **Joe Meehan**
November 12, 2013

Midnight fog comes unannounced
Spreading stillness
Over the dark landscape.
It rolls through deserted streets
Like gray tumbleweeds.
The fog is a rising tide
Settling a blanket of mist in its path.
Streetlights are halo'd
In tarnished pewter,
No more beacons on the way.
Dense night air is heavy, water beads
The Ladd and Whitney monument and its City seal,
"Art is the Handmaid of Human Good."
It fades fast in the sun
Burning the fog's dark silent beauty.

Patterns of a Prayer Town

By **Paul Marion**
December 16, 2013

Our Lady of the Bathtub shines white.
A flagpole becomes a stack of gold eggs.
The small dogwood vanishes—in its place a floating rosary.
There's a chain-link gate festooned with gaudy bulbs,
shrubs lassoed blue, dormers lined in radiant jelly beans—
every other house turns into a birthday cake.
City folk do it for you and me, for their
kids and kids of passing strangers.
But what do the Martians think,
gazing at us through super-powered telescopes?
What do they make of this season
when it looks like a carnival has spread like
flu through the neighborhoods?

Manny

By **Tom Sexton**
January 7, 2014

He was a minor god of the underworld
whose euphonious name brought no reply
if mentioned during the day, a lounge
singer, a god of sirens and bleary-eyed
last calls, of broken hearts and hands.
Still wearing his brushed velvet jacket
and heavy rouge, he joined us at the diner
that never closed, where laughter rang hollow
and everyone who came in eyed the clock.
His hair was dyed the color of Apollo's,
and his voice was raw from singing requests.
He would sit on a stool at the long counter
or in a booth with men who might turn on him
once the night melted like lard on a griddle.

Billerica, Midnight

By **Jean LeBlanc**
January 18, 2014

We begin to have an interest in sun, moon, and stars. What time riseth Orion? Which side the pole gropeth the bear? East, West, North, and South—where are they? What clock shall tell the hours for us?—Billerica, midnight.—H.D. Thoreau, journal entry of August 31, 1839

Rowing out to the island, rowing around
to find the best spot to scramble up the granite,
slippery with needles from the pines, laughing
at the suddenness of being there, being far away
from the known world—how could you not
fall in love with that boy whose arms were brown
from weeks of summer? "We are being watched,"
he whispered, arching an eyebrow to indicate
the school of fish just below the surface.
All you heard was his breath close to your ear.
A little campfire would have been nice,
but would have attracted attention from shore.
Better, then, to unroll sleeping bags
and watch the lights come on and dance
across the lake, and the moon rise. Better, then,
to sleep. You both would promise to do this again,
maybe next weekend, maybe next, and on
through the years. Every time you look up
into a winter night and see Orion dominating
the sky, you think, Maybe next summer,
if not back home in Ashby, Fitchburg, Ripton,
Billerica, Concord, Hollis, if not there, then
another lake, another bed beneath the pines,
another moonrise, another school of patient,
watchful, knowing fish and stars.

HISTORY AS IT HAPPENS

Letters

By **Kate Hanson Foster**
January 24, 2015

It was easy
to lock them in the safe—

pale and luckless
as the bills, vanished

into the back of the closet.

Sometimes I still picture you running
down the streets of Lowell,

past the arena, the Brewery,
the Aiken Street Bridge.

Throw all my letters away.

POEMS

2012

Lowell Police Account of Downtown Riot

By **Dick** on February 10, 2012
—

The Lowell Police Department has posted an account of the riot inside Fortunato's (corner of Middle and Palmer streets) early Friday morning in which three officers were injured and which led to 14 arrests. The full report is online at the Lowell Police blog, but I've reproduced it in part below:

"Numerous individuals were arrested in the City earlier this morning. At 1:30 a.m. every on-duty Lowell Police Officer was summoned to the Downtown area to assist officers who had requested immediate back up. Officers from Lowell, Dracut, Tyngsboro, UMass Lowell, and the Massachusetts State Police responded. This incident started inside Fortunato's, also known as Club 44, which is located at the corner of Palmer and Middle streets. Two officers stationed on the corner noticed a large fight occurring inside the bar. Officers observed a large group of people fighting on the dance floor, throwing chairs, tables, and beer bottles. Officers called for assistance and entered the establishment to restore order. Once inside, officers realized there was only one point of entry/exit for the establishment, as the other doorways were locked from the inside. Back-up officers who were assisting the initial officers on the scene had difficulty entering the establishment. Inside, officers observed approximately 170 to 200 people inside the establishment. At this point some patrons began trying to leave. Officers assisted those who wished to leave. While some officers assisted patrons to leave safely, other officers were focused on ending the fights that were occurring within the establishment. Patrons began throwing bottles at officers who were attempting to affect an arrest inside the bar. Several individuals became violent towards the officers and resisted arrest. At this point, several individuals who had left the bar attempted to get back into the establishment to continue fighting. These individuals were subsequently arrested. This incident led to the arrest of 14 individuals and three Lowell Police Officers being injured."

XFest and Puck Fest

By **Paul** on February 26, 2012
—

Somebody once said that Lowell is a "little big city," and that character is due in part to the spectrum of activities on any given day: small to large, low to high, basic to extravagant, local to global, traditional to experimental, common to cosmic—you get the idea. Yesterday was a "little big city" experience for me from afternoon to evening, with the activity tipping the scales toward the "big city." In the storefront art space that announces itself with blaring color on Chelmsford Street in the Lower Highlands, the second day of 119 Gallery's XFest got going around 2 p.m. with an opening set featuring Lowell writers Ryan Gallagher and Derek Fenner, accompanied by Walter Wright on drums (whose array of percussion components included an upside down cupcake pan atop one of his tom-toms), Rick Breault on laptop (yes, he was operating this device for sonic effect), and Stephanie Lak on another electronic audio instrument that was a cross between a keyboard-synth and a short-wave radio.

Ryan approached the standing mike and proceeding to unroll a short epic poem from his inner drive that pulled the audience toward him in held-breath mode for at least a third of a scuba tank of air. He kept saying his long lines with images of marmalade and jazz, his sentences surround-sounded by the rumble and snap and melodic static and voicings of the trio backing him. Next up was Derek Fenner who crouched at a portable typewriter wired to a speaker that turned the machine into an alternative drum, bang-banging as he punched out a poem on the spot. When his poem-on-paper rolled off the typer, he picked it up and stood up at the microphone to read that one and ten other short pieces, many of them Lowell-inflected in the way Sandburg's early poems spoke Chicagoan, strange and reverent vignettes of life on the local run. He closed with two poems, one a howler, from a friend who couldn't be there. On the howler, the musicians raised the volume roof with their post-mod version of a Salvation Army band. In the compact gallery a few dozen people from Lowell and beyond were locked in on the performances.

For this festival, 119 Gallery is the magnet to which the iron filings of edgy cultural taste are drawn. This weekend, visiting artists traveled from Berlin, Montreal, Asheville N.C., Brooklyn N.Y., and other places. In the second set, musicians Chris Welcome (guitar) and Shayna Dulberger (upright bass) of Brooklyn and sax and flute player Ras Moshe put music to the smooth testimony of spoken-word artist Anthony Febo, one of Lowell's favorite poets, a master of performance, who, like Ryan Gallagher, has a lucid memory of his own compositions. Anthony and I alternated in our set, each of us putting four poems on the table. Mine were the audience participation piece "December Canticle," "Crazy Horse" (about the maker of a huge stone monument out west), "Make Words," and "The Sandbank on Riverside" (set in Pawtucketville).

For Part Two of the day, the location shifted to downtown and the Tsongas Center at UMass Lowell, where the high-achieving River Hawks wouldn't let the nearly 6,000 people go until they had tied the Merrimack College Warriors, who had whipped the locals the night before. I sat with four friends two rows behind the Merrimack bench, where the ice action is in your face, including the random clearing shot plunking off the durable glass. The Tsongas has become everything the campus leadership imagined was possible in the complex and daring days when the transition from City to University was being worked out. It is a full-on sports experience in sound, light, video, and live athletic drama. This is big-time college sports. Nationally ranked. Top tier in all respects. The student shouters were out in force. The seating bowl was the definition of family entertainment. The Lowell Bank Pavilion was jammed. In the lobby a dozen or more *Star Wars* characters posed for pictures with the kids and parents. Rowdy the River Hawk starred in a clever film mash-up that turned the Death Star into a war ship of downriver Merrimack College that got obliterated on the jumbo-screen high over center ice. Each time UMass Lowell tied the score the building rocked on its pins. We would have liked to walk down Martin Luther King, Jr., Way with a win in our pockets, but it could have been worse. It's been a super season, with more to go. What a difference a couple of years makes. And kudos to the traffic controllers. They got the max crowd off the property in good order.

Automobile Races, Technology, and the Lowell Connection

By **Marie** on February 27, 2012
—

It's all about the cars! Big NASCAR races are the current focus of aficionados of the sport—although for the first time ever the opening of the Daytona 500 was rescheduled due to the heavy rain and dangerous conditions down in Daytona, Florida, yesterday. It's a pageant, a festival, if you will, wrapped around the races. It harkens back to a different kind of automobile racing when Lowell, Massachusetts, hosted its first "automobile carnival and road race" in 1908. Locals won't be surprised to learn that the twists and turns of a roadway along the Merrimack River in the Pawtucketville neighborhood created a natural and attractive raceway. Another factor in the Lowell race was that John O. Heinze, president of the Lowell Automobile Club and owner of the Heinze Electric Company that made parts for Detroit car manufacturers, was a major advocate for racing. He knew that to have racing sanctioned, issues of safety had to be addressed. Lowell was a proving ground for his technology—Lowell partnered again with those in the forefront of new technology.

In his essay "Race Along the River," former Lowell Historical Society President and Pawtucketville activist Ray Hoag gives us the "front and back stories" on the 1908 race. While an entertainment for both the drivers and the spectators, as Heinze planned, the races were really a testing ground for the emerging technology of the automobile. Just what could these "machines" offer both the racer and the public? What could they withstand on a long trip or for that matter even on a rigorous short trip? Motor car touring was becoming popular, and New England with its scenery, charm, and challenging roadways was a magnet for these new "tourists." Back in 1908, as now, Lowell seemed ripe for marketing as a destination city for the new motoring tourist back in that day. There is another connecting thread, consider that the American Automobile Association (AAA), celebrating its 110th birthday on March 4, was organized from regional groups in response to a lack of roads and highways suitable for automobiles. The AAA was an early sponsor of races and later turned to meeting the needs of the touring and vacationing public.

Tweet and Greet

By **Dick** on March 2, 2012
—

Thanks to the nearly 50 people who came to Lowell Telecommunications Corporation this morning for our Tweet-n-Greet. The attendees covered a wide range of Twitter abilities and personal and professional backgrounds, reflective of Lowell. Thanks to everyone on the staff at LTC who worked on the event and thanks especially to LTC Board President Mimi Parseghian who donated the refreshments. Before we went our separate ways, I asked attendees for suggested "next steps" for the Lowell Twittersphere. Here are some ideas: Don't wait six months to have a follow-up activity; create a public online list of Lowell Twitter users to make it easier to find folks to follow; make a list of "writing prompts" for those struggling to find things to Tweet about; offer a workshop with intermediate users to brainstorm uses of Twitter's advanced functions; and envision a space with wi-fi where people can connect via laptop, iPad, or smart phone.

'Dickens and Massachusetts' Exhibit

By **Dick** on March 30, 2012
—

More than 100 people gathered at the Tsongas Industrial History Center at the Boott Cotton Mills Museum earlier this evening for the opening reception for "Dickens and Massachusetts" commemorating the author's 1842 visit to Massachusetts, which included a day in Lowell that made a deep impression on the acclaimed English writer. The exhibit, in the first-floor gallery of the museum, will be open every day through October. The program opened seven months of lectures, demonstrations, walking tours, and all manner of activities—75 in all, around the city. Tonight's program opened with UMass Lowell Chancellor Marty Meehan thanking the project partners including Lowell National Historical Park, the Tsongas Industrial History Center, Worcester Polytechnic Institute (WPI has a world-class collection of Dickensian artifacts—who knew?) and the Charles Dickens Museum of London. The Park's David Blackburn, who co-curated the exhibit, introduced co-curator Diana Archibald, professor of English at UML, who thanked everyone and said the final days of setting up the exhibit made it feel like Dickens had returned to Lowell. Being around so many artifacts from his life was very special. Dr. Florian Schweizer, the executive director of the Charles Dickens Museum of London, said the exhibit shows how Dickens influenced America and America him. Schweizer acknowledged that while much of the attention on Dickens writings about America focused on some negativity expressed by the writer, it was time for us to re-evaluate the relationship between Dickens and Massachusetts.

HISTORY AS IT HAPPENS

'This Is Dalton Jones'

By **Paul** on June 6, 2012
—

Last Friday, I received a surprise call at my UMass Lowell office. I was in a meeting off campus, so was not there to pick up the phone. Later in the day, I got an email message explaining what had happened and telling me to check my voicemail.

I joined the Facebook universe in January 2011. That spring, when baseball season came around, for fun I changed my Profile picture on Facebook (for non-users, that's the one that identifies you on all your postings). I put up an image of a Topps baseball card from 1965. It was Dalton Jones, the infielder with the beautiful left-handed swing who played for the Red Sox in the mid-1960s. He was my favorite player. He wasn't a superstar, but he was a valuable contributor to the team. As my friend Jack Neary said recently, "He got a lot of big hits in 1967."

I played baseball for Dracut High School for four years. I wasn't a regular starter. I played shortstop, second base, and wherever I could help. I was a much better hitter in neighborhood games and in pick-up softball later in my life, but I held my own in high school—one time broke up a no-hitter with two outs in the last inning in Billerica.

In 1965, when I was 11 years old, my favorite Red Sox player was Dalton Jones. He batted .389 in the 1967 World Series, playing third base in games one through four. He was 7 for 18 with a .421 on-base percentage in the Series. Boston lost to St. Louis, as we all recall. I remember a newspaper cartoon the day after the series showing a sad kid in a Red Sox cap who had scrawled these words on a wall: "Julian Javier is a Jerk" (you have to say it with the j's as h's)—Javier was the Cardinals' shortstop. Dalton had been such a good prospect coming out of high school that the Red Sox asked another great left-handed hitter to recruit him: Ted Williams.

When my Facebook and real-life friend Bill Lipchitz saw Dalton Jones on my Facebook page, he wrote to me and said, You probably don't know this but Meredith Fife Day went to high school with Dalton Jones in Louisiana around 1960. Bill said she still talks to him and visits when she goes back to her hometown. Meredith has been the artist-in-residence at the Whistler House Museum of Art for several years. One of her paintings hangs in my family's living room. Bill is a friend of Meredith's, so he told her about Dalton and me. Meredith wrote to me and said it was great to hear, and that she would tell her baseball-playing friend that he had a big fan in Lowell. She said Dalton was expected to attend the Fenway Park centennial celebration in April 2012. As it turned out, he was not able to get to Boston this spring.

Imagine my surprise and happiness when I listened to the voicemail message last week. "Hi, Paul. This is Dalton Jones. I'm sitting here with a good friend, Meredith, and we're talking about you. Sorry I didn't get through to you. She's going to bring back a couple of things for you. Goodbye."

Texas Jack, Peerless Morlacchi, and the Lowell Connection

By **Tony** on August 14, 2012
—

Here is another one to place in the category, "There is always a Lowell Connection." I'm almost through reading a book about Buffalo Bill Cody titled *The Colonel and Little Missie* written by Larry McCurtry, author of the Pulitzer Prize-winning novel

Lonesome Dove. In one of the later chapters, McCurtry mentions John Omohundro and Giuseppina Morlacchi. These two are the Lowell connection. McCurtry's book on Buffalo Bill only briefly mentioned that Morlacchi had been buried in Lowell—but I became curious about the "Lowell Connection"—so I Googled it. The Center for Lowell History at UMass Lowell served as a great source of information about Omohundro and Morlacchi.

The famous Lowell couple is better known as Texas Jack and Peerless Morlacchi (Josephine). For many years, Texas Jack performed alongside Buffalo Bill Cody in both his Wild West Show and some independent stage productions. During one of these stage shows Jack met Josephine, and they soon married.

Peerless Morlacchi was one of the most famous dancers in America. Before the marriage, she often performed in Boston even though she didn't want to live in the city. The solution? Morlacchi bought a "summer house" in a rural town not far from Boston, Billerica. While living in Billerica, Morlacchi often visited Lowell and became well known in the Mill City. John Baker Omonhundro (Texas Jack) was a renowned scout for the U.S. Army, considered as able as Buffalo Bill himself. His fame spread rapidly. Texas Jack, like Bill Cody, became the subject of many dime novels.

After their marriage, Peerless Morlacchi and Texas Jack continued to tour but eventually tired of the road. They purchased a second piece of property in the Merrimack Valley—on the corner of Market and Suffolk Streets in Lowell. Not long after, Texas Jack died while on a trip to Colorado. He was only 33 years old. His wife returned to Billerica and spent her time either in Lowell or at "the summer house" in Billerica. Peerless Morlacchi died in 1886, six years after Texas Jack. She is buried in St Patrick's Cemetery in Lowell.

Nobody Beats the Fizz

By **Bob Forrant** on August 28, 2012
—

INTRODUCTION

For 37 years I've lived and worked in Massachusetts industrial cities, and for the last 25 I've thought a lot about how cities like Springfield, Holyoke, Lawrence, and Lowell can move beyond their mill legacies and generate new waves of economic and social growth and vitality. One new book wrestling with these issues is Mario Polese's *The Wealth and Poverty of Regions: Why Cities Matter* (U. of Chicago Press, 2011). He wants to know, as do I, why certain places prosper while others can't seem to get out of their own way. He starts a chapter with a quote from one of the world's preeminent urbanists, Sir Peter Hall. "[As] always in human experience since the invention of the telephone, the dissemination of electronic media may paradoxically even increase the need and the incentive for face-to-face contact. . . And so, surely, this time around: the likelihood is that places with a unique buzz, a unique fizz, a special kind of energy will prove more magnetic than ever (1999)."

In an article in *The Atlantic*, urban studies theorist Richard Florida sought the fizz. During the economic depression at the end of the nineteenth century, he noted, "the country remade itself from an agricultural power into an industrial one." After the 1930s Great Depression, the country once again remade itself. "It discovered a new way of living, working, and producing, which contributed to an unprecedented period of mass prosperity. At critical moments, Americans have always looked forward, not back, and surprised the world with our resilience." The country had the fizz. So, can the Lowell region be reconfigured? Yes, because it "has the fizz," thanks largely to the efforts of the

UMass Lowell and Lowell National Historical Park.

THE POLICY QUESTION

For the past 20 years, policymakers have studied mid-sized cities like Lowell, cities struggling with job loss, decaying infrastructure, tight budgets, and the loss of a good deal of their middle-class. In 2007, MassINC and the Brookings Institution studied the challenges such cities face in Massachusetts. They concluded that many of them feature walkable downtowns and affordable housing. And, these places have growing, entrepreneurial immigrant populations and vibrant cultural and other community organizations, including churches, youth organizations, and immigrant social clubs. These things are enhanced in Lowell with twin engines for long-term, thoughtful development, UMass Lowell and the national park.

THE UNIVERSITY OF MASSACHUSETTS LOWELL

In response to challenges in their neighborhoods numerous urban universities recognized the common interests they shared with residents in the creation and preservation of stable communities. In the mid-1990s, under then Chancellor William Hogan, UMass Lowell focused on the development of a regional economy predicated on the notion that a sustainable economy required a skilled and ever-replenished workforce, innovative products, environmental protection, and strong public health and public education infrastructures. Integral to its mission, the university fostered the enhancement and protection of the historical fabric of the community, supported K-12 and continuing education, and worked to strengthen the region's social and cultural life. This work was continued under Chancellor Martin Meehan. For example, the 2009 opening of the Inn & Conference Center in the former DoubleTree Hotel marked UMass Lowell's commitment to the downtown.

The words of Eugene Trani, president of Virginia Commonwealth University (1999-2009), are instructive here: "Twenty or even ten years ago, universities may have pared back their community-engagement activities in periods of fiscal uncertainty on the grounds that they were valuable expressions of the university's social commitment but not essential to teaching students and contributing to the scholarly community. But today we need to engage with our communities to meet our instructional goals, equip our students with discernment and judgment, and enable them to be productive citizens." UMass Lowell, even as its state funding was cut, did not pare back its engagement. On the contrary, faculty, staff, students, and the administration are more engaged than ever, with co-op learning, internships, expanded study and service abroad, and the like. Engineering students take part in service-learning, and for the past three years the University has made President Obama's Higher Education Community Service Honor Roll.

LOWELL NATIONAL HISTORICAL PARK'S RICH CANVASS

Established in 1978, the park holds some of the most significant restored properties in Lowell that create a platform for telling Lowell's stories. In its 30-year anniversary report, the park reported the extraordinary fact that 77 percent of the five million square feet of the city's historic mills have been rehabilitated. The mills become the backdrop for the Industrial Revolution story told to hundreds of thousands of visitors annually. Sixty thousand school children and hundreds of college and university student ride the rails of historic replica trolleys and experience the noise of a working weave room and museum at the Boott Mills. Visitors can experience the canals on boat tours; some $43 million has been invested to create the Canalway and Riverwalk system. Much of this work is done in partnership with UMass Lowell's Tsongas Industrial History Center.

Frederick Coburn, in his 1920 *History of Lowell and Its People* observed that when the labor supply from New England's rural towns was exhausted employers sent recruiters to places like Quebec and Greece for workers. "Adventurous folks from other lands," Coburn writes, "seeking the advantages of a political democracy, are welcomed as workers. A few members of a nationality establish themselves, and these are quickly followed by others from the same foreign town or countryside." In other words, Coburn's immigrant story is part of our present-day one and shapes how we respond as a community to the current economic malaise.

Absorb the words of a 1977 Lowell profile prepared by Boston University's Sociology Department. "To walk from one end of Merrimack Street to the other is to experience the mosaic and vitality of ethnicity in Lowell. In what was formerly referred to as 'Little Canada,' the elderly on the street discuss in French the visit of a politician. Not far from there, near the court house, a Greek family still makes phylo pastry 'like in the old country,' and others come and go handling in Greek the daily business of living. Next to the recently arrived Jordan Marsh Department Store is a small Lebanese and Syrian restaurant where the customers as well as the owners speak Arabic. At the top of the street the Puerto Rican 'bodega' sell[s] plantains and mangoes, ripe from the Caribbean sun, to the Spanish-speaking community." A similar description—with the names of some groups changed—could be made if we made that walk today.

I've often heard people in Lowell say, "Lowell National Park is the city, and the city is the park." I believe we are moving to the point where the metaphor should be expanded to read, "The park, the University, and the city's rich variety of educational and creative institutions are the city, and the city is all of these." Many of my friends living and working in other mill cities would love having a national park or a growing research university; we have both. From this happy coincidence, I offer a new slogan: "Lowell, the City of Knowledge, Old and New."

On the Road with Apologies to Everyone

By **Tom Sexton** on September 9, 2012
—

Our friend, faithful reader, and occasional contributor Tom Sexton is driving across the continent with his wife, Sharyn, headed from Alaska to Maine for the fall and winter. He will send us dispatches from the road while they are out there. Following is the first report. Tom is on the list of Distinguished Alumni of Lowell High School and is a former Poet Laureate of Alaska. He has a new book of Lowell poems, Bridge Street at Dusk *(Loom Press).*

I thought when I told Paul Marion that I would send a few reports about our drive from Alaska to Maine, I would report on how the Alaska Highway has changed since we first drove it in 1968 in a Volkswagen bus. This trip, our tenth in ten years, is being made in a 2007 Volkswagen Passat. On day three, I was wishing we still had the bus, but more about that later. Our first stop after leaving Anchorage is Tok, with a population of about 1200, and pronounced Toke, for some reason. It began as a construction camp during the building of the highway in 1942 because of a fear that the Japanese would invade Alaska, which, in fact, they did, but far from Tok. They landed in the Aleutians where Mr. Nason, who lived across the street from us on Oak Street when I was a small boy in Lowell, spent several years during the war. I've written four poems about the poor man so far. He doesn't seem to be able to escape me.

An interesting but seldom mentioned fact about the Alaska Highway is that most of the actual building of the highway was done by African-American soldiers working in minus-60 degree temperatures during the winter and mosquito-infested swamps during the summer. When we first drove the highway, it was still a winding narrow primitive road lined with roadhouses where they could repair anything. Most of the curves are gone, and you can drive as fast as you want most of the time. All but two of the roadhouses are gone, so don't break down. If you do find yourself in Tok, eat at Fast Eddy's. Good food and interesting customers. I watched a guy visit the all-you-can-eat salad bar eight times.

Now, for our first and perhaps last Lowell connection. In Tok we stay at Caribou Cabins. They have four beautiful log cabins built by owner Chris Beeman and his wife, Carrie, who appear to be in their mid-30s. Chris was born at Lowell General Hospital and grew up in Chelmsford, Mass. Carrie grew up in Worcester, Mass. He attended Middlesex Community College in Lowell and once applied for work at the nearby Radisson. Carrie works for Head Start, and Chris runs the successful business. Their children are Alaskan-born. It's pretty clear they miss Massachusetts though.

The first city down the highway is Whitehorse, the capital of the Yukon Territory. It's about 750 miles from Anchorage and always a pleasure to reach. Right on the Yukon River, it has a 10-mile walking trail. It was a sleepy government town, but now it's becoming a jumping-off point for oil and gas exploration. It's more liberal than most of Northern Canada, but that's changing. Like Alaskans, many Yukoners consider themselves to be exceptional because of the riches beneath their feet. You can get sushi and German food as well as vegetarian. Whitehorse must be closing in on 30,000 people.

After you leave Whitehorse, you can see the Northern Rockies to the east, and before long you are climbing summit after summit. This is buffalo country, and they own the road. This is also where our Passat's computer had a nervous breakdown. Warning light after warning light came on telling us to get to a dealer. The only problem was the closest dealer is in Grand Prairie, Alberta, about a thousand miles down the road. I called Volkswagen, and they offered to have us towed to Grand Prairie from Fort Nelson, B.C., because we were passing through

Canada. No one in Fort Nelson could scan the computer, and we were faced with renting a car, which came with a $900 fee to return the car to Fort Nelson as well as $89 a day while we were driving to Grand Prairie, plus 79 cents a kilometer. All in all, about $3,000 to get us there, not counting hotel rooms. Did I mention we have a 12-year-old Airedale?

Now the good news. I started the car just before the wrecker arrived and things seemed to be back to normal, so we drove on. Sharyn, calm as calm can be; me, in a state of panic. Tomorrow, I'll report on our adventures from Fort Nelson to Dawson Creek.

Marcel's Laws of Politics

By **Paul** on October 25, 2012

My father, Marcel R. Marion (1919-1982), was an enthusiastic observer of American politics and world affairs. He never ran for anything except union steward when he worked in a textile mill in Lowell in the 1940s. He was a wool sorter, meaning he classified types and quality of wool by examining samples from bales of fleeces shipped to the mill. He never skipped a vote in a local, state, or national election. He watched the news on TV every evening and read two papers a day and three on Sunday. He had a way of cutting to the chase on political arguments. When I think back on what he always said about the two major political parties, it is kind of amazing to see that it pretty much still fits today, even admitting that both parties have a corporate tilt.

My father was a Democrat, going back to the days of President Franklin D. Roosevelt and the New Deal. Born in 1919 in Lowell, my father knew what a Depression looked like and never forgot what government programs like the Works Progress

Administration (WPA) and Civilian Conservation Corps (CCC) meant for people who needed jobs.

I posted a few of Marcel's Laws in the last election cycle, such as "Everybody should take a turn running for office," "There is always something you can do to help," and "There are always more workers than bosses." He would say around this time of year, "The Republicans are for Big Business, and the Democrats are for the Little Guys" (Marcel's Laws, No. 9). I know this way of describing the difference is a cliché, but, fair or not, if you boil down and sift through a lot of what is being said by the Obama and Romney campaigns, the messages sound very much like this. The one percent, the 47 percent, the 99 percent, the two percent, job creators, illegal immigrants, moochers, wealth generators, taking responsibility for their lives, Forward, taking our country back—all these figures and phrases that get tossed around are embedded with ideas, values, and policy positions. Time to sort 'em out, like the old wool sorter did.

Remembering Peter Stamas

By **Marie** on November 16, 2012
—

I got to know Peter Stamas in the mid-1970s. He was a colleague at Lowell High School first—then as Headmaster he was my boss. I had great respect for him. As the representative of the Teachers Advisory Committee I sat across from him expressing teacher concerns—he was always respectful, concerned, and understanding. After I retired a year or so later, I was much happier sitting beside him as we worked on community projects as activists with the Human Services Corporation (HSC) and later the Greater Lowell Community Foundation and the Lowell

Heritage Partnership.

This was the kind of man who devoted a year of his life to work locally and then nationally and internationally with an important youth church group—GOYA, Greek Orthodox Youth of America. So, to note his intense activism with AMNO, the Acre Model Neighborhood Organization, and its Education Component is no surprise. His commitment to Lowell and the Acre was deep and wide, encompassing the educational, social, cultural, and work-life aspects of a city that many saw as poor in reality as well as in mood and perception. He worked very closely with Dr. Patrick Mogan, seeking opportunities to revitalize the city, rebuild the confidence and spirit of the citizenry, and to have outsiders respect the city and its place in the history, and as Pat described them, the process and consequences of industrialization. We and you know that story!

What I know and saw about Peter was his leadership skill—his ability to really listen, to understand, and then synthesize and distill what he heard to make things work. Peter was a thinker as well as a doer. He had a passion for his work—both vocational and avocational—and a compassion for people in all situations. His relationships cut across all ages, stations, experiences and positions: with priests and politicians, bankers and coaches, high school kids and university presidents, the erudite and the struggling. And so importantly to me, he respected, appreciated and worked well with women. I note Sr. Lillian Lamoureux, Kay Georgalos, Clemmie Alexis, and Mary Bacigalupo as examples. (Me, too).

For more than 30 years, Peter guided and inspired Human Services Corporation as the organization worked on urban planning, education, children's services, the plight of the mentally challenged, and respite care. Yet it is the HSC role in the realization of Lowell National Historical Park that Peter saw as its most significant achievement. When HSC was celebrating its 30-year anniversary, he was asked about its most important contribution. He said "I suppose the achievement that is most spectacular and the one most talked about is the role that we played in keeping the idea of the Urban National Park alive once it had been conceived, and being the catalyst that brought it through to fruition." (By the way, knowing just how important Peter was to HSC, we once took a vote that he be president-for-life!)

HSC had a strong commitment to preserving, protecting, and celebrating Lowell's heritage through its buildings, the surrounding nature, and its vast culture. This goal was cultivated and realized though a highly successful design charrette and follow-up activities leading to what we called "Lowell: The Flowering City." Peter nurtured the concepts and the activities; the Lowell Heritage Partnership was soon created and is now partially funded through the annual distribution from the HSC endowment at the Greater Lowell Community Foundation.

Having a community foundation was long a goal of the HSC board of directors. As far back as 1991, there were strategic planning sessions with Peter spearheading years of searching and researching the various community foundation concepts and actual organizations. Speakers came to Lowell from Connecticut and elsewhere. We traveled as well, learning about Worcester and Lawrence. We read the literature and the legislation. Others saw Lowell as fertile ground—Lawrence wanted us to join them! Peter diverted that discussion and met with Lowell movers and shakers about a community foundation for Lowell concept and what support was vital. Then, with people like Richard K. Donahue and George Duncan backing the community foundation concept, the Greater Lowell Community Foundation was born. Endowments were established and grew. Peter was a founding member, a trustee, and for a while the treasurer. I had a vested interest through my role as an HSC board member with Peter as our leader. I was proud to chair the Distribution Committee for many years, where I still serve. The strength of Peter's commitment and his determination to have the Lowell High scholarship money as part of the GLCF funds, where those funds and the foundation corpus could grow, was critical to the current success of the Foundation.

Let me say that Peter Stamas was and remains a role model for me; he was a mentor and an inspiration for a certain style of community activism that I adopted and that I still espouse.

When, in 1997, I nominated him to be honored as a Distinguished Democrat, it was not only because he was a good and committed Democrat—it was his dedication to people and to doing his part to bettering their quality of life that tipped the scales. He was humble in his acceptance. He might have been a Harvard-man, but in substance he was molded by his Bartlett School days, Lowell High experience, his faith, and his family.

I had the opportunity to talk with former Massachusetts Governor Mike Dukakis two weeks ago. I told him about the tribute event. He noted his respect for Peter, "A good guy, a smart guy," whom he appointed to his innovative Judicial Advisory Committee. Peter, by the way, wasn't sure he as a non-lawyer was the right guy to appoint. As Dukakis noted, he was a very valuable adviser!

For the nearly 30 years that I knew Peter Stamas, I saw a leader who played a pivotal role on the Lowell scene. A leader who was always part of a team! In the late '60s and early '70s, Pat Mogan and Peter were a team. When Peter took over as Headmaster at Lowell High School in a time of transition, expansion, and changing student population, Peter assembled and led a team of educators, staff, and partners to get the job done. In the '80s at Human Services Corporation, it was always a team—Peter, Kay, Lillian, Clemmie, Anne, George, Mary, Paul. Then at the Greater Lowell Community Foundation, the trustees, donors, distribution committee, another team effort. And amid all this there was Peter Stamas calling the plays. Peter Stamas was a Lowell Treasure! Peter Stamas was my friend. I honor him and I miss him.

HISTORY AS IT HAPPENS

Stephen King at UMass Lowell

by **Paul** on December 8, 2012
—

In the same year that UMass Lowell and the National Park Service celebrated Charles Dickens's famous visit to Lowell in 1842, the University hosted the author who is arguably the Dickens of our time when it comes to readership and popular interest—that would be Stephen King, the guy who grew up in the gritty dooryards of northeast Maine with an outsized passion for reading, writing, rock'n'roll, and the Red Sox. He brought his one-man literary power station to the Tsongas Center at UMass Lowell last night. "This is my first stadium show," he shouted to the capacity crowd of 4,000 people (The area behind the stage was blocked off). There was a lot of yelling, arm waving, and fooling on stage as he bantered, reflected, and preached. He was both pitcher and catcher to his friend and fellow author Andre Dubus III, who was magnificent as the primary questioner and listener—and the face of the school's English Department, which gained $100,000 for scholarships on this night. Five thousand dollars came from a raffle of the two signed armchairs that the guys used on stage.

When I was growing up as a writer, I read about the mass audience for poetry in the Soviet Union. Poets could fill sports arenas for their readings. In Lowell, I've seen 1,000 people show up for a group reading by Allen Ginsberg, Lawrence Ferlinghetti, and fellow Beat writers. Maya Angelou read to 1,000 in the Smith Baker Center for Middlesex Community College. The Lowell Memorial Auditorium drew 2,000 or more for David Sedaris last year, and had a similar-sized audience for Garrison Keillor. Robert Frost and T.S. Eliot in their prime filled large performance halls. I've never seen anything like the scene last night. King joked at one point that it felt like a Lynyrd

Skynyrd concert. He'd mention a book title like *The Shining* or *The Tommyknockers* as if name-dropping "Free Bird," and cheers and applause would erupt. Both he and Andre plugged in to the electric author-love.

The program came in three sections: Steve and Andre talking shop, King reading a new story about death and regret, and audience questions. About 20 lucky people got a chance to ask a question, including people who had traveled from Chicago and Pennsylvania and an 11-year-old girl who charmed everyone when she said out loud, as if pinching herself, "I'm speaking to Stephen King," before posing her question. To the woman who asked about Red Sox management decisions, Steve said re-signing David Ortiz was an act of good faith that Red Sox Nation needed.

Stephen said you have to get a buzz off what you are doing as a writer in order to stick with the solitary work. He told touching, gossipy, funny, inspiring, and profane stories about his journey from a rookie writer whose devoted wife fished his first novel *Carrie* out of the trash (he got $2,500 for an advance payment on the hardcover publication... and then $200,000 for his share of the paperback publishing rights) to the rarified air of cultural royalty who honored a request from Bruce Springsteen to meet for dinner in Greenwich Village. "Yes, I'd like that," he told his Rock and Roll Remainders-bandmate and music critic Dave Marsh who had carried the request from The Boss.

Andre closed out the first part of the program by reading a passage from Stephen's book about writing in which the author describes regaining his strength and capacity to create after being run over by a car many years ago. "Writing isn't about making money, getting famous, getting dates, getting laid, or making friends. In the end, it's about enriching the lives of those who will read your work, and enriching your own life, as well. It's about getting up, getting well, and getting over. Getting happy, okay? Getting happy."

Farewell, Dr. Patrick J. Mogan

by **Paul** on December 14, 2012
—

We learned earlier today about the passing of Dr. Patrick J. Mogan—teacher, planner, dreamer, and tireless enthusiast for Lowell. I had the privilege of working for him and with him. He was a mentor and guide to me. His purposeful and joyful commitment to bettering his adopted city inspired countless people. He could be a tough critic when he saw something that he considered to be unfair or wrong-headed. He knew where he wanted to go with a good idea. He amazed people with his relentless advocacy of the core concepts about learning and community redevelopment that he had arrived at through experience, study, and imaginative analysis. He was forever citing nuggets of wisdom and sensible insights that he had picked up through reading or meeting other smart people; he seemed at times to be speaking in proverbs, many of them based on his own observations. A nimble thinker, he was especially good at synthesizing complex thoughts and applying them to the situation at hand. He was the type of person who could see around the corner or over the edge of the horizon, figuratively, which invested his proposals with a depth of importance that made people pay extra attention. He didn't suffer fools, and he wasn't fooled by self-righteous experts and officials, but he sought out and welcomed substantive expertise and serious scholarship.

He always remembered that he was working for sincere Lowellians in whom he had so much confidence—and for whom he had so much respect. One of his central worries was that the revitalization of Lowell would turn Lowell residents into "spectators of their own culture." It was important to him that the cultural revival upon which he had staked so much maintain its authentic Lowell character and be animated by

Lowellians—without lapsing into provincialism or becoming stale. As a teacher, he favored learning by doing and place-based learning. He said, "Don't confuse knowing something with understanding something."

A couple of years ago, at the wake for his wife, Mary, he thanked me for attending and two minutes later gave me a homework assignment having to do with starting a foreign-language academy in Lowell that would be a sure-fire bet for public funding because of the national-security angle. He never stopped imagining ways to make Lowell "a good address" even after the address had been substantially improved. I will miss him. We will miss him. There is zero chance that he will fade from our collective memory. Lowell was lucky to have him for as long as it did. Thank you, Pat.

Top Ten of 2012

By **Dick** on December 31, 2012

—

Here are my Top Ten events and developments in Lowell in 2012. Please add your own using the comment feature:

1. Elizabeth Warren defeated Scott Brown in the contest for the United States Senate seat, 54 percent to 46 percent. Warren won Lowell by nearly 6,000 votes. Many of those who voted for Warren have not regularly participated in City elections. Whether these voters can be persuaded to vote in City elections or whether they just show up for the Presidential election will have a substantial impact on local politics.

2. Patrick Murphy was elected mayor by a five to four margin at the City Council inauguration. He received votes from himself, Kevin Broderick, Marty Lorrey, Bill Martin, and Vesna Nuon. Councilor Rodney Elliott voted for himself and received the votes of Ed Kennedy, Joe Mendonca, and Rita Mercier.

3. Changes in City government: Kevin Broderick resigned from the City Council and was replaced by eleventh place finisher John Leahy (tenth place finisher Armand Mercier passed away in January). Mike Lenzi resigned from the Vocational High School Committee after moving to Dracut. He was replaced by Ray Boutin, who received the most votes at a joint meeting of the Lowell City Council and School Committee.

4. John Kerry was nominated by President Obama to serve as Secretary of State. Lowell has had a love/hate relationship with John Kerry for 40 years, beginning in 1972 when he moved to the city to run for the Congressional seat formerly held by Brad Morse, a Republican. Kerry won a tough Democratic primary, beating such established Lowell figures as John Desmond, Helen Droney, Fred Finnegan, Robert Kennedy, and Paul Sheehy, but then he lost the general election to Andover Republican Paul Cronin. In 1984, Kerry defeated then Fifth District Congressman Jim Shannon for the U.S. Senate seat being vacated by Paul Tsongas. In 1996, Kerry held onto that seat in the face of a strong challenge by then-governor Bill Weld, who had the support of much of the Lowell establishment. Kerry's departure will cause a special election in early summer of 2013 to fill the Senate seat.

5. UMass Lowell continued the amazing reinvention of its campus and its own emergence as a nationally recognized

institution of higher education. The Saab Emerging Technologies and Innovation Center opened on the North Campus; construction of a new parking garage began on the South Campus; and the demolition of the old St. Joseph's Hospital to make way for the University Crossing student center was well underway. UMass Lowell became a major player in state and national politics with its polling and political analysis operation, and with its hosting of a crucial debate between Scott Brown and Elizabeth Warren at the Tsongas Center.

6. The cultural life of the city remained vibrant throughout 2012 with speaking appearances by Stephen King (UMass Lowell) and Michael J. Fox (Middlesex Community College); another successful Folk Festival; and musical performances at the Lowell Summer Music Series by musicians such as Kenny Loggins, Lyle Lovett, and k.d lang. A major exhibit on "Dickens in Lowell" hosted by UMass Lowell, the national park, and others with related programming produced to celebrate the 1842 visit to Lowell by Charles Dickens. The 100th anniversary of the Bread and Roses Strike in Lawrence, Mass., had a big Lowell component thanks to UMass Lowell history professor Bob Forrant. The Angkor Dance Troupe celebrated its 25th anniversary with the world premiere of *Apsara Dancing Stones* at Lowell Memorial Auditorium. A tribute to Mary Sampas in April had an overflow crowd at the Whistler House Museum, and the first annual Lowell-area publishers roundup was held at the Old Court in January. At the national park, Celeste Bernardo succeeded Michael Creasey as superintendent, and "the Father of the National Park," Patrick J. Mogan, passed away in December.

7. Unruly behavior by patrons of downtown drinking establishments became a major issue in 2012, set off by

what was described as "a riot" at Fortunato's restaurant in February. Criticism of the Lowell License Commission's handling of this issue led to the departure of two of its members, but the problems persist as seen in a major altercation at Brian's Ivy Hall in December. Rowdy behavior in bars was tolerated for years because Downtown mostly emptied out at the end of the business day. Downtown is now a residential neighborhood whose residents are rightly intolerant of such behavior. The resolution of this conflict is critical to the continued success of Downtown.

8. The United Teen Equality Center (UTEC) opened its new headquarters on Warren Street, combining a vintage church building with a modern addition to create a fabulous example of environmentally friendly reuse of a century-old downtown structure. UTEC also led the community response to a wave of shootings that struck the city with a Rally Against Violence in September.

9. Mill City Grows burst on the scene, promoting the ability of Lowell residents to grow, purchase, distribute, and consume healthy, locally produced food on land in the community. Its September Harvest Festival was a great success, and the organization remains active year-round. Mill City Grows is forward-looking, but it also taps into Lowell's agricultural heritage: most immigrants long ago came here from farming communities. While their primary employment in Lowell was in the mills, anyone with a spare plot of earth, no matter how small, cultivated it, both to supplement the family food supply but also to remain connected to their rural ways. The pattern of newcomers with roots in rural places remains a strong one, but people's origins vary more these days.

10. Social networking and new media continued to thrive in Lowell. *Howl in Lowell*, a culture and entertainment publication launched in March, continues going strong. New blogs include Jen Myers' *Room 50* and Paul Belley's *Captain's Log*. A "Tweet-Up" at Lowell Telecommunications Corporation in March attracted a large crowd interested in refining their skills on Twitter, which, along with Facebook, keeps growing as a channel of community engagement. Also, Comcast switched the City's government access channel from 10 to 99.

2013

2013

Dylan in Lowell, Another Side

By **Paul** on April 10, 2013
—

I'm glad I went down to the river last night. The preacher was in town, and the congregation was called to assemble. He made his fourth tour through the city of smokestacks and steeples, the small city with the world on its streets. The people arrived with eager, happy looks on their faces, a blend of loyalists who grew up with the artist and younger adventurers. We had a beautiful scene outside the Tsongas Center as music lovers streamed toward the arena and the regular Tuesday night Riverwalk runners wove through clusters of people on the pathways. I met a woman, whose name I can't recall, who had been with Dylan on the 1975-76 Rolling Thunder Revue tour from the Plymouth, Mass., concert through Lowell and Madison Square Garden and on to the Zimmerman homestead in Hibbing, Minn. Mysteriously, she said, "I was one of the unknowns."

 A couple of the fans had been to Kerouac's grave earlier in the day, making the pilgrimage to the grave the same way Dylan himself paid respects to one of the writers who influenced him as a young man. We had a reporter from San Francisco who writes a daily column on Dylan for an online publication. I met a teacher who told me he is the person he is today because of Dylan's music and ideas. I haven't seen so many gray ponytails in one place in a long time, probably since the last Dylan concert. I was reminded of the Gray Panthers elder activists from the 1970s. Dave Lewis teaches business at UMass Lowell; he had his green 1965 VW bus parked outside the Tsongas with doors open as a living artifact of the root-times of Dylan. Dave, Mary Lou Hubbell, and I handed out 700 copies of a commemorative pamphlet about Dylan, UMass Lowell, and the city to appreciative concert-goers—an instantly collectible essay by writer Dave Perry with

263

pictures of Dylan in Lowell. In the parking lot, I talked to a guy who had been to the two previous shows, and he extolled the performance: "You're going to enjoy this tonight, but he will only play about three songs from the old days." The event had something of a feel of a high-school reunion, a gathering of the faithful for another dose of the sound and the voice that have already gone down in history. In the same way we drop the names of Edgar Allan Poe and Abraham Lincoln as legendary visitors to Lowell, this man will be spoken of for a hundred years or more when the cultural chronicles of Lowell are consulted.

Bob Dylan was in good spirits last night on the UMass Lowell stage. I've seen him perform about ten times, and he offered a fine show, better in my view than in his last appearance at the Tsongas. He leaned into the songs and honored the words, shaping the phrases to fit his older throat. He opened strongly with "Things Have Changed," and on the sixth number thrilled the audience with the first notes of "Tangled Up in Blue." The floor was semi-packed and the seating bowl filled about a third of the way around—not a capacity crowd or even close, but the people who attend now are connoisseurs or new converts; the recreational rubber-neckers have been drained out of the "endless tour." I understand the reason for the smaller crowds; this edition of Dylan is an acquired taste, and, honestly, I take some of it like medicine. But it's a unified field of creative work. You are there because you need to be there now—nobody is "making the scene" to be seen or to chase a celebrity. The preacher comes to town. The congregation gathers. "So let us not talk falsely now/ The hour is getting late."

Review of *Lost Child: Sayon's Journey*

By **Dick** on April 18, 2013
—

On Thursday, April 4, several hundred supporters packed theater 13 at the Showcase Cinema in Lowell for the New England premiere of *Lost Child: Sayon's Journey*, a documentary about the experience of Sayon Soeun as a child soldier in Cambodia and his search decades later for the surviving members of his family. The turbulence of the early 1970s touched every part of Cambodia, including the rural home of six-year-old Sayon where he lived with his parents, brothers, and sisters. Although he had been instructed by his mother to stay close to home, one day Sayon climbed aboard a military truck that was already filled with dozens of his friends. That was the last day he would ever see his parents. Taken to a military camp, Sayon and the other children were trained as Khmer Rouge soldiers despite their young age. For the next few years, Sayon served as a soldier and became an eyewitness to the horrors of the "Killing Fields" of Cambodia.

As circumstances in Cambodia changed, Sayon and thousands of others could leave the country, first for refugee camps and then for the United Sates. Thirteen-year-old Sayon was adopted by a family in Connecticut. After graduating from high school, Sayon was drawn to Lowell by friends and remained in the city because of difficulties with the law. A six-month jail sentence gave him time to think about his future, and as soon as he was released he devoted his life to helping Cambodian youth in Lowell.

In recent years, after marrying and becoming well established in Lowell, Sayon thought more and more about the family he left behind in Cambodia. His investigation put him in contact with men who claimed to be his brothers. Although he was skeptical of that claim, he decided to return to Cambodia to explore further. He was accompanied by his sister-in-law, Sopheap Theam (also a survivor of the "Killing Fields"), and a documentary film crew.

Back in Cambodia, Sayon met the three men and one woman who claimed to be his brothers and sister, along with dozens of nieces and nephews. Each talked about their experiences during the war and the fate of their parents. Although he was treated warmly by everyone, Sayon still had doubts about whether he was their brother and subsequently persuaded them to have their DNA tested to establish the relationship for sure.

The tensest moment in the film occurs when the envelopes with DNA test results are delivered to Sayon in Lowell. Regardless of the test results (which I will not disclose here), Sayon felt as though there would always be something missing in his life. Perhaps the title of the film, *Lost Child*, also means a lost childhood because that was something taken from Sayon that could not be replaced.

Directed by Janet Gardner and co-produced by Gardner and Sopheap Theam, *Lost Child* is a thoughtful and informative film that should be seen by everyone, especially those who are not from Cambodia or of Cambodian descent. It gave me valuable insight into the experience of many of my Cambodian friends and neighbors and increased the respect and appreciation I have for their accomplishments here in Lowell.

Some Thoughts on the Marathon Bombing

By **Dick** on April 22, 2013

With the past week's tragic and dramatic events now a part of history, life in Lowell can start edging back to normal. The primary for the special election for the U.S. Senate seat is a week away (Tuesday, April 30), and conflict at the City Council meeting will grab center stage for some. During the crisis, I found it hard to write blog posts: things unrelated to the bombing seemed trivial, and things about the bombing were coming in overwhelming waves from other sources. Best to stay silent. Before moving on, however, I wanted to post some observations from the week past, more for archival purposes than anything else.

News of the Boston Marathon bombing arrived at 3:00 p.m. last Monday, Patriots' Day. More than a decade after 9/11, my first reaction when told there had been an explosion at the Marathon wasn't "terrorist attack," although that reality set in fast. The death toll was quickly set at three and the injured toll at 50. My expectation was that the former number would creep upwards, but it did not (from bomb injuries, at least). But the number of wounded did rise to around 170. Given the packed surroundings, it is amazing more were not killed by the two explosions. That is attributable to the construction of the bombs (at ground level, they propelled shrapnel outward not upward, causing massive injuries to legs but few to vital organs) and the instant availability of top quality medical care at the nearby marathon runners' tent.

As is often the case, connections to Lowell were soon established. The photo of a gravely injured Lowell High School student being treated by two bystanders dominated the Tuesday front pages of both the *Boston Globe* and *New York Times*. A surprising number of the injured were from Greater Lowell or had close ties to this area, and there was Ed Davis, a calm, authoritative voice throughout the crisis as Boston's police commissioner (and Lowell's former police superintendent).

Wednesday was spent reading of the victims, of those who responded to them first, and speculation about who had done it. One website had pre-explosion crowd photos with every isolated male with a backpack annotated as the possible terrorist. (As someone who routinely carries a backpack, I found this crowd-sourcing exercise creepy and, while possibly of some assistance, a source of potential harm to the reputations of many innocent bystanders).

Thursday was the interfaith memorial service featuring President Obama. As is so often the case (in my view) his public remarks struck the right note of comfort for the injured, defiance towards the perpetrators, and inspiration to everyone else. After the service the President visited victims at Massachusetts General Hospital.

Throughout Thursday, the media spread the word that the FBI had photos of the bombers and would be releasing them to the public soon. That happened in the late afternoon: it was a video loop of two men striding relaxed but purposely down the sidewalk in column, the first with a black baseball cap and a black backpack squarely strapped to both shoulders (Suspect #1), the second with a white ball cap worn backwards, with a grayish colored pack slung casually over his right shoulder. Still photos were grainy but clear enough to allow the persons to be recognized. I went to bed at about 10:30 p.m. with no further news.

Waking up Friday at 4:30 a.m., I glanced at my phone for overnight news. Two emails from my son Andrew, who lives near Harvard Square in Cambridge, grabbed my attention. The first was at 11:41 p.m.: "There was just a shooting near MIT. Some injuries. No threat here." The second at 2:06 a.m.: "I'm sure you'll see all the details when you wake up. Eventful night. They're not done sweeping the area of Watertown, but it's a lot less chaotic than it was. I think I'll be going to bed soon." The first thing that popped up on my computer was Facebook. I locked onto Andrew's feed: "There was a shooting around MIT. Then there was a car hijacked in Central Square. Pursued by police. I heard sirens, then turned the police radio on. I heard an explosion and gunshots in the distance from my room. . . they're now saying grenades and automatic gunfire in Watertown. Second officer down."

After that, news came rapidly from the TV and the computer. The Marathon bombers had been identified as two brothers from Cambridge. The news Friday morning was that the brothers had ambushed and killed an MIT police officer, robbed a 7-11 store (an erroneous report), hijacked a car, and been stopped by police in Watertown where a massive firefight ensued. A Mass. Bay Transportation Authority (MBTA) police officer had been badly wounded in the gunfight, one of the terrorists (Suspect 1) had been killed, and Suspect 2 had escaped.

By 6:30 a.m., Governor Patrick had shut down the entire MBTA. The communities of Watertown, Cambridge, Newton, and several others were all locked down, which meant people were to remain at home and businesses were not to open while a massive manhunt was conducted. Within minutes, the lockdown was extended to the entire city of Boston. Here in Lowell, the work day continued uneventfully, but all eyes and ears were trained on whatever "breaking news" source was available. An Amtrak train in Norwalk, Connecticut, had been evacuated, and a bomb squad in Buffalo was searching a car with Massachusetts plates. Nothing came of it.

Twelve hours later, exhausted and disheartened elected officials and police announced at a news conference that the suspect continued to elude them, however, the lockdown would be lifted and the MBTA would resume operating. With that announcement, the local TV news morphed into Diane Sawyer and the national news, something I hadn't watched in months. She broke for a commercial at 6:50 p.m. After the ads, the local news anchors on Channel 5 were back on screen, telling of breaking news in Watertown. Suspect #2 had been located hiding in a boat stored in a yard just outside the day's search perimeter. Gunfire broke out and then faded. Wave after wave of police of all types arrived. At 9:00 p.m., they announced that Suspect #2 had been captured, alive but badly wounded.

The media has had a mix of stories about the terrorists and their motivations and actions as well as other reports about the victims, the funerals, and their recoveries. For most of us, returning to work today will be a chance to talk about the news of Friday night and share nuggets of information picked up over the weekend. I suspect that those involved in K-12 education who are returning from a week of vacation will have a different experience. With the news profiles of the younger terrorist all reporting that he was a fine student, an excellent athlete, a good friend, and many other superlatives, those who work with and educate young people must be struggling with the question of what makes someone who by all appearances was a "good kid" morph into a murdering terrorist and how can that transition be identified, diverted, and derailed?

2013

Holding On to Those Self-Evident Truths

By **John Wooding** on July 3, 2013
—

It's Independence Day. A few weeks ago, I became an American citizen. No big deal, really. Thousands of people do this every year. But I have been here for more than 30 years, hanging on to my Green Card (it isn't green) for no real reason—perhaps clinging to a British identity, maybe a certain arrogance, perhaps inertia, probably ambivalence about going through the process. I really don't know. But now I am an American, and this will be my first Independence Day as a citizen.

The ceremony took place at Faneuil Hall (the irony here was not lost on this Brit). I did not expect to be moved by the event, but I was—deeply. I was one of 262 people from 86 countries who sat staring at paintings of George Washington (he looks a bit pissed off), the Adams (John and Sam, both a tad grumpy) and of Webster (in full debate mode) while waiting to become citizens. There we were—from Azerbaijan to Zambia and from everywhere in between. We were young and we were old and all the colors of humanity. And lots of kids and families and friends. We were in party mode—full of expectation and a little bit intimidated by the setting. When the judge arrived (a woman, herself an immigrant) we quieted down, a little scared by the court being called to order. The judge was remarkably friendly, asking each of us to stand up when our country was named and each getting a cheer when we did so. On stage a bunch of young children (volunteers from the newly inducted mums and dads) led us in the oath. We happily renounced and abjured all allegiance to foreign potentates (I had been meaning to do that for ages). The young woman from the Dominican Republic sitting next to me whispered, "What's a potentate?" I mumbled something about not having my PowerPoint slides available to explain.

We pledged, we sang "The Star-Spangled Banner" (with a lot of looking down at the handy-dandy lyrics, thoughtfully provided) and we listened. The judge, with warmth and humor, let us know how seriously we should take this event. She pointed out that we had just sworn to defend this country from foreign enemies, but that it was equally important that we defend it from those who would limit its freedoms in the name of that defense. I was shocked, and I was pleased that she said this. She told us to use our newfound ability to vote, but chided that this was not enough, that democracy requires work and not just a mark on a ballot. She stressed that true democracy demands engagement, participation, and struggle and that this, and only this, will insure the greatness of this country. The critical listener in me was vigorously nodding agreement. It got me thinking.

Born of a generation used to slamming the U.S.—the Vietnam War, Watergate, Civil Rights, the Cold War, the Gulf Wars, and the too-often arrogant posing—I tended to take what we academics like to call a "critical stance." Having for years called the U.S. to task for supporting tin-pot dictatorships in the developing world, where military regimes committed the most appalling acts while the American government turned a blind eye, saving the world from the Soviets; having puzzled over the obsession with guns, the debate over abortion, the resistance to socialized medicine, and the mindless advocacy of individual over collective rights, I have done my share of tut-tutting and complaining. Like many others, I have been outraged by the lies about weapons of mass destruction, the stupidity of pretending climate change ain't happening, by the horror that is Guantanamo, and (with many American friends) perplexed by a government system that works about as well as a Ford Pinto. Oh, and the strutting America: bigger, better, and so terribly right about everything. It is no wonder that so many (myself included) are quick to damn and so unwilling to praise. So, you can imagine I had a certain skepticism about becoming an American, and I wasn't expecting to feel so moved or to feel so much pride that morning as I joined the huddled masses in downtown Boston.

And yet that day, in that historic hall, I realized that the core values of America are incredibly important and unique. The Declaration, by insisting that we are all equal, that we have inalienable rights and that life, liberty, and the pursuit of happiness should always and everywhere be protected, is a magnificent statement. The assertion that governments derive their powers from the consent of the governed should never be forgotten nor eroded. These ideas, these claims, are the foundations of democracy, and they mean much more than I often thought. The Constitution and the Bill of Rights, too often misused and misquoted by scoundrels, build on this foundation, demanding protection from tyranny and enshrining rights that are absolutely critical. I guess we sometimes forget the power of these words and the passionate core held by these ideas.

On that morning, in a too hot hall, with hundreds of others, I thought about these things. The need to defend the liberties and the rights that sit at the heart of the American experience became evident to me in a new way. I was proud to be part of this, to become American. I realized why so many want to be in this country, to feel this country. I now know why I have stayed here and all the many ways this country has been good to me. More than anything it touched me and made me understand that we all need to pay attention, all the time. If we don't do that, if we don't pay attention, democracy will wither and collapse. Paying attention means that we must know stuff about the world, celebrate diversity, speak truth to power, and argue—with each other, with the powerful. We need to be informed and engaged and stand up for what is right. And yes, sometimes take to the streets. Democracy is an obligation. We need to make sure that Jefferson's ringing words of self-evident truths remain vibrant and alive. Being an American demands it. I will try to do my bit.

HISTORY AS IT HAPPENS

Edward Snowden and Secret Intelligence

By **Dick** on July 20, 2013
—

It was last Wednesday, our first afternoon in Berlin. Struggling to stay awake against the effects of losing a night's sleep by flying across the Atlantic, we found a peaceful café with outdoor seating along the banks of the Spree River in the heart of Berlin for a late lunch. Once our 40-something waitress determined we were American, she became quite talkative, explaining that she had spent time in Florida doing winter waitressing jobs and asking where we were from. When we had finished eating, she approached the table to begin clearing and asked, "May I ask you a political question?" Anticipating something about the President, the economy, maybe health care, we invited her inquiry. "What do you think about Edward Snowden." I almost blurted out "Who?" but how could I not be aware of America's most recent traitor or patriot, depending on one's point of view.

Roxane (my wife and traveling companion) and I answered simultaneously and similarly: neither of us were all that concerned by his revelations since we assumed the government was conducting that type of surveillance anyway. (By way of background, when we first met in the early 1980s, Roxane and I were both serving in U.S. Army intelligence units in Germany that were doing the kind of electronic intelligence gathering that we're still not supposed to talk about). We asked the waitress what she and others in Germany thought of Snowden. "He is a great hero," was her reply, although she seemed a bit disappointed by our lack of concern (not all that disappointed though because when she spotted us back at the café on our final night in Berlin, she rushed over and greeted us like long-lost friends).

In retrospect, our Berlin waitress's celebration of Snowden's disclosures should not have been surprising. She lives in a country, after all, that is just two decades removed from two successive regimes that elevated spying on their own citizens to levels unimaginable to us. And running afoul of the government meant death in the case of the Nazis and prison terms and loss of economic security under the Communists.

So, what exactly is it that Edward Snowden disclosed? As I understand it, he revealed that the National Security Agency is tracking all conversations, voice, video, and typed, made by everyone, everywhere. They're not monitoring the content of the communications (although they have that capability). They are monitoring who is talking with whom. If you make frequent phone calls to someone in Pakistan, they make note of that. And if the person at the other end is a suspected terrorist, they will note who else you are talking to here in the U.S. They may even request a warrant from a Federal court for permission to see what it is you are saying to these others. If you are just calling Espresso Pizza to order a large pepperoni for pick-up, they won't pay attention to that.

While I'm concerned about this process, I'm not outraged by it. I greatly value the protections provided to us by the Constitution, but the Constitution is a living document that should evolve as society evolves. The means of communication available to us today are flexible and ubiquitous and have greatly improved our quality of life. They've also made it easier for bad guys to avoid detection. Not that we needed a reminder of the effects of a terrorist attack, but we sure received one with the Boston Marathon bombing. While communications surveillance didn't stop that one, I suspect it has prevented others. That counts for a lot, as does the fact that this program is overseen by all three branches of our government. Show me an actual instance where the information has been abused, and I'll be more concerned. For now, the practical benefits outweigh the threat of theoretical abuses. Besides, as I am eerily reminded every time a targeted ad pops up in my internet browser, corporate America is already monitoring our every online move in the name of capitalism without a lot of showings of outrage; why shouldn't we tolerate the government doing the same to protect us from terrorists?

As for Snowden, until I see evidence of actual abuses of this information, I don't see him as a hero. Traitor is too strong and inaccurate a word to use to describe him. Suffice it to say that he has probably done grave damage to our ability to detect and prevent terrorist attacks. What I've written above is based on a very general understanding of the program involved. Snowden disclosed many details both substantive and technical. Electronic intelligence is a precarious commodity. As soon as the bad guy realizes you can monitor his communications, he can easily change the means of communicating and cut off your information flow. That's why the product of these programs and the very existence of these programs is so highly classified. I may not have scrutinized the details of what was disclosed by Snowden, but I am certain the bad guys did.

Lowell's Hidden Epidemic

By **Derek Mitchell** on August 22, 2013
—

Lowell is suffering from an epidemic that is draining community resources and takes more lives than car accidents and shootings. No neighborhood is unaffected by what Wayne Pasanen, former Emergency Room Chief at Lowell General Hospital, calls "the most severe public health crisis in our community." With 34 lives lost in 2011, coupled with estimates that for each fatal overdose there are 825 additional non-medical users, we cannot afford to ignore opioid addiction.

Opioid users challenge many stereotypes about substance abusers. Statistics indicate a disproportionate amount of those addicted are tradespeople, whose habits spiral from initial, legitimate medical use related to on-the-job injuries. State Rep. Tom Golden has seen the impacts of this crisis firsthand. "The people who are affected by opioid addiction are spread throughout the entire community," Rep. Golden says. "It is a growing epidemic that affects us all." He has been an advocate at the state level to address addiction, and there is more work that we can do at the municipal level.

Opioid addiction is an issue of public health and public safety for Greater Lowell. Former Lowell Police Superintendent Ken Lavallee says, "You can tie 80 to 90 percent of crime in the city, everything from petty theft and car breaks to violent crime and prostitution, back to substance abuse." Lavallee's assessment is consistent with a finding that the average addict commits 230 crimes per year.

Associated costs for police enforcement, legal proceedings, and property loss and damage make this an issue that affects us all. Community-wide problems require community-wide solutions. In addition to training for law enforcement officers, both police and community agencies can educate Lowell residents about early signs of addiction in family members or employees.

While early intervention is vital, prevention is even more cost-effective. Educating students about the physical effects of addiction may reduce initial use among youth. Much of this crisis is fueled by the availability of legally prescribed opioid-based pain relievers—sales of which have increased 300 percent since 1999. The City of Lowell operates an unwanted pill drop-off kiosk, a program that can be expanded and for which grant funding may be a resource.

Remaining silent about opioid addiction will continue to leave us vulnerable. Focusing on prevention and early intervention now will reduce crime-related costs in the future. As individuals and as a community, we must prioritize resources to fight this epidemic.

Cambodia Town of Lowell

By **Sengly Kong, Ph.D.** on August 23, 2013
—

The following article appeared in the latest edition of Khmer Post USA *and is reposted here with permission of* Khmer Post *and of the author, Sengly Kong, Ph.D., who is the chair of the Cambodia Town committee.*

In 2010, City of Lowell officials designated a Cambodia Town district to recognize the Lowell Cambodian-American community's contribution during the past three decades to revitalizing the partially blighted Lower Highlands neighborhood. This action elevated interest in the area's stores and restaurants, attract new businesses, bring in tourists, and increase civic pride.

The designation was a timely response to the aspirations of the community and businesses as reflected in their positive responses to a brief survey in 2010 conducted by the Cambodian Mutual Assistance Association (CMAA) of Greater Lowell. On October 29, 2011, a Cambodia Town Committee composed of volunteers was set up with the support of the Cambodian community and businesses. The committee works closely with the City and other local organizations to advance a vision for an economically, culturally vibrant, and prosperous Cambodia Town.

Lowell is home to the second largest Cambodian-American community in the United States after Long Beach, California. Richard Howe, co-author of the book *Legendary Locals of Lowell*, writes that Cambodian refugees were attracted in large numbers to Lowell by relatively plentiful jobs in the mid-1980s and the already vibrant Cambodian community in the city. The 2010 U.S. Census states that Lowell has about 22,000 Cambodians; however, it is widely agreed that Cambodians in Lowell were seriously undercounted. Community leaders, who have lived and worked for decades in the community, estimated that there are approximately 35-40,000 Cambodians, about one-third of the city population; the estimate is quite consistent with extrapolated school enrollment data. Lowell has a large proportion (20.2 percent) of Asians compared to only 5.3 percent statewide. Also, Lowell businesses are 14.8 percent Asian-owned compared to 4.5 percent statewide (Census 2010).

There are at least 200 Cambodian-American businesses of all sizes and kinds, most of which are concentrated in Cambodia Town. Cambodian restaurants are ubiquitous; each offers a variety of authentic ethnic dishes, and each also tends to have its signature dish based on customer preference. For example, customers usually like a sour beef stew (Samlor Machu Sach Koa) at Red Rose restaurant; roasted duck at Phnom Penh restaurant; steamed soy sauce Tilapia (Trey Cham Hoy) at Mekong restaurant; or Rice Field Sour Fish Soup (Samlor Machu Srae) at Piphup Thmei restaurant. All ingredients are authentic and available at Phnom Penh Market on Branch Street, Hong Kong Market on Westford Street, and Bangkok Market on Chelmsford Street.

Authentic jewelry stores are also omnipresent in Cambodia Town. You can find, for example, Asian Jewelry on Westford Street and on Middlesex Street you will see Phnom Pich Jewelry, Pailin Jewelry, or Apsara Jewelry. You can buy a necklace with a lucky charmed pendant or a bracelet with artistic design or earrings of Angkorian style or contemporary Cambodian fashion.

During summer weekends, you can see traditional wedding receptions at Cambodian restaurants with bride and groom wearing a set of dazzling jewelries, wedding crown, costumes—and changing each set every hour through the evening. A traditional wedding is customarily organized in two parts: the first part takes place in the morning at a bride's home with invited monks chanting blessings for a couple. The reception is generally held in the evening with invited guests from the bride's side and the groom's. One can also buy traditional costumes, jewelry, lucky charms, and other souvenirs at local costume and souvenirs shops throughout the Town.

Religion plays important roles in most Cambodian-American lives. From birth to death, Cambodians involve Buddhism one way or another. Buddhist monks chant the blessing for a newborn, although this practice is rare nowadays. There are Buddhist ceremonies all year: Phjum Ben, New Year, funerals, etc., each of which involves monks chanting blessing. Three Buddhist temples offer religious services: Glory Buddhist temple is in Cambodia Town off Chelmsford Street while two others, Trairatanaram and Khmer Lowell Temple, are in a neighboring community. There are scores of other cultural entities that make Lowell's Cambodia Town culturally vibrant. The Cambodian Mutual Assistance Association provides culturally appropriate social services; Metta Health Clinic of Lowell Community Health Center provides culturally competent healthcare services; and Angkor Dance Troupe and Tep Niyum Musical offer classical and folk dances for various occasions, etc.

Cambodia Town offers great opportunities for tourists to experience authentic culture and for investors to invest in new businesses, and for Cambodian Americans to be proud of their community. Visiting Cambodia Town of Lowell gives you not only great memorable experiences, but also helps promote sustainable economic growth that will help this former refugee community realize its vision of a prosperous Cambodia Town, economically and culturally vibrant.

Lowell's Cambodia Town is easily accessible from I-495, exit 35, A-B-C; Route 3; and I-93. The commuter rail from Boston's North Station is a 40-minute ride.

2013

Remarks at Lowell Plan Breakfast

By **Francey Slater and Colleen Brady** on September 26, 2013
—

The final speakers at this morning's Lowell Plan Breakfast were Francey Slater and Colleen Brady, two participants in the 2013 Public Matters leadership development program, co-sponsored by the Lowell Plan and Lowell National Historical Park. Neither Slater nor Brady was born in Lowell; they both came to the city by separate paths and they have both chosen to stay. Throughout this morning's program, a recurring theme of the earlier speakers was that the key to success for cities like Lowell in early twenty-first century post-Industrial America is to attract and keep the age cohort called the Millennials (i.e., those born from 1980 to 2000). Slater and Brady are emblematic of how Lowell is succeeding in this effort. They kindly consented to allow me to post the remarks they jointly gave this morning.—RPH

So, you might ask, "What is our intention in sharing our Lowell story with all of you?"

We are both recent graduates of the Public Matters program, and Colleen and I share a common sense of stewardship and civic responsibility regarding Lowell. This place is our home, even though we were not born here nor do we have deep family roots here. This place is our home because we have chosen it to be the place we build our careers, families, relationships, networks, and life experiences.

We hope that in sharing our stories with everyone we can deepen our resolve to better our city and build upon the greatness that has come before us.

Colleen's Background: I moved to Lowell from the United Kingdom as a sophomore in high school. I disliked Lowell in the same way teenagers dislike everything—it wasn't specific—but within a year, I began to love Lowell, making the social adjustment to my new home. I chose to stay here because I had a base here; I set my life up with a community that I felt I belonged to. I love the people of this city; they are truly themselves without necessarily feeling the need to put on airs and graces.

Francey's Background: I moved to Lowell in 2009 out of geographic convenience—it was the mid-point between my job in Cambridge and my husband's job in New Hampshire. For the next two years, I basically came to Lowell to sleep; but even in the small pockets of time I had to explore and get to know the neighborhoods, I was seduced by the city, and we decided it was home. We bought a house in the Highlands, with space for a garden and a rental unit to help us cover the mortgage. Two years later, I am firmly rooted here, having launched Mill City Grows—an urban food justice initiative aiming to transform communities through growing food and growing relationships

Lowell is a city of stories, a city with a true sense of place, grounded in the people who have built this city and continued by those who now call it home.

I never tire of hearing stories of the remarkable Irish immigrants who settled the Acre, and how St. Patrick Church made the Acre home. I feel a deep sense of recognition when someone references Jack Kerouac growing up in Pawtucketville, which, as a new immigrant from England was my first home, and I knew as "Potatoville."

The stories of fellow Lowellians who have survived the unspeakable acts of the Khmer Rouge never fail to remind me of the character, the grit, the tenacity, and the fighting spirit of the residents of this city.

We draw from these stories an unbreakable strength to propel us through many of the challenges that we face as a mid-sized, post-industrial city.

The Lowell that started the Industrial Revolution, which changed the American way of life, is still a city of innovators, leaders, and collaborative creators. The great projects underway in our city, from the transformation of the Hamilton Canal

District, to the growth of the institutions of higher education, to the reinvestment in our neighborhoods by local businesses, are proof that these innovators and do-ers still call Lowell home.

Every time I pass the new Jeanne d'Arc Credit Union buildings on Merrimack Street, I see a company that is truly investing in Lowell and people putting their money where their mouths are.

But our work is not done. We still face challenges that will require us all to act. The call to action for the residents of this city is to be responsible.

We must take responsibility for the way we speak about Lowell—how we portray this community is how we come to see it ourselves, and how others will perceive it. Many problems we face here are not intrinsic to our city but are universal challenges faced in urban centers across the country. As residents and representatives, leaders, and initiators, it is our responsibility to be ever conscientious in the words we choose when talking about the city.

We must take responsibility for the civic process, not only participating in order that our interests be heard, but also speaking up when we witness inequality. Are we advocating for the disenfranchised? Are we working towards creating an inclusive process of decision-making where all members of our community have a voice and a platform?

We must take responsibility as creative problem-solvers, pulling together to work towards solutions, and resisting the pitfalls of infighting and blame.

We must take responsibility for the safety of our streets and address the devastating presence of substance abuse and addiction in our community. From fights in downtown bars, to drug-related gun violence in some neighborhoods, to domestic abuse in others, crime impacts all households. We have to find solutions that engage all residents in creating a safe and healthy community.

How do we move towards a Lowell where all residents feel safe and comfortable, feel they have options and opportunities to advance, whether they are professionals, students, families, artists, new immigrants? Whatever their path, we need to create opportunities for positive momentum to advance and grow. It is incumbent upon all of us to be our brothers' keepers.

The problems we face are not easy to solve, nor are they problems we can continue to live with if we hope to grow and prosper as a city-renewed.

Lowell's story of this moment is filled with challenge, hope, and choice, and the next chapter will depend upon us all.

What is your vision for this city? What specific effort are you committed to make your vision a reality?

Life's greatest challenges offer the greatest opportunities for growth, and therefore we must relish the chance to address any challenge presented to us, as the outcome will benefit us all.

. . . And Howe

By **Paul** on November 19, 2013
—

The morning began with dark purple clouds bumping in the sky lanes above a sherbet-rinsed sunrise of raspberry and peach. Wind kicked the brittle leaves every which way, and the frigid air made you feel extra alive in your skin. All good for a big day in Lowell. Spirits were up for an event that doesn't come often in a lifetime: the dedication of a permanent bridge over a serious river.

It was no ordinary time at 10 a.m. at the northernmost curb on Merrimack Street. These folks could have been gathered for the launch of spaceship. The scene turned majestic when the milling-around crowd of hundreds was signaled forward by the construction workers who waved everyone ahead towards the middle of the span where a podium was set up for the ceremony. What a collection of people: political figures, public administrators, writers and reporters, photographers and filmmakers, ardent citizens and family members of the honoree, university personnel, neighbors from the Acre and Pawtucketville, the bridge builders themselves, state transportation agency officials, and the kids kept out of school, along with the proud, the curious, and the devoted locals.

City Manager Lynch said this bridge has been coming for decades. Decades. He reminded us that former City Manager John Cox and his team outlined a vision for this bridge at the head of Merrimack Street. It was fitting that the man who in January is expected to be the community's next mayor, City Councilor Rodney Elliott, had made the motion to name the bridge for Richard P. Howe. History was cycling in the wind.

Today we honored a man who became a kind of monument in front of our eyes. Chancellor Meehan praised his courage and integrity, describing how he had saved local control of the city's school system at a critical moment. Rep. Kevin Murphy extolled his legal acumen. Rep. Golden brought congratulations from state Sen. Donoghue and saluted him as the true dean of city's political brotherhood and sisterhood. Rep. Nangle thanked Mary Howe for sharing her husband with us and counted out the 2,000 Tuesday nights on which he made "government" an action word in the Council chamber. Mayor Patrick Murphy spoke for every citizen in recognizing the contributions of an uncommon man. Congresswoman Tsongas sent a flag flown over the dome in Washington, D.C. And his daughter Martha called him a living bridge for the public work he had done as a representative of the people and a leader of the people. She said his example illustrates how politics can be a noble profession. All this was said about a high-grade baseball player, honorable family man, and dedicated attorney who made time in his life for civic duty. A record of 40 years of service, including four terms as mayor of his city, shows up about as often as a new huge blue bridge across the Merrimack.

In my mind, I keep coming back to the crowd. What a tribute in the form of showing up. Not only quantity, but quality. Talent attracts talent, and the senior Dick Howe brought out a highly enriched collection of admirers. None of us there today will probably ever stand again in the middle of that bridge, which for its first few open hours existed as a scenic overlook. We feasted on spectacular views of the rushing rocky river, the new Saab building for emerging technologies on the north campus of UMass Lowell, and the glassy University Crossing under construction on the opposite bank. At our backs was the long stretch of Merrimack Street as far as we could see. On the open roadway, we, the people, occupied the structure, railing to railing, lingering a bit to remember what it felt like as a pedestrian way. Once the cars and trucks get at it, the vehicles will shape the experience of going over the water. This is something new for Lowell. We have been cutting a lot of ribbons these past few years. Historians will notice the beginning of the twenty-first century in this city. We got a new bridge today. We dedicated it to Mr. Howe of Lowell.

Lowell Celebrates Nelson Mandela

By **Dick** on December 13, 2013
—

The African Cultural Association of Greater Lowell in collaboration with the Lowell Community Charter Public School organized a memorial celebration in honor of the late Nelson Mandela tonight at the Charter School on Jackson Street in Lowell. The fast-moving program consisted of speeches, music, dancing, and a video tribute. Pastor Jerry Menyongai said everyone is placed on Earth for a reason and that by celebrating the life of Mandela, we are all reminded that one person can make a difference. State Senator Eileen Donoghue praised Mandela as a shining example for Lowell because our city's greatness has been based on the integration of people from many countries and cultures as well as on the preservation of those cultures. In honoring Mandela, she said, we must remember the importance in society of fairness, equity, and justice. One of the masters of ceremonies, Bowa Tucker, said just because we are free that does not relieve us of the responsibility of working to make all people free. Mayor Patrick Murphy reminded us that poverty is not addressed through charity but rather through justice. He quoted Robert F. Kennedy in South Africa speaking about the way great men like Mandela can bend the arc of history. While most of us do not have that power, we have the capacity in our lives to emulate Mandela in small ways, and that many ripples can build into a giant wave. The program included music by the Lowell Community Charter Public School Percussion Band; singing by Daniela Deny and Samone Cobb of Lowell High school; traditional African music by the Osibi Drumming & Singing Group of Lowell; and traditional music and dancing by the Singo Dance Troupe of Vermont.

Goodbye to Recycling Boxes

By **Dick** on December 28, 2013
—

Yesterday morning, I lugged my green rectangular recycling box out to the snowbank that serves as a curb and plopped it down on a level surface to prevent it from sliding away. The weight of accumulated newspapers and torn-up wrapping paper held it in place. A half dozen cardboard tubes, once the innards of that wrapping paper when it was in its pristine state, protruded from the box. I paused to take a picture of the box in its final day of service. It needed to be replaced anyway, since it had a growing fracture at one corner. I'm looking forward to the switch to the new 96-gallon recycling bins on wheels. There will be a lot less bundling of newspaper and cardboard because the new container will allow me to toss it inside. I understand the concerns about the size and weight of the new containers, especially for elderly persons, but I hope that won't be a problem. I have a green-topped lid on my recycling bin and have my trash picked up on Thursdays (in non-holiday weeks). The color-coded calendar on the City's recycling page shows my first recycling pickup as next Friday, January 3 (the New Year's Day holiday causes all trash pickup to slide back a day).

Lowell Political Year in Review: 2013

By **Dick** on December 29, 2013
—

With no City Council meeting last or this week due to Christmas and New Year's Day, there's not much new to report on politics in the city. That's good because with this being the final Sunday of 2013, it's time to review the year in local politics. Here are some observations to consider:

Counter-Revolution in Lowell: I'm convinced that much of the political conflict in Lowell flows from deeply held philosophical differences between those who embrace change and those who embrace the past—progressives and conservatives to use the common labels. In that, the city is a microcosm of the entire country. It's been this way for a long time, and will continue to be so well into the future with momentum shifting from one side to the other. The pendulum swung dramatically in the progressive direction in November 2012 when Elizabeth Warren defeated Scott Brown to win the election to the U.S. Senate. In Lowell, Warren beat Brown by 17 percent despite much of the city's power structure, Democrat, Republican, and unenrolled, being firmly behind Brown. Warren's victory in the city was the result of a lot of hard work by people young and old, many of whom were either immigrants or just new to the city. Few of those who were most active in that campaign had ever participated in city politics.

In the aftermath of Warren's trouncing of Brown in Lowell there was much speculation that the city had pivoted politically in a new, much more progressive direction. That caused a reaction, a counter-revolution if you will, by conservative elements in the city led by the *Lowell Sun* and radio station WCAP. Mayor Patrick Murphy, one of the few elected officials in Lowell who had vigorously campaigned for Elizabeth Warren and the foremost proponent of progressive policies for City government, became the prime target of the conservative struggle to regain dominance. The attacks reached their peak on April 2, 2013, with Councilor Rita Mercier's motion of "No Confidence" in Mayor Murphy and then tapered off with the knowledge that Murphy would not seek reelection to the city council. But there were many other skirmishes in this struggle: backyard chickens, bike lanes, disdain for "professional" management, Jack Mitchell and his "Taliban" comment about neighborhood power jockeying, Gerry Nutter and the Election Commission, the list goes on.

There are many explanations for the city council election results, but part of the outcome, at least, was attributable to the conservative elements in the city fighting hard to strengthen their long-time grip on City government, a grip they feared was slipping away after the Warren victory in Lowell in 2012. That 2012 election, just like the 2013 city council election, was just another chapter in a long and ongoing struggle over the city's direction. The length of time someone has lived here has nothing to do with this conflict other than the fact that many of the people who have been drawn to Lowell by its embrace of the arts, its higher education opportunities, and the high value placed on its immigrant culture and heritage are progressive in their politics and their outlook on life. This is all about change. It's a struggle between those who embrace change and see it as a positive thing and those who resist change and look to the past for comfort and guidance. That's what it's about in Lowell, and that's what it's about across the United States.

City Council Election: City government is involved in our daily lives in so many ways that any time four new councilors are elected, it's big news. The newly elected councilors are Dan Rourke, Jim Milinazzo, Bill Samaras, and Corey Belanger. Those who are leaving the council are Mayor Patrick Murphy, who did not seek reelection, and Marty Lorrey, Vesna Nuon, and Joe Mendonca, who all failed to win reelection. Returning to the council are Rita Mercier, Rodney Elliott, Ed Kennedy, Bill Martin, and John Leahy.

Violence and Public Safety: Although the police and the City administration assured residents that statistically there was less crime this year than last, many residents felt differently. In some cases this was based on personal knowledge, but in others it was a perception that was fueled by various sources with a variety of motives. While the most noteworthy incidents of violence involved shootings in the lower Highlands and Centralville, Downtown also became the focus of the public safety debate, first in a search for ways to hold downtown bars accountable for the behavior of unruly patrons and then because of something commonly referred to as "aggressive panhandling." A vote to enact an ordinance banning panhandling in the downtown will be one of the first orders of business for the new council. Strategies for dealing with violence and crime will also be high on the new agenda.

UMass Lowell's continued expansion: There are almost too many good things to say about the continued growth of UMass Lowell. There are new buildings such as the Health and Social Sciences Building and a new parking garage, both on South Campus, and the rushing-to-completion University Crossing on the site of the former St. Joseph's Hospital. Then there is the increasing recognition of the university for its academic programs and the great value received for cost of tuition. The University continues to raise its profile in other ways, moving its sports teams to Division I, hosting a debate between Congressmen Ed Markey and Steve Lynch in the Special U.S. Senate Primary Election, and presenting a great public interview of outgoing Boston Mayor Tom Menino by former *Lowell Sun* and *Boston Globe* reporter Brian Mooney in a Lunchtime Lecture at the Inn and Conference Center. However, lurking just beneath the surface is friction between the University and some elements in the city. Some councilors have latched onto a theme that the University taking ownership of so many properties is a bad thing, since it deprives the City government of potential property tax revenue. Chancellor Meehan launched a preemptive attack on that notion at the Lowell Plan Breakfast with a detailed presentation and pamphlet documenting all of the economic benefits afforded Lowell by the University, but the talk will persist into the new year.

Change in Lowell Public Schools: Steve Gendron, who served on the city council in the 1990s and on the planning board for the past few years, ran for school committee and won a seat. With all six incumbents running for reelection, the odd man out was Bob Gignac, who finished seventh. Gignac, who is only in his mid-20s, has a promising future ahead of him in Lowell politics and public service despite this slight setback. In other school news, Brian Martin, former city councilor, mayor, City Manager, pro hockey team GM, and Congressional district director, was hired as the new Lowell High School headmaster and wasted no time in putting his imprint on LHS. In perhaps the biggest news, the school committee embarked on a comprehensive study of its facilities including Lowell High School.

Senator Markey: When former Lowell resident John Kerry was confirmed as Secretary of State, it triggered a special election to replace him. Longtime Democratic Congressman Ed Markey defeated Republican nominee Gabriel Gomez in the June 25 special election. Markey beat Gomez in Lowell, 58 percent to 42 percent.

Sustainable Lowell 2025: The City Council unanimously adopted "Sustainable Lowell 2025," a comprehensive master plan that "establishes long-term policies and a shared vision for smart, responsible development within the city." Enormous effort went into the creation of this plan, both by the City's planning department and many community volunteers in numerous working sessions. "Sustainable Lowell 2025" is a comprehensive and progressive document that provides a road map for the city going forward. Unfortunately, since the council voted to adopt the plan, I can't recall it being mentioned again during council meetings. Perhaps that's because it's silent on the issue of double telephone poles and similar issues that occupy so much of the council's time during meetings.

Personnel Turnover: Chief Financial Officer Tom Moses recently left Lowell when he was hired to be town manager in Hudson. He has not yet been replaced. Ken Lavallee retired as superintendent of police in March. He was immediately replaced on an interim basis by Deputy Superintendent Deborah Freidl, and in November the city manager chose veteran captain Bill Taylor to be the new superintendent. Although not based at City Hall, the company that had run Lowell Memorial Auditorium for decades, Mill City Management, did not seek renewal of its contract and was replaced by a company called Global Spectrum, which may have lacked the local political connections of Mill City but which already manages the Tsongas Center for UMass Lowell. Other personnel changes with Lowell connections included Ed Davis resigning as police commissioner of Boston; Dennis Piendak retiring after 28 years as town manager of Dracut; Tom Menino not seeking reelection as mayor of Boston, and state Representative Marty Walsh winning the election to replace him; and Dan Rivera beating Willie Lantigua to become the new mayor of Lawrence.

Greater Lowell Vocational in the news: The Greater Lowell Vocational School Committee had much difficulty agreeing on a new superintendent for the school (although they did ultimately select one who has already started work). The school faces a more significant challenge from a dispute with the City of Lowell over the Constitutionality of the current method of selecting vocational school committee members.

No Slots: Our Tewksbury neighbors rejected a proposed slot parlor when 61 percent of the 2500 residents who participated in an August town meeting voted against the proposal. The Tewksbury outcome seemed to empower other communities around the state to stand up to the pro-slots momentum.

2014

Moody Gardens

By **Mehmed Ali and Beth Brassel** on January 7, 2014

Between 1950 and 1970, Lowell, Mass., saw its status as an industrial dynamo erode. The textile industry shrank to almost nothing, and many residents quit on the city, moving to the suburbs or leaving the area in search of good jobs. In 1950, native son Jack Kerouac published his coming-of-age novel *The Town and the City*, set partly in a fictional Lowell, and followed it in 1957 with the best-seller *On the Road*, a book that altered the national culture. During these two decades Lowell also saw its first Greek-American mayor, its first Polish-American mayor, and, in 1964, Mayor Ellen Sampson became the first woman to hold that office in Lowell. Meanwhile, during these years the early seeds of what was to become a national civil rights movement were being sown at a small bar on Moody Street.

In 1933, a common victualer license was issued to Frank Dondero and Henri St. George to operate a bar at 294 Moody Street. Both men were sons-in-law of Louis Berube. The Moody Gardens Café stayed in the Berube family until its closing in 1964. From the start, the owners were often at odds with the City's license commission. In 1936, the bar's license was suspended for opening before 1:00 p.m. on Thanksgiving Day. A year later, the *Lowell Sun* reported that a complaint was made against Dondero for distributing "paper matches containing 'double meaning' pictures of a lewd nature." The complaint was dismissed when Dondero convinced the commission that he realized the matchbooks were "a big mistake."

By the 1950s, the Moody Gardens was, as one former patron stated, "at rock bottom." However, in 1957, the bar's fortunes changed. Eugene Berube, the manager, invited an all-women's Country & Western band to play at the Moody Gardens. The band had been performing across the street at the Silver Star and was drawing a crowd of gay and lesbian patrons. When the gay crowd was, as a former member of the band put it, "pushed aside," Berube invited the band to play at the Moody Gardens. Along with the band came lesbians from not only Lowell, but also Lawrence, Wilmington, Chelmsford, Dracut, and as far away as Worcester. The women began staking out a place for themselves in Lowell and, ultimately, a presence in the larger society.

In a 2004 interview obtained from Boston's History Project archives, a lesbian who was a Moody Gardens regular described the experience of being gay in the 1950s: "Everyone who I have talked to said that they thought they were the only one who was gay." As another Moody Gardens regular wrote in a letter housed at the Lesbian Herstory Archives in New York, "You were an ugly duckling in a world of swans." Without a place to gather, it was difficult for gay people to meet and gain a sense of community. When gay people did meet at a bar, there was always "that fear of being asked to leave or physically being hurt when you left at night."

Thus, by inviting the band and opening the bar to its gay and lesbian following, Berube provided an opportunity for a community to form. Describing the importance of the Moody Gardens to the lesbians who called it home, the same woman wrote, "It was our world; yes, a small world, but if you're starving you don't refuse a slice of bread, and we were starving."

Despite the police vice squad and the state Alcoholic Beverage Commission aggressively monitoring Moody Gardens, Berube ran the bar as the haven that it had become for area lesbians. Describing police surveillance of the bar, one woman said: "The vice squad used to come in like two and three times a night. They'd come in the bar side and look all around, and they'd walk in the other side and look all around, and they'd go out. You'd figure, well, they're gone. Fifteen minutes later, there's three paddy wagons at both doors and they'd throw us all in the paddy wagon, . . . take everybody, clean the whole place right out."

When asked if the police would pick up the straight patrons, the woman said, "No." After being arrested, the lesbian patrons would be held for three hours and then allowed to bail themselves out for ten dollars each. The charge was usually "being drunk," regardless of whether a person had consumed alcohol. If there is doubt as to why the vice squad was targeting Moody Gardens, minutes from a City License Commission meeting make it clear that the presence of lesbian clientele brought the police attention. The August 3, 1964, minutes include a statement read to the commission by Superintendent of Police Peter D. Guduras.

Objecting to a request by Berube to transfer the bar's license to a different location, Guduras notes:

" . . . on diverse dates between October 1962 and July 1964, despite many warnings from members of the Liquor and Vice Squad and other police officers, the manager, Mr. Berube, has allowed persons of dubious character, whose actions while on the premises indicated a suggestion of sexual promiscuity between persons of the female gender . . . ."

Among the complainants at the 1964 hearing were Father Conroy representing Father Horgan of St. Patrick's Church and a host of Acre neighborhood residents. In 1964, the bar closed, and Berube invested in another establishment, The Lantern, in Tyngsboro, Mass.

Fifteen years after the Moody Gardens closed, 175 women gathered at the Pulaski Club in Lowell for the first reunion of what would come to be known as the Old Moody Gardens Gang. In the days prior to email and Facebook, a handful of former Moody Gardens patrons scoured New England looking for lesbians who had been a part of the bar's community. The gathering at the Pulaski Club would be the first of several reunions. These women understood that their willingness to endure routine harassment and arrests by the police paved the way for future generations of gays and lesbians to claim an identity and a place in society.

There are other pieces of Lowell's gay community history that have yet to be uncovered. In 1950, Manny Dias, a well-known local entertainer, was barred from performing in Lowell because of previous appearances as a female impersonator. Dias's case was taken up by Brad Morse, a local lawyer who would eventually go on to become the U.S. Congressman representing Lowell and its district. After multiple hearings before the License Commission, Dias won back his right to perform in Lowell. Although his case did not repeal the commission's "no female impersonator" rule, he could continue performing. In 1958, he performed at Happy Helen's, billed as "Chiquita, the Cuban Bombshell."

The history of Lowell is a tapestry of smaller, diverse pieces: immigrant, working-class, industrial, and women's history. The story of Moody Gardens and the role the bar played in the shaping of the identity of many people, an emerging community, and a larger social movement, has been well documented in the canon of gay community history. The legacy of persecution and perseverance of Manny Dias, the Moody Gardens Gang, and many other Lowellians over the decades helped to win the civil rights of today and should not be forgotten.

Farewell, Joyce Denning, Teacher

By **Paul** on February 5, 2014
—

There was a disturbance in the Learning Force this week when Joyce Denning passed away. She was Professor Joyce Denning of the Political Science Department at UMass Lowell. I am one of the lucky ones who can say she was my teacher. There are hundreds of us. Thousands. She is still my teacher because what she put in my head and soul is part of what guides me day to day.

I looked for a photo of Joyce on the internet. I could not find one, so I went to my notebooks where I knew I had a picture of her cut out of a yearbook from 1975. It was on a page with other faces, so I had to block it off with paper to get a scan of Joyce alone. It was just like her not to have a bunch of pictures on the web—it wasn't about her, ever—it was about the students. She gave everything. She gave her knowledge, boundless time, genuine attention, and her money (she and her longtime co-conspirator, history professor Dean Bergeron, created a fund to help students with special projects and later for the International Relations Club activities). In lieu of other acts of sympathy and generosity, Joyce suggested that people, if they wish, should send a contribution to the fund in her honor.

When I transferred from Merrimack College to Lowell State College in the fall of 1974, Joyce and Dean welcomed me into their classes and office clubhouse in Coburn Hall. I bonded with them immediately, and took every course they offered. Joyce's political sociology sessions were full of insights about American political culture. She'd say, "Listen for the instructions because sometimes they mean the opposite: 'The least you can do is vote' meaning, perhaps, 'the most you should do is vote because the establishment doesn't want a lot of activists out there mucking up the system they control.'" She used a political theory textbook titled *Community and Purpose in America* by Mason Drukman that dug deep into the tension between community and liberty that defines us today—think, Moveon.org vs. Tea Party. When there was no course in the catalog that covered political economy, she let me design one and work with her one-on-one, reading Marx, Schumpeter, Heilbroner, and others.

For a time, Joyce managed the Second Chance program at the University, which allowed older persons to register for classes and continue their education. One of my aunts signed up for that. Joyce was an institution in Coburn Hall for a long time. Her door was always open. Her mind was always open. She'd say, "Don't do something just to get your ticket punched—follow your passion." She encouraged us to be curious, to be wise, to be kind, to be engaged. Joyce lives in all of us.

A Fun Bazaar at Mill No. 5

By **Dick** on February 5, 2014
—

Last Saturday, I visited Mill No. 5 on Jackson Street for "Love Buzz," a pre-Valentine's Day shopping and entertainment bazaar at a great new Lowell venue. I'm a big fan of Western Avenue Studios and the other artist outlets in the city and was pleased to discover that the retail outlets at Mill No. 5 form a nice complement to the existing creative-economy outposts. Words like quirky, eclectic, and funky describe a lot of what you find on Jackson Street. It's the kind of stuff you don't see at malls or come upon online by accident. Here it's all in one place, which allows you to wander around and make exciting and fun discoveries. Best of all, many of the vendors I spoke with not only do their work in Lowell but live here, too. The best place to get current info about what's going on there is at the Little Bazaar blog.

Bernie: Ideas Matter

By **Paul** on March 5, 2014
—

I appreciated the farewell remarks of City Manager Bernie Lynch at his final City Council meeting as Manager last night. Especially this part, recorded by my colleague Dick Howe's notes:

> "Through all of that, I was hoping to build a sense of community. Lowell is a great city. Every place can become a better community. Hopefully that came through. That we act like a business, but retain our humanity. I've had great support from the City Council. I've been very fortunate that as I walk the streets of the city, the response I get is almost always very positive. Hearing from people in the city who have expressed appreciation has really been heartwarming. I've said that I fell in love with the city in the 1970s when it was at its low point and am fortunate to close out my relationship when the city is at a high point."

Bernie, UMass Lowell Chancellor Marty Meehan, and I all learned from some of the same professors in the political science department at UMass Lowell before it was so named. We were interested in politics, government, democracy—and we absorbed the ideas we were introduced to, wrestled with difficult policy questions, and gained an intellectual foundation that would help guide our future application of civic concepts. Academic life deals with theory and practice. It's interesting to note that our discipline is called political science and lives in the social sciences side of academia. Behind the politics and the public administration in government are beliefs and values, as well as statistics, analysis, and evidence.

Representative democracy, our system, can't work without a sense of community among the citizens. If people don't have a stake in public life, they are less likely to participate, minus a crisis. Political science as a social science has no soul without a commitment to humanity. That humanity is expressed in the countless decisions made every day by people who make the government work in any city.

I was glad that Bernie Lynch framed his efforts in high-minded terms. It is noble work to be in government, even if it doesn't look like it sometimes. With the chaos and coarseness that are part of our messy but indispensable democracy, the fundamental ideas sometimes get crowded out or twisted for short-term gain. We had a textbook in the Coburn Hall classrooms of the 1970s which I go back to now and then to read about "community and purpose" and remind myself of what is at stake.

Paul J. Sheehy: A Remembrance

By **Marty Meehan** on March 16, 2014

It was Irish Cultural Week in Lowell. As the family prepared for his wake and funeral, Paul Sheehy's voice was heard at the Acre Forum as he recalled growing up in his beloved Acre. As St. Patrick's Church filled with hundreds of family, friends, colleagues, and admirers to mourn, celebrate, and remember Paul Sheehy, a group was being led through the Acre to learn about and experience the Acre of his birth, his baptism, his education, his nature and nurture. As the Mass ended, Fr. Dan Crahen, OMI, invited three people to the altar to offer words about Paul Sheehy: Marty Meehan (an admirer, a former colleague, former 5th District Congressman, and now Chancellor of UMass Lowell); Attorney Victor Forsley (Paul's longtime friend and fellow Lowell State College/Suffolk University Law School alum); and Paul's daughter and youngest child, Elizabeth Sheehy. Here are Chancellor Meehan's remarks from March 15, 2014.—MS

Paul J. Sheehy was born in the Acre section of Lowell on November 1, 1934. He was the youngest of seven children. The Sheehys were everything Irish, Catholic, and St. Patrick's Parish.

I always marveled at how tough and strong Paul could be in dealing with adversity. It's a trait he had to learn early. His father, Joe Sheehy, a Lowell firefighter, was killed in the line of duty when Paul was only nine years old. His mother Mary was left to raise her family on her own.

After graduating from St. Patrick's School and Keith Academy, Paul earned his bachelor's degree in education from Lowell State College, where he was a standout baseball and basketball player. Paul began teaching in the Lowell public schools while attending Suffolk University Law School, where he earned his Juris Doctorate in 1964.

Paul set his sights on making a difference in public service, running for state representative later that year. And, Paul didn't pick an easy race either. In those days, two representatives were elected per district. Paul ran against two popular incumbents, Connie Kiernan and Archie Kenifick. But Paul's brothers and sisters and their huge group of friends and family had become a true force in the city. Some people at the time thought that Connie Kiernan was vulnerable, but when Paul topped the ticket it was Archie Kenifick who was left out.

Paul rose quickly in the House of Representatives, forging relationships, earning a seat on the powerful Ways and Means Committee and the Vice Chairmanship of the Education Committee. And it was in the House where Paul began his lifelong commitment to provide a high quality public education for anyone who was willing to work at it, regardless of race, gender, or economic status. He wrote the legislation creating Middlesex Community College in Bedford. He wrote a law establishing the Greater Lowell Regional Vocational Technical High School. He wrote legislation and was the chief architect of the merger of Lowell State and Lowell Technological Institute. And, make no mistake about it, we would not have a world-class public research university in Lowell without Paul J. Sheehy. The doctoral program in education at UMass Lowell that has produced some of the finest educators in the state was advocated for by Paul and funded as a result of his efforts.

Paul left the legislature to run for Congress in 1972. It was the most hotly contested Congressional race in the country that year, and Paul finished second in a crowded field of nine candidates. Paul finished far ahead of five other Lowell candidates in the race, establishing himself as a political force in Lowell for years to come.

Paul served as Lowell City Manager in 1974 and 1975 and served on the staffs of Congressman Joe Early of Worcester and Congressman Jim Shannon of Lawrence. In 1984, Paul was elected to the Massachusetts state Senate where he continued to advocate for public education, delivering funding for the construction of 14 new public schools in Lowell and proposing and securing funding for a permanent Middlesex Community College in downtown Lowell. I remember being thrilled but stunned when Paul got Middlesex Community College to open a campus in downtown Lowell. I asked him how he did it. He explained that Frank Keefe, the planning director in Lowell when he was City Manager, was now the Governor's top secretary, Administration and Finance, and that he set up a meeting and went to see him—and those of you who know Paul, well, let's just say he could be persuasive. If we had an audio recording of that meeting it probably went something like this: *Marty in his own way then did his best Paul Sheehy voice and recreated the conversation—it was warm, funny, and right on! Lots of laughs from those in the Church, especially from Paul's family.*

Lowell has had a lot of great legislators over the years, and I was having lunch with one of them last week, Steve Panagiotakos. Steve made the point that Paul Sheehy arguably did more for Lowell as a legislator than anyone who ever served. What would Lowell be like without the University and the Community College? Hundreds of people who never knew who Paul Sheehy was went to college, succeeded, and have a better life because of his commitment to public education.

Paul was an incredibly effective legislator because he worked relationships. He was intensely loyal, and he always kept his word. If Paul told a Governor or Senator he was going to do something, he did it, no matter what. Paul didn't care about getting credit.

I think we have entered an era in government where politicians seem to care more about optics and how things appear, rather than substance and how things actually are. Paul didn't care about optics; he was always about the substance—and it is a good thing he was.

Paul also changed the lives of everyone he worked with—for the better. Young people on the staffs of Congressman Early and Jim Shannon, as well as his own staffers at the State House—ALL

STILL TALK about the lessons of life that Paul Sheehy taught them. I know, I was one of them! Paul influenced my life more than anyone, except, perhaps, my own father. Paul pushed all the young people around him to get an education—to go to Law School, to get your master's or why don't you get your doctorate?

Paul gave advice and counsel; he'd give you every dollar he had in his pocket if you needed it. He might give you the push you needed, and with me, more often than not, a good kick in the pants—all to get you headed in the right direction.

Paul was known as a conservative Irish Catholic, but Paul always fought discrimination based on race, gender, or sexual orientation. And I have never met anyone more pro-woman, pushing young women staffers to go and get an advanced degree, go for positions of power, and better careers—and Molly and Paul's three daughters are an example of that.

So, as we say goodbye to Paul, I want to say, Thank you, Paul—for leaving this world better than you found it—for positively impacting so many people you met—as well as positively impacting hundreds of thousands you never met. And through it all, as the lyrics of one of your favorite song goes—You did it—You did it your way.

I, we, love you.

Dismantle the South Common? Hands Off

By **Paul** on April 15, 2014
—

Early in 2014 there was increasing chatter from some circles in the city promoting the replacement of the downtown Lowell High School with a new one on the South Common.

The South Common was created for the enjoyment of all the residents of the city. The South Common is not an empty lot waiting for a better use. The South Common is functioning well for its designated purpose, thank you.

The South Common is scheduled for a major renovation, based on a thoughtful plan put together for the City of Lowell by a well-respected landscape architecture firm—and with significant community input. We have been waiting for years for a major investment in this park. The South Common is part of the South Common Historic District, and the Lowell Historic Board has a say in the razing of existing structures and design of new structures in the district.

The South Common is not a good location for a new high school. I live on Highland Street. No secret. The idea of injecting many hundreds of additional cars of teachers and students into already thickly congested Thorndike, Gorham, and Highland streets is not a good idea. In addition to enhancing the quality of life of neighbors and recreational users, as an active green space the South Common can be an asset for Sal Lupoli's planned residential development at the former Comfort Furniture/Hood Co. complex and for the future Judicial Center in the Hamilton Canal District.

Who speaks for open space in the city? Who speaks for Nature? Who speaks for the current users of the South Common? Who speaks for this important part of Lowell's heritage?

HISTORY AS IT HAPPENS

Chicago Lessons

By **Paul** on May 21, 2014
—

I'm back from a family vacation in Chicago, Illinois, one of the great cities of the USA. It was my first visit to a city that I associate with Carl Sandburg, Barack Obama, Studs Terkel, Albert Halper, Poetry *magazine (founded by Harriet Monroe and Alice Corbin),* Cloud Gate *by Anish Kapoor, the Cubs and Blackhawks, skyscrapers, Ferris Bueller,* The Fugitive *with Harrison Ford, and the Democratic Party's 1968 national convention. All this and a lot more was packed into three days on the ground on the shore of Lake Michigan. I came back with some observations about what we in Lowell might learn from Chicago's way of presenting itself as a city, no matter the vast difference in scale. Certain lessons can be customized for a smaller historic city and do us some good.—PM*

1. Mark your special buildings. The Chicago Landmarks Commission has a program of simple building plaques fabricated in durable materials that provide basic information about historic buildings (name, date, when built, when restored, purpose, architects, developers). Lowell could do this now. A friend of mine from London who teaches "urban regeneration" said Lowell could add another whole layer of public story, the revitalization, by marking the preserved buildings, which would not only raise the profile of the world-class preservation work but also draw in another segment of visitors.

2. Do more with the waterways. The Chicago Architecture Foundation and a few other groups offer daily guided boat tours of the city on the Chicago River, which runs from Lake Michigan (Chicago's waterfront) through downtown (The

Loop) and branches in two directions, eventually connecting to the Mississippi River. Like Lowell, much of the old building stock backs up to the river, but the recent adaptive reuse of commercial buildings now emphasizes the water view, especially with new residences outfitted with balconies. Chicago is building about 20 miles of a river walk on both sides of the river, which is not wide at any point downtown (maybe half the width of the Merrimack River where it swings around our downtown). The boats, which hold about 200 people, were loaded on the sunny day we were on board. On the residential boom in downtown Chicago, there are now about 150,000 people living in the upscale waterfront area, with more buildings planned (one at 96 stories)—and this is a new phenomenon in the past 20-25 years.

3. Give people beautiful, clean parks with ambitious public art, flowers, and active-living features. There is no better example of a successful public space in the USA than Millennium Park in Chicago. The crowning glory of this new park is the most successful work of public art I have ever witnessed, *Cloud Gate* by Anish Kapoor, a wondrous shiny object that is a cosmic selfie-generator for the city, the sky, and all who come near. Its appealing organic shape (nicknamed "the bean" by locals) and ever-changing surface make this sculpture new every minute. Several other monumental artworks, including a fountain colored by light after dark, contribute to the park's personality. There's a large outdoor performance venue, acres of flowers and prairie plantings, extensive children's play areas, wide lawns, a serpentine bridge that could be a model for making the connection across Thorndike Street (from Dutton Street to Middlesex Street and Western Avenue), two-story climbing walls in the form of multi-sided sculptural blocks, and more. Maintenance and security workers were highly visible on a Sunday when we walked through.

4. Put your museums up front in your tourism promotion. Again, by comparison the scale is not fair, but the concept is applicable. Chicago boasts about its world-class museums: The Art Institute of Chicago and Field Museum of Natural History being the two most prominent. For the 40 million visitors to Chicago each year, the museums are high on the priority list of places of visit. We saw an all-star array of masterpieces at the Art Institute and met "Sue" the T. Rex at the Field Museum. The surprise of the visit was the Chicago Cultural Center, an exhibition, performance (small), presentation, and educational space, including offices for groups like StoryCorps, in a stunning restored building that was once the public library. And like a public library, the City of Chicago opens the doors of this Cultural Center to all for free every day. We saw exhibits of paintings of the 1920s-1930s jazz-era by African-American painter Archibald Motley; the distinctive graphic art of Valmor Products, a beauty product maker in the city from 1920 to 1980; and documentary photographs about preserved architecture in the city. The morning we were there, a crowd was gathering for a free concert by high-school musicians that was a tribute to Louis Armstrong. The building also houses offices for various community organizations and services. On a Lowell-scale, the Smith Baker Center has the potential to do some of the things that are being done in the Chicago Cultural Center. Also, being across from our Pollard Memorial Library, there's a nice public library link in our city, too.

5. Give people a view of the city from above. At least two of the immense skyscrapers (Hancock Observatory/360 Chicago and Sears/Willis Tower) have top-floor viewing that is mind-blowing and not for those of us who get weak in the knees at that height. At 360 Chicago, a person can actually lean out over the edge in a tilting glass encasement. I could hardly look

at those looking down. Lowell is a low-lying city. Fox Hall, Merrimack Plaza, Cross Point, the old SUN building—these are among the high-rises. Because of the historic city plan with the mill layout and canal system fed by the river, Lowell's urban plan is best understood via an aerial view. It would be great to have some place open to the public where people could take in the arrangement of the city, some high place we could call "Above Lowell" or something. People like being in the bird's nest. Where could we do this?

6. Push the world-cuisine menu of your city. Chicago is an ultra-ethnic city with something like 80 sub-neighborhoods and a plethora of peoples from every race and nationality, all of whom brought their food to town. This is one of Lowell's strengths. We can do more with this natural resource of world foods and American standards.

7. Put on a good face. Everywhere we went we met people who were glad to see the visitors to their city. "Welcome to Chicago," one businessman said on the sidewalk outside our hotel, after using our camera to take our picture with a friend who was showing us around.

HISTORY AS IT HAPPENS

Vigil in Memory of Fire Victims

By **Dick** on July 10, 2014
—

The Cambodian Mutual Assistance Association organized a candlelight vigil and prayer service this evening in memory of the seven victims of this morning's fire at 77 Branch Street. Tonight's event began at 5:30 p.m. with a gathering at Pailin City business district, a short distance on Branch Street from the fire scene. More than 150 neighbors and community members gathered there and were led to the site of the fire. Because it is still considered an active fire scene, the group stayed across the street from the building. Orange-robed Buddhist monks chanted prayers while crowd members held lit candles. Mayor Rodney Elliott spoke briefly, offering his condolences and praising the entire Lowell community, but especially the Lowell Fire Department, for the response to the fire. More than a dozen television cameras and an equal number of photographers and reporters covered the event.

'More For Your Dollar'

By **Paul** on August 28, 2014
—

Who wins with this resolution of the Demoulas drama? Out of the gate, it looks like everyone wins after six weeks of pain. When a lot of us in this region go back to Market Basket as full- or part-time shoppers and/or employees, let's hope that the "more" in "More For Your Dollar" says something about more fairness for people who go to work every day with something meaningful to do. In the end, that's how I see the outcome. The people of Market Basket Nation saw something fundamentally fair in the exchange of labor and compensation, in the exchange of goods for payment, and in the solidarity at a place of business when they looked at Market Basket. Can a common experience like this be a catalyst for larger change? We all watched it day to day, and many of us took part in some way. We have to wait for events to play out to know that answer. I've never seen anything like it in Greater Lowell. Those empty parking lots week upon week spoke volumes. People stuck together on this one. It was an astounding example of collective action. Community became a verb, an action word, in this case.

Market Basket Deal: Time to Celebrate

By **Marjorie Arons-Barron** on August 29, 2014
—

Since this blog post, the writer and her husband have become weekly shoppers at a Market Basket that opened just after the demonstrations.

It's hard not to be happy that the Market Basket board approved Arthur T. Demoulas' buyout of the supermarket company. Not that I shop there; there isn't one near me. But my sister does, and praises its bargains. What makes a mere onlooker happy is the sense that for once the little guy won, that is, a bunch of little guys, the employees standing in solidarity without a union and refusing to bend to moneyed corporate power. Refusing even though it put their jobs in jeopardy and, for six weeks, affected their family income.

This does seem to be a victory for time-honored (too often

ignored) corporate values of appreciating the employee, sharing profits through better benefits, and reinvesting in the company rather than having all profits go back to the shareholders. It is a triumph for the notion that CEO's can really care about the ordinary folks who work for them.

The *Boston Globe* just posted video of the pickup in activity in the warehouse. The mood is celebratory, though for some weary protesters this resolution seems to have come just in time. It's unclear, notwithstanding their dedication to CEO Artie T, how much longer they could have held out. Beyond the grit and determination they have all shown, employees and customers alike now have to have patience. The *Globe* reports that it will take seven to ten days until Market Basket shelves are 80 percent full, and it will take two weeks to be back to 100 percent.

It may be that some shoppers have found other places to buy their groceries, but I suspect some newcomers will try Market Basket for the first time. The outstanding question is whether Artie T's purchase of the "other side's" 50.5 percent leaves him with debt service so large it renders impossible the low low prices for shoppers and generous employee benefits. There may well have to be adjustments there. For the immediate future, at least there are 25,000 workers who will have a boss who seems to care about them and understand that they are the core of the company's success. Can you imagine Bank of America or American Airlines (substitute your own favorite ice-water-in-the-veins corporation) dealing with customers and employees as Market Basket has?

Rita Mercier Gets It Right

By **Dick** on September 23, 2014

—

Crime was a topic that dominated City Council meetings in the first half of 2014. There was much "tough on crime" rhetoric that ignored reality until Rita Mercier got right to the heart of the problem. Here is what I wrote about her remarks.—RPH

I commend Councilor Rita Mercier on her remarks this evening regarding crime in Lowell. My notes from the entire meeting are available online but I want to single out Councilor Mercier's comments, partly because she and I haven't shared a lot of common ground on issues, but mostly because she's right.

Here are the main points she made:

> People who are addicted to drugs don't belong in jail; they belong in treatment centers.

> There should be more treatment centers.

> There should be more and better-paying jobs.

> Many children in our city are on their own and receive no love or respect at home so they seek it out in gangs or use drugs to escape.

> One of the reasons children lack support at home is because so many parents must work two jobs to make ends meet, something caused by an overall lack of jobs that pay enough to cover basic expenses.

> Neither the police nor the council can solve this problem alone; it takes everyone in the city working together.

She said some other things, but the above is the gist of it.

Over the past few months as the temperature of the rhetoric has risen on the floor of the City Council, I've responded on this site to assertions that the problem is lenient judges who aren't enforcing the law. From 1986 to 1994, I did mostly criminal defense work in the Lowell District Court and Middlesex Superior Court, and I never encountered such leniency. If a crime has a mandatory minimum sentence as with illegal gun possession, you get sentenced if you're convicted. Period. The only discretion the judge has is to give you more than the minimum. The District Attorney has the power to reduce the charge to a lesser offense, but as anyone who was paying attention to our recent state primary election knows, District Attorneys are elected officials, so they've never been generous in dispensing get-out-of-jail-free cards to accused criminals. And if the defendant is found not guilty, he's not supposed to go to jail. Can we agree on that, at least?

My time as a defense attorney also coincided with an escalation in our "war on drugs." Remember when Bill Weld got elected governor back in 1990 on a tough on crime platform in which he famously said he wanted to introduce criminals to "the joys of making little rocks out of big rocks." Not wanting to be left behind in the "who can be tougher on drugs race," the state legislature instituted mandatory minimum sentences for repeat drug distributors. Fantastic. Lock up all the cartel traffickers. But that's not what happened. The people getting locked up for five full years were street junkies in Lowell who sold a few bags of heroin to finance their own use. The junkie would get arrested on a first offense, plead guilty for a sentence of probation, and be right back out on the street doing the exact same thing because he was an addict and nothing in the criminal justice system even attempted to deal with that. Arrested a second time for the same thing, he was carted off to state prison for five years, a sentence more onerous than many who committed serious, violent crimes which had no minimum mandatory sentence. So, the state paid to incarcerate all these people only to have them emerge from prison five years later and begin the cycle all over again because their addictions were never effectively addressed.

As Councilor Mercier asserted tonight, if they were effectively treated for their addiction right from the start and helped to find a decent job, the cycle of crime and incarceration might end. It's not simple, and it's not cheap, but true leaders of the community don't duck complicated issues and hide behind cheap rhetoric to score political points. True leaders use their stature in the community to persuade their fellow citizens that there are no easy solutions to such complex problems and that the only hope we have of improving the situation is to all work together in a mature, rational way. That's what Rita Mercier did tonight. More public figures in the community should follow her example.

… HISTORY AS IT HAPPENS

For Cassie

By **John Wooding** on September 28, 2014
—

It felt like the summer of death. So much grief and mayhem in the world. So many examples of the ways in which we have become adept at killing and maiming each other: Syria, Iraq and Egypt, the Gaza Strip, Ukraine, ISIL, Boko Haram and, now, the scourge of Ebola. On top of all this we lost our dog. The death of a dog cannot mean much in a context of such global violence. But, with the distance of a few weeks, losing Cassie got me thinking about what it means to lose those whom you love—the now all too common experience in the world.

Cassie was a constant companion for over 16 years. But she didn't just die—we put her to sleep, as the phrase goes. But that's not true. She's not asleep. She's dead. She didn't "pass away," didn't simply expire. We had her euthanized. How brutal that sounds with its hygienic and, let's face it, fascist overtones. Assisted suicide? I don't think so. She did not directly ask for that. "Put down"? Even worse.

We do not have good words for what happened to her. We do not have good words for such losses. She is no longer here. No longer the constant presence that filled our life. I will never again feel her head on my knee, looking pathetic and endearing, trying to get me to share my food. I will miss the gentle warmth of her head. I will never again rub her belly or tousle her ears. She will never again greet me when I get home, tail-wagging, eyes expectant. I will never watch her run through the woods, vibrant with the joy of being a dog. I will never again see those ears go up when something catches her attention, never hear her bark or growl when she got a message from the dog planet.

It is the absence of theses things that hurts. In 16 years there were thousands upon thousands of small interactions, moments that pile up upon each other, building small mountains of memories. It is this way when a loved one dies, be they animal or human. Something goes missing, and you know you will never find it again. Some might say, "Well she was just a dog," but would we say that about a friend, a child, a mother? No, of course not. They are not "just a human being." Those we love are a relationship, a history. They are familiarity and comfort, they are the continuity of ourselves when so much else seems strange or threatening.

    I walked Cassie in the woods near our house innumerable times. I watched her bound through the grass when she was a puppy, chasing the squirrels and chipmunks she never caught. I called for her helplessly when she was gone too long and, when she eventually came back, smiled at the dirt and leaves on her face and her doggy happiness at being out and running free. I smiled, too, for having her safely again at my side. I watched while she dug holes in the ground; butt in the air, dirt flying from her paws like some manic backhoe. I spent hours fixing the seat belt and gearshift knob in a car we leased after her puppy enthusiasm for chewing left them ragged and beat-up. God knows, we still have the sofa that we had to have covered when she decided to make a meal of the cushions. I have thrown balls for her to chase and never bring back, sticks for her to catch and to chew, and given her a million treats—sometimes as a reward, mostly for just being her.

    Like most dogs, she was sad when you left the house and ridiculously, insanely happy when you returned. You could be gone a week, or merely taking out the trash—it didn't matter, the welcome was always the same. Dogs have no sense of time; at least that's what they say. They also say that dogs can learn about 160 words. Maybe. I have no idea how many words Cassie knew but I sure as hell talked to her like she understood everything. Did she have emotions? I am pretty sure she did—she really could seem happy or sad, or guilty or angry, or loving—at least that's what I think. Who knows? But her eyes were deep and brown and they watched constantly. They made her seem human. She may never have spoken, but in those eyes I swear there were answers to questions I dare not ask.

She slowed down as the years went by; the greeting was still there but it transformed to a slight raise of the head and a quick thump or two of the tail. She didn't gallop through the woods like a miniature deer any more, but she still ran and sniffed and investigated. Later still, watching her climb stairs, I could see how the old joints were beginning to seize up. She took to hopping down. It was easier for her and slightly comical to watch. But the eyes remained bright and knowing, and that never changed right up until the end. In the last few months it took her longer and longer to get herself upright. Stairs became impossible. I took to carrying her up so she could sleep in the bedroom with us, the way she always did. It was the least I could do. In the last few weeks she could hardly move, couldn't hear or see too well. Eventually, she could no longer stand. It was time.

So, she's gone. We played God. I only hope someone will love me enough to do the same thing when I can no longer stand or wash myself, or when I can no longer figure out where I am. Let me go from this world with some scrap of dignity left. I hope we gave that to her.

So, why share all this? Does the world need another sad tale of a dog that died? Probably not. But losing Cassie made me see this summer in a different and darker light. We have all watched as the world has staggered from one senseless act of violence to another. It has been made more poignant and tragic in this, the anniversary of that most senseless and stupid of human slaughters—World War I. It feels like 1914 all over again. No wonder we turn back to family and friends, to our dogs and cats, to home and to comfort. It is good that we do. And we can learn lessons from the animals we have in our lives, who are never just a dog or a cat, never just anything—for we share this world with them as we do with every other human being and every other animal. Our love and our concern for them make us better human beings, ones who know that the welfare of others is our concern. And yes, this past summer was just yet another long trail of death and destruction across the globe. And yes, I can explain this, discuss the politics, make the arguments. But, in the end, what does that really do? Losing Cassie made loss real. It made me realize, in a new way, why we need to demand peace and an end to war. So, this is all for those who have lost someone dear to them. And for Cassie, never just a dog.

Glass Half-Full and Filling Up

By **Paul** on October 3, 2014
—

For those able to attend yesterday's Lowell Plan Breakfast at the UMass Lowell Inn & Conference Center, a person would have to be hard-hearted not to have come away feeling better about the city and more optimistic about what's over the wooded horizon. The 300 people in the room heard two young bankers, graduates of the Public Matters leadership program, describe why they feel good about living and working in the city—the comments kept coming around to the high quality of community engagement they see every day. They care about Lowell because they see other people so invested in making this city a good place to be. They feel the energy that comes from people working the city like people work the land to make a garden. They take advantage of opportunities to enjoy being in the city, whether that is going to a baseball game or singing in a play.

And then one of our most enthusiastic businessmen shared a big idea that has the potential to lift a lot of spirits this winter. He said, "Why don't we take the wonderful example of the giant Christmas tree that strings out from the towering smokestack at Wannalancit Mills each holiday season and replicate the tree on smokestacks at all the mill complexes?" He showed an artist's conception of what it could look like. Somebody said it looked like the line of mountaintop beacon fires in a scene from *The Lord of the Rings*. Brilliant. Earlier, the retiring long-time president of our downtown community college got a standing ovation. She walked everyone down memory lane with before-and-after pictures of all the building projects that have borne success in 25 years or so. She gave a virtual tour of the new fine arts center coming at the old Boston and Maine Railroad depot on Central Street, and then let everyone know that she has another $10 million to spend on one more building for the downtown campus. The City Manager announced three big business developments that will bring scores of jobs to the city, including a medical devices company and a restaurant with a familiar Merrimack Valley name.

Finally, an acclaimed urban planner who has been helping to re-boot the city's downtown spoke in-depth about strategies designed to set the city on a course of greater vitality and stronger appeal as a distinctive American city. He said, There's no city like Lowell in the country. You have something special here. It's handsome, and a little rugged, and full of surprising special places and structures. Lowell is poised to attract more people to live and work in the city, especially "the millennials," those up and coming women and men with the kind of talent, ambition, and imagination that every city in Lowell's category wants to keep (among its own residents) and pull in from the outside.

He talked about the Downtown Evolution Plan and urged everyone to stick with it. So far, so good. This was coming from someone from away, somebody who works all over the country and travels across the globe doing the business of city planning. And he's feeling good about Lowell. Which is just what one elected official said to me today after thinking about what he had seen and heard yesterday. He said, I'm feeling like the glass is half-full and filling up.

Open Campus: 1970s Lowell High

By **Jim Peters** on November 15, 2014
—

More than forty years ago, when I was at Lowell High School and when Dick Howe, Jr., was in elementary school, I was very active in school. Many of my friends agreed with me about the Open Campus program at the high school, which was brought about partly to ease overcrowding. In 1969, Lowell had 17,000 students in 32 schools. The *Lowell Sun* reported that some members of the local government wanted to tear them down. My father was the School Superintendent, and he knew that, while some schools were severely dated, the city did not have the money or the resources to get the money, to rebuild all the schools. To ease overcrowding at the high school, he proposed an alternative plan in which students would be allowed to leave the campus for a half hour or forty-five minutes at a time to alleviate the crush of people.

There was not necessarily a strong legislative team, which Lowell now enjoys, to obtain state funding for school construction. Therefore, we were stuck in place. We had few resources, a great demand for action, and little pressure to put on the Boston-run legislature to help us. Boston was having its own problems with court-ordered busing for desegregation, and very few state legislators felt a strong compunction to solve problems in Lowell. My father had left a tenured position in Chicago (Harvey), Illinois to run the Lowell school system. There were those who thought he did a good job, including the *Lowell Sun* whose editor wrote, "Since coming to Lowell, Dr. Peters has effected some meaningful improvements in the school system" (3/7/72) and "He has also been confronted by the impossibility of promoting any major program for modernization and construction of new schools because the city simply cannot afford to underwrite too much at once." In the high school, he was stymied by a stronger union than that in the elementary schools. When he introduced an Open Campus for high school students, the policy was roundly criticized by teachers and it did not work well.

The simple idea had worked in Illinois, where students could go home for lunch. In Lowell, they were not afforded that luxury, and many students, seeing an opportunity to miss afternoon classes after their break, helped bring the system to a halt. It was largely interpreted in Massachusetts that the school system had run out of viable options. Perhaps it had.

I had always attended my father's schools, except for two years in Superior, Wisconsin, where I went to a Catholic school for a year-and-a-half. In every school, we had the option of going home for lunch. For us, Open Campus meant a half an hour to eat outside the building and a requirement that we go back to class. To the teachers and administrators in Lowell (not all, obviously), it was chaos.

The Open Campus plan was not an effort to undermine the teachers or the administrators at the high school. At that time, more than 2,000 students at the high school did not have the new building that came later. When my father tried to talk about building above- ground tunnels such as we have now to a new wing of the high school on the lot across the canal, the Proprietors of the Locks & Canals said that was not possible because the company owned the air rights over the waterways.

The Open Campus movement was an attempt to free up space in the cramped Lowell High School for students to use in an adult manner. Senior Class President Michael Viggiano told the *Sun* that a small walkout by students opposed to the plan had "no support" from members of the senior class or the "rest of the school. . . ." He said, "Their protest would increase administration and teacher disgust for the full Open Campus plan, which both the rebel students and the more moderate class officers would like" (Delia O'Connor, *Sun* staff). A group of students visited the newspaper office and said, "If the students do not work for the Open Campus plan by wearing their I.D. cards, picking up their litter, and showing respect for the rules, then they can kiss goodbye any plan they had for the Open Campus."

Most moderate students supported the plan. Some did not and were pegged as "the moderates." Even students who were doing well with their behavior would go to Study Hall under the Open Campus plan. That would be determined by their grades. If they were failing a subject, they had to go to Study Hall and could not participate in the Open Campus. School Committeeman George D. Kouloheras said, "Open Campus is not to make it easy for the students, but to make it easy for us to house the students. If we had a new school with lots of space, then I'd be all for the traditional school pattern (*Lowell Sun*). Mr. Kouloheras said it best. The idea was not to reward ignoble student behavior, but to reward good behavior and good grades. My father and Mr. Kouloheras were destined to land on opposite ends of many spectrums, but on this they agreed. The Open Campus was an attempt to make up for shortages that the schools were battling. Space was the major one. Self-discipline was the other. On March 7, 1972, the newspaper called for my father to get tenure. "We think that parents and the rank and file of Lowell's citizenry are willing to have him continue his work here in our city." I have many strong and good memories of my father. He was the only person in Plan E form of municipal government to finish first in both School Committee and City Council races. He beat his second-place School Committee challenger by more than 5,000 votes. He stayed here to provide us a good city to call home.

Parties

by **Jack McDonough** on Dec. 20, 2014
—

Well, here we are at the end of the year again. And you know what that means.

That means parties. Office parties. Neighborhood parties. Family parties.

Parties are nice, but when they all come within about three weeks of one another, it's a bit tiring.

There are problems, too. Not big problems—but party problems.

One of the first things I think of when I ponder these annual get-togethers is napkins. You never get cloth napkins at parties. That would be unreasonable. You can't expect the person giving the party to provide linens. So, of course, when you work your way down the buffet table you pick up a paper napkin.

That's fine with me. Except that paper napkins at holiday events are always too small and they always come with a seasonal greeting printed on them. You know, Merry Christmas or Happy New Year, or something like that.

It's not the message I mind. It's the ink. You can't wipe meatball gravy off your face with a napkin coated with ink. The best you can do is turn it inside out so the ink is on the other side. But you still have the size problem. Those printed napkins are always too small to do much good.

I'd be much happier with a big paper towel. Maybe two of them.

Then, of course, there is the problem of juggling the food on a paper plate and trying to cut a piece of chicken with a plastic knife. And it's impossible to do while you're standing up. There's never enough room for everyone to sit down. I understand that. That can't be helped. But even if you can find a chair, cutting up food on your lap is a dicey procedure.

And if you somehow have managed to juggle a plate of food and pick up a drink at the same time, you've got to find a place to put that drink down so it won't get knocked over. If you're standing up and you put it down on a table somewhere, someone is likely to pick it up by mistake and walk off with it. And if you're sitting down and you put it on the floor, someone—probably you—will end up kicking it over.

The quantity of food itself is never a problem at these parties. There's always plenty. The trouble is that there may be a lot of duplication. If it's a potluck kind of event, you can be sure that before the night is over, there will be four huge bowls of salad on the table.

And lasagna. There's always lasagna in a serving dish that's about the size of Rhode Island. I'm not a lasagna fan. Don't get me wrong. I love Italian food—and I guess lasagna is Italian. The word sounds Italian, and it's made of pasta. It's just that there's way too much pasta there for me. And then there are those layers of cheese. Most people must like lasagna though, because it's always there.

My strategy is to pick out only the kind of food you can eat with your fingers. Like chicken wings. Or pepperoni and cheese. Or ripple potato chips that you can use to scoop up a lot of dip. If you fill up on all that, you can skip the difficult stuff and just walk around with your drink.

Desserts are always plentiful. And there's almost always a big plate of brownies. Brownies are good. Especially if they're made with that dark, semi-sweet chocolate. As Rachael Ray would say, "Yum."

But that brings up the issue of gaining weight in December. That's why all the health club memberships go up in January.

HISTORY AS IT HAPPENS

Lowell Year in Review: 2014

by **Dick** on December 28, 2014
—

At its inaugural ceremony in January, the new city council unanimously selected Rodney Elliott to be Mayor of Lowell. The new council consists of reelected members Elliott, Rita Mercier, Ed Kennedy, Bill Martin, and John Leahy and newcomers Dan Rourke, Bill Samaras, Jim Milinazzo and Corey Belanger. (Prior council incumbents Marty Lorrey, Joe Mendonca and Vesna Nuon had failed to win reelection, and Patrick Murphy did not run).

At the first meeting of the new term, City Manager Bernie Lynch announced that he would leave the manager's post at the end of his contract in March. For most, this was a bolt-from-the-blue surprise.

Kevin Murphy, who had served as a state representative since 1997, was selected to replace Lynch as the new Lowell City Manager.

Rady Mom was elected to replace Murphy as the representative for the 18th Middlesex District.

Superintendent of Schools Jean Franco announced that she would not seek a new contract and retire at the end of the 2014-2015 academic year, making her the third consecutive superintendent to leave under similar circumstances (the other two being Karla Brooks Baehr and Chris Augusta Scott).

An early morning fire on July 10 at a multifamily apartment building on Branch Street left seven people dead and brought the community together in mourning for their loss.

An attempt by the board of Market Basket to oust Arthur T. Demoulas from the office of president of the company sparked a walkout by employees and a boycott by customers that lasted for weeks until the parties agreed to resolve the dispute by selling the entire company to Arthur T.

Violence continued to plague certain Lowell neighborhoods, especially in the first half of the year, despite more resources being devoted to the police department.

The Cambodian Mutual Assistance Association celebrated its 30th (not "25th" as originally posted) anniversary in Lowell.

A lightning bolt that struck and fatally damaged the brick smokestack at the Thorndike Factory Outlet (formerly the Hood Patent Medicine Company) brought to the surface a simmering discontent with the city's Historic Board and prompted a vigorous response from advocates of historic preservation.

Above are my top ten Lowell political events of 2014, but here are some other notable developments during the past year:

In January, workers at Lowell Memorial Auditorium discovered a Civil War battle flag that was encased in a frame that memorialized Solon Perkins, a young soldier from Lowell killed in action during the Civil War.

In April, students from the UMass Lowell Honors Program organized and hosted the first TEDx Lowell event at UTEC.

In May, Governor Patrick came to Lowell to proclaim Asian American Heritage Month, and Bill Nye the Science Guy was the commencement speaker at UMass Lowell.

In July, the Cross Point commercial complex (formerly Wang Laboratories' office towers) sold for $100 million.

In August, two-way traffic returned to downtown Lowell. (It has generally been well-received and was not as disruptive as some had predicted).

In September, UMass Lowell and Queen's University Belfast co-sponsored an Irish-American History Conference at the UMass Lowell Inn & Conference Center. Also in September, University Crossing held its grand opening, as did Café UTEC. The American Textile History Museum and Lowell Telecommunications premiered their *Lowell: Place of Invention* video that will be featured at the Smithsonian in the summer of 2015.

In October, Jeff Speck returned to speak at the Lowell Plan Breakfast about the progress of his "Downtown Evolution Plan" for Lowell. Also in October, Governor Patrick delivered $15 million for the redoing of the Lord Overpass; and *Mill Power*, a new Lowell history by Paul Marion, was launched with several readings in the city.

In November, the Kirk Street Clock alongside Lowell High School was rededicated thanks to the efforts of LHS Headmaster Brian Martin.

In December, the 2nd annual Lowell Social Media Conference was held at LTC; and La Boniche, a fixture of the downtown dining orbit since 1988, served its last meal.

At various times, voices were raised in the city council chambers about a Christmas Crèche, panhandlers, snow removal, bicyclists, and marathoners.

In the fall and early winter, several pedestrians were struck and killed by motor vehicles providing poignant examples of the need to pay more attention to pedestrian safety in the city.

After Erik Gitschier was hired to be the new Lowell Water Department Superintendent, Curtis LeMay was selected to replace him on the school board of the Greater Lowell Vocational Technical High School.

Republican Charlie Baker defeated Democrat Martha Coakley for governor (although Coakley won Lowell). Two exciting new Democrats won offices: Maura Healey was elected state Attorney General, and Seth Moulten defeated Democrat John Tierney and then-Republican Richard Tisei for the Congressional district that includes Tewksbury and Billerica.

Notable political figures who passed in 2014 included Paul Sheehy, Bill Taupier, and Arthur L. Eno, Jr.

2014

2015

Whistler's Father

By **Juliet Haines Mofford** on January 5, 2015
—

When I stayed with my grandparents in Zanesville, Ohio, my bed faced the picture of a seated lady who always seemed ready to reprimand me. Sometimes she rode into my nightmares on a broomstick. Grandmother refused to remove her to the attic. "That portrait's too heavy. Anyway, she's the mother of a great artist named James McNeill Whistler."

"One does like to make one's mummy look as nice as possible," he said after painting *Arrangement in Grey & Black, No.1* in London in 1871. The flamboyant expatriate was born in Lowell on July 10, 1834, though he denied it, stating, "I do not choose to be born in Lowell." When asked why he happened to have been born here, he replied, "The explanation is quite simple. I wished to be near my mother."

Because of this familiar portrait, Whistler's father has been largely overlooked. Yet George Washington Whistler was described as "witty and charming" by contemporaries. He was considered a man of "spotless integrity," with polished manners and a military bearing. His skill at playing the flute earned him the lifelong nickname "Pipes."

One of fifteen children, George Whistler was born in 1800 at Fort Wayne, Indiana, a military outpost commanded by his father. George entered West Point at fourteen, placing first in the class in drawing and fourth in geometry. Following graduation, Whistler briefly taught mathematics and was a lieutenant in the artillery with the Army Corps of Engineers. The young army officer became interested in railroad construction when there were no viable passenger lines in the country and only a few miles of track for hauling freight.

In 1828, the Baltimore and Ohio Railroad sent Whistler to

England to learn more about railroad technology. He became a railroad engineer when Americans still laughed at anyone who said a locomotive could go faster than horses pulling stagecoaches. By 1831, Whistler was in New Jersey overseeing the construction of the Paterson and Hudson River Railroad and two years later, lines between Providence and Stonington, Connecticut, and Baltimore & Susquehanna.

Whistler was a widower with three children when he married McNeill's sister, Anna Matilda in 1831. They eventually had five sons, the artist being first-born. The southern lady dressed in grey & black was indeed strict, "since no toys were permitted on Sundays and the only book allowed was the Bible."

More interested in civil engineering than the military, Major Whistler resigned his commission in 1833. The Proprietors of Locks and Canals had hired him as chief engineer and supervisor of the Machine Shop in the new city of Lowell. On June 1, 1834, the family moved into the residence at 243 Worthen Street, now the Whistler House Museum of Art (home of the Lowell Art Association since 1908). The house had been built for Paul Moody, first engineer at the Locks and Canal Company, who had lived there since 1824.

The large, red-brick Machine Shop developed equipment to produce cloth and created turbines and steam engines for water power. Whistler helped design Lowell's canals and aqueducts and learned how to design and build locomotives. He took apart a British locomotive to figure out how it was put together and worked with Patrick Tracy Jackson to open the Boston & Lowell Railroad.

Whistler and his family left Lowell in 1837 to take charge of the Stonington Railroad in Connecticut and soon was considered America's preeminent "Railroad Man." At one point, he supervised six lines. Russia's leading engineer, Pavel Melnikov, was sent by Czar Nicholas I to interview Whistler, who subsequently was hired to construct Russia's first major railroad between St. Petersburg and Moscow. Educated Russians regularly conversed in French, a language Whistler knew well. Whistler had full charge of all construction and supplies, a challenging job in a country short of machinery, mechanics, and domestic materials. Machine shops had to be built, and there were bridges, depots, and miles of tracks to map and construct. It was said no other American except former Ambassador John Quincy Adams was so respected by the Russians.

Although Whistler refused to wear the Russian uniform required of all noblemen and militia, a grateful emperor honored him with the Order of Saint Anne in 1847. Just before he turned 50 in 1849, George Washington Whistler contracted cholera, recovering only to suffer a fatal heart attack.

Note: Sources consulted include Whistler's Mother *by Elizabeth Mumford (1939) and* Whistler's Father *by Albert Parry (1939).*

Mayor Elliott and Human Rights

By **Dick** on January 21, 2015
—

Although nothing was mentioned at last night's City Council meeting about the recent trip to Cambodia by a delegation from Lowell led by Mayor Rodney Elliott and Councilor Rita Mercier, the group did make the news in that country. The Cambodia Daily newspaper reported over the weekend that Mayor Elliott plunged into Cambodian affairs to bring attention to several activists who had been jailed for demonstrating against substandard housing.

The article begins:

> The mayor of Lowell, Massachusetts—which has the second-largest population of Cambodian-Americans in the U.S.—on Friday visited 10 anti-eviction activists inside Phnom Penh's Prey Sar prison, emerging to announce that he would lobby the government for their release.
>
> Wrapping up a five-day visit to Phnom Penh, Rodney Elliott spent about an hour inside the maximum-security facility, where the female activists have been detained since their convictions over a pair of protests in November.

The full article is available on *The Cambodia Daily* website. Undoubtedly, this was a touchy issue for the Cambodian government, but it was probably wise for Mayor Elliott to address it on behalf of his constituents in Lowell. Hopefully, we'll get more information about this issue and the eventual outcome in the days and weeks to come.

Anyone who has dealings with the Cambodian community in Lowell quickly learns that current political divisions in Cambodia have a profound impact on the Cambodian community here. I'm not qualified to explain those divisions or identify who is on what side, but there is ample evidence that they directly affect what happens in this city. Consequently, it's important for everyone in Lowell, especially the City's elected leaders, to gain a better understanding of Cambodian history, culture, and current affairs—the good and the not so good.

It seems that this recent trip and especially the mayor's foray into Cambodian domestic affairs may be a good starting point for a community-wide discussion in Lowell about these divisions on the other side of the world and how they impede efforts to build a stronger sense of community in Lowell among all of our residents.

The Blizzard of 2015

By **Dick** on January 26, 2015
—

At 6:30 a.m. on Monday, it's eight degrees and cloudy in Lowell. By this time yesterday, the National Weather Service had already issued a blizzard watch for eastern Massachusetts and Rhode Island (since upgraded to a blizzard warning). Just moments ago, Matt Noyes on *New England Cable News* said snow will begin late this afternoon and will intensify later in the evening. Snow will continue throughout Tuesday and into Wednesday. Travel tomorrow will be "nearly impossible." By the time the storm is over, parts of southern New England will have received two to three feet of snow. Throughout the storm, electricity permitting, I'll use this post to collect observations, so please use the comment function to provide updates over the next couple of days.

From Marie at 1:40 p.m. on Monday:

> With a temp of 23 degrees, small snowflakes are falling softly in North Tewksbury. A phone call came, noting that schools are closed tonight and "No-School" declared for tomorrow. All in keeping with Governor Baker's declaration at noon today for a State of Emergency across the Commonwealth as of 12 midnight. BTW—he was wearing a suit and tie, and not a vest in the bunker!

From Paul:

> UMass Lowell not only closed early for the storm, 3:30 p.m., but also announced the school will be closed until Thursday morning, which is an extraordinary

announcement. This response to the predicted storm is what separates wheat from chaff in the world of blizzards. I had previously planned to be off this afternoon because today is my birthday, so I was on Rte. 495 South around 2:00 p.m. dropping off Rosemary's aunt in Westford when the first snow began to blow around. I turned off the Lowell Connector to stop at Target for a few last-minute household items, and the store was not crowded. There were milk, bread, and eggs on the shelves, along with just about anything else you might need in a hurry. On impulse, I bought a three-quart sauce pan (stainless steel), thinking I may cook something unusual while buttoned up inside for the next two days. On your birthday, you can do unexpected things. When I walked out of the store, snow was ticking heavily through the air, reminding me of my mother-in-law Mary Noon's old saying, "Little snow, big snow," meaning just what is says, the smaller the first snowflakes, the more likely the storm will be heavy-duty. Back home, I got the cars lined up in the back driveway to allow our trusty plowman to make the most of his visits. Elpidio Espinola of Tewksbury—I recommend him highly if you need plowing or home improvements.

From Dick at 6:00 p.m. on Monday:

20 degrees with light snow, which began at 3 p.m. Harvey Leonard on Channel 5 just said this will be all snow, and at times tonight it will fall at rates of three to four inches per hour with wind gusts up to 60 m.p.h. The City of Lowell at noon declared a Snow Emergency parking ban that went into effect at 6:00 p.m., and the Lowell Regional Transit Authority

announced it would be closed all day tomorrow. Lowell schools have been cancelled for tomorrow, and state courts, including the Registry of Deeds, will be closed all day. The city council meeting has been cancelled. Governor Baker announced a statewide travel ban starting at midnight.

From Marie at 6:55 p.m. on Monday:

As an inch or so of snow covers our North Tewksbury driveway—all local channel anchors and meteorologists kept us up to date in the news hours including an update from the Governor. Yes, he assured us, most residents of the Commonwealth will be handling two to three feet of snow and seriously dangerous winds. The Merrimack Valley looks to be, as Channel 7 weather guy Pete Bouchard describes it, a "sweet spot" for at least two feet and blizzard conditions.

Once home, unless you are a first-responder or healthcare provider, you should hunker-down according to all the experts. Most if not all Greater Lowell area town meetings, schools, and other activities are cancelled for this evening, all day tomorrow, and for some Wednesday as well. The courts will also be closed. The local news did cover the Patriots arrival in Arizona, while the national news followed this storm called "Juno" up the coast with a focus on New York City and New England. As we look to the overnight, the worst aspects of the storm ramp-up—gusty winds, heavy steady snow accumulating inches per hour, and the possibility of power outages—although more likely on the coast and on the Cape. Daylight should reveal a Winter Wonderland!

From Dick at 9:30 p.m. on Monday:

> Temp down to 17 degrees, intensity of snow increasing, but still not enough accumulation to go out and shovel. Anxious to see what the morning brings.

From Paul at 3:37 a.m. on Tuesday:

> Up early or up late in The Flats, as some people call this general area. Could also be the South End, the backside of Uptown, the edge of Back Central (I prefer to call it the Garden District), old St Peter Parish, the South Common Historic District, and a few other names, maybe Sal's Reach someday when we see the hulking Hood medicine factory restored and re-occupied.
>
> The dump truck-plows rumble down Highland Street in pairs. I see twirling amber lights on Thorndike from heavy equipment that's beating back the storm as much as possible. I don't know if this is the peak of the blizzard, but conditions are near white-out. Snow in a billion bits whips east to west, from Gorham Street and across the Common to the train station. The street lights are just bright enough to keep the scene visible.
>
> It's difficult to tell how much snow has fallen. The National Weather Service map online shows about eight inches for the Lowell area, but because of the strong steady wind the amount varies on our property. The driveway is clear to the black-top in the middle, but some of the drifts in the yard look about two feet high. The street is passable due to the constant plowing. We are fortunate here to be in a high-traffic zone with a school, the court, satellite

police precinct, Gallagher transportation terminal, and two streets that funnel vehicles to the Lowell Connector. I'm sure the situation is tough on narrow side streets in dense neighborhoods all over the city.

A "weather event" like this one puts in perspective a lot of things that all of us take for granted day to day—clean running water, a heating system, power for lights and appliances and this laptop computer, a functioning bathroom, and four walls anchored in a foundation and topped with a roof that's holding. Check, check, check, check, check. We hardly notice until there is a problem.

The other thing about these extreme weather events is that they put everyone in the same boat for a while. When I was growing up, Boston's three TV network affiliates (plus Channel 2/PBS) provided a linking experience for most of the people I knew. These days the social fabric is stretched thinly. We are drawn and pulled in many ways because of technology, dispersed employment, the movement of peoples, the information overload, etc. The social fabric shrinks back and thickens when we find ourselves in an "emergency," such as encountered in extreme weather. The weather covers us all. It's the ultimate broadcast network. It is sending, and we are receiving.

I remember the Halloween nor'easter of 2011, when the power was out for days, and trying to get local news from WCAP Radio with a battery-run radio. What was happening out there? It was wild, and people were disconnected. But everyone was experiencing the same thing.

Here comes my own plow-guy, Elpidio, his yellow truck light shining in my kitchen window. 4:13 a.m. He's been out since 11:00 p.m. straight, he just told me. I gave him an envelope with payment for the season so far. He's such a reliable guy, and he never sweats the payment. He knows we'll settle up when the snow is cleared. Another one of those things that translates into a sense of community. It snows. He shows up. I don't have to call him to make an appointment. I'm on the list. Amazing, really. All informal. Based on trust. Something to feel good about.

From Dick at 5:45 a.m. on Tuesday:

Temp 13 degrees, strong gusty wind. Snowing heavily with fine, light flakes. I measured 12 inches in my driveway at 5:15 a.m.

From Marie at 6:26 a.m. on Tuesday:

Our area of Rte. 495 is in the red zone right now—heavy fine flakes falling, gusty howling winds, blowing, drifting snow, and a measurement of 18 inches outside my back door in North Tewksbury. The storm continues as a plow lumbers by on Fiske Street.

From Marie at 6:52 a.m. on Tuesday:

The gusty winds are ferocious, causing near white-out conditions as the snowfall is more intense and heavy. The brunt of this phase of the storm is on top of us in North Tewksbury along Rte. 495.

From Marie at 8:00 a.m.:

In North Tewksbury—gusty winds, blowing, drifting heavy snow—at over 20 measurable inches at driveway door and nearly off the yard stick at backyard door to garage—and the Governor in his recent update thinks we'll get less snow than predicted—not up here in my backyard, Governor—our part of the Merrimack Valley is getting slammed. Time for tea and some breakfast!

Marie at 2:00 p.m.:

A frigid 16 degrees as the snow continues to fall sideways from the northeast, whirling, swirling, and drifting but lighter in North Tewksbury. Opening the garage door revealed a nearly 34-inch drift of snow and a high drift against the backdoor area. The driveway is socked-in as we await plowing and shoveling. Hours more before the snow stops here in the Merrimack Valley. In Western Mass., the snow has let up, and the Governor has lifted the driving ban for some local roads. The swath of geography from Worcester up through Lawrence to Newburyport continues to feel the heavy brunt of this storm. This snow event may not be historic elsewhere but it could top many past storms totals in Worcester. Could see third highest snow totals. In the Merrimack Valley, a blizzard warning is in effect until 8:00 p.m. Mounds of snow are growing in the cities.

Photos of folks shoveling a runway for pets are all over Facebook and Twitter as officials warn us to clean heating exhaust pipes from homes to the outdoors and to clear a pathway to our fire hydrants. It's very quiet along Fiske Street with an occasional town plow and sander sweeping up the street, and only a few private plows seen. *Channel 7 News* with former Lowell cable TV newsman Steve Cooper and Dan Hausle is keeping us abreast of our neighbors in Andover. The large parking lot at The Chateau restaurant located alongside Rte. 93 and River Road in Andover has long been a weather reporting spot not just for local TV reporters but nationally for The Weather Channel.

Amid this weather crisis Wall Street noted the Dow tanking 350 points this morning, but it has since rallied and is down only 250 points. Oil prices, while up a $1, may be the cause along with retail numbers. Closing the roads in states along the Northeast corridor (N.Y., Conn., Mass.) doesn't help. Remember the effects of Hurricane Sandy on the market. Check out our house snowdrift/window photos posted here: the first from this "Blizzard of '15" ongoing storm and the second from the "Blizzard of '78."

Tuesday at 4:30 p.m. from Dick:

The National Weather Service is reporting that Lowell has 28 inches of snow on the ground as of 1:00 p.m. It hasn't stopped snowing since then, so I expect we got at least enough to push us past the 30-inch threshold. Earlier today the Lowell Police tweeted that City Hall and all municipal buildings (as well as the schools) will remain closed tomorrow (Wednesday). No word on the courts and the Registry of Deeds yet; the Trial Court website says a decision will be made tonight. The MBTA and Commuter Rail haven't announced when service will resume.

I made my second pass of the driveway with the snow blower at 2:00 p.m. About six inches more had fallen since my effort this morning, which was more challenging due to the 20 inches that had fallen. I'll go out again after dinner, hopefully for the last time for this storm. Up until a few years ago, I would also have to clear off portions of my roof due to ice dams.

That was crushing work, especially after clearing the driveway and the dog's area in the backyard. Three years ago, I smartened up and installed some electric heating cables along the edge of the roof in a couple of key spots. The cables melt channels through ice backups that otherwise cause thawing snow to leak into the house.

As I was dragging the snow blower into the garage, two pre-teens from a nearby street walked into my driveway with a plastic grocery bag. Girl Scout cookies? No, they offered to sell me a newspaper, a self-produced one, for 25 cents. Because of the travel ban, the usual paper copies from the mainstream media didn't arrive today, so I was happy to purchase this one and added a decent tip for their efforts and initiative. The lead story in *The News Splash* is that Tom Brady and the Patriots have been falsely accused of wrongdoing ("Maybe the other team should just be quiet."). Also, *Bella and the Bulldogs* is going to be a great new TV show. There were two pages of comics, too.

Wednesday (Jan. 28) at 8:30 a.m. by Dick:

The National Weather Service reports that Lowell received 31 inches of snow in this storm, a figure I won't dispute. It began Monday night and ended on Tuesday night, so we had almost 24 hours of continuous snowfall with the temperature never rising above 16 degrees. Strong, gusty wind caused the light, fluffy snow to drift into artistically sloped piles. I was disappointed to awake to a slate gray sky this morning. Brilliant sunshine bouncing off the new fallen snow gives you a day of visual enjoyment before the hassles of narrow streets, high snowbanks, buried sidewalks, and disappeared parking spaces bring you back to the drudging reality of life in the aftermath of a big snowstorm. City Hall, the courthouses, the Registry of Deeds, and all schools in the vicinity are closed today. The MBTA and commuter rail are back in operation, but my MBTA alerts this morning made me think otherwise. There are several cancellations and delays.

Lowell Week in Review: March 8, 2015

By **Dick** on March 8, 2015
—

JACK'S CORNER AT THE POLLARD LIBRARY

About 40 people gathered yesterday on the first floor of the Pollard Memorial Library to dedicate "Jack's Corner." Musician and composer David Amram, who first met Jack Kerouac in 1956 in New York City, said that Kerouac knew more about more things than anyone Amram had ever met. Asked to explain his wide and deep knowledge base, Kerouac attributed it to the many days he spent reading in the Lowell Public Library. Amram went on to say that Kerouac was a true intellectual and a great scholar. As evidence of that, he pointed to *Atop an Underwood* (1999), a collection of 60 previously unpublished works that Kerouac wrote before he was 22. Our co-blogger, Paul Marion, edited *Atop an Underwood*.

Paul became a key party in the creation of today's event by donating 400 books of poetry to the Pollard Library. The books are shelved in a section called "The Young Prometheans Poetry Collection," immediately adjacent to the area favored by Kerouac.

(The book section is named for the literary "gang" that Kerouac hung out with in high school and just after.) And Kerouac occupied that space for a considerable amount of time. Roger Brunelle of the local group called Lowell Celebrates Kerouac! explained that during his junior year at Lowell High Jack was absent 32 days; during his senior year, it was 44 days. All of them were spent at the library, a place he frequently referred to as a temple.

Kerouac himself documented the importance of the Lowell Public Library in this passage from his book *Vanity of Duluoz: An Adventurous Education*, 1935-1946, written largely in Lowell when he lived for a while in the Highlands neighborhood in the mid-1960s and published in 1968, the year before he died:

> "Bragging still, but telling the truth still, . . .during all this time I was getting A's and B's in high school, mainly because I used to cut class at least once a week, to play hooky that is, just so I could go to the Lowell Public Library and study by myself at leisure such things as old chess books with their fragrance of scholarly thought, their old bindings, leading me to investigate other fragrant old books. . .loving books and the smell of the old library and always reading in the rotunda part of the back where there was a bust of Caesar in the bright morning sun. . . ."

Yesterday's event was ably organized by Sean Thibodeau, the library's Coordinator of Community Planning, who also served as the master of ceremonies. Also speaking was Bill Walsh, who gave a brief history of the library, and Mayor Rodney Elliott, who read a citation from Governor Charlie Baker proclaiming that March 12, 2015 (Kerouac's birthday), would be observed as "Jack Kerouac Day" in the Commonwealth of Massachusetts. This is an annual recognition for Kerouac by the state, a significant statement reserved for persons of extraordinary achievement.

Robert Frost, who grew up in Lawrence, is similarly honored.

Also attending were City Councilors Rita Mercier, Corey Belanger, and Bill Samaras; School Committee member Dave Conway; state Representative Rady Mom; Library Trustee Marianne Gries; Pollard Memorial Library Foundation board members Mary Johnson-Lally and Rosemary Noon; many members of the library staff; Lowell and area residents; and a young woman who is writing her Ph.D. dissertation on Kerouac at Laval University in Quebec. While waiting for the ceremony to begin, she engaged in a friendly conversation about snow and its removal, politely observing that Quebec City seemed to have the snow removal drill down better than Lowell based on what she has seen during her visit thus far.

OPIOID EPIDEMIC

Everyone in Lowell knows a family, often more than one family, that has lost someone to drug addiction. Most everyone has an opinion about why this is so, but such opinions, however, logical, don't always match reality. The City Council got a heavy dose of reality last Tuesday night during a presentation on the city's opioid epidemic from Health Department Director Frank Singleton and John Chemaly of Trinity EMS at the Council meeting.

Discussing causes of this epidemic, Singleton repeatedly returned to the over-prescription of powerful pain killers by doctors. He said that the potent pain killers that now get people hooked weren't available ten or 15 years ago. Besides those drugs being available now, doctors are prescribing them in amounts far beyond what is needed to control pain, Singleton said. He said the pathway is well known: a person is injured at work, obtains a large amount of prescription pain killers, becomes dependent on them, and when he or she can't afford to buy them on the street then turns to cheaper but more dangerous heroin. Singleton said that if 25 people had already died from meningitis this year in Lowell, there would be an uproar and concerted action, but because that many deaths have been caused by overdoses of opioids, no one seems too excited.

The comments by Chemaly and Singleton were accompanied by a report from the Trinity company about its staff's response to overdose calls and the number of opioid-related deaths. The report will be posted on the City website, but for now you can download it from the March 2 Council meeting packet. Here is some data: First is the number of Trinity EMS emergency calls where the chief complaint was an overdose (excluding alcohol). In 2012, there were 599 such calls; in 2013, there were 693; in 2014, the figure grew to 917.

Calls came from across the city. Of the 2,209 overdose calls from 2012 through 2014, here are the numbers from each neighborhood: Acre, 380; Back Central, 245; Belvidere, 96; Lower Belvidere, 75; Centralville, 303; Downtown, 443; Highlands, 155; Lower Highlands, 197; Pawtucketville, 170; Sacred Heart, 97; South Lowell, 29; and Unknown, 19.

As for deaths from opioid overdoses, from 2003 to 2013, there were 244, with 176 being males and 68 being females. The age breakdown: 18 between 18 and 24 years old; 59 between 25 and 34; 78 between 35 and 44; 9 between 45 and 54; and 20 were 55 or older.

Anam Cara Honor: Irish 'Soul Friend'

By **Marie** on March 13, 2015
—

Last night I was among the 2015 Anam Cara honorees—this award recognizes local "soul friends" who have made significant contributions to the preservation of Irish Culture and Heritage in Greater Lowell. After listening to the Acre Forum panelists, I felt so much a part of their experience that after the presentation I asked forum moderator Dick Howe if I could add my story.—MS

Why am "I" in this place tonight? What is my story? Let me give you a little bit of the story. I'm proud to say that these are my people:

Patrick Meehan (1847-1913) and Margaret McDermott Meehan (1849-1916) arrived from County Sligo in 1864—when married they settled in the Acre on Worthen Street—he was a bookkeeper and a grocer. Patrick was noted in his obituary as a "man of magnetic personality with a host of friends, a man ready to lend a helping hand to anyone in need." It notes that he was a prominent factor in the growth and success of several well-known societies of St. Patrick's Church—and his passing "a cause of genuine grief to all." Margaret or Maggie as she was called—had nine children—they raised a family of the six surviving children. Patrick and Maggie died young—each at 60.

Patrick Kirwin came from County Dublin—and by way of Blackstone, Massachusetts, came to Lowell early in the 1870s—he had a valuable skill—he was a wool sorter, and he had management skills. Ellen Courtney—a bit younger than Patrick—also from Dublin by way of Blackstone—came to Lowell and married Patrick in 1876. They raised a family of eight children—first, in what we call the Flats—but they soon moved up to 30 Agawam Street in what would be called the

Sacred Heart Parish. Patrick was considered one of the pioneers of the Sacred Heart Parish as he was one of the committee who met often in the Lyons Street School to organize this new Catholic parish. His son—William J. Kirwin, Oblate of Mary Immaculate—would later become its Pastor. Patrick had a large circle of friends—he was known as a loyal friend and family man. With Ellen—who survived him by many years well into the mid-1930s—and their children, they formed a solid part of their community—but were NOT—as was made clear to me many times—of the 400!

Thomas Deignan—a six-foot-tall red-headed man came to Lowell from County Leitrim—by way of Liverpool—to the Acre. He was a laborer—he was into wood and coal and being a teamster. The lively Elizabeth "Lizzie" Charles came to Lowell from Ireland with her sisters. She married Thomas at the Immaculate Conception Church in 1885 (I'm wearing her wedding ring tonight). They had ten children and raised eight into adulthood. Lizzie lived for many years—to 1940—and was the center of the Deignan home on High Street—ensconced in her rocking chair in the family kitchen. Only three children married—and just two had children—the others lived at home well into adulthood and not surprisingly—bringing home the paycheck to Lizzie. (I suppose then it was a pay envelope!)

Joseph Burke and Matilda Montgomergy Burke emigrated from Newtoncunningham, Londonderry, Ireland, to the United States in November of 1898—arriving on-board the Nebraska with two children in tow—Katherine and Bill. They had their first child in America, in Lowell, in 1900, and that was my grandmother "Tillie." They raised their eight children—first, in the Sacred Heart Parish on South Whipple Street, Gorham Street, and then on Moore Street before settling by the late 1920s in the Highlands on Stevens Street. Joe Burke was a physically strong man who could do the hard work of many. He walked long distances for most of his life, usually with his dog Rigger—I'm told there were many Riggers—and Joe "Pa" Burke lived to be

100. Matilda sailed and traveled back to Ireland many times to visit her brothers. She enjoyed life, she was a fashion-plate in her time and worked as a saleswoman in a department store for many years. Joe outlived her.

My grandparents were of these beginnings (the Meehan-Kirwin wedding was at St. Patrick's as was the Deignan-Burke). Both grandmothers were women of strong faith and family: Agnes Meehan (Notre Dame Academy, Lowell alum, trained for business and sales) and Tillie Burke (homemaker, great cook, and founding member and President of the Ladies Ancient Order of Hibernians, Division #46). Both grandfathers, Patrick "PJ" Kirwin and James "Jimmy" Deignan, were charmers. They both worked in government: Papa Kirwin, born in 1884, for over 50 years at the Lowell Post office, and Papa Deignan, born in 1895, a WWI Army veteran, at the Watertown Arsenal. Then for "PJ" there was the Meehan and Kirwin funeral business with his brother-in-law the postmaster and former mayor, and for Jimmy Deignan, with the beautiful tenor voice, Irish wit, and repartee, there was the B.F. Keith Vaudeville circuit. Appearing in local shows, he even produced Keith Academy Shows, and in the late 1930s he served a few terms on the Lowell City Council! What a heritage!

These men and women—my great-grandparents who came to Lowell—left their mark and their legacy through their children, grandchildren, and great-grandchildren. Their influence brought men and women into all walks of life—education, military service, public service, service to the Church, medicine, healthcare and public health, government service. They became teachers, doctors, nurses, businessmen and businesswomen, laborers, librarians, maintenance workers, car salesmen, accountants & CPAs, a mayor, a city councilor, a school committeeman, a postmaster, organists, pianists, music teachers, priests, sisters, funeral directors, social workers, CCD religious teachers, computer and technology workers, writers, lawyers. Some of them "Got on the City" or the telephone or electric companies.

They worked at the *Lowell Sun*, the bank, the hospitals, and the Lowell Housing Authority; managed nursing homes; or were in private practice. They became Tewksbury Hospital medical and nursing directors, got into food service, were civically and culturally active, and so much more.

For me, it's always been as I was taught, as was role-modeled for me: the legacy of faith, family, community, our Irish heritage and culture, and service. And, well, a little Democratic politics thrown in.

I want to thank the committee, on behalf of myself, my husband Bill (my partner of over 47 years whom I met in Sister Rita's kindergarten at the Sacred Heart School), and my sons Bill and Ted, daughter-in-law Nicole, and granddaughters Abby, Hannah, Eva, and Mae, and all those who came before me—I want to thank the organizers for including me in tonight's honors. To be included with this group of people is a great part of the honor. *Anam Cara*—it is a high honor to be deemed a "Soul Friend" of Irish culture and heritage—along with Peg McAndrews, an old friend so committed to her Irish heritage, St. Patrick's Church, the work of Catholic Charities, and to whom I had the pleasure of giving the Greater Lowell Area Democrats "1999 Distinguished Democrat" award; with Leo Mahoney, a good man, a humble and generous man, "the salt of the earth," as they say, whose son and nephews and our sons and nephew share a friendship and a bit of history; with Mike Demoulas, another humble and generous man of the Acre whose friendship with my dad lasted more than 50 years of business and shared beginnings; and lastly, with the great leader Paul Sheehy, a colleague, a mentor, and actually my boss for a while, but most of all my longtime friend—and as with the others—greatly missed.

Thank you all very much!

HISTORY AS IT HAPPENS

Lowell's Nelson Mandela Overlook

By **Dick** on April 29, 2015
—

The Africa America Alliance, Inc., (AAA), an organization "dedicated to the pursuit of human rights and equality for all," held an inaugural breakfast event for its proposed Nelson Mandela Overlook yesterday at the Paul E. Tsongas Center at UMass Lowell. The AAA believes Lowell is a fitting site for this monument because the city is home to thousands of individuals from more than a dozen nations in Africa. The Mandela monument will acknowledge the presence and contribution of the local African community while celebrating a global icon in the never-ending struggle for freedom and justice. Members of the local African community including Gordon Halm, Janice Johnson, Bowa Tucker, and others, developed the concept and approached university officials about creating a Mandela tribute.

UMass Lowell Executive Vice Chancellor Jacqueline Moloney said the idea for a permanent monument honoring Nelson Mandela at UMass Lowell gained momentum during the time spent in Lowell by Justice Albie Sachs of South Africa, a 2014 UMass Lowell Greeley Scholar for Peace Studies and a close associate of President Mandela's. Sachs, a fellow freedom fighter and friend of Mandela's, encouraged the AAA leaders to pursue their fledgling idea as a Pan-African tribute in Lowell. UMass Lowell Athletics Director Dana Skinner, an admirer of Mandela's, recommended that the monument be placed on the grounds of the Tsongas Center because Nelson Mandela used sports to rally and unite people.

The next milestone of the project came when UMass Lowell Art Professor Jim Coates organized his undergraduate sculpture class around a competition to design the Mandela tribute. Three student teams engaged in extensive research of the concepts and objectives of public art and came up with excellent designs. The winning proposal was submitted by the team of Erin Cahill, Rebecca Dolan, and Josh Rondeau.

The team's design elements represent Nelson Mandela's cause and beliefs. The memorial site is along the Western Canal on the Tsongas Center grounds. They have proposed a two-tiered granite circular base that will be a seat and support for the sculpture. At the center of the granite base will be a globe-like object which symbolically suggests that racism and oppression are global issues. The globe will be an open negative form made of bent iron bars, alluding to Mandela's time in prison. A springbok (resembling a gazelle), the national animal of South Africa, as well as the name of the national rugby team, will support the globe. On the base will be a quote from Mandela: "Sport has the power to change the world. It has the power to inspire. It has the power to unite people in a way that little else does. Sport can awaken hope where there was previously only despair."

Lowell Week in Review: Sept. 13, 2015

By **Dick** on September 13, 2015

—

Thanks to Dave Ouellette for a great tour yesterday in the final Summertime Lowell Walk of 2015. He led the 105 people in attendance up Moody Street to the Armand Mercier Center on Salem Street, to Decatur Way, and finished inside St. Jean-Baptiste Church. Along the way, he shared the kind of inside stories that have helped make these walks so popular.

Here's a review of the tours and the number of people who attended each:

June 25—Preservation Success Stories with Fred Faust *(81)*

June 13—Lowell Public Art Collection with Paul Marion & Rosemary Noon *(107)*

June 20—Inside Lowell High with Brian Martin *(86)*

June 27—Literary Lowell & the Pollard Library with Sean Thibodeau *(76)*

July 11—The Irish and the Acre with Dave McKean *(125)*

July 18—Green Lowell with Jay Mason *(43)*

Aug 1—Abolitionists in Lowell with Bob Forrant *(119)*

Aug 8—Hamilton Canal District with Allison Lamey *(129)*

Aug 15—Natural Lowell with Jane Calvin *(75)*

Aug 22—Lowell Artists with Jim Dyment *(86)*

Aug 29—Lowell Monuments with Dick Howe *(167)*

Sept 5—Trains & Trolleys with Chris Hayes *(120)*

Sept 12—Renewing the Acre with Dave Ouellette *(105)*

That's 1,319 people total for an average of 101 per tour. Today, I presented "perfect attendance" awards to six people who came to every tour. One thing that contributed to the large turnouts was the fantastic weather. July 18 was the only rainy Saturday. Another thing that contributed was the attractiveness of downtown Lowell. When you get out of your car and walk around with your eyes open, you see the payoff of all the preservation work that's been done over the past forty years. Finally, the volunteer tour guides were fantastic. Each brought great stories to the walks.

We're already planning next summer's tours. On Monday, October 26 at 6:30 p.m. at the Pollard Memorial Library's Community Room, we will have a 2015 Lowell Walks Retrospective that will feature slide-show followed by a discussion about the walks.

But Lowell Walks tours are not over for 2015; they are going on the road. In two weeks, the fall tours of the Lowell Cemetery begin (Friday, Sept. 25 at 1:00 p.m.; Saturday, Sept. 26 at 10:00 a.m.; Friday, Oct. 16 at 1:00 p.m.; and Saturday, Oct. 17 at 10:00 a.m.) all stepping off from the Knapp Avenue entrance.

In three weeks, we'll have our first Lowell Walks neighborhood tour. On Oct. 3 at 10:00 a.m., we'll gather at Clemente Field on Middlesex Street for a tour of Cambodia Town and the Lower Highlands. The tour will be led by Paul Ratha Yem, Sengly Kong, and me. I'll cover the nineteenth and early twentieth century history of the neighborhood, and Paul and Sengly will talk about the area's recent history.

Salute to Women Remarks

By **Bopha Malone** on September 17, 2015
—

At Tuesday's Lowell Sun *"Salute to Women," event, the three award recipients who addressed the crowd were excellent and inspirational. The remarks of one of them, Bopha Malone, were especially moving and profound. Bopha kindly shared them with me for posting here.—RPH*

Over the past few weeks, a devastating and shocking picture has been on my mind. It's a picture of a body of a small boy, no older than three, washed up on the shore—a life destroyed by circumstances he and his family couldn't control. That boy was Aylan Kurdi, a little boy who drowned as his family tried to escape the Syrian conflict. This picture prompted me to become more knowledgeable about the horrific situation facing Syrian refugees today.

As a former refugee, it made me somber and sad, and incredibly thankful that my family was able to survive our escape from Cambodia to Thailand years ago—when I was the same age as Aylan. It made me reflect about my own family's journey and how far we and our fellow survivors have come since.

Imagine what life is like for someone fleeing from their home country.

Imagine living through an atrocity in which your own people starved you, tortured you, and killed the people you love.

Imagine the trauma of losing everything, of living in fear that if you say or do the wrong thing, that you will be harmed.

Imagine having to sacrifice everything to escape, walking your three-year-old through the jungle in the dark, praying that you wouldn't step on any landmines, begging your child to stop crying so you don't get caught by patrolling soldiers and killed.

These were some one of my earliest memories as a child.

After a couple of days, we finally reached Thailand, where we were placed in a refugee camp. Although it was better, it still was not safe. Instead of hearing lullabies, we'd go to bed most nights being scared by the sounds of gunfire and bombings. Most nights we'd go to bed listening to our parents talking about their escape plans—which child they would take and where they would meet if they were to be separated. It became normal for us to run into a hole we had dug beneath the floor of our home to hide from the Thai soldiers when they came raiding each night. We lived like this for five or six years, praying every day that we would have the opportunity to immigrate to America.

When we finally made it to the U.S. in 1989, it was a blessing. But the adjustment was not easy.

We settled in Harrisburg, Pennsylvania, where we were one of the only two Cambodian families in town. I was nine years old, starting second grade. I stuck out like a sore thumb. The only English words I knew were "yes" and "no."

I was very fortunate to have people who helped me overcome that. Caring teachers spent extra time to teach me English. They even came to our home to show our family what Thanksgiving and Christmas were all about.

It was even tougher for my parents to adjust and find jobs to support us.

We later resettled in Lynn, Massachusetts, where we lived in a tough neighborhood. My parents had to work all the time, so my brother and I were often on our own. I adapted to American culture, and began to speak and understand less Khmer. Because my parents were very traditional, they were very strict, especially with me because I was a girl. They wanted me to stay home, do housework, stay away from boys, and study. I now understand that what my parents did was out of love and wanting me to be successful. But at that point, due to our lack of communication and not understanding each other's world, I thought they were unfair. Not knowing who to turn to, I felt depressed, intimidated, and alone.

Luckily, when I got to high school, I learned about Girls, Inc. Because it was a safe place I could go to after school—and because it was for girls only—my parents were open to allowing me to attend. Initially, I joined the teen program, just wanting to get out of the house, but what I learned there and the experiences that I had changed my life and helped me to become the woman I am today.

At Girls, Inc., I had women mentors who understood my struggles and helped me to overcome my challenges and fears. They saw potential in me that I didn't see in myself. They took the time to listen and to encourage me to be brave. They showed me what it takes to be a successful woman, and they empowered me to help others. With their support, I gained confidence, I was happy, and I no longer felt alone.

With the help of Girls, Inc., applied for and received a full scholarship to college. I began to appreciate my Cambodian roots more and to reconnect with my language and culture.

I have been very fortunate to have had many opportunities given to me, and I learned the importance of giving back and helping others, as so many people have helped me in my life.

After college, I spent a year doing volunteer work in Cambodia, where I helped open a school for disadvantaged children. When I returned, Carol Duncan of Girls, Inc., in Lowell introduced me to George Duncan and Enterprise Bank, and I became a part of the Enterprise family.

At Enterprise, I've not only learned about all aspects of the banking world, but I've also had an opportunity to get involved with this wonderful city and our vibrant Cambodian community. Most of all, I am inspired every day to do what I love doing—helping people.

One example of this is my involvement with the Cambodian Mutual Assistance Association. As a member of the CMAA board, I'm a part of helping other Cambodians and minorities adjust to new life in a new country. I know how scary it is when you don't know the language, the people, the culture, and where to turn to for guidance, and it makes me so happy to be able to return in some small part the kindness I received as a child.

This kindness was never more evident than last summer, when a devastating fire struck our community. The entire city of Lowell—Cambodians, City officials, and community organizations—came together to make sure that those affected by the fire had everything they needed to get back on their feet. I was incredibly proud to be a part of this citywide effort.

This past winter, I had an opportunity, as part of the City of Lowell delegation, to visit Cambodia. There, for the first time since I was a little girl, I returned to the refugee camp on the Thai border where I spent part of my childhood. It was a very emotional experience. Seeing the poor conditions that we lived in, remembering the fear we endured, reminded me of how fortunate I have been and how thankful I am for my parents' courage, and the sacrifices that they made to give our family freedom, and a better life.

The experience made me more determined than ever to do all I can to improve the lives of Cambodians and other refugees in the Lowell area. As the story of Aylan Kurdi reminded us, every refugee has his or her own story, and is deserving of respect, understanding, and care.

Thank you again for this recognition. I look forward to continuing to do all that I can to help make Lowell an even stronger and better place for us to live and work.

HISTORY AS IT HAPPENS

The Christmas Fruitcake: An Ageless Tradition

By **Henri Marchand** on December 16, 2015
—

Like its subject this essay has been around, appearing first as a Sunrise *radio essay, re-wrapped as a "Guest Column" piece in the* Sun, *and showing up on this blog last year. I re-gift it once more to all who either love or loathe the fruitcake. Merry Christmas!*—HM

I think there is no yuletide tradition so endlessly lampooned and so deliciously mocked as the once-esteemed fruitcake. Everyone loves chestnuts roasting on an open fire, and even plum pudding gets an annual endorsement by the beloved Cratchits, but mention fruitcake, and people giggle. Johnny Carson suggested that there exists but one fruitcake in the world; it just passes from one unappreciative family to another. Calvin Trillin is reported to have commented that "There is nothing dangerous about fruitcakes if people send them along without eating them." And in Manitou Spring, Colorado, the Chamber of Commerce sponsors an annual Great Fruitcake Toss. The record is 420 feet, the waste immeasurable.

Unpopular as they may appear to be, a web search turns up more than 2,000,000 fruitcake hits. Mail-order bakeries began selling them in 1913, and now sell thousands every year. There were times when the fruitcake was revered. Early recipes date to ancient Rome, but evolved over the years. The modern fruitcake originated in the Middle Ages with honey, rare spices, and hard-to-get preserved fruit from the Far East. In the 18th century nuts were incorporated, the cakes eaten for good luck with the following year's harvest. Due to the expense of the ingredients and a difficult baking process, fruitcakes were once restricted by law in Europe to special events like weddings and Christmas.

Today the fruitcake is pretty much a Christmas tradition. (Has anyone ever heard the refrain, "The bride cuts the fruitcake!"?) There are many types of fruitcake, but they're all basically a pile of fruits and nuts glommed together with a minimum of batter and often soaked in liquor for added flavor and shelf life, and then dusted with powdered sugar.

When it comes to fruitcake, everyone takes sides. As in politics, there are two camps, each sharply opinionated—those who have bitten the hallowed fruitcake and those who would rather die. Of those with a taste for this yuletide dessert a number partake openly while others do so surreptitiously, stealing a morsel when they think no one is looking. Among those few bold enough to discuss their addiction, there are preferences. Some fancy the lighter, citron-based variety, while others crave cakes with a higher nut content. Some drool over the dry, crumbly variants, others lap up the glazed and gooey sorts. In my early years, I never cared for the bland flavor of citrus bits or their texture, which I found not unlike that of pencil erasers.

I developed an affinity later in life and I have baked a pair of cobblestone-sized loaves annually for more than ten years. I do so with great holiday cheer despite loud family protestations. The recipe I follow is out of a dog-eared cookbook, a dark molasses-rich block chock-full of candied cherries and pineapples, dates, and golden raisins. But I've modified the mix over the years and use shelled walnuts instead of Brazil nuts. Mainly it's because I prefer the taste of walnuts. It's also because shelling Brazil nuts is like disarming grenades. You need a deft touch, applying just enough pressure, otherwise the crescent-shaped, steel-like shells explode, scattering shrapnel all over the place and turning the nutmeat to mush. A pound of nuts produces a measly two-to-three usable undamaged pieces. Cutting up the fruit is no less challenging; thickly sugared pineapples and tacky dates stick to knives, cutting boards, and fingers. Many end up in my mouth. This year, I'm going to add dried apricots to the mix and drown one of the finished cakes in brandy or bourbon, an added inducement for those who have yet to indulge themselves.

I'll do this because I've noticed that there are not many takers when I wheel out the fruitcake on Christmas Eve. I don't push it on anyone or suggest that they try "just one little piece." I just slice it and let it speak for itself at the front of the buffet table under a small spotlight. Oh, several guests are polite and praise its jeweled appearance and my stubborn adherence to tradition, but there aren't many slices missing by midnight. Others shake their heads, and say, "No thanks, I don't do fruitcake," as if refusing a casual offer of an illegal substance. Some groan and cry, "Oh, no, no, I'd love to but I just couldn't eat another bite," even as they shovel down handfuls of peanuts and mouth another meatball. Still others simply sniff in mock derision, roll their eyes, and say things like, "Yeah, right, Dad!" Apparently, Santa's no fan either as the thick slices left for him by the tree are still there Christmas morning while the chocolate milk is gone.

I know the merry barbs are coming from the anti-fruitcake faction and the remains of my effort will linger long after the holidays, but I don't care. I like fruitcake! I'll enjoy slivers of these ageless bricks for the next six months. Or until the spirit of the season abandons me in April, and I toss the lot of what's left to the squirrels and birds.

Lowell Year in Review: 2015

By **Dick** on January 3, 2016

—

Rather than a week in review, today we have a year in review. Here are some memorable events from 2015.

SNOW

The record amount of snow that fell in January and February was the biggest story of the year. For the winter of 2014-15, Lowell received 111 inches of snow, more than any other city of 100,000 or more residents in the United States including Alaska. A blizzard on January 26-28 got things started with 33 inches of snow, followed by big storms on February 2, 8, and 15. By the time it all ended, driving resembled a game of chicken due to high snow banks; too many people learned about ice dams; and the "snow farms" on the South Common and Hamilton Canal District resembled slate-gray mountain ranges.

EDUCATION

Lowell School Committee incumbents Kim Scott and Kristin Ross-Sitcawich chose not to seek reelection, and colleagues Dave Conway and Jim Leary ran for the city council. Incumbents Steve Gendron and Connie Martin were reelected. They will be joined by new members Jackie Doherty, Robert Gignac, Bob Hoey, and Andy Descoteaux. With a new mayor to be elected tomorrow, five of the seven members of the school committee will be new, an extraordinary turnover. Before leaving, the old members of the school committee selected Dr. Salah Khelfaoui to replace Jean Franco as Lowell School Superintendent. Khelfaoui received four votes to three votes for Deputy Superintendent for

Finance Jay Lang (who shortly thereafter became superintendent in Chelmsford). The state's School Building Assistance Bureau selected Lowell's proposal to build a new high school for further study, and a group of parents reactivated the defunct Citywide Parent Council. In higher education, Marty Meehan became the president of the University of Massachusetts system, and Jacquie Moloney was chosen to succeed him as chancellor of UMass Lowell.

CITY GOVERNMENT

All eight city councilors who sought reelection won (Bill Martin chose not to run). The ninth council seat was won by Jim Leary, who made the leap from the school committee. The City ended its relationship with Trinity Financial and issued a new request for qualifications (RFQ) for the Hamilton Canal District. In a big breakthrough, the City reached an agreement with the Lowell Regional Transit Authority (LRTA) that will allow tour buses visiting Lowell National Historical Park to park on LRTA property on YMCA Drive, permitting the soon-to-be-constructed City parking garage in the Hamilton Canal District to have more space for ground-floor retail partners than parking for buses. In November, Governor Charlie Baker came to Lowell with a big check for the Lowell Judicial Center, suggesting that the long-delayed court building will open before the end of this decade. In other city news, the Markley Group purchased the former Prince Spaghetti manufacturing facility in South Lowell for use as a state-of-the-art server farm to provide cloud-based computing services to businesses all over the world. With the help of a $13 million federal TIGER grant, the City reached an agreement with Enel Green Power to take over eight Enel-owned canal bridges. City leaders also held several meetings on the future of the Lord Overpass.

OPIOID CRISIS

Heroin and opioid overdoses in Lowell and the state are at the highest levels in history. All levels of government have struggled to find ways to effectively deal with this epidemic. Lowell's fire and police departments began carrying Narcan, an overdose antidote. City councilors addressed the epidemic almost weekly. Both Governor Charlie Baker and Attorney General Maura Healey made the opioid crisis a top priority. Despite these efforts, the epidemic continues with no end in sight and little cause for optimism.

CREATIVE ECONOMY NEWS

Western Avenue Studios and Mill No. 5 continued to thrive, but downtown retail had mixed success with some businesses doing well and others not so much. Winterfest was rescheduled because of too much snow, and the St. Patrick's Day charity breakfast became a dinner. The American Textile History Museum announced that it would close its public spaces on January 1, 2016, as a cost-saving measure. The Coalition for a Better Acre responded to a City request for proposals (RFP) for the reuse of the Smith Baker Center, but the outcome is still pending. UMass Lowell with the Africa American Alliance dedicated a portion of the lawn on the west side of the Tsongas Center to be used for the erection of a memorial to Nelson Mandela, and the Pollard Library dedicated a section of the first floor to Jack Kerouac (called "Kerouac's Corner"). Lowell Walks, a series of guided walking tours, drew more than 1,300 people to downtown Lowell on Saturday mornings.

REAL ESTATE

Statistically, real estate in Lowell was stable during 2015. The number of deeds recorded in 2015 was statistically the same as in 2014. Mortgages were up 20 percent, but then declined in November and December. Although foreclosure deeds were down slightly, the number of orders of notice, the document that signals the start of a foreclosure proceeding, was up 65 percent, which does not bode well for 2016.

Looking at specific properties that changed hands, UMass Lowell continued to increase its real estate holdings, purchasing a nine-unit wood-frame apartment building on Salem Street for $815,000 in March; two adjacent wood-frame apartment buildings on Pawtucket Street adjacent to the Howe Bridge for $1 million each in October; and the Notini property on Aiken Street for $5.8 million in December.

Notable downtown transactions included the sale of 40 Central Street to United Teen Equality Center (UTEC) for $1.2 million; several floors of the Hamilton Mills to the Lowell Community Charter School for $8 million; a portion of the Massachusetts Mills for $1 million; 29-35 Market Street (Savannah Palace) for $1.5 million; and the Howe Building at 11 Kearney Square for $720,000.

Commercial properties outside of downtown that sold included the St. Hilaire Car Wash on Middlesex Street for $1.4 million; the old Prince Macaroni facility on Prince Ave. (to the Markley Group) for $3.9 million; the M/A-Com facility on Chelmsford Street for $8.25 million; the Polish American Veterans Club on Coburn Street for $600,000; the CVS drugstore on outer Middlesex Street for $2.8 million; and the former St. Peter's Rectory (most recently Cooney Insurance) for $702,000.

The parking lot of JJ Boomer's Pawtucket Blvd sold to Market Basket for $1.3 million. Several apartment buildings outside of downtown also changed hands. They were located on Middlesex Street (adjacent to the Lord Overpass) for $929,900; Hildreth Street for $5.9 million; Middlesex Street (at the foot of Livingston) for $1.6 million; at Stevens and Princeton Boulevard for $3.7 million; Nesmith Street for $2.3 million; and Mammoth Road for $1.2 million.

STATE, NATIONAL, INTERNATIONAL

The Boston 2024 Olympic effort flopped, dragged down in part by the poor performance of the Massachusetts Bay Transportation Authority during last winter's heavy snow. Terrorist attacks struck Paris twice and San Bernardino, California, just before Christmas. Mass shootings that many people would also call terrorist attacks occurred in cities across the United States.

Videos of police interacting with citizens had a profound impact on how people viewed law enforcement and on how law enforcement does its job. In the span of 48 hours, the United States Supreme Court upheld Obamacare (the Affordable Care Act) and extended the right to marry to same-sex couples across the country. The United States and several other countries reached an agreement with Iran on limiting that country's nuclear program. Dzhokhar Tsarnaev was found guilty of the 2013 Boston Marathon terrorist attack and was sentenced to death. Aaron Hernandez was convicted of first-degree murder and sentenced to life in prison.

The Patriots won the Super Bowl, 28-24, on an incredible last-second interception by Malcom Butler. The Patriots accomplished this despite being bogged down in the "Deflategate" controversy in which quarterback Tom Brady was accused of tampering with the air pressure of game balls. Red Sox star Pedro Martinez was elected to the baseball hall of fame. Providence College defeated Boston University to win its first-ever NCAA men's hockey championship. The United States won the Women's World Cup.

Jon Stewart left the *Daily Show*, and *Star Wars: The Force Awakens* broke box office records.

Initiative

Sovanna

By **Fred Faust** on Sept. 21, 2015
—

In 2015, Fred Faust wrote a series of profiles of Lowell people who have demonstrated extraordinary initiative in community affairs. Their contributions range across city life, from business and health care to social services and the environment. Following are five in-depth posts about these inspiring leaders. This series added a new dimension to the RichardHowe.com blog, long-form journalism, at least relative to our standard practice. Because the profiles were so compelling on first reading and remain so, we grouped them in a section of their own, "Initiative."—RPH

Sovanna Pouv savors the satisfaction of a job that helps people daily. Yet he continues to feel the weight of a genocide that casts a long shadow over family life for all Cambodians. At 34 years old, he has come a long way through his perseverance and initiative.

> "Initiative to me means taking the extra step. It's a challenge, but you want to take it. I'm in this work to give back because the community took a step for me."

Today, Pouv is the executive director of the Cambodian Mutual Assistance Association (CMAA). He is credited with bringing stability and good will to the organization. CMAA was founded in 1984 to help assimilate new immigrants into a new and very different environment. Because of church-based resettlement efforts after the genocide in their country, many Cambodians came to Lowell seeking a new life. The country had been destabilized by the impacts of the American involvement in Southeast Asia. In the resulting takeover by the Communist Khmer Rouge, Pol Pot and his army attempted to kill all professionals, government workers, and other skilled citizens with the excuse of trying to bring back an agrarian culture. Among the millions killed were Pouv's maternal grandmother and grandfather. Pouv believes he inherited their commitment to social good. His grandmother assisted with the development of agricultural programs. Pouv's grandfather was a teacher.

ESCAPING CAMBODIA

During her attempt to escape the "killing fields" in Cambodia, Pouv's mother was shot in the ankle by the Khmer Rouge. While the group she was with continued their escape, she was left behind in a ditch. She was eventually rescued by a group of Cambodians now fighting with the Thai army. One of these soldiers ultimately became Pouv's father. Pouv was born in 1980 in a Thai refugee camp. The family was there for nearly two years before settling in Chicago. They relocated to Lowell in 1988 when Pouv's mother and sister reunited.

Growing up in a single-parent home with three other siblings was not easy. The family moved frequently. Customs and language were unfamiliar. Pouv was held back in second grade. Cousins and peers joined street gangs. At one time, one of Pouv's cousins was tried but not convicted of attempted murder. Pouv described himself as a "nerdy student" who got along with everyone. Over time, he did well in school. Unlike others, he resisted dropping out or getting involved with gangs. He credits his mom's sacrifices and the Big Brother-Big Sister's Adam Project for directing him towards more productive activities. But other circumstances would intervene after graduation from high school.

THINGS HAPPEN

"I had some things happen in my life," Pouv says. This is the way he introduces becoming a father at age 20. "I was blessed," he stated. The blessing was Bryanna Honor Pouv, who is now a happy and radiant 14-year-old student at Lowell High School.

Bryanna's mother was in and out of their lives for the first year after Bryanna's birth. She was younger than Pouv and initially forbidden by her parents to interact with either Sovanna or Bryanna. Over time, this situation resolved itself and, while not together, Bryanna now has the active support of both parents.

To care for Bryanna, he dropped out of Middlesex Community College and left his job at a toy store. For the first year, he and his baby daughter lived in a friend's basement. His brother and his mom helped. It was hard, and he became depressed. But he decided that he owed more to his daughter and himself.

LEFT-HAND MAN AT UTEC

Eventually, Pouv applied for a training program and drew a job as a street worker and administrative assistant at the United Teen Equality Center (UTEC). In addition to first-hand experience with gang environments, Pouv had the ability to handle administrative issues and technology. He was hired minutes into his interview with UTEC Executive Director Gregg Croteau. According to Pouv, it was a "turning point for the better" in his life. Because Pouv was left-handed, Croteau branded him his "left-hand man." Croteau became his mentor and remains an inspiration today for his social commitment and teaching skills. "I learned so much from Gregg about non-profits. It was about working with young people, with trade people, architects, and other professionals."

A GOOD HEART

After 12 years at UTEC and a brief stint at a Lowell tech company, he heard that the top job at CMAA was open. It was a little intimidating. CMAA was a longstanding organization and well known in the Cambodian community. Many elders had served on the board. Some of the angst and conflicts within the community had also impacted CMAA over the years. While stabilized recently, Pouv wondered if he had the stature and qualifications for the job.

In fact, friends urged Pouv to apply for the executive position at CMAA. "I didn't think I was ready to take on this big a job," he recalls." As he was thinking about the matter, one of his friends told him, "You are a good person. You have a good heart. You have a good soul." He thought about it over and over. One month later, he applied for the job.

"Initiative to me means taking the extra step. It's a challenge, but you want to take it. I'm in this work to give back because the community took a big step for me."

What skills did he rely on to bring calm and direction to CMAA? "I can be naïve even when I've done my research and have a good sense of what is going on. I might say, Oh I didn't realize that." The strategy gave him the ability to learn and to approach issues on a merit basis. "After a while I gained trust." That trust has enabled him to be a leader that the board has rallied around. He's worked closely with partners and built bridges to the mainstream community.

THE 1.5 GENERATION

"We have a new generation in Lowell," Pouv says, referring to what he calls "the 1.5 generation" of younger Cambodians. At 35-plus years since the first Cambodians arrived in Lowell, he and his generation are more assimilated in America. The members of this generation, born in the United States, speak English as a native language. But he is distressed that many of his peers do not fulfill their potential. The challenge he is taking on is of great importance in seeking to understand the Cambodian culture.

"How can we get more young people involved? I want to recruit people for management jobs and new ventures. Too often we are intimidated because of the fear of rejection and because parents cautioned us to be careful. By being careful, they meant anything having to do with the government, police, and people we didn't know. It was like a form of PTSD, Post-Traumatic Stress Disorder. I want to see more young Cambodian Americans stepping up and taking larger roles. Many other immigrant groups have done the same thing."

WHITE MEN IN SUITS

"My group of friends is a good example of how we were brought up. Of the 10, maybe two of us work in an office setting. The rest all work in manufacturing. They are skilled, smart, but never take that extra step of going to college. It's the fear of unknown and intimidation. That's a challenge I want to address."

Pressed to explain that feeling of intimidation, Pouv recounts some of his first efforts back at UTEC to work within the mainstream business community. "In my early 20s, I was intimidated. I felt so uncomfortable. It's being the only person of color in a room of white men in suits," he says.

Sovanna Pouv is trying to change this mindset. Working with board members and staff, he intends to do it through social interaction, partnering, and building confidence in general. He is concerned that the recent backlash against immigration may hamper these efforts. "I think this country needs to focus more on celebrating the lives that are created here and the opportunities for everyone to benefit. Immigrants contribute their skills and experience and have helped to grow this country."

DEFINING SUCCESS

At 34 years old, Sovanna Pouv is a success story. He has demonstrated heart, grit, and initiative. A discussion with Pouv imparts a quiet but powerful message. The lesson is that time has come for self-respect and community respect for all. Pouv has seen the CMAA turn a corner. He looks forward to more collaboration and further success.

HISTORY AS IT HAPPENS

Sisson and Slater: Mill City Grows

By **Fred Faust** on Oct. 5, 2015
—

"To be in the farm industry as a young woman, you have to work really hard. You have to make sure that everyone knows you're for real."—Lydia Sisson, co-founder, Mill City Grows

Francey Slater and Lydia Sisson are modest about it, but they want to change the world. They see healthy foods, healthy families, and greater community participation as changing health trends for the better, including a way to combat the frightening increase in childhood obesity. Fortunately, they decided that their healthy start would be made in their adopted city. They named their organization "Mill City Grows." To be sure, it is growing. After hearing their serendipitous story, it is hard not to think of these two young women as the proverbial two peas in a pod.

At the start of the recorded discussion about the organization, Slater helpfully suggests noting the contents of each speaker's remarks with their names. "Are you going to be able to tell us apart? People say we sound alike," Slater states.

The history of Slater's and Sisson's work together supports a theory of predestination.

Both women have strong social commitments. Both had majored in college in aspects of agriculture. Both had acquired practical experience by getting their hands dirty. Though in different schools and at different times, both had chosen food-related internships or farm work in Italy. These types of experiences gave them a sense of food in a culture that valued quality, presentation, and natural, healthful ingredients.

A SEED GROWS AT UTEC

"We first met at a job interview in Lowell," Slater explains. "I guess once we spoke, we found out we were cut from the same cloth." The details are that Slater interviewed for a job at a food program at UTEC in Lowell. She had graduated in 2003 from the University of Pennsylvania, majoring in psychology and biology. Sisson graduated in 2006 from Vassar College with a degree in environmental studies.

As of 2007, Sisson was departing a farm-support job at the non-profit youth group and was asked to be part of an interview team. Slater was one of the candidates interviewed and offered the position, but decided to continue working in Cambridge. Subsequently, they kept running into each other at events and social gatherings. At another such encounter in Jamaica Plain, Sisson says they laughed about these continuing occurrences, remarking at about the same time, "Hey, we should be friends."

When Slater and her husband decided to find a more central apartment location because of their commutes, Sisson and her spouse offered to rent them an apartment. According to Slater, "They owned a two-family house in Lowell and asked, 'Do you want to rent the upstairs apartment?' And that worked out well. That was really the fertile ground for all of this."

The conversations about working together picked up steam given their new proximity.

They cemented their relationship and agreed that they should give up their full-time jobs. They laugh about their income for the first six months, but credit their spouses for enthusiasm and full support. In 2011, they founded Mill City Grows.

Today, the non-profit organization's assets include eight full-time and five part-time employees and a budget of $550,000. They have a farm site and multiple neighborhood gardens. They have also acquired a retail food van, farming equipment, and many, many enthusiastic volunteers. They have won grants, started school programs, and have been generally recognized as having achieved dramatic successes quickly. Recently, they held a fundraiser at UTEC's auditorium and function hall that drew more than 200 people to celebrate their success. This year, they each had their first child—about one month apart. At 31 and 34 years of age respectively, Sisson and Slater lead busy lives.

WE KEPT COMING BACK

Professionally, Slater and Sisson encountered immediate skepticism about their plans. When they had tried to meet with the former City Manager, two assistant city managers were delegated to speak with them. Slater recalls, "They said, you want to do what? A farm in Lowell? A garden? Oh sure, cool. But so many people had come to them with interesting ideas," Sisson says. "We were not going to be persuaded otherwise. We kept coming back, trying to figure out what we needed to do to make this idea a reality."

Interestingly, the City Hall skeptics ended up being some of their strongest supporters. Sisson explains. "One day, Henri Marchand suddenly called back and asked, 'Do you still want to do that garden thing? I think I found you something.'" Adam Baacke, then assistant city manager for Planning and Development, caught the enthusiasm and later joined their executive board. The City supported collaboration with the active Back Central Neighborhood Organization, rewarding them for their interest and initiative.

Sisson also described their first meeting with Tom Bellegarde, the longtime public parks overseer in Lowell. "When he first met us, he just said, 'No way. This is never going to work.' Now he's really supportive. He does so much to support us and help us succeed. Tom is great."

"So, that probably is the kind of thing that happens to everyone," Sisson recalls, "but we were not going to be persuaded otherwise. No, we were going to do this." Slater and Sisson procured a grant from Lowell General Hospital to focus on the health benefits of diet. They had enough now to pay themselves for five hours of work each week. They kept moving forward, participating in an accelerator business program offered by E-for-All, a non-profit organization that advances innovation and entrepreneurship in the Merrimack Valley.

Meanwhile, the first project with the Back Central neighborhood had kicked off. The neighborhood and their supporters were a great fit. Dave Koch and his large family and their friends had already been planting fruit trees and reclaiming abandoned property in the area.

Explains Slater, "So to get started we had set up a board, build a model, and establish a brand. We were going to quit our jobs. Wow, we said, we're going to go through with this. The City had the money to put in a garden through the City Manager's Neighborhood Impact Initiative. David Koch and the neighbors were great, but they didn't know where to start." Sisson continues the story. "And we were like, we can do this." Slater just smiles. "And you know what? Neither of us had ever even started a community garden."

COMMUNITY GARDEN NO. 1: SUCCESS

The development of a community garden in Back Central commenced a new building program. In an urban community with a history of post-industrial waste, a community garden—especially a large one as you see on Middlesex Street downtown—is not a simple or inexpensive matter. The bed needs to be framed and raised and significant clean soils must be brought in. Irrigation is needed. There is a need to till, plant, fertilize, and separate crops. And of course, there is watering, weeding, and the harvest. Training sessions, volunteer recruits, and "guardians" of the gardens all were needed. To date, there are four community gardens in Lowell.

Mill City Grows has also developed educational programs and events, such as the Annual Harvest Festival that recently took place at the North Common in Lowell. An astounding 1,000-plus people attended the harvest event that brought life and attention to the historic North Common. The organization also has a truck with walk-in trailer that sets up as a portable fruit and produce stand. Weekend booths have been a success as well. Slater and Sisson, however, point to partnering with the Lowell school system and school children as the potential game changer.

CULTURE SHIFT

"The partnership piece for us has been a huge opportunity," says Sisson. "Working in the schools, for example, is the kind of thing that's become so much larger than us. It's part of a culture shift. That way, we'll be able to influence hundreds and thousands of kids."

The satisfaction of starting a new and successful endeavor is just the beginning for Slater and Sisson. They're working on a strategic plan for the next five years. They expect to up their budget by about 25 percent next year. They are strong believers in the need to scale up to be able to make an impact on the health and wellness of entire communities. As people are more conscious of food and health issues than ever before, they say modestly that they just happened to be here at the right time, and that Lowell has been the "right place."

Slater credits the openness of Lowell to new ideas. She also says that the ability to seize on existing contacts and partnerships is essential. Sisson continues: "Healthy food, healthy eating, and healthy communities. If we achieve that with the schools, it means that our mission has leapt forward without having to build the infrastructure from the ground up every time we start out. Leveraging existing partnerships is what it's all about."

Because two positive, dynamic, and socially committed women decided to get their hands dirty, and because they never gave up, Lowell has a most inspiring story and healthier future.

DEFINING INITIATIVE

"What is initiative," asks Sisson, mulling the question. "Initiative can be refusing to say no. But it also can mean showing up, too." Partner Slater agrees. "Yes, for the gate to open, you have to be constantly trying. I think we've been able to thrive just because, again, we keep showing up."

Finally, Francey Slater and Lydia Sisson credit their husbands, Aaron Slater and Derek Mitchell, as among their strongest and most committed supporters. At the recent Harvest Festival or on another crisp autumn day, you will expect to see Aaron and Derek, likely with babies, Julian and Layla, in their front packs. You can also expect to see Lydia and Francey, the Mill City Grows co-founders, enthusiastically planting new seeds wherever they go.

George Duncan: The Kid and the Kool-Aid

By **Fred Faust** on Oct. 14, 2015
—

As a kid in Lowell's Back Central neighborhood, George Duncan didn't drink the Kool-Aid, he sold it.

"I started when I was very young on Back Central Street. I realized that you could make a lot more money selling things than by waiting for your parents to give you your allowance. I realized that by taking initiative and offering a product or a service, you could find a way to make money and then do other things with it. So, I started very early in business."

His Kool-Aid stand, according to Duncan, gave him his first business lesson. That included "organization, follow up, customer service, just putting things together." Later endeavors included raising and training homing pigeons with his dad. This developed into a successful breeding business. "Right there in the back streets of Lowell we were selling champion homing pigeons to people around the country and even the world," Duncan remembers. As another indication of future enterprise, Duncan single handedly organized an entire neighborhood carnival with 30 booths. "It was a lot of fun."

Duncan attended Lowell High School. He describes himself as "drifting" through his courses. For a time, he even considered applying for a job at a local shoe manufacturer. His professional career may not have happened at all if a history teacher at the high school, Wyman Trull, had not sensed potential in a young George Duncan. Trull befriended and challenged George to work harder and to focus on academics. Duncan cites Trull as his earliest mentor. That close and meaningful relationship lasted for many decades, according to Duncan, until Trull's passing. After graduating from Lowell High, Duncan attended and received a business degree from Lowell Technological Institute, the future UMass Lowell.

Duncan found employment at the then-dominant local financial institution, Union National Bank. There he encountered the ultimate local banker and civic leader, the legendary Homer Bourgeois. Bourgeois was not just the president of the bank; he was the major player in the Lowell community. Duncan says that when someone needed to get something done—from a loan to an apartment to a job, they went to "Uncle Homer." Duncan recalls, "That was the way it was done; people would send you to Mr. Bourgeois and tell you, Uncle Homer will take care of that." It was said that Bourgeois controlled banking, the hospitals, major businesses, and, occasionally, City Hall. Duncan took advantage of the overall learning experience at Union National Bank to better understand the benign side of community linkage.

Another key in Duncan's career was his association with Edward Redstone. Redstone owned First Bank in Chelmsford and Lowell. Redstone, whose father created the theatre chain that brother, Sumner, leveraged into a billion-dollar media powerhouse, was brilliant, but could have daily mood swings. Duncan had a sense of calm and patience that complemented Redstone's force of personality. Duncan became president and eventually CEO of First Bank. As bank mergers swept out smaller banks, Hartford National Bank purchased First Bank, and then was merged into Shawmut Bank. Redstone retired, but Duncan bided his time, gathered a core of former associates and on January 3, 1989, launched Enterprise Bank and Trust. Located on Merrimack Street, in the Old City Hall Building, it had no drive-up and no suburban branches.

Did Duncan ever have doubts about starting a bank at a time other financial institutions were failing? "I didn't really have doubts. Did people tell me I was a little crazy to start a bank? (He doesn't answer but laughs.) First, I got to know a lot of people in the community. Second, I knew how to run a bank because I'd picked up knowledge and experience over the years. I had also put a lot of people into business. So, I knew I could go to these people and ask them to be customers and shareholders."

Duncan's instincts and contacts proved critical to success. He and his team raised sufficient capital and built a very local board of directors. A key board member Duncan credits is businessman Arnold Lerner. "Arnold was and continues to be invaluable as a board member. In terms of leadership and counsel, Arnold is one of the advisors and mentors I've always relied on."

The Enterprise "Statement of Values" includes a very basic principle:

"We play an active role in making every community in which we operate a better place to work and live."

Why was Duncan confident that a new, small community bank could compete?

"I saw that the banking industry was going the wrong way. The big banks were eating up all the community banks, and the merged banks weren't treating customers well. Locally, one of the larger banks had failed, along with several others. So, the timing happened to pay off. We were there as a new bank, but with a lot of experienced staff people and a great board. That ability I had as a young person to organize was there, and I picked good people. Those are the things that I had the experience and confidence to do."

Duncan was asked why his was willing to take a risk on downtown Lowell.

"I was highly invested in the rebirth of the downtown. I drank the same Kool-Aid that people like Paul Tsongas and Pat Mogan drank. There was really no compelling reason to build a bank in downtown Lowell. It would have been much easier to build an operations center on some big piece of land and not cope with many kinds of urban issues."

The commitment to Lowell ultimately delivered a major bank operation to the downtown. Duncan, who has been described as a self-made architect, has added first-class design, flowers, and art to the mix at the bank's 21 branches. Every bank has original art and plantings, when possible. It's not so much a brand but a personal ethic.

"My daughter, son, and friends have kidded me that the reason we've done so many banks and branches is not really about business, it's about gardens and art and architecture. And I say, well, those are really three very important things."

Duncan's modest office is located close to the main teller line at the Merrimack Street bank. It has glass panels and a door that is almost always open. When Duncan stepped down as CEO, the board of directors designated Jack Clancy as successor in 2007. Clancy, along with Duncan and President Richard Main, have worked collaboratively since the founding of the bank. Assets now exceed $2 billion. There are more than 400 Enterprise Bank employees. To his self-professed dismay, despite stepping down as CEO some eight years ago, Duncan's pace seems not to have slowed. At 75 years old, Duncan says he is still "one of those people who gets up early in the morning with a head of steam and looks forward to going to work."

What motivates Duncan today?

"I like people," he says. "I enjoy the company of my family, people, and friends. Beyond whatever I learned as a young kid, I was very lucky to have teachers, business people whom I learned from, and a lot of great mentors."

Duncan links the commitment of the bank and other businesses to further progress downtown. He is positive about Enterprise Bank's continued growth and Lowell's as well.

"Given all that's going on with Middlesex Community College, UMass Lowell, and the Hamilton Canal District, I feel Lowell is really about to pop. It's going to be based on innovation, new businesses, and start-ups. I see new people moving into the city. The culture is going to grow and change. That will be a benefit to the city as a whole."

Duncan is proud of the growth and evolution of the bank.

"We've gone from being a small company to a business that's listed on the NASDAQ stock exchange. It is still a local bank. Going forward, we have a big empty parking lot. If the bank continues to grow and prosper, I can see us building a large corporate headquarters on that parking lot next to Old City Hall."

While classically understated, to Duncan the bank's success is a corollary to the best that Horatio Alger had to offer.

"My father always said never underestimate America. I feel the same way about investing in business and investing in Lowell. I feel that Lowell has a great future. There are lots of terrific things going on. I'm very proud of the fact that as a nationally listed business we're located right here on Merrimack Street in downtown Lowell."

From Merrimack Street to Duncan's childhood Back Central Street home, it's just under a mile. George Duncan, though, has come a long way.

HISTORY AS IT HAPPENS

Local Heroes Made a Splash

By **Fred Faust** on Nov. 27, 2015
—

A neighborhood parents' group—mostly moms with young children—made a $700,000 "splash" and created a major playground attraction at Lowell's Shedd Park. "We might be the most successful unsuccessful people you've ever met," says Kelliann Bazemore, from the Friends of Shedd Park.

Recently, Meg Chase, Carrie Carolan, and Kelliann Bazemore gathered to recall a story that began some ten years ago with a simple question from a friend from Andover: "Why do you put up with a playground that's so awful?" When they took a closer look at the old monkey bars, asphalt base, and the long metal slides that sent children hurtling to the ground—or burnt them on hot days—they agreed it was a "disaster."

Bazemore, Carolan, and Chase were among a group of 13 parents with young children who decided to tackle that question themselves. As neighbors in Belvidere, they spent a lot of time on the ball fields at Shedd Park. The group, mostly moms, started with the modest goal of replacing a "decrepit and dangerous playground," according to Chase.

Today, Shedd Park is a destination for reasons other than just the ball fields and tennis courts. The historic pavilion has been restored. In the summer, children whoop, laugh, and dance through the water jets of the varied Splash Pad features. Children of all ages and physical abilities can also take advantage of the imaginative and colorful playground next door. Covered picnic tables are present as well for moms and dads trying to keep up with their energetic children.

How the group surpassed its goal goes back to Kelliann

Bazemore's definition of success and the commitment of the group. "We were like the little train that could. We just kept on chugging along." The group gained momentum early because of their history of working together, affection for Lowell as a community, and formed partnerships.

"While a couple of people looked at us funny, and said, Oh, you want to build a park, good luck with that," Bazemore remembers, the group's familiarity and contacts within the city "made all the difference."

THE MOMS AND THE MARKETING GUY

Rob Fardin, a neighbor and part of the parents' group, has professional marketing credentials. This includes an MBA in sports management from the University of Oregon. Fardin and his wife had two young children at the time. His counsel was, "Think big."

Fardin recalls, "I said, if you want to run a golf tournament, I'm out of here. If you want to run a bake sale (one of the original ideas), that's going to be a lot of cake and cookies." He advised them to go local and to use ideas and themes that would be successful in attracting attention and building a loyal audience.

It was mostly us women and Rob," says Bazemore. According to Carolan, "He contributed all the crazy, creative ideas."

"Well, for example, I saw that everyone loved *Dancing with the Stars*," Fardin says. One of the first so-called "crazy" ideas was to draft famous local "stars" and to hold the contest at the neglected pavilion at Shedd Park. Thus, the "Cotillion at the Pavilion" was born. Fardin not only named it and sketched the invitation, but also went to the pavilion with volunteers to clean a fireplace that likely hadn't been cleaned for decades.

Fardin describes the group in sports terms. "We came together as a team. You have to in order to be successful. We said it was time to do something for the community and to think big. Kelliann and I went to grade school together, and she was great. So, I said this is what we need to do. We need to start with $100,000. I mean how many bake sales can you do? It was pretty quiet for a moment there. I challenged them to think bigger. Hey, the people will come out and support it. I'm a believer in copying things that work. I mean, don't reinvent the wheel, retread it."

Fardin's large vision also included keeping people focused on the park and its needs. "Find your lane," he intones. "Find something related to what you're doing. They focused on the park and their retread was a local version of *Dancing with the Stars*.

DANCING WITH THE STARS

Amazingly, the "Cotillion at the Pavilion" attracted some 400 attendees. "It was fun and talked about," according to Fardin, "including several articles in the *Lowell Sun*. We grossed $30,000 at one event. It was our big "Oh my God!" moment. By the time the next year came around, people were asking, When are you going to do that again?"

Meg Chase described that first night as taking place in a driving and chilly rain. Setting up that afternoon, they wondered if anyone would show up. The pavilion is open on the sides and offered little protection. "Fortunately, someone came up with the idea of getting giant posters to decorate," said Chase. "That was the thing that saved us. It saved the event."

In fact, the attendance was amazing. That first year a dazzling champion also emerged on the dance floor. A good-humored City Councilor Rita Mercier and partner swept to victory. Despite the weather, it had been a great night for all, and the *Lowell Sun* followed with an article that caught people's attention and imagination. The event was repeated for three years straight. It was continuously successful and produced other memorable scenes: a poignant father-daughter dance team of Connie and Larry Martin, who has since passed away, as well as the bravado of local business person James O'Donnell channeling John

Travolta in very tight white suit. What more can you say about a prominent funeral director dancing to the song "Staying Alive"?

It was the just start of continuing publicity and several unintentionally comic experiences. This included a near frozen Santa (Rob's dad), a failed Guinness World Record stunt involving not quite enough water pistols, and a Winterfest float that suffered black-outs and mechanical failures.

FRIENDS OF SHEDD

During an earlier fundraising effort, Bazemore had been introduced to Thomas Bellegarde, the City's Commissioner of Parks and Recreation. Everyone involved in the efforts at Shedd mentions Bellegarde. "He was incredibly helpful and positive." Bellegarde enlisted early, cut through red tape and championed the endeavor. He helped to rally the local legislative delegation that ultimately won a major complementary grant. Former City Manager Bernie Lynch and many private citizens such as John and Linda Chemaly stepped forward in support. Nancye Tuttle and Mary Sampas of the *Lowell Sun* contributed articles about events that built momentum and credibility.

Many other events followed. The women laughed as they remembered "frozen Santa" at the Shedd Pavilion and frostbitten volunteers as their Winterfest float went dark before its scheduled cruise down Merrimack Street. They dispatched Fardin to purchase multiple flashlights. They also knocked on doors, conducted raffles and silent auctions, and found other ways to solicit funds.

The Shedd legacy was also used as a rallying point. In 1910, Freeman B. Shedd bequeathed 50 acres to the City of Lowell and added an endowment of $100,000 to develop fields and other enhancements in order to create "Shedd Park." The first condition of his letter, referring to the land, stated:

"That it shall forever be used as a park and recreation

or playground for the citizens and children of the City of Lowell, and for no other purpose."

In addition to the legacy argument, the group stressed the condition of the playground and now-closed swimming pool, which engineers had determined was beyond repair. Within the first two years alone, the group surprised itself with the extent of their fundraising. They had brought in nearly $200,000. This inspired them to do even more. Lowell had been successful in attracting funds for a Cawley Stadium remake, including new turf. They worked with state delegation members. "Those relationships were key," says Bazemore. They were eventually awarded an "amazing" grant of $500,000. The new grant allowed the park improvements to include the addition of the Splash Pad. Not only were they having unexpected success, "As a group," says Chase, "we had fun. We learned. It was like a sounding board. I think this is where people got their feet wet."

LESSONS

Looking back, Bazemore says, "Our kids are older, and we've gone on to other things, community things. But we're all still involved and friends. The great thing was it was really about building relationships and making things happen."

Chase agrees. "Everybody had different strengths. We shared responsibilities, and everyone had something they did to contribute. It all came together in the end." Chase also gives a lot of the thematic credit to Fardin. "If it wasn't for Rob and his crazy ideas, big ideas, and a background in marketing, we might not have been successful."

Of course, Fardin disagrees on the factors that defined success. "What made this group successful is that they were willing to get out of their comfort zones. Who wants to ask for money? Hey, know your lane. Ask yourself, what can you do well? What is going to help draw attention to what you want to do?

Think big ideas that raise exposure. Try to do something new and interesting." He repeats again, "This was about teamwork."

Bazemore attributes the group's success to other factors as well. She describes "an underlying pride in Lowell" and the desire to help Lowell succeed. Her advice to others is to "Write down ideas. Ask for help. In this city, you'll get it. If someone sent me an invitation for a fundraiser for a playground, I'd really feel that I'd have to go. I mean anything to keep improving our city. I think we're all rooted in the city, and we want our kids to do well here and to want to come back."

Freeman Shedd's last condition for acceptance of the land by the City of Lowell stated that he should have the "right to erect... a suitable gateway and entrance, with a tablet or tablets thereon with the following transcription: "Shedd Playground. A gift to the City of Lowell by Freeman Ballard Shedd, A.D. 1910."

The Belvidere neighbors' group and their friends have also made a "suitable addition" to Lowell's largest and most famous park. No doubt that Mr. Shedd, watching the trials, tribulations, and ultimate success of the group, would be appreciative of their efforts to make Shedd Park and Lowell a better place.

HISTORY AS IT HAPPENS

Dorcas Grigg-Saito: Low Key, High Success

By **Fred Faust** on Dec. 14, 2015
—

The Lowell Community Health Center takes care of more than 500 patients every day, whether the people can afford health care or not. The non-profit organization includes 400 employees who speak 28 different languages, reflecting Lowell's diverse population. The new 100,000-square foot Moses Greeley Parker building opened two years ago. It offers medical, behavioral health, and community health services to about one half of Lowell's population every year. The new health center resides on a street that not long ago was known largely for drugs and prostitution.

Dorcas Grigg-Saito sits at a conference table in a modest office with an appropriately long view of the city. Despite her impressive resume and success, she admits to being a shy person from childhood.

SHY AND GUTSY

With a track record that includes elevating and inspiring a health care institution and entire city, how does she explain the dichotomy between shyness and obvious success? "I am a member of what we call the shy, gutsy group. I just try to focus on what needs to be done."

Grigg-Saito is low-key, with an easy smile and self-deprecating sense of humor. "You get up, come to work, and plug every day. Every day is busy. We used to have someone here who'd say, 'Just give me one dull moment.' That sort of captures it. For 18 years, I don't think there's been one dull moment." Keeping busy apparently helps to keep your knees from knocking. Grigg-Saito describes that as a common experience when she was first asked to speak to groups in public.

GROWING UP IN THE SOUTH: BLACK AND WHITE

The 68-year old CEO's upbringing is reminiscent of the novel *To Kill a Mockingbird*. She might have played the role of Scout, learning about racism and prejudice—in this case—at the knee of her Baptist minister father.

"I was born in North Carolina. Growing up, I lived in Georgia and Louisiana, too. I probably went to something like five schools before I was in seventh grade. We moved all the time. If you're a Southern Baptist minister, whenever you're going to make a change, a new church, new job, the phrase in our house was usually that God called me. That's truly what he (my dad) felt. So, when I was in the fourth grade, we were at breakfast, and he got a telephone call, and he said God had called him to go back to North Carolina. At the time, I thought that was pretty cool, that God would call him like that on the phone.

"My father was a minister, but after I was about six years old he wasn't a minister of a particular church. His job was to improve relationships between black and white Baptists. So, I spent a lot of time in churches. When he did preach, it was usually in an African American church. When we lived in Louisiana, I was probably 10, and that was in the late 1950s. Alexandria, Louisiana—you can imagine that it was very segregated. So, when I was in junior high school and high school, my parents would have friends over who were African American. Recently, I was in North Carolina visiting a friend and she said, 'You know, I never sat at the dinner table with anyone who was African American until I came to your house.' For our family, that was the way it was." As a result, she says, "We weren't the most popular family in town."

Grigg-Saito remembers her father receiving death threats. Her mother, too, was strongly committed to issues of equality and fairness. "My mother and father one time were traveling in rural Louisiana, and they stopped at a gas station. They had pamphlets in the back of their car that had a black hand and a white hand that read 'God, make me color blind.' So, the attendant came over to my mother and asked what the pamphlet meant and she said, 'Just what it says.' And he glared and said, 'If you weren't traveling with him, I would have got my shotgun out and I would have shot him.' That was the kind of thing that was happening then."

The experiences growing up shaped Grigg-Saito's moral judgment and career choices.

"I told this story when I received the Girls, Inc., award in Lowell. I remember as a kid going shopping in a Sears and there was a "colored" water fountain, as it was called then, and a white one. I remember going over to the colored one and drinking out of it. So, I guess my being conscious of these things was around that age, knowing it was wrong."

A VARIED RESUME

The future Health Center Director had a lot of her own stops professionally. She attended the University of North Carolina at Chapel Hill where she was trained as a physical therapist. She then moved north, initially to Yale-New Haven hospital. She worked as a physical therapist and taught English in Japan for six months. Eventually, she received a master's degree from Harvard University's School of Public Health with a degree in Health Policy and Management. After working at Brookline Health Department and starting a rural health center in North Carolina, she took up physical therapy once again and became a childbirth educator and doula, which is a professional who provides support to an expectant mother before and just after childbirth. She raised two daughters, as well, with husband Yoshio. The couple met when she visited Tokyo. They were married several years later, in 1975. Japanese style and culture made a formative impact as well on Grigg-Saito.

"There was something about Japan that I just loved. My personality fits in very well in Japan. Quiet. It was a great opportunity to learn what it's like to not be the majority. That culture is so different than ours. All of that certainly had an impact on what I've ended up doing."

Grigg-Saito also worked for Planned Parenthood, did legislative advocacy, and then held a position with the Massachusetts Department of Public Health, assisting with refugee resettlement and health promotion. There she was fascinated and motivated by the different cultures she was working with, along with the added benefit of "a lot of good food." She also received a fellowship from the National Association of Community Health Centers, which brought her to the nearby Greater Lawrence Community Health Center.

THIS IS MY PLACE

Grigg-Saito was offered the director's position at Lowell Community Health Center after having accepted another job in Cambridge just weeks before. "I'd been to Lowell a lot," she recalls. "I remember the first day that I came for an interview." She had arrived very early and waited outside the building before meeting the board. There she witnessed some of the things that were often common to that upper Merrimack Street neighborhood at the time. She thought, she recalls, "This is my place!"

As for her interview, Grigg-Saito says, "I'm sure I thought I didn't do very well. I had two great job choices. This one really brought it together." What does she remember about the early days at the Health Center? She smiles again. "Well, there wasn't much of a finance system." She also remembers hearing stories about the former director practicing putting in the hallway. "It was a health center that was in need of some stronger infrastructure and improvement in its culture. It needed to be respectful and more welcoming."

Developing an identity and culture was one of Grigg-Saito's first tasks. Clients were diverse and often intimidated by institutions and authority. She was conscious of this need—again, a sea change for the health center.

"I think it came from my family life. In addition to my father's work, with my mother, it was always that it didn't matter how rich or poor, the color of your skin, but she was always welcoming and warm to everybody. So, there's working to understand people who are different. I went to a lot of cultural awareness and racism training, and it helps you understand how you come across to other people. So I think it's about being able to be open to others and to find out from them how you're being received."

At the health center, the attitude of the staff was also critical. "It starts in recruitment and interviewing; making clear what's important. We provide a variety of cultural competence training, and if problems arise, we try to bring people together and talk about differences."

Having experience with prejudice and given recent national issues, Grigg-Saito is asked whether she believes racism can be overcome. "Sure, I think it's teachable," she says without any pause. "There's a whole spectrum from stereotyping to discrimination to racism. Part of it is exposure to others. Certainly, racism is alive and becoming more obvious," though she believes that "progress has been made."

THE BIG INITIATIVE: A NEW HEALTH CENTER

The new health center is the product of an amazing fund-raising campaign that generated some $5 million in private and public contributions for what was a $42 million project. Grigg-Saito gives credit to her board, development director, and her team of committed professionals. She sums it up simply. "A lot of people who learned about our story and helped us." She also mentions positive coverage in the *Lowell Sun*, which featured more than

20 articles envisioning the potential of a new and improved health center for Lowell.

The new building consolidates multiple properties that were developed piecemeal over time. Rather than constructing a new building on an outlying parcel, Grigg-Saito and the board chose to preserve and renovate a portion of the historic Hamilton Mill—located in the heart of a longstanding urban renewal district. Both the funding and construction involved monumental challenges. The resulting facility is striking in design, respectful of clients and employees, and has helped to energize the area known as the Jackson-Appleton-Middlesex (JAM) area.

The property bears the name of a prominent Lowell physician known for his national contributions as a Civil War physician and administrator. Later, Moses Greeley Parker returned to his hometown and endowed various community initiatives including the current Parker Lectures. A major supporter of the health center was the Parker Foundation, founded by a nephew of Dr. Parker's, Theodore Edson Parker.

The health center provides family and women's health, tackles substance abuse, offers a teen program, two school-based health centers, a Southeast Asian-oriented Metta Health Center, mental health services, outreach, and training programs.

THOUGHTS ABOUT LIFE AND RETIREMENT

Grigg-Saito recently announced that she is retiring in May. She is not yet done, however, with the health center's growth. Another 100,000-square foot expansion project was recently announced. The additional space will provide expanded medical and behavioral health services as well as dental and vision services and housing, increasing the space by 60 percent.

Asked about how she made her retirement decision, Grigg-Saito comments, "I guess the main thing that went into it is that life is short. I have a daughter Katrina, son-in-law Jonah, and new grandson Taiga, who are living in San Francisco. We'll be able to spend more time with them. Jonah got a great job offer to work for Google. That's a piece of it. Another piece of it is that Yoshio has lived in the country for about 45 years now, and we'll be able to spend time in Tokyo and travel in the next several years.

"Sometimes I think you're taking a chance financially when you retire, but you're also taking a chance if you don't retire and you lose your ability to think or to travel. The health center has changed so much over the years. Whenever I left I wanted it to be at a time when the health center was stable, had accomplished a lot, and able to move to the next chapter. We have a great board that understands the health center and really understands the community. We have a great management staff and leaders throughout the health center. In addition, we're developing the building next door, and that planning and financing should be done before I leave. It seemed like a pretty good time for the health center to make a transition."

EMILY

When Grigg-Saito says, "Life is short," it has a poignant meaning for her and her family.

"In 2011, our daughter, Emily, who was 28 and had suffered from depression through the years, and was amazingly bright, intelligent, funny, outgoing—a student in landscape architecture and urban planning at the University of Washington, Seattle—died by suicide. And that certainly changed our lives. So we learned a lot of things from that. In terms of depression, the thing we came to understand is that people who suffer from depression don't see the world the way we do. Things that we might be able to incorporate into our lives, they're not able to do. There's a trigger. It was the depression that caused her to die.

"One of the things I learned after I came back to work was how many people suffer from depression. Suicide is much more common than most people think, and attempted suicide is even more common. Mental health issues and suicide are certainly not things we talk about. But they are things we need to talk about. If depression was handled the way diabetes is, as an illness, then more people would be able to manage their depression."

Grigg-Saito has focused her grief on helping others. "One specific thing we did was to provide training for faith leaders to provide services for people who have lost someone. We brought people together to talk about the problem." The 20 clerics attending found ways to talk about common issues, and the health center responded as well programmatically.

"When Emily died we asked people to donate to the health center for 'Emily's Room.' On the third floor we have behavioral services with a plaque for Emily." To remember her design and creative side, the health center duplicated a college design project and placed swiveling benches on the main entry bridge over one of Lowell's most dramatic spots, the so-called Industrial Canyon.

"We thought about benches that Emily and two of her classmates had designed. We got the plans. There are three benches in Seattle at a bus stop, and our architect added more benches here that move and twirl. The idea at the bus stop is that you could twirl around and talk to a friend. You could turn to see the bus coming. And the benches on the bridge twirl. It's great to see little kids and big kids and adults swivel and twirl around. That's in Emily's memory as well.

"I think for us as a family we've been pretty good at appreciating every day and the beauty of life around us, and the value of our friends and family. But losing someone who shouldn't have died at that age makes you realize the importance of people around you—the people you love and who love you."

Describing her health center family as very supportive, Grigg-Saito says, "One of the difficulties of leaving the health center, all those people who know me, and I know their stories, well, we all have what my brothers would call 'cross-eyed bears.' The alternate meaning is a 'cross I'd bear.'" She continues. "We all have our burdens that we carry with us. I think of mothers, particularly in the Cambodian community that have lost children, young children. We have come to appreciate that we at least had Emily for 28 years. She was a loving and vibrant part of our family. You go through this would'a-could'a stage. Emily knew that we were a family that shared our love for each other. Emily knew that we loved her."

The recent birth of grandson Taiga has helped the family move forward. "It's very special to have grandchildren." Taiga means "Great River" in Japanese. Rivers are vital in many world cultures. Great rivers flow with life and find their own paths forward.

JUST DO IT

Dorcas Grigg-Saito is inspiring in many ways. She is a teacher, conciliator, leader, and builder. Perhaps she is also a role model for those whose knees may shake just a little before meeting an audience. For Grigg-Saito, the "shy, gutsy" type, it's just part of doing your job.

The key to doing her job, according to Grigg-Saito has been "Hard work and showing up. Developing the important partnerships," as well, she says. "For the health center, I think as we started to develop the building, it really forced us to become more visible. We had a lot of support. We went from no donors to 1,400 donors. We were able to get to know people in Lowell who came to believe in our mission, and gradually we came to believe we could do it."

"Just do it," is the Nike trademark. Nike pays millions to feature athletes like Michael Jordan and LeBron James with their products. If Nike wanted to add a real-life achiever, they might ink a contract with Dorcas Grigg-Saito. But then again, Nike would need to know, hers would be very large shoes to fill.

INITIATIVE

2016

Anti-Trump Rally, 6:00 p.m. Report

By **Paul** on January 4, 2016
—

About 200 people rallying in the Free Speech Zone at 6:00 p.m. Happy to see the second shift show up outside the Tsongas Center at UMass Lowell. After 45 minutes, frostbite was setting in, so I gladly handed off my piece of the stand-out to the next group. Thousands upon thousands in line from the arena doors all down John Cox Circle and wrapping around the post office. It's an orderly process for so many people. Some shouting back at the demonstrators, but nothing nasty. Typical political give-and-take. Twenty reporters and camera people swarmed the first group of demonstrators, interviewing and filming every person they could pull in. Then the media headed inside. Good signs in the demo crowd: Dump Trump, No H8, Shut Up Donald, Black Lives Matter, and more. Chants of "No hate in our state," "Be nice," "Massachusetts's not for sale," and the like. Lots of students, some Boston area folks with signs and a flag, Lowell artists with bright posters, UMass faculty and staff, local activists, everybody cold, cold, cold—but hot with resistance to DT.

HISTORY AS IT HAPPENS

Lowell Week in Review: Jan. 10, 2016

By **Dick** on January 10, 2016
—

DONALD TRUMP RALLY

Last night I finished reading *Foreign Correspondent: A Memoir* by H.D.S. Greenway who wrote for *Time*, *The Washington Post*, and *The Boston Globe* in a career that spanned five decades. Greenway's specialty was reporting from war zones and he visited plenty of them, from Vietnam to Afghanistan. After his time in Bosnia in the early 1990s, Greenway consulted academics in search of an explanation for why neighbors who had lived peaceably for so long suddenly turned on each. Here is what he learned:

> "Among human beings, the stress and fear of losing something, whether it be social position, livelihood, sometimes racial dominance, or one's very life, brings forth xenophobia [i.e., intense or irrational dislike or fear of people from other countries] . . . In times of stress, or when a threat is perceived, people tend to define themselves more narrowly, sharply distinguishing friends from enemies. . . Economic difficulties play a big role in provoking hostility toward ethnic minorities. . . Another common phenomenon [is] 'the egoism of victimization.' So caught up does each group get in its own sense of hurt that it cannot conceive of the hurt it could be doing to others."

That made me think of the Donald Trump rally in Lowell last Monday night. I didn't go, but I watched his speech live online. His folksy, relaxed, almost conspiratorial (with the audience) style was very powerful. Had he gone to law school, he would have been a tremendous trial attorney. Coincidentally, I was reminded of a trial attorney saying as I watched Trump speak: "If the facts are on your side, pound the facts; if the law is on your side, pound the law; if neither is on your side, pound the table." I witnessed a lot of table pounding. Let me share two examples. To get car manufacturing back to the U.S., Trump will "impose" a 35 percent tax on every Ford imported from Mexico. Everyone cheered, but are they also willing to pay 35 percent more for their next automobile? Probably not, but it sounds—strong. The second example is Iraqi oil. Trump promised "to take it." He never explained how we would do that. I think that was the Bush administration's purpose in invading Iraq, and we know how that worked out. But no matter, Trump sounded—strong. I doubt many in the Tsongas Center were there in search of substantive solutions. Some, I assume, were there for the spectacle; others were drawn to Trump's "not a politician" incarnation; still more were there to assuage their sense of grievance described so well by Greenway above. Here's a random Facebook post that illustrates that third group:

> "People may think [Trump] is nuts, but if you get past it and listen to what his ideas are, you might just say, Wow, he's right. I don't hear any other candidate out there saying they would tax Ford motor company 35 percent for each car they bring into this country if they move [factories] to Mexico. And tell me you're not tired of paying billions for all the illegal immigrants in this country. You go to work every day so they can have everything for free. At least Donald wants to do something about it. Your kids have to pay $50,000 to go to college. They go for free. You're paying for them to go. So maybe you all should just listen a little bit."

The mainstream media seem to have latched on to this view, too. On Friday, political reporter Jenna Johnson of *The Washington Post* wrote: "[Trump] is increasingly defined by the rallies held in cities that rarely see presidential candidates... [These towns] lag behind the country and their home states on a number of measures. Their median household incomes are lower, and they often have lower rates of homeownership or residents with college degrees. Even though most of these cities have sizable minority populations, the crowds at Trump's rallies are nearly entirely white." In "The Upshot" data analysis column in the December 31, *New York Times*, Nate Cohn similarly wrote: "[Trump's] very best voters are self-identified Republicans who nonetheless are registered as Democrats. It's a coalition that's concentrated in the South, Appalachia, and the industrial North... In many of these areas, a large number of traditionally Democratic voters have long supported Republicans in presidential elections... Mr. Trump appears to hold his greatest strength among people like these—registered Democrats who identify as Republican leaners...."

"Registered Democrats who identify as Republican leaners"— yes, that covers a wide swath of Lowell politics, and not just when it comes to Donald Trump. Fortunately, we won't have long to wait to see how candidate Trump does with actual voters. The Iowa Caucus is on February 1; New Hampshire Primary on February 9; South Carolina Primary on February 20; and Massachusetts and all the other "Super Tuesday" primaries are March 1.

David Bowie and Bob Martin: The Lowell Connection

By **Paul** on January 11, 2016
—

There's always a Lowell connection, right? Farewell, David Bowie, rock star, pop star, culture star, endlessly inventive artist. When I heard the news today, I was reminded of a story told to me by Lowell singer-songwriter extraordinaire Bob Martin. He was breaking into the music business in the early 1970s, paying his dues in clubs and coffeehouses right around the time the top record companies all wanted the next James Taylor, who had hit big in 1970-71 with "Fire and Rain" and "You've Got a Friend."

As the cliché goes, timing is everything, and it looked like Bob was catching a wave after a few years of playing the Cambridge hotspots like Club 47, later Passim, church basements, and folkie round-ups. In 1972, with Nashville musicians he recorded his first album, *Midwest Farm Disaster*, for RCA, one of the heavyweights. And I hope I have the details right here. His record company brought him to New York City for a showcase event with a line-up of artists who had new work. Bob played his set, drawing a strong response from those listening. Next up on stage was something different. A young Englishman. It was David Bowie introducing *The Rise and Fall of Ziggy Stardust and the Spiders from Mars*. Bob said he just knew when he saw the glam-rock act that the music buzz was about to change. It was going to be platform shoes and glitter make-up instead of work boots and faded denim. But Bob survived the shift of taste and kept making songs and playing music, a half-dozen albums worth and still going, touring coast to coast and into Europe.

As a kid, Bob saved a piece of brightly colored wire from one of the carnival trucks that had set up in Lowell. He kept that hunk of plastic-covered wire on the table next to his bed as a kind of magic link to the traveling world of entertainers and performers who brought the carnivals to all the small places in America. He wanted to go where the carnival was going. He wanted to be in that vivid truck bashing down the highway to the next show. He and David Bowie both chased the carnival and caught up with it. And we all got something good out of it from them. Bob, thanks for the music and the stories.

Lowell: The Next Initiative

By **Dick** on January 29, 2016

—

"The Next Initiative" was renamed "The Lowell Waterways Vitality Initiative" later in the year.

Yesterday afternoon I joined 97 other people at Mill No. 5's Luna Theater for a presentation called "Lowell: The Next Initiative," and effort organized by Fred Faust and Paul Marion of the Lowell Heritage Partnership in cooperation with the City of Lowell and with substantial support from George Duncan of Enterprise Bank. Here's what this project is about: Lowell has 5.6 miles of canals and two rivers that flow through the city. Around the world, such water features have been central to urban revitalization. In Lowell, however, these water features have been underutilized. Coincidentally, powerful, vibrant LED lighting is more affordable than ever. This "next initiative" is a citywide effort to make great use of our rivers and canals as cultural resources that will lead to more economic development.

The gathering began with remarks from Mayor Ed Kennedy who recalled traveling to Washington, D.C., in the 1970s with Pat Mogan to testify in favor of a national park for Lowell. Back then, Mogan emphasized the canals as a unique aspect of the Lowell story. Kennedy said it was fitting and consistent that the city help use these canals in the best way possible and he promised to do what he can to make this project work. City support was also evident by the presence of so many city councilors. Besides Mayor Kennedy, also present were Councilors Rita Mercier, Jim Milinazzo, Rodney Elliott, Jim Leary, Corey Belanger, and Bill Samaras.

Councilor Samaras, an early backer of this project and the chair of the City Council's economic development subcommittee, spoke next. Samaras recalled his father frequently referring to Lowell as "the Venice of America" because of the city's canals. Early in his career his mentor was Pat Mogan, whom he described as a dreamer who made dreams come true. But he said Mogan also understood that to accomplish anything, you need a community with great vitality. Samaras said that by linking historic preservation and economic development, Lowell will thrive as a community. Having had a preview of the presentation, he promised the audience that it would show them the great potential of our canals to become a place that people from around the region and the world will want to visit.

City Manager Kevin Murphy said that when he and his wife go on vacation, they don't go to Caribbean resorts, they go to great cities. In his experience, the common element found in great cities is their attractions and the festivities that spring up around those attractions. He sees the canals of Lowell as such an attraction and said the city can make this happen. As an example of the City government's support for this initiative, he cited the LED lighting that was this very day being installed on the Merrimack Canal alongside Lucy Larcom Park. Mounted on the railings alongside the canal, these fixtures will project multicolored light on the canal, its embankments, and the surrounding trees and structures. Expected to be unveiled at Winterfest, Murphy said that the lighting at Lucy Larcom Park is a great start and that this Next Initiative presentation is the next step.

With that, the lights dimmed and the presentation began (much of it the work of Dan Koff, a recent graduate of the Harvard Graduate School of Design and someone I first met a decade ago through his great work in Lawrence, Mass.). Wonderful photographs of Lowell scrolled on Luna's big screen to the accompaniment of Paul-and-Fred's narration. They explained that canals had long been a central element of the plans for Lowell's revitalization, but that we had never realized the full potential of these waterways. In helping the audience envision the potential, scenes of brightly lit and vibrant water features from cities around the world flashed across the screen. The key to the Lowell effort, Faust and Marion said, is to build on the great assets that already exist here such as Lowell National Historical Park's canal boat tours, the miles of existing walkways along our canals and rivers, recurring events such as the Folk Festival and the Lowell Walks series, and many others.

What's next? Anyone interested is encouraged to attend a follow-up meeting on Thursday, February 11, 5:30 p.m., at the UMass Lowell Innovation Hub at 110 Canal Place, which is in the middle of the Hamilton Canal District, just a block from Mill No. 5. Three subcommittees—on tourism, culture, and economic development—will meet to formulate tangible next steps in the process.

The Optics of Sanders: Is Bernie a Gandalf?

By **Paul** on February 2, 2016
—

The media commentariat and political insiders seem astounded that U. S. Senator Bernie Sanders is attracting vast support among young voters on the Democratic side. Setting aside Bernie's views on government policies and social values, remember that people in their 20s grew up watching movies that featured a wise old man with special powers and elite fighting skills taking on the forces of evil in the world of Tolkien. They like Gandalf.

Lowell Week in Review: Feb. 14, 2016

By **Dick** on February 14, 2016
—

TROLLEY EXPANSION DIES QUIETLY

For nearly a decade, there has been talk of a greatly expanded trolley system for Lowell. Conceptually, the project would expand the national park's existing 1.5 mile trolley system to connect the Gallagher Terminal with downtown and with UMass Lowell campus centers. A consortium of local partners including the City, UMass Lowell, Lowell National Historical Park, the LRTA, and others, has met for years in pursuit of this objective. A memo in this week's City Council packet, written in response to a motion asking about the status of the trolley expansion, makes it clear that the project has been taken off life support. In making the case to abandon the trolley project, the memo makes it clear that the cost—$100 million to build and $3 million per year to operate—greatly exceeded the capacity or the willingness of the partners to undertake the effort. There is a $1.5 million federal grant from several years ago that was appropriated for the trolley system but not yet used. The partners will work with Congresswoman Tsongas to allow for the repurposing of that grant so that it can be spent on other "multi-modal options" for connecting the Gallagher Terminal to downtown and the UMass Lowell campuses in a way that is compatible with "the City's current projects at South Common and reconstruction of the Lord Overpass."

Amazing Vision for a New Lord Overpass

By **Dick** on March 29, 2016
—

Lowell City planners hit a home run—make that a grand slam—with a radical new concept for the Lord Overpass, unveiled tonight at a public meeting at the Lowell Senior Center. City Manager Kevin Murphy opened the program by saying he felt a little like William Shatner because we were about to "boldly go where no planning department has gone before." He wasn't kidding. City planners and consultants from VHB Engineering then walked the audience through the process that included an earlier public meeting in November, detailed analysis of traffic accidents, an extensive site visit that helped visualize the problems inherent in the current design, and much debate in the drawing room.

Their conclusion: the Lord Overpass should be filled in, with Thorndike Street in both directions rising at the same elevation as the existing up and down ramps to form twin intersections with Middlesex Street and with Chelmsford/Appleton Streets. Coming from downtown, you will be able to turn left or right onto Middlesex Street or go straight ahead. Coming from the Lowell Connector, you will be able to turn right onto Appleton, left onto Chelmsford, or go straight ahead. Most importantly, the safety and convenience of bikers and walkers will be greatly enhanced.

At several points during tonight's presentation, the 70-plus people in attendance broke into spontaneous applause. That's not the usual response to the rollout of a new traffic pattern. There was applause because those in attendance recognize that this proposal undoes 50 years of failed traffic planning that centered on highways and fast-moving cars at the expense of people and neighborhoods. I've compared the Dutton/Thorndike Street corridor to Lowell's version of the Berlin Wall. It separates the western half of the city from the eastern half, and attempting to cross it puts your life at risk. This asphalt gash has been a major impediment to economic development for decades. With forthcoming construction in the Hamilton Canal District, a proposal to rehab the Thorndike Factory Outlet for apartments and business use, and the tremendous potential for tying that in to the Gallagher Terminal, South Common, Lower Highlands, Acre, and the rest of downtown—with all this potential, we desperately needed an innovative plan for the Lord Overpass that broke from the highway planning mold.

HISTORY AS IT HAPPENS

Lowell City Council Meeting: March 29, 2016

By **Dick** on March 29, 2016
—

For decades, Lowell City Council meetings have been televised live on cable television and archived for later-viewing on Lowell Telecommunications Corporation's website. But meetings typically take several hours, so not many people watch them. I do, and while I watch them, I type much of what is said at the meetings and then post the content to RichardHowe.com as soon as the meeting ends. (Who knew that typing would be the most valuable course I took in high school?) The result is not a stenographic transcript; it is instead a string of word bursts presented in raw form without regard to quotation marks, other punctuation or sentence structure. We have included two such posts in this book. This one, from the March 29, 2016 council meeting, and the other from May 17, 2016. Although my "transcripts" of the full meetings are available online, both posts that appear in this book omit relatively mundane, municipal matters, and focus exclusively on a controversial issue that emerged each night.

With more than 20,000 residents from Cambodia or of Cambodian descent, Lowell has the second largest Cambodian-American community in the United States, after Long Beach, California. Although several Cambodian-Americans have held elective office—Rithy Uong and Vesna Nuon on the city council, and Rady Mom as state representative—the Cambodian community has mostly steered clear of involvement in day-to-day Lowell politics. That was not the case on March 29, 2016, when several hundred Cambodian-Americans attended the Lowell City Council meeting to protest the planned visit to City Hall of Hun Manet, a general in the Cambodian Army and the son of that country's prime minister, Hun Sen.

Coming to power in 1985, Hun Sen has controlled the Cambodian government ever since, despite strong opposition within the country.

There have been elections, but a 2013 U.S. State Department Human Rights Report called them "flawed and poorly managed" and criticized the Cambodian government for "a flawed and politicized judiciary" and "constraints on freedom of the press and assembly." The conflicts in Cambodian politics also manifest themselves in Lowell in ways that are difficult for those outside the community to discern and understand. The conflict was in full view at the March 29 council meeting.

Petition by Residents to Speak re: Proposed Visit of Hun Manet (23 people registered to speak).

The first speaker condemns Hun Sen (Hun Manet's father and the ruler of Cambodia) and urges the council not to receive him at City Hall—much applause from the several hundred people in the crowd.

The next speaker urges the council to meet with the visitor regarding a sister-city link with Phnom Penh. (Throughout this gentleman's remarks, which are in Khmer but translated into English, but the crowd boos and shouts). Mayor Edward Kennedy interrupts and chastises the hecklers. The speaker points out the commonality of the Cambodian people and urges them to come together and act in a unified way.

The next speaker describes the statue the Hun Sen government is giving to Lowell as a unifying symbol that should not become a political issue. He points out that the future speaker is a candidate for state representative who is politicizing this issue for his own benefit. He points out that the gift was motivated by the visit to Cambodia of Councilor Rodney Elliott when he was Mayor of Lowell—and that he signed a sister-city agreement between Lowell and Phnom Penh. He says many people in Lowell support this and will be deeply offended if the city rejects it. He says the businessmen who will accompany Hun Manet are looking for trade and business opportunities in the United States and especially Lowell. He cites how American presidents have normalized relationships with Cuba, Vietnam, and China. Cambodia wishes to normalize relations in the same way.

The speakers continue, with the majority opposing the visit. Several speak in Khmer with occasional translation into English. The crowd understands what is being said; the councilors I suspect do not. Passions are running very high. Mayor Kennedy begins invoking the five-minute rule for speakers. It appears that several decades of accumulated grievances against Hun Sen have found an outlet tonight.

Now former City Councilor Rithy Uong speaks. He says he won't say much because he will let the crowd and their signs speak for the community. He says that since the Cambodian people have come to Lowell, they have achieved great success. He says the Cambodian community of Lowell doesn't need any gifts from the current government of Cambodia. He then mentions the abuses practiced by that government. He suggests the visit is a pretense to promote business relations between Lowell and Cambodia, when really it is an attempt to strengthen and promote the Communists in Lowell. He says Lowell does not need this "blood money" from "land grabbers" from Cambodia.

Former Councilor Vesna Nuon speaks next. He reminds councilors that both Niki Tsongas and Elizabeth Warren have been critical of the current Cambodian government. He says it's alright with him if Hun Manet visits Lowell, but City officials should not honor him or welcome him to City Hall. If the statue arrives in Lowell, the community should pay for it, he says.

One speaker criticizes state Representative Rady Mom for having previously met with Hun Sen in Cambodia and the local Cambodian Mutual Assistance Association (CMAA) for staying neutral on this issue. This speaker compares Hun Manet to a Trojan Horse coming to Lowell. He says people here will be at risk because the regime will have "so many spies in Lowell." He says those who welcome Hun Manet "are criminals, too."

The final speaker has a petition signed by 500 Lowell residents. She alleges Hun Sen has a long record of human rights violation, corruption, persecution of opponents, and many other wrong-doings. She also alleges that Hun Manet's objective for his visit is to build support for the regime among young people living outside of Cambodia. She says many people in Lowell fear Hun Sen and believe the statue will represent oppression.

Another speaker, a business owner who has been in Lowell for more than 28 years, expresses his gratitude to the United States for welcoming him and teaching him about real democracy. He says the CPP (Hun Sen's party) represents the interests of Vietnam, not the interests of Cambodia. End of speakers.

Councilor Elliott is the first to speak. He explains that when he visited Cambodia, he was unaware of the politics there but has since learned more about it. He talks of how Lowell people and the Cambodians who came here learned much from each other. He says we continue to work together and respect each other. He recalls the experience of visiting ten women unjustly imprisoned in Cambodia. He and Councilor Mercier at the time spoke out about the injustice. That was met with an irate letter from the Cambodian Secretary of State. He contacted U.S. officials, and the women were released several weeks later. He says he stands with the community and add that while in Cambodia he specifically refused the offer of the statue.

Councilor Mercier speaks next. She says, "This is what it is all about—freedom of speech." She says she believes in majority rule and that the majority clearly opposes this visit. She explains she went to Cambodia to learn more about the culture and history of Cambodian people in Lowell. She closes by saying she will stand with the people and will not honor Hun Manet.

Councilor Milinazzo says the "powerful message tonight will stay with me for the rest of my life." He says he will stand with them. He asks the mayor to explore how to rescind the invitation.

Councilor Leary says he will support rescinding the invitation. He adds that we do tolerate other opinions and says everyone should respect those who were in the minority who spoke in favor of the visit.

Councilor Samaras says tonight is an example of how people who are new to the country sometimes have a better appreciation of democracy than those who were born here. Mentions that he has visited Cambodia and learned much from his visit. Says that the job of councilors is serve the people. He says there were two points of view expressed tonight, but we should respect the wishes of the majority and not allow the official visit to go forward.

Councilor Leahy thanks people for coming and says he supports them. Councilor Rourke says the same.

Mayor Kennedy, speaking from the chair, says he came into the office of mayor not knowing much about the politics of Cambodia or conditions there, but he's learning fast. He says five weeks ago, he had a visit from the honorary Counsel General who said Hun Manet was visiting Lowell along with the Cambodian Ambassador and the Cambodian Secretary of State and about 40 others. He says the City government did not ask for the visit, did not ask for the statue. Says the statue is supposed to arrive sometime next week. The Counsel General asked that the statue be placed in front of City Hall. After speaking with the City Manager, the two of them decided it would be best placed in Pawtucketville along the riverbank where the Southeast Asian Water Festival takes place. The Cambodian delegation is scheduled to meet with dignitaries at City Hall on Saturday morning. He says doing that on a Saturday was not his first choice of how to spend a Saturday, but he felt it was his responsibility as mayor to meet with them. He feels it is still his responsibility to meet with them. However, if the city council votes unanimously that he should not meet with the delegation, he will respect that vote.

Councilor Belanger says he supports the mayor's initial decision, but that we have since learned a lot about Cambodian politics. He says that based on what was said tonight, we should denounce the visit and the gift. He makes a motion to do that.

The motion passes 8 to 0 with Mayor Kennedy abstaining. Mayor Kennedy says, "So, we won't be greeting the general." The councilors take a three-minute recess.

Clemente Park: A History

By **Dick** on April 29, 2016

More than 100 years ago, today's Clemente Park in the Lower Highlands neighborhood was the site of one of the most modern baseball stadiums in America. Built in 1906 and named Washington Park, the baseball stadium had more than 3,000 seats and was home to the Lowell Tigers of the professional New England Baseball League.

In *Bricks and Bats*, his 2002 history of professional baseball in Lowell, Chaz Scoggins writes that the Tigers had been playing on Spalding Park since 1902, but Spalding Park—now Stoklosa-Alumni Field on Rogers Street—was too far away for fans living near downtown. Al Winn purchased the Tigers in 1906 and decided to build a new ballpark closer to downtown. He chose a site along the Pawtucket Canal in the Lower Highlands that was near the city's main train station on Middlesex Street underneath today's Lord Overpass (named for Louis J. Lord, father of one-time Lowell mayor Raymond Lord).

At a cost of more than $10,000, Winn built a state-of-the-art ballpark with 3,500 seats, 1,500 of them under a roof. All were opera-style seats and not the traditional backless benches of other parks. There was indoor plumbing and locker rooms with hot showers for the players (a novelty at the time). Because of the dimensions of the lot, the right field fence was closer than usual. A contest was held to select the park's name. Washington Park was the winning name, for President George Washington.

Washington Park opened on April 27, 1907. The team was initially successful, but the owner's abrasive personality soon turned people off and attendance dwindled. In the midst of the 1909 season. The New England League ordered Winn to sell the team. He did, offering to rent Washington Park to the new owners, but they instead chose to play home games back at Spalding Park.

Without a baseball team, the stadium at Washington Park was neglected and later torn down. On December 8, 1921, the city of Lowell Board of Park Commissioners took the 120,000-square foot parcel by eminent domain for a public playground, paying $30,800 to Mary L. Saunders, Annie G. Saunders, and Edith St. Loe Saunders, whose family had owned the land for at least 50 years.

The 1922 Annual Report of the Board of Park Commissioners reports:

> "Washington Park was given attention during the year. Two plots of land were acquired near the Franklin School and graded, making a more convenient entrance from Middlesex Street. Considerable grading was done in this park which brought the surface to an even grade. Some 1,800 yards of good filling which we obtained gratis, was used in this work. A baseball diamond was laid out, and a good backstop built as well as an 8-foot wire fence constructed to protect the adjoining property."

The park kept the name Washington Park until July 10, 1973, when the Lowell City Council passed a motion by Councilor Phil Shea to change the name from Washington Park to Roberto Clemente Park. Shea recalls that he made the motion at the request of one of the priests at St. Patrick's Church, which had become a gathering place for many in the expanding Latino community.

Born in Puerto Rico in 1934, Roberto Clemente played professional baseball for the Pittsburgh Pirates from 1955 until 1972. His Pirate teams won the World Series in 1960 and 1971. He was the Most Valuable Player of the 1971 series and had been the league's MVP in 1966. He had a career batting average of .317 with 3,000 hits, 240 home runs, and 1,305 RBIs. He was a 15-time All Star and four-time National League batting champion. Throughout his career, Clemente involved himself in charitable work in Puerto Rico and throughout Latin America. He died on December 31, 1972, at age 38 when a plane he had chartered to fly relief supplies to earthquake-ravaged Nicaragua crashed, killing all aboard. Clemente was posthumously elected to the Baseball Hall of Fame in 1973, making him the first Latin American baseball player so enshrined.

The same summer that the city named the park for Clemente, the city council also voted to install powerful "arc-lights" that would allow adult softball teams and Little League baseball teams to play night games at Clemente Park, which joined St. Louis Field as the two city parks illuminated for night softball games. Lowell today has a Roberto Clemente League for youth baseball whose mission is to help kids "stay healthy in body and mind."

In the 1980s, thousands of Cambodian refugees came to Lowell. Many settled in the lower Highlands neighborhood. Clemente Park became an important gathering place for members of the Cambodian community. They did not play baseball or softball, so those fields were replaced by volleyball and boule (bocce) courts. There is a playground for children, and the City in 2011 built a concession stand. Members of the Cambodian community refer to the park as Pailin Park, because of its proximity to the Pailin Plaza retail-and-restaurant complex named for the region of Cambodia that was once home to many of Lowell's residents. On any night in good weather there are scores of people at the park, one of the busiest in the city.

The local Latino community in late 2016 appealed to the city council to assign a new home baseball field for the Roberto Clemente League. As this book goes into production a new Roberto Clemente Field is in play.

HISTORY AS IT HAPPENS

Lowell City Council Meeting: Transgender Bathroom Debate

By **Dick** on May 17, 2016
—

Like the March 29 post on the Cambodian community's protest of a planned visit to the city by a Cambodian government official, this entry offers the raw transcript of remarks made at the city council meeting on May 17. The catalyst for this episode was a joint motion by Councilors Rodney Elliott and Rita Mercier—although Mercier immediately withdrew her support of the motion—that the city council adopt a resolution opposing a bill recently passed by the Massachusetts Senate that would allow transgender individuals to use the bathroom of their choosing. This is not a verbatim transcript. The notes were typed as the words were spoken, without regard to quotations marks, punctuation, or sentence structure.

Motion by Councilors Elliott and Mercier: Request city council vote to adopt a resolution to oppose the transgender bill adopted by the state Senate, which allows transgender people access to women's bathrooms and locker rooms.

Councilor Mercier informs the City Clerk she does not wish to co-sponsor the motion. Councilor Mercier seconds the motion.

Councilor Elliott suggests allowing the registered speakers to proceed first. There are 25 people registered to speak.

Following are sample remarks that are unattributed because it was difficult to hear the speakers' names (or get proper pronouns or the correct spelling of names) on the cable TV broadcast; a tape of the meeting is available at Lowell Telecommunications Corporation, the community access organization. The numbers associated with the remarks do not reflect the order of speakers. Public figures are identified as known.

Citizen 1: It is ironic that today is worldwide anti-transphobic day. Also, that a big project (the private dormitory being built opposite Lowell High School) is presented in front of people who find this motion hurtful. Commends City Manager and councilors for pushing the city forward. The only thing that can hold the city back is fear. This is not the first time that the toilet has been the battle ground for civil rights. This bill will not magically create a class of sexual predators. Instead it will say to every trans person that they are not welcome and will push them further to the periphery of society.

Citizen 2: Supports the Commonwealth's attempts to help trans community. Concerned with women's safety, too, and cites statistics on rape and sexual assault for all women. Says trans women face much higher rates of sexual violence. Trans people are members of our community who face great challenges because of the intense stigma society attaches to them. They are some of the most vulnerable among us. Don't they deserve our support too?

Citizen 3: Thanks the council for hearing them and thanks the speakers who will "educate you on something you know nothing about." Identifies as a member of the LGBT community. Says the trans people are the ones who need protection. Says the bill offers no protection to predators. "Let knowledge pave the way rather than baseless fear." Says the idea of separate bathrooms for trans persons does not work. Shares the terrible experience of not being able to use either bathroom because of the risks involved. Urges the council to adopt a motion commending the state Senate bill.

Citizen 4: Says having to use the "wrong" restroom exposes trans people to great risk of violence. Forcing businesses to have separate bathrooms for trans people makes no economic sense. This bill also addresses many other aspects of life for trans people that are critically important. Supporting this motion will mean you are turning your back on the most vulnerable people in this city. Speaks of discrimination she has experienced. This motion will have unintended consequences—that people who have discriminated against me are in the right. Please support the bill.

Citizen 5: Recalls the summer of 1992 when he was at Lowell High. He secretly attended a gay pride event in Boston, but a photo appeared in the *Boston Globe*. Parents kicked him out of the house. The ignorance of 1992 still exists today. Recounts how Massachusetts has been the first to protect gays, to recognize same-sex marriage. Lowell should stand on the right side of history on this proposal.

Citizen 6: Supports this motion and opposes the state bill. Says it opens the door to sexual predators to pose as trans people to access spaces reserved for the other sex. Says this will lead to increase in sexual assault. Says this bill will do more to help sexual predators than trans individuals.

Citizen 7: Reads a letter from a trans friend who did not want to appear in person. Tries to assure everyone the trans people are not predators. Says women and trans women have been sharing bathrooms for years without incident. It is trans people who have been the victims of assault. Says there is a lot of concern for a "non-problem" and not enough concern for real problems (assaults on trans people).

Citizen 8: Three young girls speak, introducing themselves by stating the pronouns they use to identify themselves which they do to make trans people feel comfortable. They support the trans bill because we've been raised to support everyone and treat everyone equally. Everyone should have the right to use the bathroom they identify with.

Citizen 9: Lives in Lowell with his family; they have embraced the community. But he's not comfortable with the bill passed by the Senate because it puts women and children at risk. Says there have been documented cases of men dressed as women assaulting women in restrooms. Says there should be separate bathrooms for trans people. This bill only replaces one risky situation with another. Asks to postpone the vote to get a better feel for the community.

Citizen 10: Owns a house here, works here, identifies as transgender. Knows what it's like to be a victim of harassment, to not feel comfortable in a restroom, to be denied service in a public space. Has been trans for 30 years, and is an ordained minister and licensed social worker. Sees many trans-gendered identified clients who live in Lowell. Has voted for Councilor Mercier for a decade because she is a "strong woman" and is the first person to speak out in favor of helping senior citizens. Trans people are the most vulnerable people in this city. Says my work involves teaching people how to stay safe when they need to use the restroom. I'm tired of doing that. As for the option of creating a third restroom, does not think officials are prepared to pay to build new bathrooms in every public place in the city. As a Christian, believes we are all created in the image of God, including trans people. Urges councilors to defeat this motion and instead pass a motion supporting the state Senate bill.

Citizen 11: The real issue is a lack of education about trans people. Has taught at Lowell High for ten years. Created the first gender identity class. Understands the intent of this motion is to protect people from sexual predators and not from trans people, but it perpetuates the marginalization of trans people. Implores councilors to "stand on the right side of history" and to advance human rights.

Citizen 12: Quotes attorney general Loretta Lynch to North Carolina: "This is about far more than bathrooms; it's about the dignity and respect we afford all of our citizens." Has been a psychiatrist for 30 years and is head of the department at Leahy Clinic. Says there is no basis in fact or in science for the objections to this bill. Urges councilors to support a substitute motion that supports the Senate bill.

Citizen 13: Goes to school in New York City where everyone is comfortable being themselves. She identifies self as part of the LGBT community. Hurts very much to learn that the city might support something that is so hurtful to the cause of human rights.

Citizen 14: Has always lived in Lowell and identifies as a

lesbian woman. This is all grounded in sexism. The designation of sex at birth is only "a powerful predictor" of gender.

Citizen 15: A student at UMass Lowell and veteran of U.S. Army, describes self as gender-fluid.

Citizen 16: Denying people the right to public accommodations is to deprive them of the right to participate in public life. "You wouldn't put up with being treated that way; why should trans people?" UMass Lowell, the community of artists, status as a Gateway city all could be harmed if a fear-based anti-trans motion makes Lowell the focus of the wrong kind of attention. A motion like this sends a signal to the haters that it is acceptable to treat trans people differently.

Citizen 17: Says is appalled and embarrassed by this motion.

Citizen 18: Here in her capacity as Asst. Director of Community Relations of UMass Lowell. Reads a statement from UMass Lowell which says individuals should use the restroom that complies with their gender identity.

Citizen 19: The city is fortunate to have a councilor like Rita Mercier. Talks about God creating the world and then creating Adam and then Eve. "The animals today still work with male and female; what happened to us? I say this in a biblical way; you've heard of Sodom and Gomorrah. Fire came down and destroyed cities because of this type of activity. All I'm saying is . . . we don't want fire to come down. We don't want to go against the Ten Commandments or against God."

End of public speakers.

Councilor Elliott: I know this is a very difficult issue. It's very emotional. I know the issues faced by the LGBT community. That's not what my motion is about. It's about the bathrooms. I understand this motion will probably fail, and I could have withdrawn it, but people had registered to speak. The people I represent are genuinely concerned about allowing males in women's bathrooms and so am I. It's already been proven to be a place where assaults take place, and this will open the floodgates of such assaults. Cites statistics of sexual assaults.

He says he takes pride in the melting pot of Lowell. Says that equating a policy that allows trans people use the bathroom of their choice to the Civil Rights movement cheapens the Civil Rights movement. Says he filed this motion for the safety of children and women and of those who are preyed upon by perverts. "I'm not saying that the trans community are predators. This is not about transgender people attacking women—that's a bait and switch." This law "opens the door for any creep to go into a women's room and claim he's transgender. I have to live with my conscience."

People interrupting with shouts. Mayor Kennedy insists that they listen to people speak, otherwise he will clear the chamber.

Councilor Elliott cites instances from across the country of men assaulting women. He understands trans people are often victims, but says you don't solve one wrong with another wrong. He says a separate bathroom is not discriminatory.

Councilor Mercier says she wants to clear the air. "I made a promise some months ago that I would always second a motion by one of my colleagues." She says she admires Councilor Elliott for having his opinion. He has every right to express it. But "I think you may have misunderstood me when you told me about your motion when I said, 'Go for it' meaning I would second it." When people say that we are all created equal, I don't think that's true. When children are born blind, of drug-addicted parents, they're not all equal. Years ago, I may have thought of the "perfect family," but it's my opinion that some babies are born males who are trapped because they feel like they are in the wrong body. I don't know how that torture affects you, but that doesn't make you any less of a person. I'm no better than you. If a man identifies as a woman and needs to go to the bathroom and comes into the lady's room, "I'm thinking it's a woman." I don't buy that this bill will lead people to go into bathrooms and sexually assault kids. There are bad people in the world; that's a separate issue. I don't want to support a motion that harms trans people even further. Sexual predators go to the YMCA, and we don't close the YMCA. She says she supports the Senate bill.

Councilor Belanger: Thanks people for the several hundred emails and the speakers tonight. I know far more on this issue now than I knew 72 hours ago. This issue is complex, and it's evolving faster than people are evolving. He confesses that he should have been more aware of it than he was. The stories have been very compelling. Sees some parallels to opioid issue; there is a stigma attached to users and addicts. The council is working to change that. Similarly, this council has a responsibility to do the same thing for the trans community. He commends Councilor Elliott while he was mayor for being so inclusive; assures everyone that Councilor Elliott is not a hateful individual. The councilor has a concern that "I may not agree with him on," but he's sincere about it. He says we represent 110,000 people, and we must take a step back and look at what's best for everyone. He says he won't support anything that will be harmful to the LGBT community. They are part of the city. The city has come a long way, and we can't be set back by the perception that we may be discriminatory.

Councilor Belanger makes a substitute motion in support of the transgender bill adopted by the state Senate.

Councilor Samaras seconds it. Samaras speaks: Says that when people talk about complex issues, things can get heated but we must respect the opinions of others. My position here is simple: I follow Senator Eileen Donoghue when she said this is a civil rights bill. Says he will support Councilor Belanger's substitute motion. We talk about Lowell being a place that is accepting. We must show that it is an accepting city.

Councilor Milinazzo thanks everyone who came tonight and says he will support the substitute motion. He says law enforcement and major employers overwhelmingly support the bill.

Councilor Leary: He says he will support the substitute motion. He says it's the council's job to support those who are most vulnerable. I think it's important for the council to take the lead on this to send a message to the city and the rest of the state. It's not an economic issue; it's about doing the right thing. I understand that there are people who will disagree with supporting the bill, but we must set the example and take the lead.

Councilor Rourke requests a roll call.

Councilor Leahy says, "We're here to try to do the right thing. We must remember that the House has a bill and then it goes to the governor, so the final result might be very different."

Roll Call on Substitute Motion for a resolution supporting the Senate bill: Passes 8 to 1 with Elliott against.

Council takes a brief recess.

HISTORY AS IT HAPPENS

Lowell Week in Review: Memorial Day Edition

By **Dick** on May 29, 2016
—

It being Memorial Day weekend, instead of writing about Lowell politics this morning, I'd like to share the stories of some Lowell residents who gave their lives while in the service of their country.

DONALD ARCAND—VIETNAM WAR

Born in 1946, Donald L. Arcand grew up on Ford Street in Little Canada, where Father Morissette Boulevard is now. Donald graduated from St. Joseph's High School in 1963 and volunteered for the Army. Trained as an infantryman, Arcand was assigned to an aviation battalion where he served as a door gunner on a UH-1 Huey helicopter. On September 1, 1965, his helicopter was hit by ground fire and exploded in midair, killing all aboard. His funeral took place a week later at St. Jean-Baptiste Church and he was buried in St. Joseph's Cemetery. On May 25, 1969, Arcand Drive was dedicated immediately following the Memorial Day parade. The memorial plaque sits in Monument Square, alongside the Ladd and Whitney Monument. It reads:

> City of Lowell, Massachusetts Northern Canal Renewal Area ARCAND DRIVE Dedicated on November 11 to the memory of PFC Donald Leonard Arcand Born in Lowell on February 13, 1946 Killed in action in Vietnam, September 1, 1965

LORNE CUPPLES—CUPPLES SQUARE—WORLD WAR ONE

Lorne Lee Cupples was born on January 12, 1882, in Canada,

the son of James and Salome (Babcock) Cupples. In 1886, the Cupples family immigrated to the United States and settled in Newport, New Hampshire. By 1908, Lorne Cupples had moved to Lowell and eventually became the superintendent of Whitall Manufacturing Company on Rock Street. Whitall produced "corset-covers, drawers, night robes, shirts, chemises, and dressing slacks." The 1910 census identified Cupples as "superintendent, underwear company." On August 17, 1908, he married Marion J. Corner. They lived at 116 Grove Street.

Cupples enlisted in the U.S. Army's reserve officer training corps (ROTC) at Fort Plattsburgh, New York. After training, he was commissioned as a Second Lieutenant and was assigned to the 303rd Machine Gun Battalion of the 76th Division which was stationed at Camp Devens, Massachusetts. Cupples landed in France with that unit in the summer of 1918, but was soon transferred to Company C, 101st Machine Gun Company, 26th Infantry Division, which was made up of men from Connecticut, mostly. The 101st was involved in heavy fighting during the St. Mihiel and Meuse-Argonne offensives in the fall of 1918. At Brabant Wood north of Verdun on October 23, while firing in support of an attack by American infantry, the 101st came under heavy German artillery fire. In Company C, the German shelling killed three men and seriously wounded Lt. Cupples and three others. His severe stomach wounds proved fatal, and he died on November 2, 1918, in the 15th Evacuation Hospital. He is buried in the Meuse-Argonne American Cemetery, Romagne, France.

His widow, Marion, became a nurse and moved to 441 Westford Street. After the war, the intersection of Pine and Westford Streets was named Cupples Square in his honor.

NORMAND BRISSETTE—WORLD WAR TWO

Enlisting in the Navy in 1943 at age 17, Normand Brissette became a gunner/radio operator on an SB2C Helldiver flying from the carrier *Ticonderoga*. On July 28, 1945, Normand's plane, piloted by Lt. Raymond Porter, was shot down off the coast of Japan. Both survived and were imprisoned with ten other American flyers at the Chugoku Military Police Headquarters in Hiroshima. There they stayed until August 6, 1945, when the *Enola Gay* dropped the atomic bomb less than a kilometer from their jail. All but Brissette and one other died instantly. Ten days later, the newly captured crew of a downed B-29 were imprisoned with Brissette and the other survivor, who were gravely ill from radiation poisoning. Both died the next day, but the B-29 crew survived to relay their story. Brissette and the eleven other aviators are now memorialized by a plaque erected by the city of Hiroshima. Normand Brissette's story is poignantly told in the recent documentary, *Paper Lanterns*, by local filmmaker Barry Frechette. The film also features Shigeaki Mori, himself a survivor of the atomic bomb, who has dedicated his life to identifying and commemorating Brissette and the eleven other U.S. prisoners who perished from the bomb. When Barack Obama became the first sitting American President to visit Hiroshima, he sought out and embraced Mr. Mori for his kindness to these deceased American service members.

SCOTT FINNERAL—GULF WAR

A Lowell native who enlisted in the Navy after graduating from Lowell High in 1988, Scottie Finneral and five comrades were killed when their MH-53 mine-sweeping helicopter plunged into the Persian Gulf on September 14, 1991, during the first Gulf War. In 1996, the Massachusetts State Legislature named the walkway along the Merrimack River within Lowell Heritage State Park the Scott Finneral Memorial Riverwalk.

ADRIAN BILODEAU—KOREAN WAR

Adrian L. Bilodeau, born in New Hampshire on May 10, 1907, became a career non-commissioned officer in the United States

Army, enlisting in 1928. He served continuously on active duty through World War II during which he served with the 526th Armored Infantry Battalion. After the war, he lived with his wife at 26 Crawford Street in Lowell.

When the Korean War began, he was stationed on the island of Okinawa near Japan with lightly armed occupation troops. Four hundred barely trained recruits were rushed from the United States to join the men in Okinawa to form the 3rd Battalion of the 29th Infantry Regiment, which immediately deployed to Pusan, Korea, landing there in July 1950. Almost immediately, the battalion wandered into a massive North Korean ambush at Hadong that left half the American battalion killed or wounded. In the immediate aftermath of that attack, Sergeant Bilodeau organized an ambush that inflicted heavy casualties on an advancing North Korean unit, slowing the enemy advance.

Because of the high rate of casualties suffered, the 3rd Battalion should have been deemed combat ineffective, but the desperate situation demanded that the survivors go back into action almost immediately. Sergeant Bilodeau, then 43 years old, should have been assigned to a rear area job because of his age. Instead, he remained at the front, where he was killed by enemy fire on September 10, 1950. Adrian Bilodeau's body was returned to Lowell. He is buried in St. Joseph's Cemetery in Chelmsford.

LUTHER LADD AND ADDISON WHITNEY—CIVIL WAR

A 25-foot high granite obelisk on a small grassy island in front of Lowell City Hall commemorates seventeen-year-old Luther Ladd and 22-year-old Addison Whitney, two Lowell mill workers who, along with Sumner Needham of Lawrence and Charles Taylor of parts unknown, were the first soldiers to die in the American Civil War. Known as Monument Square, this parcel is also the final resting place of Ladd and Whitney.

Born in Waldo, Maine, on October 30, 1839, Whitney had

lived in Lowell for two years prior to his death. He worked at the Middlesex Company, one of the textile businesses. Ladd, born in Alexandria, New Hampshire, on December 22, 1843, had been in Lowell long enough to enlist in the 6th Massachusetts Volunteer Infantry Regiment along with Whitney and several hundred other men from Lowell, Lawrence, Groton, and Acton.

On April 14, 1861, the day after the U.S. Army personnel at Fort Sumter surrendered to secessionist troops in South Carolina, President Abraham Lincoln called for 75,000 volunteer troops to come to Washington, D.C., to put down the rebellion. One of the first units to mobilize was the 6th Massachusetts. As the regiment passed through Baltimore, Maryland, on its way to Washington on April 19, 1861, the soldiers were attacked by a mob of pro-Southern civilians. Ladd, Whitney, Needham, and Taylor were killed, and about 32 of their comrades were wounded. The regiment pressed ahead to Washington, and the bodies of Ladd and Whitney were returned to Lowell. The monument that bears their names was dedicated on June 17, 1861, in an elaborate ceremony attended by an enormous gathering of people.

'A Special Place and a Special Park'

By **Dick** on August 25, 2016
—

More than 100 people assembled at City Hall this morning for the raising of the National Park Service flag as part of the centennial celebration of the service, founded 100 years ago today. Speakers included Mayor Edward Kennedy, former Mayor Armand LeMay, Congresswoman Niki Tsongas, Fred Faust (who as an aide to U.S. Senator Paul Tsongas played an important role in the creation of the park), and park Superintendent Celeste Bernardo.

Linda Sopheap Sou, Chief of Interpretation and Education at Lowell National Historical Park, was master of ceremonies. After the flag-raising, everyone adjourned to the Market Mills Courtyard to enjoy an enormous birthday cake while the U.S. Air Force Heritage Band, Rhythm in Blue, performed.

Fred Faust said the Lowell park reminded him of Aaron Copland's musical piece, *Fanfare for the Common Man* because the park is intended to celebrate the men and women who worked in the mills and enriched the community with the culture and customs of their countries of origin. He praised community leaders like Armand LeMay who, along with Patrick J. Mogan and Paul E. Tsongas, helped make the park a reality.

Lowell Park Superintendent Celeste Bernardo spoke of the future of the Lowell park, saying a major goal is to create greater access to the rivers and canals of Lowell. She cited the coming September 1 "lighting up the canals" event and mentioned plans to illuminate buildings and other structures. The National Park Service plans to extend the existing Riverwalk to the east side of Bridge Street and a new walkway, to be called the Pawtucket Falls Overlook. At the same time, the park will work cooperatively on new city developments, especially those in the Hamilton Canal District, to preserve the historic character of the district and to attract more tourists.

A special place and a special park—a pretty good slogan.

HISTORY AS IT HAPPENS

Compensation for Councilors

By **Mimi Parseghian** on September 7, 2016
—

The City Council this week took steps to encourage more residents to run for municipal office. The Ad-Hoc Subcommittee on Charter Changes and Elections discussed three council motions pertaining to local elections. The subcommittee, Councilors Jim Leary, Bill Samaras, and Rita Mercier, were joined by the six other councilors. The first motion focused on a salary adjustment for the Mayor, councilors, and school committee persons. The last salary increase was approved 20 years ago.

A councilor now receives $15,000 a year; the subcommittee suggested an increase to $25,000. The Mayor's compensation would rise to $30,000 from $20,000. As for the school committee, the suggestion is to adjust their salaries to $12,000.

I am strongly in favor of raising their compensation. I believe that it will attract those who want to serve but cannot afford the sacrifice. It is also the right thing to do for those who are currently serving and want to continue to serve.

We expect a councilor to attend the weekly meetings, subcommittee meetings, ethnic and national flag-raisings, community activities, non-profit fundraisers, and civic events. In effect, it is a second job.

The current council is composed of individuals who are self-employed, retired, or work for a government agency. It is almost impossible for a young person, who is on a career track and employed by a private firm, to be able to devote the time and effort to serve.

A vote is set for the next City Council meeting (September 13), and if the subcommittee's motion passes, a public hearing will be held on September 27, when the final vote will be taken. The ordinance change, if approved, will be effective January 2018, when the next council takes office.

Lowell has seen many positive changes in the past 20 years. Our compensation for elected municipal officials needs to keep up with those changes.

Carrying a Torch for *Ti Jean*

By **Paul** on October 24, 2016
—

We were talking about Bob Dylan getting the Nobel Prize for Literature last week and ole Jack Kerouac having received nothing in his life by way of awards and prizes, and so my friend and I went to the famous gravesite in Edson Cemetery and presented to dead Jack a gold trophy-top from my grandfather-in-law's jewelry-store leftovers in my cellar in recognition of Jack's contribution to world literature, an athlete-figure in a cape and holding a torch, maybe some kind of Prometheus, after all, for the man who stole fire from his book-writing heroes to light the literary underbrush in America in the mid-20th century, including a blaze that warmed the artistic heart of young Robert Zimmerman from the Iron Range in upper Minnesota, the same Bob who is living his own solo legacy in his 70s on the Endless Tour that has run from the White House to Las Vegas and quite a few truck stops in between, the same Bob who was excited to read Kerouac's "breathless, dynamic bop phrases" and gave a nod to Jack in his towering "Desolation Row," the same Bob who sat on the ground where my friend was standing today back in November 1975 when he barnstormed through the city with his Rolling Thunder Revue, which I was lucky enough to see-and-hear for myself just down the street from my apartment in Pawtucketville, that neighborhood of tenements and broad boulevards across the river from center-Lowell and just this side of the Dracut wild woods, the neighborhood where young Jean/John/Jack patrolled the streets and invented his Doctor Sax atop the sandbank—all this in mind in the autumn sun amid dry leaves red and also gold like the trophy that we set into the earth right by the simple flat granite marker that bears his name, a name that was not spoken from high podiums for his benefit, a name that was not pulled from a sealed envelope at any New York or Swedish ceremony, a name that only rose in the chorus of his readers then and again today, a name and a presence that was strong when we stopped by to say, "Take this for what you gave us."

And when we turned to go more readers from two cars parked nearby were heading Jack's way.

School Daze Lost in Time

By **Bob Hodge** on October 26, 2016
—

"Books have a unique way of stopping time in a particular moment and saying: Let's not forget this."—Dave Eggers

The first race, a cross-country race, opened my imagination and sent me into and out of a dream continuously.

"Hey, Hodgie, what the hell were you doing in Trull's class" asked Emo, my friend from the neighborhood. "What do you mean," I said. "Man, it was like you were a manikin or some *Twilight Zone* character when Trull called on you and had to come over and wind up his pointer and whack your desk to get your attention." Emo was nonplussed with my behavior lately.

"I was thinking about Thoreau, a quote he uses in *Walden*."

"I am Monarch of all I survey, my right there none to dispute."

"Emo, I love this idea, you dig?"

"Hodgie, quit that hippie talk and snap out of it. You worry me, boy." Emo meant well, but I did not think like most other people and I accepted that.

I had another friend ask me once, "Hodgie, how do you manage to stay above it all?" Well, "it all" seemed like terminal silliness to me, just lowbrow. Of course, this kind of thought process didn't matter much in the "hood," so mainly I kept it to myself.

I realized early on that possessions were not important to me, only experiences. There was that letter jacket though, so proud when I got it with the grey leather sleeves and red cotton with a grey letter L. The first night that I wore it out with my friends I got drunk sitting around in some field drinking quarts of Schlitz, and then when it got late I started running home and threw up on the jacket, which I then deposited in a garbage can.

It was just a stupid jacket.

I also had a thing about my hair, and I never combed it or washed it often enough and it got to be a massive mess of curls. I had some weird phobia about the barber, who I thought had insulted me once, and so I started cutting my own hair and continued to do so for many years. The results might be awesome or atrocious according to my whim.

Much later I won a marathon race in Japan, and my photo from the after race with a laurel wreath on my head and my wild hair blowing out all over was in the papers back home. I spoke with my brother when I returned, and he said "Ya, Bob, me and Dad saw your picture in the papers. Dad figured you must still be cutting your own hair, ha ha."

I wore flannel shirts (or I should say "shirt"), cords, and construction boots usually with white socks. This mode of dress for public high school students was not unusual in the 1970s.

I was in love with Lulu who sat two rows away in math. She was aware of my running exploits and asked me about it class.

She wanted to go out for the fledgling girls track team.

One day I walked into class, and she was not there and had not been there for a week. "Hey, Wally," I asked my friend "Where's Lulu?"

"You didn't notice?" he said.

"Notice what?"

"She's pregnant, pecker-head. Everyone says it's somebody from Dracut."

Women and girls are nothing but heartache.

A thousand kids in my high school, and I am probably the only one who didn't know. I lived a lot in my own little world. Running and reading were my passions in that order.

"School daze." When would they end, and what I would do? I knew not. I still had senior year, and it was looking easy since I had not made any college plans and few colleges showed an interest in me even though I was among the best runners in the state.

I took Driver's Education with Ray Riddick, a legendary football player and now coach of our high school football team. I would meet coach and the other students one morning a week behind the school where the cars with the big "Student Driver" signs attached were parked.

We drove a Plymouth Satellite (like the woman from "Planet Claire" for you B-52's fans) a 1972 model, a monster of a car. It still had that new smell and just a few hundred miles on it. Ray, Mr. Riddick, or coach—I was never sure how to address him—beckoned me to get behind the wheel, and he slid across the front seat and sat right up against me. The man was enormous. My hands got all sweaty.

"OK, Bobby," and he started quizzing me on everything on the dashboard and steering column, which was pretty basic in those days. He continued to sit next to me, and he put his left arm over the seat back, so his enormous hand sat right behind my head.

"OK, Bobby, put it in reverse and ease it back." I started to go in reverse, and he said, "Have you ever driven before?" As I was about to answer, I lightly touched the brand spankin' new power brakes and Ray's head, not far from the ceiling of the car anyway, bumped it. Bam!

His enormous hand then wacked me a couple of times in the back of the head. "Bobby, easy on the brakes." I nervously explained that my brother's Oldsmobile did not have power brakes, hence my heavy footedness.

There were usually three students in the car together, and we would each take a turn at the wheel. Ray was patient, but the man's sheer size and demeanor were intimidating. One young woman braked hard to avoid hitting a squirrel, and Ray bammed his head again on the ceiling of the car. He had her pull over. "It's us or them, missy."

My favorite ride was the route to the Quality Donut shop in the Acre section of the city, right across the street from where I used to live, featuring "Lowell's best coffee," and I think it was, too.

There we would all sit and drink coffee for a bit while Ray talked with the locals about the upcoming football season and his former glory days as a player with the Green Bay Packers.

After a few weeks of Driver's Ed., Ray signed off on my certificate and said I was good to go. That gave me a free period during which I would eat breakfast at a little coffee shop, if I had any money, or I would go to Prince's Bookstore or the public library.

In my senior year, I felt more comfortable in my skin. Running was going well, grades were OK (B's & C's are good enough folks). Unexpectedly, I had been offered a scholarship to Johnson & Wales Junior College in Providence, Rhode Island. That was something to ponder.

Citizenship Is an Endless Job

By **Paul** on November 9, 2016

Filmmaker and political agitator Michael Moore had his finger on the Trump uprising months ago. He predicted the wins in Penn.-Mich.-Wis.-Ohio, as well as the Jesse Ventura Effect of voters making mischief because they can. Now he says get up off the mat if you were not for Trump and get to work. That's the American way. Moore has suggested a five-point action plan in the wake of the election including "return the Democratic Party to the people" and saying, "Hillary Clinton won the popular vote." And, yes, fire all the pundits and pollsters.

President Obama today said that no matter the political party, we are on the same team as Americans. The elections are more like intra-squad scrimmages, competing against ourselves. I was surprised he had the presence of mind to say that in the face of the furious rejection of what he represents. But he has always taken the long view of his own role, as I understand it from reading interviews with him or hearing him talk about political life.

What we cannot do is hand over the keys to the car to one person or a few people who say, "Just get out of the way and let me drive. I've got this." No, it has to be, "We've got this."

I saw the following quote on Facebook, lines from a speech by Abraham Lincoln in 1838 warning about the danger of a tyrant or tyranny at large arising in the nation (his target was the acute threat to national life posed by slavery's supporters): "Shall we expect some transatlantic military giant to step the ocean and crush us at a blow? Never! All the armies of Europe, Asia, and Africa combined, with all the treasure of the earth (our own excepted) in their military chest, with a Bonaparte for a commander, could not by force take a drink from the Ohio or make a track on the Blue Ridge in a trial of a thousand years. At what point then is the approach of danger to be expected? I answer. If it ever reach us, it must spring up amongst us; it cannot come from abroad. If destruction be our lot, we must ourselves be its author and finisher. As a nation of freemen, we must live through all time or die by suicide."

HISTORY AS IT HAPPENS

President-Elect Trump

By **Dick** on November 9, 2016
—

At 10:00 p.m. last night, Twitter reported that the Canadian immigration website had crashed. It was time to go to bed. While the election outcome wasn't final, by that point it was clear to me that Donald Trump would be the next president of the United States. I went to bed, but I confess to not sleeping very well.

During the 2012 presidential campaign, Nate Silver, the data guru of *The New York Times*, seemed to provide the best data analysis of what was going to happen and what did happen. Shortly after that, Silver left the *Times* to start his own site called *FiveThirtyEight*. I continued to follow Silver and, as this election approached, paid close attention to his daily emails.

As yesterday's election drew near, Silver, who interprets polls taken by others instead of doing his own polling, wrote that aggregating all national polls gave Hillary Clinton a three percent lead in the popular vote and similar leads in state polls. But he only gave Clinton a 67 percent chance of victory while similar websites were rating her chances in the 90 percent range. Silver explained that it was not uncommon for polls to be off by up to three percent. That was the case in 2012 when the polls gave Obama a three percent lead over Romney, but Obama won by six percent. (Because the error was in Obama's favor, perhaps some of us were less likely to notice it). Silver said that a three percent error in the 2016 polls could end up as a Clinton landslide or, if the error was in the other direction, a very close race popular-vote wise, but also one that opened a clear path to a Trump victory in the Electoral College. Silver further explained that Clinton could take little comfort in state polls, because they did not exist in isolation. An error in one state poll would likely bleed across state boundaries and affect them all.

With that in mind last night, I shifted from covering the

Lowell City Council meeting (which ended at 7:12 p.m.) to following election results on Twitter and the *New York Times* website. (When the council meeting ended, I spun my TV dial to the traditional news channels, but quickly found them more annoying than informative, and so pulled the plug on television.)

At first, things went predictably. Indiana and Kentucky were called for Trump at 7:00 p.m., the same time Vermont went for Clinton. At 8:00, Massachusetts and Maryland offset Tennessee and Oklahoma. Florida was a key early indicator. Clinton could win without Florida, but Trump could not. In my mind, an early and healthy lead in Florida for Clinton would point to a solid Democratic victory. But Florida was too close to call; so was North Carolina; so was Virginia. As the votes were counted, the trends in Florida and North Carolina were towards Trump. When early returns from Ohio, Pennsylvania, Wisconsin, and Michigan showed surprising strength for Trump, it was clear that Nate Silver's three-point polling error had happened, and it had happened in Trump's favor. That's when I headed to bed.

Awake at 1:00 a.m., I reached for my phone and opened Twitter just in time for "Decision Desk HQ" to tweet, "OK all. It's the big one. We project Trump wins Arizona. . . and the state of Pennsylvania. He's President-elect."

Sorting out what happened and why will take time. The electorate wasn't just divided, it was VERY divided, so today people will either be euphoric or distraught. With the strong performance of its Senate candidates across the country—who knew Trump would have such long coattails?—the Republican Party will control the presidency, both houses of Congress, and the Supreme Court (as soon as they confirm whomever Trump nominates to fill the seat vacant since Justice Scalia's death).

If you like what happened, congratulations. If you don't like it, remember that all politics is local. The American political system is very fluid and filled with moving parts. In the past, whether it was during the tenure of Ronald Reagan or of Barack Obama, whichever party was out of power at the federal level turned to state and local government to effect change. I expect the same thing will happen this time, which makes the people we elect to represent us at the Massachusetts State House and at Lowell City Hall even more important.

With that in mind, let's take a quick look at the contested local races decided last night. Niki Tsongas defeated Ann Wofford by 38 points, 69 percent to 31 percent (in Lowell, Tsongas received 27,889 votes to 6,805 for Wofford, an 80 percent to 20 percent margin). In the 18th Middlesex District state Representative race, Rady Mom defeated Kamara Kay by 44 points, 72 percent to 28 percent (7,985 to 3,091 votes). And Clinton won Lowell, getting 23,186 votes to 10,495 votes for Trump (65 percent to 30 percent).

As for the ballot questions statewide, Question 1 (expand slot machine gaming) lost 61 percent to 39 percent; Question 2 (more charter schools) lost 62 percent to 38 percent; Question 3 (better treatment of farm animals) won 78 percent to 22 percent; and Question 4 (legalization of marijuana) won 54 percent to 46 percent.

In Lowell, the ballot question results were: on slot machines, 52 percent yes, 48 percent no; on charter schools, 57 percent no, 43 percent yes; on farm animals, 77 percent yes, 23 percent no; and on marijuana, 56 percent yes, 44 percent no.

Based on the Question 4 result, recreational use of marijuana will be legal in Massachusetts by mid-December, which may offer some comfort to those who envision difficulties dealing with a Trump Presidency.

2016

CONTRIBUTORS

Anthony 'Tony' Accardi, adjunct professor of English at Middlesex Community College, is the former assistant Register of Deeds at the Middlesex North Registry of Deeds in Massachusetts.

Mehmed Ali is the author of *The Search for a Master's Legacy: Yousuf Karsh & John Garo*. An administrator at UMass Lowell, he is also the first official City Historian for the City of Lowell.

Marjorie Arons-Barron is president of Barron Associates Worldwide, Inc., a communications consulting firm. She is the former editorial director at WCVB-TV, Channel 5, in Boston.

Colleen Brady is on the University Relations staff at UMass Lowell. She holds a master's degree from UMass Lowell and a law degree from Massachusetts School of Law.

Beth Brassel is a librarian for Young Adult books and readers at the Pollard Memorial Library in Lowell. She has a master's degree from the State University of New York, Buffalo, in American Studies with a concentration in Women's Studies, as well as a master's in Library Science (Simmons College, Boston).

Michael Casey is the author of *There It Is: New and Selected Poems*, *Obscenities* (Yale Series of Younger Poets award), *Millrat*, and *Million Dollar Hole*. His poems have appeared in *The Nation*, *Rolling Stone*, *The New York Times*, and other publications.

George Chigas teaches Asian Studies at UMass Lowell. He is the author of *The Story of Tum Teav* and editor of *Resolute Heart: Selected Writing from Lowell's Cambodian Community*. He worked in the Cambodian Genocide Program at Yale University.

Matthew C. Donahue, a lawyer in private practice with an emphasis on environmental law, is a former Lowell city councilor and co-founded the Lowell Parks & Conservation Trust. An accomplished musician, Matt's songs are available online.

John Edward is on the faculties of Bentley University and UMass Lowell, where he teaches microeconomics and macroeconomics. A past guest columnist for *The Sun* newspaper, his has contributed many essays on economics to *RichardHowe.com*.

Fred Faust, president of the Edge Group real estate consulting firm, was an assistant to U.S. Senator Paul Tsongas and the first executive director of the Lowell Historic Preservation Commission, U.S. Dept. of the Interior.

Thomas Fitzsimmons's "Rainbow Poem" was published as a broadside by Loom Press in 1982. Born in Lowell, he is the author, editor, and translator of more than 60 books, including *Becomes One*, *Iron Harp*, and *The Dream Machine*.

Robert Forrant professor of history at UMass Lowell, has authored and co-authored numerous books, papers, and articles including *The Big Move: Immigrant Voices from a Mill City*, co-edited with his History Department colleague Christoph Strobel. He was appointed University Professor, a distinguished honor.

Kate Hanson Foster's book of poems *Mid Drift* was a "Must Read" selection in the Massachusetts Book Awards for 2011. Her work has been published in *California Quarterly*, *Poet Lore*, and elsewhere.

Bob Hodge is a writer and local running legend in Massachusetts—honored in the Athletics Hall of Fame at Lowell High School and UMass Lowell. In 1982, he won the Beppu-Oita Marathon in Japan. He directs the Berlin Public Library in Massachusetts.

Andrew Howe, a graduate of Harvard University and Georgetown University, was the Lowell field organizer for Democrat Elizabeth Warren's 2012 U.S. Senate campaign.

Richard P. Howe, Jr., founder and executive editor of *RichardHowe.com*, is the author of *Lowell: Images of Modern America* and *Lowell Municipal Elections, 1965-2015*. He is the Register of Deeds of the Middlesex North District in Massachusetts.

Paul Hudon, historian and poet, is the author of *All in Good Time* (poems) and *The Valley & Its Peoples: An Illustrated History of the Lower Merrimack*.

Sengly Kong has a Ph.D. in natural resources management from Cornell University and is a research project coordinator at University of Connecticut Health Center. He is the former chair of Cambodia Town Lowell.

Jean LeBlanc is the author of *Skating in Concord*, *The Haiku Aesthetic*, *At Any Moment*, and other books. From New England, she teaches at Sussex County Community College in New Jersey.

Jack McDonough was a senior writer and editor at UMass Lowell for more than 20 years and previously wrote for United Press International news service.

Bopha Malone is a regional business advisor at Enterprise Bank and a past board president of the Cambodian Mutual Assistance Association in Lowell.

Jacquelyn Malone is the author of *All Waters Run to Lethe*. Her poems have appeared in the *Beloit Poetry Journal*, *Ploughshares*, and other journals. She is active in the Mass Poetry organization.

Henri Marchand is the Director of the City of Lowell's Cultural Affairs and Special Events Office. He has been an assistant to the City Manager and the producer of *Sunrise*, a public affairs program on WUML, 91.5 FM, at UMass Lowell.

Joe Meehan, Lowell resident, is a recipient of the Distinguished Service Award from the Greater Lowell YMCA.

Paul Marion is the author and editor of many books, including *Union River: Poems and Sketches*, *Mill Power: The Origin and Impact of Lowell National Historical Park*, and *Atop an Underwood: Early Stories and Other Writings* by Jack Kerouac.

Marty Meehan is the president of the five-campus University of Massachusetts system. Formerly, he was Chancellor of UMass Lowell, his alma mater, and a U.S. Representative in Congress from 1993 to 2007. He is a former first assistant district attorney for Middlesex County in Massachusetts.

Matt Miller, author of *Club Icarus* and *Cameo Diner*, teaches at Phillips Exeter Academy. His poems have appeared in *Slate*, *Harvard Review*, and other journals. He received a Wallace Stegner Fellowship in Poetry at Stanford University.

Derek Mitchell, executive director of the Lawrence Partnership, is the former Lowell site director of the International Institute of New England. He served in the Peace Corps in Nicaragua.

Juliet Haines Mofford, a former staff member for the Lowell Historic Preservation Commission, lives in Maine. She has written books about the Salem witch trials, Beat Generation, polio epidemic, child labor, and other subjects.

Jack Neary is a playwright (*Kong's Night Out*, *Jerry Finnegan's Sister*, and others), director, and actor who has appeared in the films *Black Mass* and *The Town*.

Steve O'Connor is the author of *The Witch at Rivermouth, Smokestack Lighting,* and *The Spy in the City of Books*. He teaches English at Greater Lowell Technical High School.

Muriel "Mimi" Parseghian is a community activist and political analyst. She was a pioneer blogger with the *Left in Lowell* team. In 2012, she received the prestigious Agnouni Award of the Armenian Relief Society, Eastern Region.

Dave Perry is a senior writer at UMass Lowell and the founder of Vinyl Destination, a record shop in Lowell's Mill No. 5. A one-time *Lowell Sun* reporter, he was nominated in 1991 for a Grammy Award for best liner notes on *The Jack Kerouac Collection*.

Chath Piersath, poet, painter, and humanitarian, is the author of *After* (poems) and *Sinat and the Instrument of the Heart* (children's book). He lives in Massachusetts.

James Peters is the creator of the "Peters' Principles" program at Lowell Telecommunications Corporation and a former history teacher at Lowell High School.

Mary (Boutselis) Sampas was a lifelong journalist beginning in high school as a reporter for the *Lowell Sun*, where her articles and columns provided a running account of life in the city.

Tony Sampas, a librarian at UMass Lowell, has organized programs such as a "Lowell Walks" exhibit and a panel talk about journalist Charles G. Sampas. He has an MFA from Lesley University College of Art and Design (photography).

Tom Sexton, a poet and former editor of *Alaska Quarterly Review*, was Poet Laureate of Alaska in 1995. He is a distinguished alumnus of Lowell High School. He taught for many years at the University of Alaska. His books of poetry include *A Ladder of Cranes, A Clock with No Hands,* and *Bridge Street at Dusk*.

Francey Slater is a seasoned educator and gardener who co-founded Mill City Grows, which is dedicated to creating urban food production in Lowell.

Joseph Smith is a community activist in Lowell who is retired from the Raytheon Company, based in Waltham, Massachusetts.

Marie Sweeney is a member of the Massachusetts Democratic State Committee, long-time chair of the Greater Lowell Area Democrats, and a former English teacher at Lowell High School.

Nancye Tuttle is a freelance writer who formerly wrote for the *Lowell Sun* and *Merrimack Valley Magazine*. She lives in Maine.

John Wooding, political science professor at UMass Lowell, co-authored, with Kristin G. Esterberg, *Divided Conversations*, about leadership in public higher education. His service work includes assisting the Cultural Organization of Lowell, SayDaNa Burmese Community Coalition, and Lowell Earth Day project.

HISTORY AS IT HAPPENS

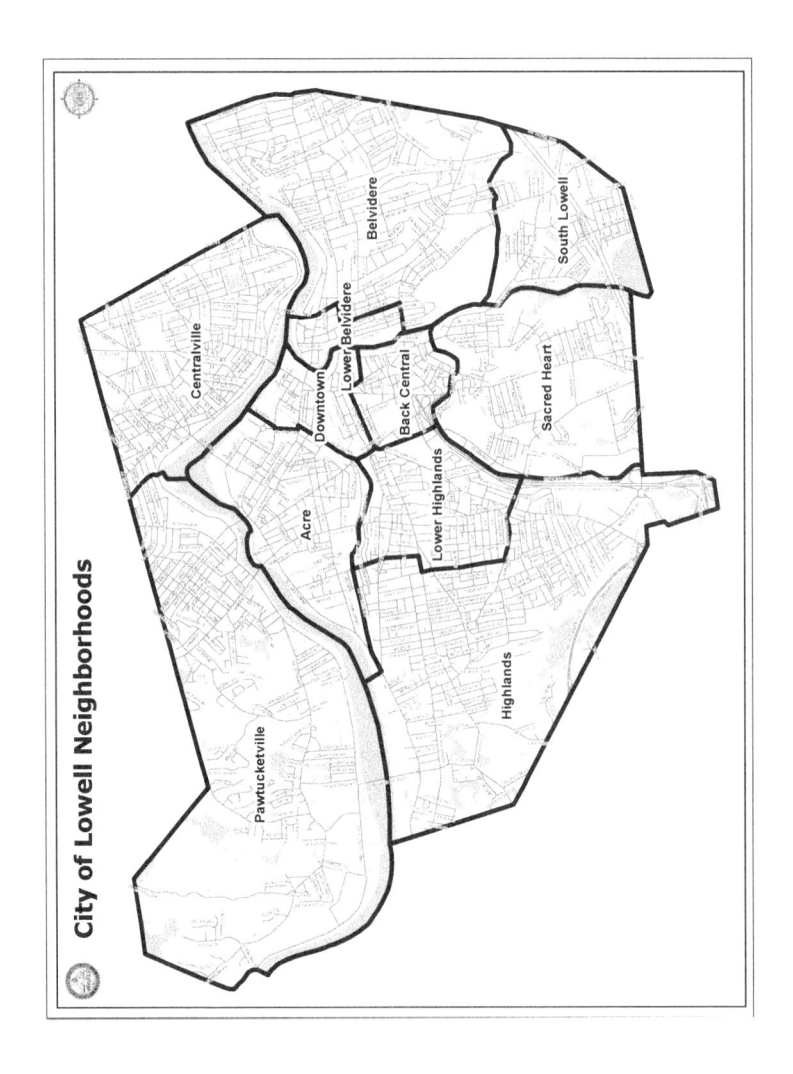

City of Lowell Neighborhoods

City of Lowell Downtown Attractions

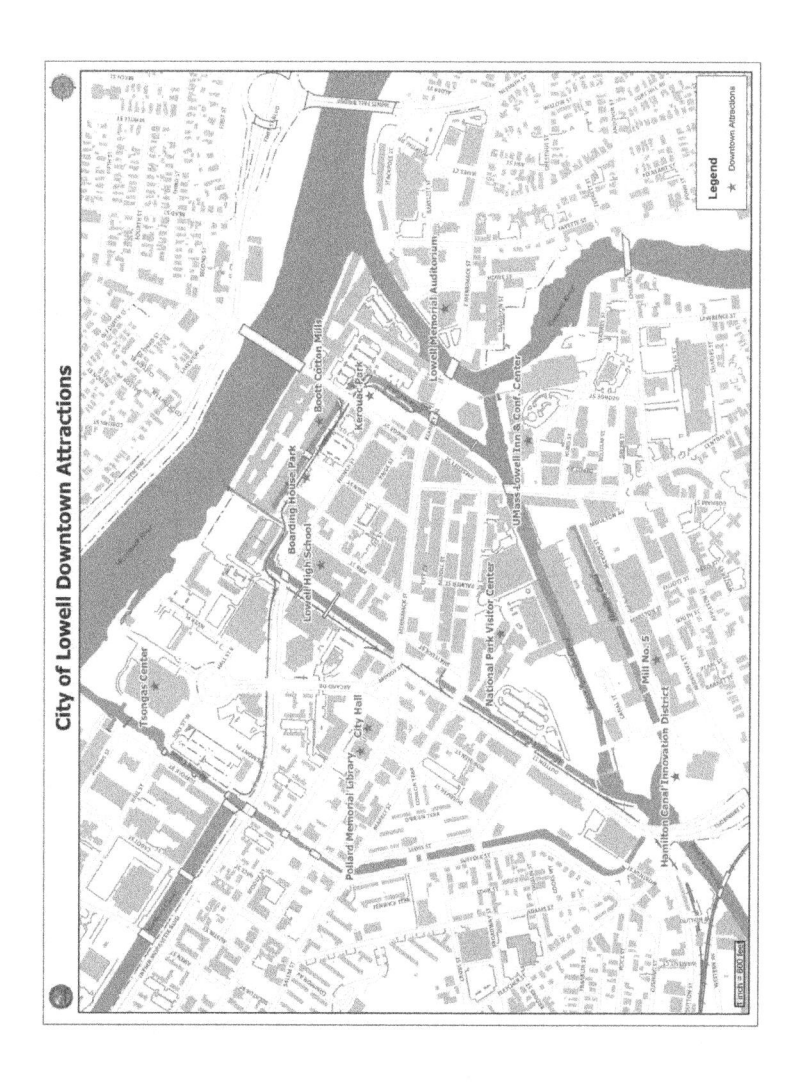